Negotiating Identities

Work, Religion, Gender, and the Mobilisation of Tradition among the Uyghur in the 1990s

The volume comprises ten chapters which present the results of extensive fieldwork carried out in the 1990s. The material has been available to date only in specialised journals and collective volumes. Six focus on important aspects of Uyghur communal life, such as production, morality, and gender relations, and rely on data collected in two rural settlements in the vicinity of Kashgar. One article examines interethnic relations and Uyghur ethnic identity in the oasis of Kucha. Three focus on popular religious beliefs; of these one draws on Uyghur indigenous sources while two provide ethnographic accounts of how these norms were played out in the Uyghur diaspora in Almaty, Kazakhstan, in 1997.

While the chapters cover a wide spatial, temporal, and thematic range, they display a number of shared features which lend the volume a sense of unity. Fieldwork data are informed by the historical context and the beliefs, values, and practices of Uyghur subjects which are shown to be embedded in and inextricably entangled with politics. Close attention is paid throughout to local actors' conceptualisations, since it is held that these remain fundamental to grasping the problems faced by this region in the twenty-first century. This collection provides both a *Zeitdokument* of the possibilities and limitations of research in Xinjiang in the 1990s – before 9/11 and local spirals of violence in the early 2000s – and a point of departure for new studies of the Uyghur and their neighbours inside and outside Xinjiang.

D1703283

Halle Studies in the Anthropology of Eurasia

General Editors:

Christoph Brumann, Kirsten Endres, Chris Hann, Thomas Hauschild, Burkhard Schnepel, Dittmar Schorkowitz, Lale Yalçın-Heckmann

Volume 31

LIT

Ildikó Bellér-Hann

Negotiating Identities

Work, Religion, Gender,
and the Mobilisation of Tradition
among the Uyghur in the 1990s

LIT

Cover Photo: Uyghur woman working in the field, Kashgar, Southern
Xinjiang (Photo: Chris Hann).

Bibliographic information published by the Deutsche Nationalbibliothek
The Deutsche Nationalbibliothek lists this publication in the Deutsche
Nationalbibliografie; detailed bibliographic data are available on the Internet at
http://dnb.d-nb.de.

ISBN 978-3-643-90745-5

A catalogue record for this book is available from the British Library

©LIT VERLAG Dr. W. Hopf   LIT VERLAG GmbH & Co. KG Wien,
Berlin 2015   Zweigniederlassung Zürich 2015
Fresnostr. 2   Klosbachstr. 107
D-48159 Münster   CH-8032 Zürich
Tel. +49 (0) 2 51-62 03 20   Tel. +41 (0) 44-251 75 05
Fax +49 (0) 2 51-23 19 72   Fax +41 (0) 44-251 75 06
E-Mail: lit@lit-verlag.de   E-Mail: zuerich@lit-verlag.ch
http://www.lit-verlag.de   http://www.lit-verlag.ch

Distribution:
In the UK: Global Book Marketing, e-mail: mo@centralbooks.com
In North America: International Specialized Book Services, e-mail: orders@isbs.com
In Germany: LIT Verlag Fresnostr. 2, D-48159 Münster
Tel. +49 (0) 2 51-620 32 22, Fax +49 (0) 2 51-922 60 99, e-mail: vertrieb@lit-verlag.de

In Austria: Medienlogistik Pichler-ÖBZ, e-mail: mlo@medien-logistik.at
e-books are available at www.litwebshop.de

Contents

List of Illustrations   ix

Acknowledgements   xi

Note on Transliteration   xiii

Glossary   xv

Introduction   **1**

Modern Xinjiang Studies   2
Rural Xinjiang   8
The Chapters   10

1   **The Peasant Condition in Xinjiang**   **21**

The Reform Context   24
The Obligations   28
The Means of Enforcement   40
The Agents of Enforcement   41
The Two Authorities: State and Religion   43
Conclusion   46

2   **Work and Gender among Uyghur Villagers in
        Southern Xinjiang**   **51**

Men's and Women's Work before 1949   52
Men's and Women's Work during the Decades of
Collectivisation   57
Men's and Women's Work in the Reform Period   61
Specialisations   63
Conclusion   67

3   **Crafts, Entrepreneurship, and Gendered Economic
        Relations in Southern Xinjiang in the Era of the
        'Socialist Commodity Economy'**   **71**

Economic Activities: *Doppa*-Makers   73
Economic Activities: Some 'Male' Crafts   78

Investment and Credit 80
The Concepts of Obligation and Voluntariness 87
Conclusion 90

4 **Women, Work, and Procreation Beliefs in Two
Muslim Communities** **95**

Baskets among the Lazi 96
Baskets and Material Culture 98
Baskets and Symbolic Culture 99
Reproduction, Patriarchy, and the Value of Work 101
The Uyghurs: No Metaphor, No Asymetry? 106
The Seed of a Metaphor 106
A Symmetrical Model of Biological Procreation 109
The Devaluing of Women's Work 113
Conclusion 114

5 **Law and Custom among the Uyghur in Xinjiang** **119**

The Pre-Socialist Period 121
The Socialist Period 136
Conclusion 140

6 **The Mobilisation of Tradition: Localism and Identity
among the Uyghur of Xinjiang** **145**

Interference with Local Practices: A Historical Overview 147
Naming Places 151
The Land 154
The House 158
Conclusion 161

7 **Temperamental Neighbours: Uyghur-Han Relations
in Xinjiang** **167**

Time and Space 171
Occupation and Education 174
Dress Code and Fashion 181
Temperament and Diet 186
Boundary Crossing and Intermarriage 189
Conclusion and Epilogue 191

8   **'Making the Oil Fragrant': Dealings with the**
           Supernatural among the Uyghurs in Xinjiang   **197**

           Rituals Pertaining to the Dead   200
           Personal Piety – *Yagh Puritish*   212
           Conclusion   216

9   **Rivalry and Solidarity among Uyghur Healers in**
           Kazakhstan   **221**

           The Setting   223
           The Teacher: Muqāddäs, the *Bakhshi*   228
           The Lesser Religious Specialist: Büwükhan, the Diviner   230
           Analysis: The Force of Tradition   240
           Nawat, the Rebel   243
           Conclusion   245

10   **The Micropolitics of a Pilgrimage**   **249**

           The Protagonists and the Social Setting   249
           Strategies of Recruitment   251
           Pilgrimage   252
           The Holy Places Visited   253
           The Pilgrim's Experiences   254
           Spirituality   254
           The Miracle: Punishment and Forgiveness   255
           Tradition and Creativity   257
           The Pilgrimage as Rite of Passage   260
           Conclusion   263

           Index   265

List of Illustrations

Map

1   The Xinjiang Uyghur Autonomous Region, China and Southern
    Kazakhstan   xvii

Plates

1   Village cadres, Kashgar, Southern Xinjiang   34
2   Farmers gathered to be told about new agricultural policies,
    Kashgar, Southern Xinjiang   35
3   Woman picking mulberries, Kashgar, Southern Xinjiang   37
4   Young man decorating wedding chests, Kashgar, Southern Xinjiang 65
5   *Doppa*-maker, Kashgar, Southern Xinjiang   76
6   Village women visiting a young mother and her new baby,
    Southern Xinjiang   112
7   Village in Southern Xinjiang   146
8   Kucha in 1996   169
9   Animal market in the dry river-bed, Kucha, Southern Xinjiang   175
10 Men gathered for a funeral outside a mosque, Southern Xinjiang 211
11 Healing ritual at home, Almaty, Kazakhstan   233
12 Pilgrims at the shrine of Aristan Baba, Türkistan, Kazakhstan   253
13 Aḥmad Yasawī's shrine in Türkistan, Kazakhstan   256

(all photographs are either by the author or Chris Hann, 1995–1997)

Acknowledgements

This volume is a collection of articles which were published previously in various journals and collective volumes between 1997 and 2011. During this period I was supported by many organisations and individuals. Most of the research was financed by a generous grant from the Economic and Social Research Council of Great Britain (R000 235709) between 1994–97. Research among the Lazi (1991–93) was also supported by the Economic and Social Research Council (R00023 3208 01). Fieldwork in China was made possible by Professors Tsui Yen Hu and Fang Xiao Hua, both of Xinjiang Normal University in Ürümchi, and by the Chinese authorities who issued the necessary research permit. My stay in Kazakhstan was a success due to the generous support of Julie and Bill Clarke, Michael Borowitz, Marek Gawęcki, Ruth Mandel, and Danuta Penkala-Gawęcka. My special thanks are due to the late Ambassador Gunnar Jarring for his comments and his generosity in allowing me to use manuscript materials held by the University Library in Lund. I also enjoyed the institutional support of my former employers, the University of Kent at Canterbury and the Orient-wissenschaftliches Zentrum at the Martin Luther University in Halle-Wittenberg. The volume was prepared for publication during a nine months' Fellowship at the Institut d'Études Avancées in Nantes in 2013–14. This stay in turn was made possible by my current employer, the Department of Cross-Cultural and Regional Studies at the University of Copenhagen, which allowed me a sabbatical term. My thanks are also due to the following publishers for granting permission to reproduce these articles: Taylor & Francis (ch. 1, 3, 6, 8; www.tandfonline.com), Bloomsbury Publishing Plc (ch. 4), and Brill Academic Publishers (ch. 9). I am also grateful to authors who allowed me to cite their unpublished manuscripts, conference organisers and participants, and numerous editors and anonymous reviewers for their useful suggestions along the way. My special thanks are due to Dr. Jennifer Cash for her meticulous language editing and numerous valuable comments, and to Berit Westwood who prepared and formatted the manuscript for final publication.

Above all I am immensely grateful to those Uyghur individuals and families in Xinjiang, Kazakhstan, and Turkey who welcomed me into their homes, taking the time and trouble to talk to me, typically accompanied by generous hospitality.

My personal thanks are due to my children, Agnes and Mark, who had no choice but to participate in much of this fieldwork. My greatest indebtedness is to Chris Hann, who was associated with both projects and shouldered most of the childcare in the field, for his professional and personal encouragement and support throughout.

Note on Transliteration

The transliteration of modern Uyghur follows the simplified system employed in Komatsu Hisao et al. (eds.) *Chūō Ajia wo Shiru Jiten* [Encyclopedia of Central Eurasia]. Tokyo: Heibonsha, 2005, 592–93.

Glossary

alwang	—	corvée, labour obligation
arwah	—	spirits
barat	—	popular religious holiday
bakhshi	—	healer, shaman
bek	—	indigenous office holder
damolla	—	learned molla, honorific title
dakhan	—	healer, shaman
dihqan	—	peasant
doppa	—	Uyghur skull-cap
guna	—	sin
haj	—	Hajj, the pilgimage to Mecca
haji	—	a person who has completed the pilgrimage to Mecca
halal	—	lawful
haram	—	unlawful
imam	—	religious office holder who leads public worship
isqat	—	payment given to strangers at the grave as a form of redemption
jan	—	soul
khoja	—	1. honorific title used for the descendents of Muhammad, 2. respectful form of address, 3. master
mazar	—	Muslim shrine
mädräsä	—	Islamic college
mähr	—	marriage payment prescribed by Islamic law
mäktäp	—	school
mäshräp	—	form of socialisation, conviviality
mijäz	—	disposition, temperament
mirab	—	official in charge of the distribution of water
mu	—	area measurement, 1 mu = 1/15 hectares = 1/6 acre
molla	—	1. mullah, title of religious office holder, 2. scholar, 3. title of respect
namahram, namähräm	—	unfamiliar, a stranger
namaz	—	ritual prayer
näzir	—	ritualised communal meal
näzir-chiraq	—	commemoration of the dead

örp-adät	—	custom, customs and habits
päri oynatish	—	exorcising the spirits
pärikhan	—	exorcist, healer
pärz	—	mandatory duty
pir	—	elder, patron saint
qazi	—	judge
qäländär	—	mendicant dervish
qumilaqchi	—	diviner
qurban	—	1. sacrifice, 2. the Festival of Sacrifice
ramazan/rozä	—	Ramadan, the ninth month of the Islamic calendar, the month of fasting
räkät	—	a complete act of worship with the prescribed postures and prostrations, a unit of the namaz
roh	—	spirit
sawap	—	meritorious deed
sädiqä	—	alms, charity
sär	—	measurement of weight, ca. 35 gr.
taranchi	—	the Turkic speaking Muslim cultivators of Northern Xinjiang
tängä	—	coin, currency unit
toy	—	joyous celebration, wedding
toyluq	—	marriage payment
yagh puritish	—	creating a fragrance by heating oil, oil sacrifice
zikr	—	remembrance, Sufi ritual

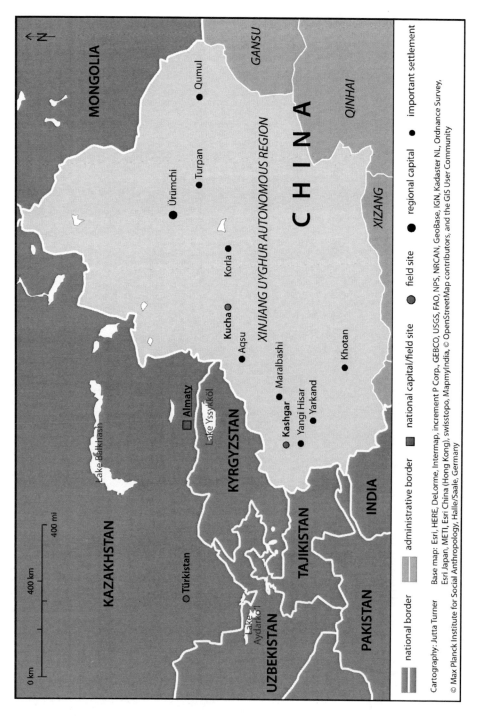

Map 1. The Xinjiang Uyghur Autonomous Region, China and Southern Kazakhstan.

Introduction

In 2013 I uploaded onto academia.edu my article titled 'The Peasant Condition in Xinjiang', originally published in 1997. The automated feedback revealed that within 48 hours it was accessed more than 200 times. This could mean only two things: a growing interest in the situation of the Uyghur minority in China, and a continuing paucity of English-language sources of information about rural Xinjiang. This was the trigger for my decision to bundle ten of my publications, all the products of one ethnographic research project carried out in the mid-1990s, into a single volume.

I first visited Xinjiang for five months in 1986, soon after it had been opened to foreign visitors in the wake of Deng Xiaoping's reforms. The reforms were launched in the late 1970s and early 1980s, but much of Xinjiang remained closed until the mid-1980s. This visit allowed me to start language work and to gain a basic orientation in Uyghur social relations, but systematic fieldwork and publications followed only in the mid-1990s, by which time more foreigners had begun research in the region. Since then multi-ethnic Xinjiang, like the rest of China, has undergone further decollectivisation, the expansion of the market and, more recently, accelerated top-down development. Since 1990, following a decade of unprecedented cultural and religious freedoms for China's 55 recognised ethnic minorities, the Uyghur in Xinjiang have experienced increasing restrictions. It was under such conditions that I embarked on the empirical part of a major project in Southern Xinjiang in the mid-1990s which resulted in the pieces collected in this volume. In order to situate my work, I shall first sketch the emergence of modern Xinjiang Studies. It will be shown that, although this field has its roots in the eighteenth and nineteenth centuries, research started gaining momentum in the 1990s, and continues with surprising vigour against the odds.

Modern Xinjiang Studies

Due to the troubled political situation in Xinjiang, in recent years the Uyghurs, the titular group of the Xinjiang Uyghur Autonomous Region, have become subjected to growing international media attention. Over the years, international media reporting on the Uyghurs has become more sophisticated (although in recent years also somewhat repetitive), but Uyghurs have failed to capture the Western public imagination and sympathies in the way that Tibetans have succeeded. This is so in spite of the fact that the two groups occupy structurally similar positions as officially recognised ethnic groups vis-à-vis the centre of power in the People's Republic of China (Bellér-Hann and Brox 2014). Contemporary Uyghur and Xinjiang-related scholarship must be understood against this background.

The modern study of Xinjiang looks back on respectable forerunners and comprises contributions to diverse disciplines. Most of the scholarship, however, is united by a common denominator in that it takes either Xinjiang or the modern Uyghurs (in and sometimes also outside of Xinjiang) as the unit of enquiry.[1] Although they are aligned to specific disciplines through a chosen methodology, these works are typically relegated to the academic periphery of area studies where China Studies, Central Asian Studies, Turkic Studies, and Islamic Studies intersect. This is demonstrated through the occasional, token inclusion of Xinjiang/Uyghur-related articles in collective volumes which have Central Asia as their regional focus. While the multiple cultural and historical connections to Central Asia are readily recognised, authors tend to shy away from focusing on comparable phenomena, be it popular religious practices, life-cycle rituals, or the nature and outcomes of Russian and Chinese colonialisms and socialisms respectively. In spite of promising beginnings (Eschment and Harder 2004), a systematic comparison of Chinese and Russian/Soviet domination in the macro-region of Central Asia is still awaited.[2] Experts in Turkic Studies do make ample references to Uyghur linguistics, but outside Xinjiang and China little interest has been shown in Uyghur literature or oral tradition; there has been even less interest

---

[1] I use 'Xinjiang Studies' because this formulation is inclusive enough to give space to studies which focus on ethnic groups other than the Uyghur.

[2] Such comparison requires more than a juxtaposition of the imperial experiences, as has been produced for the Ottoman and Chinese empires (Islamoğlu-Inan and Perdue 2009), but also a focus on more specific topics, such as private property (see Islamoğlu-Inan and Perdue 2004), under the comparable conditions of these contiguous regions which experienced colonial expansion, reform movements, and major upheavals at similar times, if not always simultaneously.

in placing this literature in a comparative perspective.[3] This regional marginalisation of Xinjiang Studies displays curious parallels with the Uyghurs' political marginalisation within China, and the two forms of marginalisation are not entirely unrelated. There can be no doubt that the choice of topics by foreign researchers has often been at least partially influenced by research opportunities in Xinjiang and access to data. The tightening political parameters within which Uyghurs are allowed to manoeuvre are directly responsible for their de facto position as a 'peripheral people' in several senses, to use Stevan Harrell's famous phrase (Harrell 1995: 3).

Recent international scholarship focused on Xinjiang has been characterised by a certain division of labour between those with a Sinologist perspective and those who had their training (as I did) in Turkic Studies. This in itself is a reflection of the marginalised disciplinary position of Xinjiang, since such individuals turned their attention to this region after having first joined a major recognised area studies discipline. This situation is changing. A younger generation of scholars is now entering the academic conversation, and many of these newcomers choose Xinjiang as a focus early in their careers and set out programmatically to accumulate competences in both Chinese and Uyghur. These scholars also contribute to overcoming the (unintended) regional marginalisation of Xinjiang in a number of established area studies, a process further promoted by the organisation of workshops and edited volumes which take Xinjiang and/or Uyghurs as their main focus. These trends mark the gradual and still ongoing crystallisation of what can be called 'modern Xinjiang Studies', much of which continues to be framed, inspired, or at least influenced by the ongoing political situation.

Modern Xinjiang Studies started to emerge when literati trained in the Confucian tradition began expressing interest in the region, following its incorporation into the Manchu Empire in the mid-eighteenth century.[4]

---

[3] A notable exception is Friederich (1997). Uyghur philology, folklore, and literature (especially of the pre-Islamic period) are, on the other hand, favourite topics for Uyghur students studying abroad. This interest is presumably high because these subjects can be pursued without touching upon politics. Uyghur and Han scholars active in Xinjiang have a much broader perspective, but their studies of more recent literary themes, ethnography, and religion either remain devoid of a historical and political context, or are subjected to external and/or self-censorship.

[4] For historical works dealing with the regions mostly on the basis of Chinese sources, see Saguchi (1963); Zeng (1986 [1936]); Yang (1991); Di Cosmo (1993); Chen (1999); *Zhongguo Xinjiang diqu Yisilan* (2000); Zhu (2000); Wang (2003); Millward and Perdue (2004); Millward and Tursun (2004); Newby (2005); Perdue (2005); Millward (2007). For a more comprehensive summary of the literature up to 2008, see Bellér-Hann (2008: 21–26).

Xinjiang first became the focus of international political and scholarly attention much later, in the second half of the nineteenth century, due to the political rivalries of the colonial powers, Russia and Great Britain, that have become known as the Great Game. The region and its populations became the subject of numerous travelogues and scholarly works which encompass a number of (often intersecting) academic disciplines, including geography, history, archaeology, ethnography, sociology and linguistics.[5] Such works were typically authored by outsiders, whose diverse political, economic, religious, and scientific activities were arguably all motivated by imperialist considerations.

At about the same time, Muslim knowledge in and about the region gained momentum due to the activities of the Mission Covenant Church of Sweden. The Mission inspired indigenous reflections on the discourses and practices of society among some members of the local elite. Employed by the Mission as language teachers, Turkic-speaking Muslim intellectuals (*molla*s) produced several collections of essays about local social practices, rituals, and institutions, performing a task for which no one was better qualified.[6] In this volume, eight of the ten chapters were at least partially informed by the knowledge gleaned from the *molla*s' handwritten normative accounts; one (chapter 8) uses these works as its main point of departure. Their descriptions of the social and cultural norms of the Uyghurs prior to the onset of modernisation were usefully complemented by the observations of foreign travellers to the region at the time of high imperialism. The emic views put forward by members of this educated elite constitute our most important source for deeper insights into the social life of the Turkic-speaking Muslim oasis dwellers of Xinjiang prior to socialism.[7] They also serve as important points of departure for much of the ethnographic work and anthropological analysis undertaken by both native and foreign scholars since the beginning of the socialist period[8], as is exemplified by the present volume and my previous book (Bellér-Hann 2008).

During the early decades of the socialist era, the region became almost completely inaccessible to international researchers, and periods of political and cultural repression impeded indigenous knowledge production in all

---

[5] Bellér-Hann (2008: 29–31). See also Iskhakov (1975); Hopkirk (1980); Chvyr' (1990, 2006); and, for a collection of articles on various aspects of travel in Xinjiang during this period, see the special issue of *Studies in Travel Writing* 18 (4).
[6] For analyses of other modes of indigenous knowledge production and transmission see Light (2012) and Thum (2014).
[7] Bellér-Hann (2008).
[8] Gunnar Jarring, the Swedish scholar who greatly contributed to the development of Uyghur ethnographic studies, was inspired by these indigenous accounts and their authors, whom he knew personally (Gunnar Jarring, personal communication).

areas of life.[9] The introduction of the market reforms in the 1980s and the simultaneous opening up of Xinjiang ushered in a new era of both indigenous and international academic interest in the region. Indigenous (both Chinese and Uyghur) language publications have remained constrained by top-down and self-censorship. Scholarship focusing on Xinjiang which has emerged outside China covers diverse disciplines, such as political science, geography, history, and anthropology (including ethnomusicology), and is not constrained in the same way. Most, if not all, the historical studies produced about Xinjiang privilege Chinese and Manchu sources and perspectives (e.g. Waley-Cohen 1991; Millward 1998; Newby 2005; Perdue 2005; Kim 2008). This trend may be reversed as attention turns to the emergence of Uyghur national consciousness and the role of Muslim reformers (e.g. Klimeš 2015).

In the 2000s, there has been growing scholarly interest in legal documents in both Uyghur and Chinese languages. This is reflected in the work of Sugawara Jun (2012), Huan Tian (2012), Eric Schluessel (forthcoming), and Onuma Takahiro (forthcoming). Their work demonstrates the emergence of an anthropologically informed social history within Xinjiang Studies. Another such social history is Wang Jianxin's study (2004) of Muslim elites and education, which is based on the skilful combination of materials discerned from conventional historical sources with ethnographic and oral history data. Wang's work also contributes to research on the study of Islam in Xinjiang, about which, in spite of the numerous restrictions, a handful of researchers continue to produce excellent work outside the conceptual framework of politics (Zarcone 2002; Papas 2005; Dawut 2007).

In the field of anthropology, Justin Rudelson's book (1997) continues to retain its significance as the first anthropological study of the region in the post-reform period. Although it is most often referred to for its emphasis on the importance of oasis identities, its other, less often acknowledged merit lies in the author's recognition of intra-regional (but supra-oasis) differences. Rudelson simultaneously stresses the cultural contiguities of Xinjiang's sub-regions with neighbouring areas that extend beyond the borders of the Chinese polity.

Dru Gladney's Xinjiang-related output concerning ethnic relations has been based mostly on observations made during repeated short visits to the region, and they continue to remain influential for subsequent studies.[10]

---

[9] Nonetheless, some excellent primarily text-based studies have been produced which allow valuable insight into different aspects of the political and cultural developments of this era (McMillen 1979; Friederich 1997).

[10] For example, see his collection of articles (Gladney 2004).

Research in the humanities and social sciences since the 1990s has increasingly favoured methods of data collection carried out painstakingly in the archives or in the course of long-term fieldwork. These tendencies are noticeable in ethnomusicology and literature (Trebinjac 2000; Harris 2008; Light 2008), gender studies (Dautcher 2009), and works which focus in one way or another on resistance, ethnic identity, and interethnic relations (Bovingdon 2010; Smith Finley 2013).

It does not come as a surprise that the topics of ethnic relations, interethnic conflict, and international relations dominate political science approaches, as exemplified by the works of Colin Mackerras (2009) and Michael Clarke (2011). Zang Xiaowei's (Zang 2012) sociological work discussing Islam, family life, and gender relations also relies on large-scale sampling. The results bear out his assumptions of interethnic difference and group cohesion. , but gain greater relevance and interest when juxtaposed with data collected in the course of long-term qualitative fieldwork. Inevitably, politics continues to frame much recent work which takes as its unit of inquiry Xinjiang (as a peripheral region of China) or the Uyghur (as one of China's ethnic minorities), often in comparison with other peripheral regions or peoples (Potter 2011; Smith Finley 2013; Brox and Bellér-Hann 2014; Leibold and Yangbin 2014). The to-date unpublished doctoral study by Rune Steenberg Reyhé (2013) marks a departure from these tendencies in the social sciences. His study shows how Uyghur kinship, a hitherto neglected field of research, can become a laboratory where classical and more recent anthropological theories of relatedness can be tested. Arguing that in Kashgar the conceptualisation of relatedness combines genealogical kinship and affinal relations which need to be confirmed and reproduced through gift exchange, verbal categorisation, and other kinds of semantic performance, Steenberg Reyhé also demonstrates that there is more to social life outside the colonial framework and away from the binaries created by ethnic conflict in Xinjiang that is worthy of academic study.

Even when scholars stick to the time-honoured methods of data collection as well as the theoretical toolbox of their own discipline, they often let themselves be inspired by work written in other disciplines about the region. The rapprochement of various disciplines is indicated, for example, in the anthropologically informed historical-legal studies mentioned above. It is further reinforced by the publication of edited volumes, such as the special issues edited by Aubin and Besson (1998) and Aubin (2008). Some efforts at inter-disciplinary complementarity have been intentional. For example, S. Frederick Starr's *Xinjiang: China's Muslim Borderland* (2004) was followed by *Situating the Uyghurs between China and Central Asia* (2007), edited by Cristina Cesàro, Rachel Harris, Joanne

Smith Finley, and myself. The editors of the latter explicitly aimed to include contributions on culture – a topic that was largely left out of the first volume. Further examples of interdisciplinary conversations include a collection on social and religious history (Millward, Shinmen and Sugawara 2010), a special issue of the journal *Studies in Travel Writing* 18 (4), and a volume edited by Hayes and Clarke (2015) on space, place, and power. These collaborative efforts also signify the emergence and gradual coming of age of modern Xinjiang Studies. As evidenced in these publications, modern Xinjiang Studies tends to put the major accent on the Uyghur, but accommodates the possible study of Xinjiang's other ethnic groups, including its Han population, who have been largely neglected in the literature to date.[11] It is envisaged that these and other works with a comparable focus will open the way to new research which draws attention to social groupings that are not necessarily ethnically defined, as well as to social inequalities that are not simply the result of ethnic belonging, but which emerge at the junctures between ethnicity, profession, generation, class, and gender.

In spite of the broad spectrum of topics, scholars specialising in Xinjiang tend to agree that they face considerable constraints in research, regardless of their chosen method of data collection, nationality, or ethnic affiliation. Ethical questions loom large especially for those who insist on employing traditional long-term ethnographic fieldwork as their main method. The difficulties which haunt both native and foreign researchers also account for the glaring gaps in research on Xinjiang. Such gaps include the economic and social history of the oases during various periods under socialism; the history of the traditional elites and of social movements; Uyghur intellectual history; various forms of micro-history; studies of the changing role of socialist cadres who, like elites in general, have been uncomfortably positioned between ordinary Uyghurs and alien power holders; analyses of the entanglement of religion and politics in the past and present; and systematic research into rural Uyghur communities. The urgency of researching such topics may be obvious to many readers; nevertheless, I consider it appropriate to illustrate in some detail the need for expanded research in rural areas.

---

[11] Agnieszka Joniak-Lüthi (2013) and Michael Dillon (2014) have started to make good this deficit by situating the Han in Xinjiang's socialist history and deconstructing their homogenous image.

Rural Xinjiang

Under the current conditions of heightened ethnic tension, foreign researchers wishing to study Xinjiang find it easier to live and work in an urban centre. Or, they choose research methods which include frequent shifting of place to avoid surveillance and restrictions by the government. Neither of these strategies allows for systematic work in the countryside. Obtaining a research permit for fieldwork in the countryside is difficult for political reasons and when it is realised, it means that the researcher is under constant surveillance. Long-term systematic research in rural areas without an official research permit is almost impossible unless affiliation to a local research team is secured. Arguments as well as counter-arguments which render a rural research site a more likely proposition for the authorities are easy to find. For example, since the government's major concern is that the researcher will gain an insight into discontent and ethnic conflict, it can be assumed that Xinjiang's numerous ethnically homogenous villages are considered to be unlikely sites of ethnic conflict. Yet it is widely known that conflict does emerge between farmers and local officials (often of Uyghur ethnicity) over the implementation of unpopular policies issued in Beijing or by the local authorities. Thus, Uyghur discontent in Xinjiang is not an exclusively urban phenomenon and, while its sources are not all exclusively ethnic concerns, they tend to be 'translated' into the language of ethnicity both by state representatives and by local actors.[12]

Uyghurs comprise about 46 per cent of the 20 million inhabitants of Xinjiang. A staggering 85 per cent of these Uyghurs are registered as rural residents.[13] This alone should indicate an urgent need to better understand Xinjiang's rural areas. Moreover, little is known about the effect of governmental policies in Xinjiang on farmers. Neither the local effects of nationwide policies implemented across the socialist period, nor those of recent policies targeted specifically at western China, have been sufficiently studied and understood.

As an example, let us take recent and ongoing transformations in rural Xinjiang. Development in Xinjiang gained momentum in the wake of the Great Western Development Drive launched in 2000, and most areas of the region have benefited visibly from investment. Yet development remains uneven, both among regions and ethnic groups as well as between urban and rural areas. My own observations made during repeated visits between

---

[12] The official scapegoating of unemployed Uyghur rural youth from southern Xinjiang for the high death toll in Ürümchi on 5 July 2009 also suggests that trouble emanates from the countryside.

[13] *Xinjiang Statistical Yearbook* 1990–2010.

2006–13 in eastern Xinjiang suggest that Uyghur villagers are subjected to irreversible, top-down changes in which they have little or no say. Such changes take diverse forms. They may include the creation of model villages in place of traditional settlements, with an ostensibly more rational use of space and the imposition of a uniform 'ethnic architectural style'; or they may even entail moving the settlement a short distance. If the traditional village is in the way of a specific development project, such as the opening or extending of a potentially lucrative mining enterprise, its inhabitants may be forcibly relocated to a new housing estate on the outskirts of a big city. At the discretion of local authorities, high rise apartment buildings may be erected in villages nearer a city, as I observed in the prefecture of Hami/ Qumul. Such projects are often accompanied by unequal negotiations initiated and carried out by the county authorities. Cadres working for the township government and village committee negotiate with developers and investors, and are in charge of issuing and administering land related contracts and documents. This situation in the Kashgar region has recently led one researcher to conclude that Uyghur farmers, whose rights to land are only weakly protected by legal documents, suffer from the changed conditions caused by relocation and only partially benefit from development (Cappelletti 2014: 20–21). This repossession of land is not limited to Southern Xinjiang, it was already well underway in Eastern Xinjiang at the time of my last visit in 2013.

Uyghurs experience this new wave of development as ethnically motivated. While many rural settlements are ethnically homogenous (either Han or Uyghur), rural townships situated nearer the city may include members of both Han and Uyghur ethnicity. Ethnic co-existence (if not mixing) may be realised through the presence of a small Han enclave or neighbourhood emerging in a predominantly Uyghur settlement. Han villages are subjected to a similar array of development strategies, but many Uyghur villagers perceive such moves not just in terms of top-down development but also as an encroachment on their traditions and consequently a threat to their ethnic identity. Uyghur villagers living in the immediate vicinity of the city are more likely to resort to administrative measures in order to contest the repossession attempts that developers initiate with cadres.

Repossession itself may assume diverse forms, such as declaring an existing contract invalid, or persuading a farmer to give up his land for an unfavourable compensation. Those who are dissatisfied with the offered arrangements follow strategies also mobilised by Han villagers elsewhere in China; they resort to the petition system. Petitions to the township or prefectural authorities are usually made through the inexpensive services of a 'barefoot lawyer', that is a local person, often himself a farmer, who has relevant experience in drawing up legal documents and a rudimentary knowledge of the necessary legal terminology. However, most of these petitions are turned down, and those who continue to seek justice in the provincial capital of Ürümchi (where they are again unlikely to succeed), may face harassment or even arrest on unrelated charges from the county authorities upon their return. Uyghur farmers perceive such landgrabbings as illegal, and while the moneyed entrepreneurs are typically identified as Han, they also suspect local cadres of corruption and complicity in such deals.[14]

The accelerated pace of development entails a rapid transformation of the social relationships I have documented in this volume, although we can be certain that many patterns persist. Both continuities and change can be understood launched better when put in the context of earlier processes which were set in motion by decollectivisation and the ensuing reforms, and which were shaped by the entanglement of local responses to these top-down policies. Six of the ten articles included in this volume deal with enduring values and their transformations among Uyghur villagers in the first decades of the reforms. These transformations immediately preceded the implementation of the Great Western Development Drive in 2000 and the declaration of Kashgar as a special economic zone in 2010. Given the paucity of this kind of data, the articles allow insight into the re-organisation of social life in rural Kashgar at a time when new opportunities were opening while significant constraints remained operational.

The Chapters

Although this volume does not offer a comprehensive description and analysis of rural transformation, the first six chapters deal with aspects of rural life in Southern Xinjiang. They address topics such as agricultural policies and farmers' agency, farmers' informal economic activities, and intra-household labour arrangements in the mid-1990s. Chapter 1 is directly relevant for understanding the implementation of top-down agricultural policies in villages near Kashgar and the related role of rural cadres who are uncomfortably positioned between the state and their fellow villagers. Chapters 2-4 deal with the gendered division of labour and the organisation of non-agricultural work in the informal sector among Uyghur villagers in the mid-1990s, with attention to historical and cultural contexts. Chapter 4 more specifically probes the limits of theorising the interconnectedness between traditional gendered divisions of labour and emic explanations of

---

[14] Such landgrabbings are reported from many other parts of China, for example see Zhao (2009) and Siciliano (2014).

human procreation through a comparison of the Uyghur in Southern Xinjiang with another Muslim community where I have conducted fieldwork – the Lazi in north-east Turkey. Chapter 5 brings together emic and etic ethnographic materials from pre-socialist and socialist Xinjiang to demonstrate both persistence and change in forms of legal pluralism. With textual and ethnographic data, I tried to outline patterns of the unwritten, orally transmitted rules which govern everyday social relations through changing political conditions, and to demonstrate how these rules undergo modifications, retain or lose their force, and reinforce or compete with other legal systems. Chapter 6, 'The Mobilisation of Tradition', also considers continuities and change among Kashgar farmers, who, due to socialist social engineering lost much of the security provided by local networks and local knowledge necessary for survival. I demonstrate how old attachments are perpetuated and merged with new attachments to produce a sense of belonging to land, houses, and local produce.

Chapter 7, 'Temperamental Neighbours', summarises my observations in the oasis of Kucha during the preliminary phase of the research project that provided the framework for most of the articles reproduced here. For two months, I waited for my research permit to be issued. During that time, I observed how interethnic relations in everyday life in the urban centres of Xinjiang were already uneasy in the mid-1990s, as expressions of discontent were becoming increasingly frequent.

Three chapters (8-10) focus on religion. Chapter 8 comprises data collected in Xinjiang, largely derived from historical texts. The other two are primarily ethnographic, but the field research was carried out among the Uyghur diaspora in Almaty, Kazakhstan in 1997. All this is no accident. Enquiring into Uyghur religious beliefs and practices during fieldwork in Xinjiang was rendered impossible by the terms of my collaborative research project in Xinjiang and through the almost continuous presence of a Uyghur-speaking Han colleague. Thus, ethnographic data pertaining to matters of religion were gleaned from the unsolicited utterances of my interview partners in the course of monitored conversations. In 1997, after cooperation broke down with my Han research partners in Xinjiang, I made the decision to relocate the last stage of fieldwork to Kazakhstan. There, I enquired into religious practices to make up for the lack of such opportunities in Xinjiang. The chapters demonstrate the differences between the two neighbouring countries in terms of research opportunities and freedom during the 1990s. My experiences of the healing practices of Uyghur women in the Almaty neighbourhood (chapter 9) and during a pilgrimage (chapter 10) document the first wave of religious revival in post-Soviet Kazakhstan, a context which does not lend itself easily to comparison with socialist Xinjiang.

Nevertheless, many of the beliefs informing the religious practices I observed in the diaspora share features with the data documented in the chapter focusing on Xinjiang: these continuities are ensured by the well-known cultural affinities of Xinjiang to Central Asia, and more concretely, by the migrations from Xinjiang to the Soviet Central Asian republics in the early 1960s. All three chapters discuss practices which rely on a shared repertoire of underlying beliefs, the common denominator of which is the veneration of the dead.

The chapters on work, gender, and religion convey beliefs, social norms, and ritual practice with which Uyghurs were generally familiar in the last decades of the twentieth century. The sentiments and emic perceptions of the in-group and of others that I documented in the oasis town of Kucha also have wider currency in the southern oases. The degree of historical contextualisation varies, but each chapter had relevance for the contemporary political situation at the time of writing. Most display a degree of gender sensitivity. Finally, they all demonstrate the significance of perceived traditions and their conscious or unintended mobilisation in the face of top-down initiatives. When taken together, these multiple, overlapping patterns of occupational, religious, and gender identifications, as well as emotional attachments to space and insistence on material displays of belonging have all contributed to the crystallisation of modern Uyghur ethno-national identity. Thus they not only assume a certain historical relevance but also testify to the deeper political significance of the everyday, often overlooked as having little or no bearing on politics.

All the chapters emerged from the same research project. With the exception of chapter 8, which constitutes text-based research, the chapters are primarily based on qualitative methods of ethnographic data collection. Seven were carried out in Southern Xinjiang, and two in Almaty. For carrying out the research funded by the Economic and Social Research Council of Great Britain (R000 235709), an official permit was obtained from the regional government. I spent the preparatory period of the project in Kucha (June to September 1995) by myself without surveillance, which did not allow for systematic interviews but made observation and informal encounters possible (chapter 7). Similarly, I carried out the last two months of the fieldwork (September to November 1997) in Kazakhstan unaccompanied, staying with a Uyghur family (chapters 9, 10).

Ethnographic data presented in chapters 1-6 were collected in two townships in the vicinity of Kashgar. These two locations as well as the neighbourhoods were selected by the local authorities who initially also wished to control which households we entered. Eventually we were allowed to carry out interviews in every household of both neighbourhoods. In the original publications I insisted on keeping the locations anonymous and I prefer to stick to this decision even today. Suffice it to say that the two townships were exceptionally prosperous in Southern Xinjiang at the time. Agriculture was the main point of identification for farmers, but it was often insufficient to satisfy subsistence needs and agricultural income needed to be augmented by engagement in non-agricultural activities. Both benefited from their geographical proximity to the city of Kashgar, and the one main difference between the two that is relevant from the research perspective was that one of them benefited from UNICEF funding.

The project was envisaged as a collaborative one and therefore most of the time I was accompanied by a Uyghur-speaking ethnic Han researcher (by training a linguist). We communicated with each other and with all our interlocutors in Uyghur. This Chinese research partner occasionally participated actively in the interviews, but most of the time he assumed a passive role. The use of the first person plural 'we' in the text is acknow-ledgement of his presence and contribution. Throughout the work I was explicitly told not to ask questions about politics, ethnic relations, and religion. Research conditions did not allow for the regular revisiting of the same families or for building up trust, and farmers often assumed that we worked for the government. Thus research conditions were far from ideal.[15] The lengths of the interviews varied but often they took two to three hours. During the main fieldwork period (April to August 1996), we conducted semi-structured interviews in about 100 households, and data was also collected in the course of numerous unstructured interviews.[16]

Further points which need clarification are as follows. The administrative divisions of socialist Xinjiang include the autonomous regional level, followed by the prefectural, county, and township levels. Below the township (*yeza*), which is equivalent to the commune (*gongshe*) of the collectivised period, we find the village (*känt*), equivalent to the production brigade (*dadüy*) of the collectivised period. The smallest unit today is the group (*guruppa*), equivalent to the production team (*shaodüy*) of the collectivised period.[17] I use the term cadre (*kadir*) in the same loose sense as did Uyghur villagers during my fieldwork: They referred to any person with some perceived or real administrative power as a cadre, regardless of whether the person was a full-time civil servant employed in

---

[15] For an elaboration on the research conditions see my summary in Bellér-Hann (2010).

[16] During the main part of the fieldwork I was accompanied by Chris Hann, officially attached to the project, and our two children.

[17] As far as I could ascertain, the *känt* or production brigade roughly corresponded to natural villages and the *guruppa* or production team was usually built around traditional neighbourhoods (*mähällä*).

government administration or a village-level official who worked for a small annual fee.

The historical periodisation used throughout corresponds to general scholarly usage and needs no elaboration, perhaps with the exception of the period starting around 1980. I refer to the period between 1980–90 as the reform period and use the expression 'post-reform' for the era starting around 1990.

Collected in one volume, these previously published pieces reflect early attempts to study social relations among the Uyghur in post-Mao China (and postsocialist Kazakhstan). Their subject matters reflect the conditions of research at the time, mapping out what was possible under controlled and strained political conditions. They also point out a number of potential trajectories further research can take, based on more diverse linguistic competences, better access to data, and more skilful formulations of research questions (see also Bellér-Hann 2008). Arguably, their current significance goes beyond their capacity to document social relations in rural Kashgar in an era gone by. Although many policies have changed, the larger patterns of access to local resources and power of the Uyghur vis-à-vis the Han population and the Chinese state remain constant. The articles also serve as points of departure for future historical studies on various aspects of the social and cultural life of the Turkic-speaking Muslims of Xinjiang. When contrasted with local ethnographers' folkloristic works, they can be used as evidence of lived social relations to make better sense of Uyghur folklorists' generalised works of Uyghur customs. They also serve as a starting point to fill out the hollow concept of tradition, a concept much used by representatives of the Chinese state, Uyghur intellectuals, and others in the pursuit of various strategies to draw the parameters of Uyghur identity.

Five of the chapters were previously published in academic journals, while the remaining five appeared in collective volumes, all meticulously peer-reviewed both by the anonymous reviewers and by the editors. While every effort has been made to correct mistakes, I have kept to the original text as far as possible although some paragraphs were abbreviated or deleted when ethnographic data overlapped between the chapters. Original bibliographical references have been retained and the scholarly literature has not been updated. I believe that, in spite of their shortcomings and the limitation of the time-frame, both the methods of data collection and the analysis have a certain added value as *Zeitdokumente*.

References

Aubin, F. (ed.). 2008. Du Turkestan oriental au Xinjiang. Quelques vues nouvelle. *Études Orientales* 25, special issue.

———., and F.-J. Besson (eds.). 1998. Les Ouïgours au XXéme siècle. *Cahiers d'Études sur la Méditerranée Orientale et le Monde Turco-Iranien* 25, special issue.

Bellér-Hann, I. 2010. Feltarbejde med forhindringer – blandt uyghur-minoriteten i Kina. *Tværkultur: Årbog for ToRS* 2: 77–85.

———. 2008. Community Matters in Xinjiang 1880–1949: Towards a Historical Anthropology of the Uyghur. *China Studies* 17: 476. Leiden: Brill.

———., C. Cesàro, R. Harris, and J. Smith Finley (eds.). 2007. *Situating the Uyghurs between China and Central Asia.* Aldershot: Ashgate.

———., and T. Brox. 2014. Introduction. In T. Brox, and I. Bellér-Hann (eds.), *On the Fringes of the Harmonious Society: Tibetans and Uyghurs in Socialist China*, pp. 1–28. Copenhagen: NIAS Press.

Bovingdon, G. 2010. *The Uyghurs: Strangers in their Own Land.* New York: Columbia University Press.

Brox, T., and I. Bellér-Hann (eds.). 2014. *On the Fringes of the Harmonious Society. Tibetans and Uyghurs in Socialist China.* Copenhagen: NIAS Press.

Cappelletti, A. 2014. Social Change in Kashgar from a Cultural and Religious Oasis along the Silk Road to the 'Dubai of Central Asia'. In S. Han, and P. Santangelo (eds.), *Proceedings of the 'Social Changes in China' Academic Workshop*, pp. 13–23. Rome: Asia Orientale.

Chen H. 1999. *Minguo Xinjiang shi.* Ürümchi: Xinjiang renmin chubanshe.

Chvyr', L. A. 1990. *Uigury Vostochnogo Turkestana i sosednie narody v kontse XIX—nachale XXv.* Moscow: Nauka.

———. 2006. *Obriady i verovanniia uigurov v XIX–XX vv. Ocherki narodnogo islama v Turkestane.* Moscow: Vostochnaya Literatura.

Clarke, M. E. 2011. *Xinjiang and China's Rise in Central Asia: A History.* London: Routledge.

Dautcher, J. 2009. *Down a Narrow Road: Identity and Masculinity in a Uyghur Community in Xinjiang China.* Cambridge: Harvard University Press.

Dawut, R. 2007. Shrine Pilgrimage and Sustainable Tourism among the Uyghurs: Central Asian Ritual Traditions in the Context of China's Development Policies. In I. Bellér-Hann, C. Cesàro, R. Harris, and J. Smith Finley (eds.), *Situating the Uyghurs between China and Central Asia*, pp. 149–164. Aldershot: Ashgate.

Di Cosmo, N. 1993. *Reports from the Northwest: A Selection of Manchu Memorials from Kashgar*. Bloomington: Indiana University Research Institute for Inner Asian Studies.

Dillon, M. 2014. *Xinjiang and the Expansion of Chinese Communist Power: Kashgar in the Early Twentieth Century*. London: Routledge.

Eschment, B., and H. Harder (eds.). 2004. *Looking at the Coloniser: Cross-Cultural Perceptions in Central Asia and the Caucasus, Bengal, and Related Areas*. Würzburg: Ergon-Verlag.

Friederich, M. 1997. *Die ujghurische Literatur in Xinjiang 1956–1966*. Wiesbaden: Harrassowitz.

Gladney, D. 2004. *Dislocating China: Muslims, Minorities, and Other Subaltern Subjects*. Chicago: University of Chicago Press.

Harrell, S. 1995. Introduction: Civilizing Projects and the Reactions to Them. In S. Harrell (ed.), *Cultural Encounters on China's Ethnic Frontiers*, pp. 3–36. Seattle: University of Washington Press.

Harris, R. 2008. *The Making of a Musical Canon in Chinese Central Asia: The Uyghur Twelve Muqam*. Aldershot: Ashgate Press.

Hayes, A., and M. Clarke (eds.). 2015. *Inside Xinjiang: Space, Place and Power in China's Muslim Far Northwest*. London: Routledge.

Hopkirk, P. 1980. *Foreign Devils on the Silk Road. The Search for the Lost Cities and Treasures of Chinese Central Asia*. Oxford: Oxford University Press.

Huan T. 2012. *Governing Imperial Borders: Insights from the Study of the Implementation of Law in Qing Xinjiang*. Ph.D. dissertation. New York: Columbia University.

Iskhakov, G. M. 1975. *Etnograficheskoe izuchenie uigurov Vostochnogo Turkestana russkimi puteshestvennikami vtoroi poloviny XIX veka*. Alma Ata: Nauka.

İslamoğlu-İnan, H., and P. Perdue (eds.). 2009. *Shared histories of Modernity: China, India, and the Ottoman Empire*. New Delhi: Routledge.

—— (eds.). 2004. *Constituting Modernity: Private Property in the East and West*. London: I. B. Tauris.

Joniak-Lüthi, A. 2013. Han Migration to Xinjiang Uyghur Autonomous Region: Between State Schemes and Migrants' Strategies. *Zeitschrift für Ethnologie* 138 (2): 155–174.

Kim, K. 2008. *Saintly Brokers: Uyghur Muslims, Trade, and the Making of Qing Central Asia, 1696–1814*. Ph.D. dissertation. Berkeley: University of California.

Klimeš, O. 2015. *Struggle by the Pen: The Uyghur Discourse of Nation and National Interest, c.1900–1949*. Leiden: Brill.

Leibold, J., and C. Yangbin (eds.). 2013. *Minority Education in China: Balancing Unity and Diversity in an Era of Critical Pluralism*. Hong Kong: Hong Kong University Press.

Light, N. 2012. Muslim Histories of China: Historiography across Boundaries in Central Eurasia. In Zs. Rajkai, and I. Bellér-Hann (eds.), *Frontiers and Boundaries: Encounters on China's Margins*, pp. 151–176. Wiesbaden: Harrassowitz.

——. 2008. *Intimate Heritage: Creating Uyghur Muqam Song in Xinjiang*. Berlin: LIT.

Mackerras, C. 2009. *China, Xinjiang and Central Asia: History, Transition and Crossborder Interaction into the 21st Century*. London: Routledge.

McMillen, D. H. 1979. *Chinese Communist Power and Policy in Xinjiang, 1949–1977*. Boulder: Westview.

Millward, J. 1998. *Beyond the Pass: Economy, Ethnicity, and Empire in Qing Central Asia, 1759–1864*. Stanford: Stanford University Press.

——. 2007. *Eurasian Crossroads: A History of Xinjiang*. New York: Columbia University Press.

——., and P. C. Perdue. 2004. Political and Cultural History of the Xinjiang Region through the Late Nineteenth Century. In S. Frederick Starr (ed.), *Xinjiang: China's Muslim Borderland*, pp. 27–62. New York: M. E. Sharpe.

——., and N. Tursun. 2004. Political History and Strategies of Control, 1884–1978. In S. Frederick Starr (ed.), *Xinjiang: China's Muslim Borderland*, pp. 63–98. New York: M. I. Sharpe.

——., Shinmen Y., and J. Sugawara (eds.). 2010. *Studies on Xinjiang Historical Sources in 17–20th Centuries*. Tokyo: The Toyo Bunko.

Newby, L. 2005. *The Empire and the Khanate: A Political History of Qing Relations with Khoqand c. 1760–1860*. Leiden: Brill.

Onuma T. (forthcoming). The 1795 Khoqand Mission and Its Negotiations with the Qing. Political and Diplomatic Space of Qing Kashgaria. In I. Bellér-Hann, B. Schlyter, and J. Sugawara (eds.), *Kashgar Revisited: Uyghur Studies in Memory of Ambassador Gunnar Jarring*. Leiden: Brill.

Papas, A. 2005. *Soufisme et politique entre Chine, Tibet et Turkestan: étude sur les Khwajas Naqshbandis du Turkestan Oriental*. Paris: Librairie d'Amérique et d'Orient Jean Maisonneuve.

Perdue, P. 2005. *China Marches West: The Qing Conquest of Central Eurasia*. Cambridge: Belknap Press.

Potter, P. B. 2011. *Law, Policy, and Practice on China's Periphery: Selective Adaptation and Institutional Capacity*. London: Routledge.

Rudelson, J. J. 1997. *Oasis Identities: Uyghur nationalism along China's Silk Road*. New York: Columbia University Press.

Saguchi T. 1963. *18–19 saeki Higashi Torukisutan shakai shi kenkyu*. Tokyo: Yoshikawa Kobunkan.

Schluessel, E. (forthcoming). Muslims at the Yamen Gate: Translating Justice in Late-Qing Xinjiang. In I. Bellér-Hann, B. Schlyter, and J. Sugawara (eds.), *Kashgar Revisited: Uyghur Studies In Memory of Ambassador Gunnar Jarring*. Leiden: Brill.

Siciliano, G. 2014. Rural-Urban Migration and Domestic Land Grabbing in China. *Population, Space and Place* 20 (4): 333–351.

Smith Finley, J. 2013. *The Art of Symbolic Resistance: Uyghur Identities and Uyghur-Han Relations in Contemporary Xinjiang*. Leiden: Brill.

Starr, S. F. (ed.). 2004. *Xinjiang: China's Muslim Borderland*. New York: M. E. Sharpe.

Steenberg Reyhé, R. 2013. *Uyghur Marriage in Kashgar. Muslim Marriage in China*. Ph.D. dissertation. Berlin: Freie Universität.

Sugawara J. 2012. Islamic Legal Order in the Northwestern Frontier: Property and Waqf Litigation of a Sufi Family in Kāshghar (1841–1936). In Zs. Rajkai, and I. Bellér-Hann (eds.), *Frontiers and Boundaries: Encounters on China's Margins*, pp. 177–201. Wiesbaden: Harrassowitz.

Thum, R. 2014. *The Sacred Routes of Uyghur History*. Cambridge: Harvard University Press.

Trebinjac, S. 2000. *Le pouvoir en chantant*. Nanterre: Société d'ethnologie.

Waley-Cohen, J. 1991. *Exile in Mid-Qing China: Banishment to Xinjiang, 1758–1820*. New Haven: Yale University Press.

Wang D. 2003. *Qingdai huijiang falu zhidu yanjiu (1759–1884)*. Harbin: Heilongjiang jiaoyu chubanshe.

Wang J. 2004. *Uyghur Education and Social Order: The Role of Islamic leadership in the Turpan Basin*. Tokyo: Research Institute for Languages and Cultures of Asia and Africa (ILCAA), Tokyo University of Foreign Studies.

Xinjiang Statistical Yearbook. 1990–2010. Beijing: China Statistical Publisher.

Yang Sh. 1991. *Huiheshi*. Changchun: Jirin jiaoyu chubanshe.

Zang X. 2012. *Islam, Family Life, and Gender Inequality in Urban China*. London: Routledge.

Zarcone, Th. 2002. *Saints and Heroes on the Silk Road*. Paris: Maisonneuve.

Zeng W. 1986 [1936]. *Zhongguo jingying Xiyu shi*. Ürümchi: Xinjiang Weiwu'er zizhiqu zongbian shi.

Zhao B. 2009. Land Expropriation, Protest, and Impunity in Rural China. *Focaal* 54: 97–105.

Zhongguo Xinjiang diqu Yisilan. 2000. Ürümchi: Xinjiang renmin chubanshe.

Zhu P. 2000. *Ershi shiji Xinjiang shi yanjiu.* Ürümchi: Xinjiang renmin chubanshe.

Chapter 1
The Peasant Condition in Xinjiang[1]

The economic reforms implemented in rural China and their repercussions have received a great deal of scholarly attention (e.g. Riskin 1987; Croll 1988, 1995; Feuchtwang, Hussain and Pairault 1988; Nolan 1988; Oi 1989; Siu 1989; Hinton 1990; Potter and Potter 1990; Davin 1991; Kelliher 1992; Liu 1994; Benewick and Wingrove 1995; Blecher 1995). Most analyses have focused on the situation among the Han majority, while changes taking place in many minority regions have been neglected. One such region is Southern Xinjiang. The purpose of the present chapter is to give a brief account of how Uyghur peasants[2], who form the majority of the population in this region, have experienced change and continuity since the rural reforms were introduced in the early 1980s.[3]

The Xinjiang Uyghur Autonomous Region (XUAR) is situated in the north-western corner of the People's Republic of China.[4] It is the home of 13 recognised ethnic groups, although the number of unrecognised groups which would like to claim such status is much higher.[5] The population is relatively small at just under 17 million, but since the XUAR makes up about one-sixth of China's total land area and comprises a strategically very

---

[1] Originally published in the *Journal of Peasant Studies* 1997, 24 (4): 87–112.

[2] I am aware of the controversy surrounding the term 'peasant'. However, in the Xinjiang context the standard word is *dihqan* which can best be translated as 'peasant', rather than farmer, villager, smallholder, or petty commodity producer. The term continues to be a primary reference point for self-identification for many rural Uyghurs. In this chapter I will also use make use of the terms 'farmer' and 'villager' for stylistic reasons.

[3] Although there is now a sizeable literature concerning Xinjiang, most studies concentrate on history or on ethnic relations in the urban setting. Few studies focus on the rural population (Hoppe 1987) or social change (Mackerras 1995), but research opportunities in the countryside for foreigners remain notoriously difficult.

[4] For a general introduction to the region see Lattimore (1962, 1975 [1950]) and Weggel (1984). For a discussion of the years of collectivisation see McMillen (1979), and for the position of the Muslim minorities there see Dillon (1994, 1995).

[5] On the politics of ethnic identity and state recognition of minority groups in China see Gladney (1994a, 1994b).

important border region, its stability is of great importance to the centre.[6] As the name of the province implies, the dominant group is the Uyghurs, people who speak a Turkic type language and profess Islam. Although the Uyghurs still form a numerical majority in the province, the rapid influx of Han Chinese from the poor inland provinces may soon change this.[7] This vast border region has had a long history of Chinese presence going back to the Han dynasty. However, for a long time the Chinese were unable to establish firm control over the region. The area first became officially incorporated into the Qing Empire (1644–1911) in the second half of the eighteenth century. Following the great Muslim rebellions of the nineteenth century it became a Chinese province in 1884 when it was given its present name Xinjiang, meaning New Frontier. During the Republican period (1912–49) the territory remained nominally part of China but little control was exercised by the centre, and the first half of the twentieth century was characterised by the unstable rule of a series of Chinese warlords. The latest de facto political incorporation of the region into China came about at the time of the communist victory in 1949.

Apart from mounting ethnic tensions, primarily between the Uyghurs and the Han Chinese, other factors also add to the growing instability of the region. Xinjiang has for a long time been perceived by the Chinese centre as a place for banishment, an imperial tradition carried into the socialist period in the form of labour camps. This is also the region where, making use of large desert areas, China carries out its nuclear tests.

The situation in the XUAR during the socialist period can be characterised as colonial. There has been a strong Chinese military presence, exploitation of mineral resources (especially oil) for the benefit of interior regions of China, and the encouragement of large-scale Han Chinese labour migration to work in construction, mining, and rural industry as a cheap labour force. Increasingly conscious of these disadvantages, the aspirations of ethnic minorities have received a great boost from the fact that Muslim groups such as the Uzbeks, Kyrgyz, Kazakh, and Turkmen, closely related to the Uyghurs in language and culture and formerly dominated by Russian imperialism within the USSR, have recently gained independence (Dillon 1995). This chapter focuses on the southern part of Xinjiang, which has the largest concentration of Uyghurs and the least developed industry.

---

[6] See *Shinjang Statistika Yilliq Toplimi* (1996: 48).

[7] In 1995 the total number of Uyghurs was 7,800,038, and that of the Han Chinese 6,318,114, see *Shinjang Statistika Yilliq Toplimi* (1996: 48).

Post-'Liberation' Xinjiang[8] has experienced all the changes which the rest of China has undergone: land reform followed by the establishment of mutual-aid teams, then cooperatives, then the Peoples' Communes, the Cultural Revolution, and most recently the reform era that began in the early 1980s. Because of restricted access to reliable information and data, foreign observers took a relatively long time to recognise the realities behind Maoist rhetoric. They emphasised the enormous achievements of the commune period in terms of eliminating poverty and realising a greater degree of equality.[9] Nowadays the Maoist period is viewed more critically, and the ongoing reform period is hailed as bringing more substantial benefits in both agricultural production and the welfare and freedoms of peasants. The unleashing of market forces under the guidance of the Communist Party has, however, given rise to new problems on the macro-level as noted by many analysts (Nolan 1988; Hinton 1990; Kelliher 1992; Blecher 1995). Though informed by these analyses, the main focus of this chapter is on how the reform era is perceived by Uyghur peasants themselves.

Although great changes have taken place in many of the villages of Xinjiang, and these are acknowledged by peasants, the reforms have not added up to a great advance for many of them. The euphoria among Uyghur peasants which followed the land reform in the early 1980s (see below) has given way to a reassessment of the present situation, which in the view of many is far from satisfactory. Peasants' accounts of their daily lives focus on continuities with past practices and dissatisfaction with the new policies, which many of them consider misguided.[10] Many aspects of the open coercion of the local peasantry by the Chinese state during the years of collectivisation have persisted and these continue to create feudal-type constraints for Uyghur villagers.[11] The term 'feudal' is used here in a loose, popular sense, to describe a situation in which peasants' freedom of movement remains seriously restricted. They have no rights of ownership over their land; they are subjected to corvée type labour obligations; and they have limited control over their harvest.[12] The term 'feudal' is also used by the socialist authorities as the official term for the pre-revolutionary

---

[8] The incorporation of Xinjiang into socialist China is known in PRC histories as the peaceful Liberation of Xinjiang. The term 'Liberation' will appear in quotation marks throughout because this description may not necessarily be endorsed by all actors concerned.

[9] For a brief overview see Zweig (1990: 39).

[10] After 1985 peasants witnessed a 'reassertion of stricter controls' (Hinton 1990: 24). See also Daniel Kelliher's comments (1992: 157-58).

[11] On continuities with the past see, for example, Oi (1989) and Kelliher (1992).

[12] According to Owen Lattimore, the most important methods of coercion in pre-industrial China used to be share-cropping and corvée. Restrictions imposed upon Uyghur farmers in this new phase of socialism meet his definition of 'feudal' (Lattimore 1962: 479).

social structure of China, including Xinjiang.[13] Local and higher level party officials still make frequent use of the term to refer to 'backward customs and ideas'.[14] A crusade against feudal customs is still being carried forward in the name of modernity and progress. Feudalism is a particularly useful idiom in Xinjiang for a Chinese state which is trying to reduce the role of Islam, perceived as the major moving force behind ethnic separatism.[15] However, while there are clear points of confrontation between the messages conveyed by religious authorities and those of the state, I suggest that at some points the two may converge and reinforce each other. The ultimate irony is that when the Chinese state seeks to weaken Islam it also inadvertently undermines a force which, in some respects, provides useful underpinnings for the acceptance and respect of secular authorities.

The Reform Context

'The Central Party Committee and the State Commission have issued a series of guidelines to reduce the burden on farmers. Various responsible organisations and local governments have also devised numerous ways to implement the spirit of these guidelines, but in many places the old situation has not changed at all and the farmers' outcry can be heard everywhere'. These lines introduce the poem 'The Peasant Cries' recorded on a tape played to us by a young peasant during an interview in his house.[16] [17] The tape contained a collection of poems written by the Uyghur poet, Rozi Sayit (1944–2001). The title of the tape and the first poem was: 'It Is Difficult to Be a Peasant'. According to our young host, the poems were an accurate representation of the peasants' position in the new economic climate. The

---

[13] As William Hinton pointed out, the revolution of 1949 was not a socialist revolution, even though it was led by the working class and the party. Its targets were feudalism (landlordism) internally and imperialism externally (Hinton 1972: 18).

[14] See for example Mackerras (1995: 111) and Rudelson (1997: 124).

[15] One of the many painful measures imposed upon Uyghurs by the state is the increasing restriction on religious freedom, which in the summer of 1996 took the form of compulsory study sessions organised for state employees.

[16] I thank Mr. Sunnat Mamtimyn and other friends in Xinjiang for helping me in transcribing and translating the tape.

[17] The data presented here were largely collected in two villages near Kashgar in the course of open-ended interviews which I conducted in Uyghur in the presence of a Uyghur-speaking Chinese academic. Occasionally other village-level cadres were also present. Although initially many farmers were reluctant to say anything other than what they thought was an officially acceptable view, after a while their suspicions receded. Many informants took the view that, even if I and my Chinese companion were working for the Chinese government (which some firmly believed), we were a potential channel through which their plight could be transmitted to the higher level authorities. The first person plural refers to my Chinese co-researcher and myself.

young man who played it for us explained that in 1996 this tape had been officially banned, soon after its release. Later I learnt that the producers of the tape had been arrested and briefly imprisoned.[18] Copies nonetheless circulated and were extremely popular among Uyghur villagers, who felt the poems to give an authentic account of their current grievances.[19]

The Third Plenary Session of the Eleventh Congress of the Chinese Communist Party (CCP) in 1978 and the land reform which was implemented in the early 1980s opened up a new era for Uyghur farmers characterised by decollectivisation and more liberal ethnic policies. Uyghurs in the Kashgar region refer to these changes as simply the 'time when land was given to us' (*yär bärghän chagh*) or land reform (*yär islahati*), while others call the period which began at this time the era of freedom (*ärkinlik*).[20] As is well known, this second land reform was not a straightforward reversal of collectivisation. Decollectivisation did not mean privatisation, because land was not returned to private ownership.[21] Land ownership was retained by the collective. Villagers were given the right to use land as household units with long-term leases (Nolan 1988: 87). Land was distributed on the principle of equality, and at varying pace in different locations. The amount of land distributed varied not only from village to village but also among production teams within each village.[22] In the

---

[18] Friends in the regional capital later told me that the tape became legally available several months later there, but farmers in the Kashgar region were convinced that its circulation remained illegal.

[19] On the increased burdens of China's farmers since 1989 and the growing unrest resulting from them see Blecher (1995: 115–19).

[20] The term *ärkinlik* refers mainly to economic freedoms rather than the exercise of democratic rights. This was illustrated in a number of instances when Uyghur peasants, who wished to explain some of their present difficulties to us, were severely rebuked by cautious local cadres. On one occasion we walked past a large group of men doing communal work on an irrigation by-channel. They wanted to know who we were and what we were doing. When they heard that we were interested in peasants' lives, one said: 'I tell you the truth. Things are better now than they used to be. Now half our stomach is full, only the other half is empty. You write about this!' His words were followed by the hearty laughter of his fellow workers. The young female cadre, the local leader of the All-China Women's Federation, angrily rebuked him: 'How can you say such a thing in front of foreigners? Are you not ashamed of yourself? You are telling them lies!' The laughing immediately died out. The men were scared. Then the one who had spoken before spoke again: 'Yes, we are very happy and content, and above all, we are free!' – he winked at us, and as the leader of the All-China Women's Federation moved on, they began to smile again.

[21] See Madsen (1991: 669–71) and also McKinley and Griffin (1993: 72) who talk about 'de facto tenancy' and the creation of de facto private property rights in land.

[22] There was a slight variation in the principles upon which land distribution was decided: in some production teams, land was allocated according to the number of persons living in a household at the time; in others the number of active workers was also taken into account. But

villages where data was collected, the average size of plot each adult received was around 1 *mu*.[23]

The limitations of the principle of equality of the land reform have been recognised by many commentators. Changes in family size, and especially variations in the number of surviving sons who will sooner or later claim a share of their father's land, lead to increasing inequalities (Bramall and Jones 1993). Freedoms to employ hired labour and to engage in specialised activities within and outside agriculture have opened the way to the accumulation of wealth for some. Farmers can also have access to land other than that allocated to them by the collective, for example, by taking over a piece from another peasant who is unable or unwilling to till his own share. The right to cultivate this land is retained by peasant A to whom it had originally been leased out by the collective, but peasant B who cultivates it will typically pay either cash or grain to the holder of the lease. Peasants view land leased from the collective very differently from land taken over for cultivation from a fellow villager. The former is seen as permanent (*muqim*) land which is referred to as one's own, over which people feel they have a degree of ownership. The latter case is seen as a temporary undertaking (*höddigä elish*) which is 'unstable' or 'temporary' (*muqim ämäs*). The leasing of additional pieces of land from the collective is another option, although there is limited scope for such arrangements because of the general scarcity of arable land in the oases. It seemed that this option was only open to a privileged few who had particularly good personal relations with the village cadres. The saying that 'no land is taken away from the dead and no land is given to the newborn' (*ölüktin yär almay tughulghanga yär bärmäydu*) is implicitly interpreted as a licence to pass on the right of land use to the next generation. This statement emphasises the total control of land by an outside force, the Chinese state. In many families, fathers have already given their married sons their share no matter how small, as pre-socialist customs required. Many other families, however, have opted for not dividing the small landholdings into smaller parcels. Rather, after the married son's separation from his parents, the two households may become separate units of production and consumption but continue to cultivate the land and share the produce between them equally. In some cases, two or even three married sons shared the land with the paternal household; in

---

the overarching desire to ensure equality was clear in the fact that each household was given tiny parcels in different locations within the common property owned by the production team to ensure that everybody had land of equal quality. In the villages where we worked, the size of allocated land was determined partly according to household size and partly according to the number of workers in the household. See Nolan (1988: 86).

[23] 1 *mu* = 1/15 hectare = 1/6 acre.

others, it was only the youngest son because his elder brothers had already received their share of their patrimony.

All peasants prioritise their own subsistence needs. But in oasis settlements land tends to be scarce and in recent decades this has certainly been the case in the Kashgar region.[24] The small parcels of land cultivated by Uyghur families are barely enough to satisfy subsistence needs and seldom provide work for all the available labour force in their households. The villages where my interviews were conducted are situated near the city, where many families could rely on other sources of income.[25] Although most of these families derived most of their income from sideline production, commerce, or wage labour rather than agriculture, they continued to identify themselves primarily as peasants. Agriculture remained fundamental for them, regarded as a basic necessity to satisfy subsistence needs rather than a source of income. When we asked about forms of cooperation, one young man said: 'We do cooperate in jobs to earn money, but we do not cooperate in agricultural work'. Agriculture is not regarded as an income-generating activity, and as Terry McKinley and Keith Griffin found elsewhere in China, farm size is not an important determinant of income (1993: 78).

Although unofficial leasing arrangements between households have made it possible for a few people to cultivate large areas through employing hired labour and thereby generating substantial cash incomes, for the majority of rural households the main sources of cash income are the crafts, commerce, and household specialisation encouraged by the state since 1983 (Croll 1988). Peasants with no skills and no means of accumulating enough capital for such sideline activities have to subsist on agriculture and many can hardly meet their families' subsistence needs. I met relatively few such people in rich villages near Kashgar, but was told that they constitute the majority in villages situated further away from cities. Such peasants typically require grain loans repayable in kind from those who produce a grain surplus. Since they have to pay substantial interest, they are rapidly entangled in a web of accumulated debts. Even in the prosperous villages where we worked[26], new problems have emerged: not only has income

---

[24] For a summary of agriculture and its resources in Xinjiang see Oskar Weggel (1984: 60–84).

[25] Both villages where the interviews were conducted were relatively wealthy because of their proximity to the city of Kashgar, though their sideline specialisations differed significantly.

[26] The two villages where we were allowed to conduct interviews had an annual income per capita around 1,000 yuan. In other villages which we visited socially, or the conditions of which had been described to us by residents visiting the city, the annual income per capita was much lower. The average annual income per capita of farmers in the Kashgar prefecture in 1995 was calculated at 882.01 yuan (*Shinjang Statistika Yilliq Toplimi* 1996: 219). In 1996 1 US dollar equalled 8.3 renminbi (Chinese yuan).

inequality risen within the framework of a supposedly still socialist economy, but social benefits such as free or heavily subsidised health care and education characteristic of the era of collectivisation have partially broken down, such that considerable expenses now have to be met by individuals.

The Obligations

The great advances of the early 1980s were halted by the agrarian 'backlash' of 1985 which aimed at re-asserting strong state control over peasants (Kelliher 1992: 132–33). Many farmers continue to feel the ambiguity of this situation. They tend to perceive the responsibility system (*mäs'uliyät tüzümi*) (a term known but hardly ever used by them) as a relationship of dependency on the state. For them the reform era means, as one man put it, very few rights in exchange for a great many duties.

Peasants' obligations to the state can be summed up in six main points:

(1)   They are tied to their place of residence and therefore to their land.
(2)   They are obliged to grow an industrial crop (cotton) and sell this to the state which holds a monopoly over it.
(3)   They are subject to compulsory grain procurement by the state.
(4)   They are required to practise methods of cultivation imposed upon them from above.
(5)   They must contribute to communal work, according to the size of their plots.
(6)   They must observe compulsory family planning policies.[27]

1. Residence

'We are the most numerous of the whole population, we are the peasants, the masters of mother earth, we are the guarantors of everyone's food and wealth, we are the hard workers of earth'.[28]

From the 1950s, the Chinese authorities imposed strict controls over place of residence in order to avoid the problems of other developing countries and to control rural migration into urban centres. In spite of some significant relaxation in the 1990s, which has led to a large influx of poor peasants into China's major cities, the household registration system ensures

---

[27] This list corresponds quite closely to Peter Nolan's list of key economic channels through which the CCP can exercise power in villages (Nolan 1988: 85).
[28] Rozi Sayit, 'The Peasant Cries'.

that rural migration into the large urban centres remains under control in Xinjiang.[29] From the peasants' point of view this policy has created a sharp dividing line between urban and rural residents, the former enjoying a number of privileges in terms of health care and access to better education, jobs, and subsidised food.[30] In modern Xinjiang, Uyghur peasants regard the registration system as a major impediment to improving their lot. They see the regulations as, in effect, a means of binding them not just to their peasant status but to their place of birth, for they have no entitlement to land in any other location.

Although some may eventually move to the city, their status of residence will officially remain rural thereby excluding them from some of the benefits of town residence.[31] Conversely, teachers and other government employees who reside in the village have no right to cultivate the land, but their residence status is essentially the same as that of urban residents, for example, in relation to social security entitlements. Thus residence regulations create tangible divisions within the village as well as serving to entrench the urban-rural divide.[32] Rural residence also means entitlement to land. For some young farmers, tiny plots which they are allowed to cultivate are more of a burden than an asset. They may consider opting out of agriculture altogether and trying their hand at business. However, such a move is very risky, since business enterprises often end in failure and most people choose to retain their small plots. A typical solution to this problem is Mijit's. He has to support his wife and two young children but has less than two *mu* of land to cultivate. He leaves his wife for many months at a time to do all the agricultural work by herself while he goes to the provincial capital, Ürümchi, where he is trying to set up a carpet business with the help of a family member.

Although few farmers view rural residence and access to small pieces of land as an advantage, losing one's rural residence without gaining an

---

[29] On the household registration system see, for example, Selden (1988: 165–68); Oi (1989); Kelliher (1992: 103).

[30] In Kashgar in 1996 there was still a considerable difference between the prices of sub-sidised foodstuffs for urban residence and the market prices peasants had to pay.

[31] Apparently under certain conditions it is possible to buy an urban residence permit: one village woman told me that she paid 3,000 yuan for such a permit for her daughter after she had graduated and got a job in town.

[32] Marriages between urban and rural residents often end in divorce as a direct result of the preferential treatment of town residents. When Aynisakhan, a village woman, married an urban man and moved to his home, her in-laws kept making demands for grain, meat, and other agricultural produce from her family, saying that she was more expensive to feed because of her lack of access to subsidised foodstuffs. Eventually her family refused to meet the increasing demands and caused her to divorce her husband.

urban registration can have very serious consequences. One woman, a native of a Kashgar village, was married off to Aqsu as a young girl. There she bore five children and after the death of her husband she remained there making a living as a peddler. As her sons were growing older, she decided to return to her native village, because, although she could do business in Aqsu, she felt that it was increasingly difficult to handle her sons. She moved into the home of one of her brothers, who provided the necessary male authority for the unruly teenagers. In Kashgar she was unable to continue her business because there peddling was not an acceptable job for a woman, and she and her children had to live off the charity of her brother. Since she had left her village during the collectivised period and returned only after the onset of the reforms when land was contracted out, she had not been given a residence permit by the local township authorities which would entitle her to participate in the household responsibility system and therefore to a piece of land. Although she and her children had birth certificates, they had no residence registration, yet without this her sons could not sit examinations for higher education or get married. Her repeated attempts to get a residence permit in her natal village had been rejected, and her eldest son had run away from home.

Even though it is widely perceived as disadvantageous compared to city registration, rural residence is the only route to access land. Farmers describe families whose members enjoy a 'mixed' residence status as the most advantaged: not only do they receive cultivation rights and through it a degree of security but also the social benefits that city residents enjoy. Furthermore, since a child's residence status is determined by that of its mother, marriage between a male rural teacher, who invariably has a residence status akin to that of an urban resident, and a rural resident female will entitle the couple to have three children.[33]

2. Cotton Cultivation

'The white gold fattens others but we still remain poor, instead we get into debt'.[34] The state continues to interfere in virtually all aspects of production. Despite the ostensible commitments to 'market economy', each year quotas specified from above determine how much land has to be used for grain production and for cotton.[35] Quotas for cotton production, which is a state

---

[33] Minority couples in Xinjiang's urban areas are entitled to have up to two children, while rural couples can have three.

[34] Rozi Sayit, 'The Peasant Cries'.

[35] Specifying the crop to be cultivated on land leased out by the state is in theory part of the responsibility contract, but farmers do not use these terms and view it as merely an obligation to the landlord state (Madsen 1991: 669).

monopoly, come from the provincial level and are then broken down at lower administrative levels until each household receives a prescribed minimum allocation expressed in terms of the area to be sown. When they first saw us, farmers often assumed that we were there to check on cotton production. They called the obligation to grow cotton a form of oppression (*zulum*) and said that if it was up to them, they would prefer to grow wheat on all the land available to them. In this way more families would be able to ensure their basic subsistence needs and profit from the sale of any surplus wheat. As it is, some families cannot produce enough wheat to satisfy subsistence needs and have to buy wheat from the market. Officials claim that the centrally planned compulsory cotton cultivation is in the peasants' own best interests, whatever they themselves say, since for many families with no sideline production or commercial activities cotton provides the only source of cash income. Peasants, however, insist that the various inputs (chemicals, fertilizer, and plastic film) for cotton plus its labour intensity mean that there is no real profit in cotton growing. They believe that the state insists on it to ensure that cultivators will have enough cash in hand in late autumn to pay tax and land rent (which neither they nor the authorities distinguish clearly) and other bills. Individual farmers calculate that the cash they receive from the sale of cotton to the state-owned cotton factory does not cover their labour and cash investment in cotton growing, which renders the whole enterprise unprofitable.

Farmers receive subsidised supplies of agricultural inputs, including chemical fertilizer, but these supplies are often not enough and many have to purchase more at market prices. The cost of these subsidised inputs is lumped together with land rent, water use, education, and other service charges in a single bill that villagers have to pay at the end of October or early in November, a few weeks after the compulsory selling of their cotton to the cotton factory. This is termed 'accounting time' (*hisaplash*). This pattern is widely perceived as very similar to the annual accounting undertaken during the collective era.

3. Grain Procurement

'We are forced to sell our grain ...'.[36] Farmers are also obliged to pay disguised taxes to the state in the form of compulsory grain procurement. This, too, has been inherited from commune times, when the struggle for the harvest was between the production teams and the state (Kelliher 1992: 157–58). According to Marc Blecher, in 1985 the grain procurement system was abolished and replaced by a contract between state and farmers for part of

---

[36] Rozi Sayit, 'The Peasant Cries'.

the harvest with free markets taking the rest (Blecher 1995: 110). For their part, peasants see this no differently from the previous arrangements, since in their experience many of them have no surplus to sell and some are forced to buy extra grain to satisfy family needs. In other words, 'the struggle over the harvest that is central to peasant politics' (Oi 1989: 227) has not been eliminated during the reform period. Uyghur farmers do not get cash from the state when they sell their quota of wheat at prices fixed by the state (and significantly lower than market prices). The amount they have sold is written on a receipt in June, and its value is deducted from their debt to the collective at the time of the annual accounting several months later.[37]

The priority of Uyghur peasants with small plots is to ensure that they grow enough wheat to satisfy their family's need: the size of their plots, the obligation to grow cotton on a certain percentage of their land, and the compulsory selling of grain to the state at fixed prices prevent many of them from fulfilling this basic aspiration.[38] This is grave since a very high percentage of Uyghur peasant families' diet is wheat-based (Hoppe 1987: 239). For families with no other source of income, this multiple state interference creates an inescapable poverty trap. Farmers who can only just fulfil their families' subsistence needs with the wheat they produce, or who have to supplement their grain store with wheat bought from the market, also have to use the market to fulfil their compulsory grain procurement obligation. Of course they have to buy this wheat at a higher price than that for which they sold their own to the state, but they calculate that this entails a smaller loss than the fine they would otherwise be liable to pay for not fulfilling their grain procurement.[39]

4. Cultivation Methods

'They say you must grow a particular crop ...'.[40] After the wheat harvest in midsummer most Uyghur cultivators plant maize on the same plots, which is made possible by the exceptionally hot and long summers. The state has no direct interest in obtaining a good maize crop, since it does not form part of the compulsory procurement. In 1996 the county government in the vicinity of Kashgar decided to enforce the replacement of the traditional local maize by another variety promising higher yields. While peasants acknowledge this

---

[37] Officials told us that the collective receives cash payment from the state for the wheat it sells; but this never reaches the villager, who does not distinguish between collective and state.

[38] This problem was also elaborated in an article in the literary magazine *Tarim* which often voices social problems in literary disguise (Tokhti 1996: 7).

[39] Similar strategies have been reported from other parts of China (Kelliher 1992: 157).

[40] Rozi Sayit, 'The Peasant Cries'.

difference in yield, most of them have a clear preference for the local variety, called white maize (*aq qonaq*), as opposed to the yellow maize (*seriq qonaq*) promoted by the authorities. They say that the bread they make out of white maize tastes sweeter, and that the traditional, local variety produces more leaves which provide fodder for their sheep. Although wheat bread (*nan*) is preferred, many households occasionally still bake corn bread (*zaghra*) especially during the winter months. Corn bread used to be the staple food of the poor before 1949, and was also an important part of local diet during the 30 years of collectivisation. For families which subsist primarily on agriculture, corn bread continues to be important since, because of the inadequate size of their plots and obligatory grain procurement, they do not grow enough wheat for their own needs and have no cash to buy what they need from the market. The importance of corn as animal feed should not be underestimated either. In all the villages I visited even the poorest households try to keep at least two or three sheep. Sheep are needed for the annual ritual of the Festival of Sacrifice (*Qurban*) but, more importantly, for poor and middle-income families alike, sheep are 'walking moneyboxes'. Although some farmers take advantage of bank loans, for many the interest rate is far too high and investing in sheep appears to be the favoured way of insuring the future against a sudden need for substantial amounts of cash in cases of family crises such as illness and death or for other life-cycle rituals.

Although observers comment on the increased autonomy of villagers, intervention in cultivation methods still seems drastic from the peasants' point of view. In the summer of 1996, following instructions from the county, township officials were actively interfering with cultivation procedures. Peasants were instructed in new, more orderly techniques: corn seeds should be sown by machine in tidy rows at regular intervals, and the newly planted corn should be covered with plastic film, a practice required in cotton cultivation for years. Rural cadres were summoned for a series of meetings with township leaders, agronomists, and other leaders, and after the new methods were demonstrated, they were told to pass on these instructions to individual farmers. The peasants themselves were not consulted before the changes were implemented. They simply received orders through the local cadres, who themselves had no say in the matter. At the same meeting, the cadres received further instructions about the completion of the wheat harvest and the procurement deadline. The tone of the township leader and the chief agronomist was stern and threatening:

> We have to employ strict measures. The wheat harvest must be finished and the wheat sold to the state within the next five days. If the maize is sown later, there will be no crop. Everybody must work. During the following fifteen days no weddings can be held, and

party officials at the township offices will not be allowed to register marriages or births. Funerals are the only exceptions, but if a death occurs, only the closest relatives will be allowed to participate in the funeral. Peasants not obeying us will be fined. Rural cadres must set a good example in all these matters. It they do not do this, they will have to account for their behaviour. These orders are for your own good. We want to make you rich. The Communist Party cares about you and it is in your best interest to obey.[41]

Plate 1. Village cadres, Kashgar, Southern Xinjiang (Photo: Chris Hann).

This meeting lasted for one hour and a half. No one took notes. Many rural cadres arrived late, and some of those sitting around were chatting or dozing. The later dissemination of these decisions was exclusively oral. In some cases, leaders used the village loudspeakers, a well-tested method of the commune period. Some production team leaders personally delivered this message to every household head[42], but another favoured shortcut was to

---

[41] Quotation from my field diary.

[42] Although in the early 1980s the names of administrative units were changed, peasants and officials alike use the designations inherited from the collectivised period: the township is still called a commune, the village a production brigade, and the smallest unit, the group, is still referred to as a production team.

announce such decisions to male household heads when they assembled at
the mosque for the Friday prayer.

Plate 2. Farmers gathered to be told about new agricultural policies, Kashgar,
Southern Xinjiang (Photo: Chris Hann).

During the two weeks that followed this meeting, I spent most of my time in
the fields monitoring compliance. Many people were late with the wheat
harvest and consequently with delivering their grain to the state. I watched a
great many villagers sow their maize: most sowed the local, preferred variety
using the old methods. Nobody in the neighbourhood, as far as I could tell,
apart from some cadres, used plastic film. Peasants grumbled that they had
to buy the new variety seed (delivered to their house by the production team
leader) whether they liked it or not, and many gave it to their animals as
fodder since the seeds provided were of particularly inferior quality. At the
time, no machine for laying the plastic film was available in the village; in
any case farmers were loath to pay for its use. They said that the plastic was
a waste of time, especially as a sandstorm could easily rip it away. Some
people resorted to a compromise and sowed both types of seeds using the old
method. But most of those with whom I talked had ignored the orders, and
claimed later that they had only learned of the orders when they had already

finished sowing.[43] At a later meeting, the results of this particular campaign were evaluated. Out of the sixteen villages that made up this township only one could report that the set goals had been fully achieved. The leader of this village boasted that in the name of increased decentralisation and autonomy he had arbitrarily imposed heavy fines (120 yuan per family) on the villagers who resisted.

5. Communal Work

'The obligation to feed silk worms was distributed among households, they are not silk worms, they are our masters ...'.[44] The right to cultivate land also entails the duty to perform communal work.[45] Such work – to open up waste-land, construct and maintain irrigation channels, build schools and even main roads – is widely resented by peasants. If the need arises, the township authorities may increase the number of workdays. The exact number of days required of each household is not decided uniformly. I heard that in some locations the number could be as high as 90 days per year, although it was more commonly between 30 and 60. In one township it was uniform for every household with rural residence until May 1996, with the exact number of workdays changing from year to year. From May 1996 the number of compulsory workdays a household had to fulfil was determined in accordance with the amount of land it contracted from the state, so families with more land must perform a higher number of labour days than those with less land. In another village, the obligation was fixed at five days per *mu*. It is a painful reminder of the times of collectivisation, when all work was both compulsory and communal; nowadays household farming, business, and sideline activities are clearly distinguished from communal work, which is known officially as voluntary work (*khalis ämgäk*). The word *khalis* is widely used in other contexts to express voluntariness or even altruism. For instance, it is often combined with the words help (*khalis yärdäm*) or additional prayers (*khalis namaz*). However, since it became a synonym for obligatory work, the expression *khalis ämgäk* has become devalued, and it is no longer used to denote truly voluntary enterprises such as the building of a village mosque. Such work is now termed 'work done of one's free will' (*öz ikhtiyari bilän ämgäk*). Many peasants continue to refer to communal work

---

[43] Feigned ignorance is one of the most common 'weapons of the weak', as identified by James Scott (1985: xvi).

[44] Rozi Sayit, 'The Peasant Cries'.

[45] Obligation to render labour services to his landlord was a characteristic trait of peasants' condition in pre-revolutionary Xinjiang, see Lattimore (1975 [1950]: 181). On communal work in the collective period see, for example, Liu (1994: 107).

as *alwang*, the expression commonly used in pre-1949 society to denote corvée.[46]

Communal work obligations are allocated from township leaders through brigades and production teams to individual households. Farmers often have to work in a different part of the township away from their own village, and in such cases they do not even feel that their work is benefiting their own community. Communal work is typically interpreted as work for the state and a form of oppression.

Plate 3. Woman picking mulberries, Kashgar, Southern Xinjiang (Photo: Chris Hann).

Communal work can be 'traded in' for other forms of obligation. For years, production teams have also been allocated quotas of silk they must produce each year and sell to the state. People who take this job may be exempt from the forms of communal work described above. Farmers in the production team where we worked apparently had hardly any training before they started raising silkworms (*pilä*). Furthermore, they complained that the work

---

[46] For a description of the hardships of compulsory communal work see Mätrozi (1996).

was labour intensive, and that conditions in their village were quite unsuited because they did not have enough mulberry trees. Instead of making a profit, in 1996 farmers in this village were unable to meet the official target and were obliged to pay a heavy fine. They boasted that they made such a mess of it last year that this year their brigade received no silk assignment, while the neighbouring village, whose performance was not so disastrous, had once again been burdened with the exploitative silk quota.

Misguided construction policies also increase farmers' resentment. One clear example was the laying down of pipes for drinking water in several villages. In one township, villagers reported that although they had to pay and contribute a great number of labour days to this job, they were initially happy to do so because they recognised the future benefits of the undertaking. Yet, although the job had long been finished, peasants had been told that in order to have the pipes extended to their own courtyards, an additional payment was required from them; many could not afford this sum. Those who had paid the additional sum came to regret doing so: although they now had a tap in their courtyard, there was hardly ever any water in the pipes because of the inadequacy of the water supply.

Communal work is allocated to all who have contracted land, and anyone who fails to meet his obligations risks a heavy fine. What farmers can do, however, is to transfer their labour obligation to others. For each workday a worker receives a chit which has no name on it and is therefore transferable. Richer people can buy poorer peasants' labour to perform the job for them. The price paid to the latter sometimes matches the price of wage labour in town, but given rural unemployment, it is usually considerably lower. All those who take part in communal work do their best to make the workday short and to work in as relaxed a style as possible, another clear legacy from the commune period. The allocation of communal work within the household is determined by gender and age. As a reaction to the collectivised period when all work was compulsory and women were also obliged to take on heavy work, not only in the fields but also at the construction of irrigation channels, communal work is now done by men only. If there are several generations available, it is always the younger men who perform the job, and lending and borrowing of labour for this purpose – as part of informal exchanges of various services between relatives and friends – have also become common. Families with financial or other resources can get rid of the burden altogether. Those with money can simply pay a certain sum per day as a fine instead of performing labour service. Others who work as cadres or who are on very good terms with cadres can also avoid it altogether. Peasants' general opinion is that low-level cadres in charge of organising communal work manipulate the system, allocating more work to ordinary people while they themselves do much less or nothing of their own share.

6. Family Planning

'In actual fact we are the slaves of fines...'.[47] Compulsory family planning for Han Chinese all over China has been enforced since the 1980s (Croll, Davin and Kane 1985; Kane 1987; Rai 1995). The policy was implemented in minority areas only in the early 1990s, but is already high on the list of Uyghur peasants' complaints. Although the policy is more generous toward minority groups, both urban and rural Uyghur families are unhappy with its limitations. Urban Uyghur couples are allowed to have two children, rural couples three. As in Han Chinese areas, many rumours circulate of forced abortions and consequent revenge taken on officials. The number of newborn babies each year is decided at county level and broken down to township, village, and group levels. If a child is born without permission (*plansiz*, i.e. outside the plan), the parents will have to pay a heavy fine, even if it falls within the three to which they are entitled. Alternatively, an abortion can be induced at any stage of the pregnancy before the child is born, and township and village officials regularly drive women to the nearby hospital against their will.[48] Peasants make comparisons with food rationing during the commune period, saying that they used to have food rationing, but now they have a prescribed quota (*norma*) of children. Others point at small children born outside the plan for whom a fine has been paid and point out sarcastically, that this is 'a child worth 700 yuan'. They find repulsive the idea of measuring children's worth in money.

Family planning in the form of various contraceptive methods and forced abortions is perceived as highly detrimental to women's health. Family planning does not extend to antenatal or postnatal care, and even county-level female cadres acknowledge a dramatic decline in women's health as a result of the indiscriminate use of the IUD, contraceptive and abortion inducing pills. To avoid being detected, many pregnant women prefer to give birth at home with no medical assistance since they fear that a hospital birth will entail sterilisation without their consent.[49] On the whole, it

---

[47] Rozi Sayit, 'The Peasant Cries'.

[48] These rumours were confirmed to me in a moving, emotional interview with a young official in charge of family planning, who was deeply uncomfortable in his role.

[49] It is a widespread belief that if a woman dies during childbirth she will go straight to heaven, while an abortion is an unpardonable sin which will condemn her to eternal hell fire. In view of such beliefs, it seems particularly insensitive and crude that slogans popularising family planning are regularly written upon the walls of village mosques, as I observed on several mosques in one village.

seemed to me that as far as family planning is concerned, local officials, themselves subject to the same regulations, allow as much leeway to villagers as possible. Peasants get around the regulations through manipulating local customs surrounding birth (one of which is that women usually give birth to their first two children in their natal home), and informal adoption within the family.

The Means of Enforcement

Villagers literally pay a high cost for defying authority openly. With certain exceptions, notably in the enforcement of abortions, the usual means of disciplining villagers in the present reform period are economic: fines are extracted for every act of disobedience. Those who refuse to plant cotton or only partially fulfil the requirements are required to pay a fine. Peasants who do not sell their grain to the state have to pay cash instead. Those who do not follow decreed methods of cultivation are fined. Avoiding communal work and having children outside the official plan also lead to fines. People recognise the legitimacy of this form of punishment, and prefer it to other forms used in the past, when beatings, imprisonment, self-criticism, and other forms of public humiliations were common. They make calculations, and when the fines are manageable they will pay to buy themselves certain types of freedom. For example, many farmers choose not to grow cotton, or to grow less than their assigned quota, and pay the fine instead. The 700 yuan charged for an unplanned child was considered a good bargain by many, but in 1996 this fine went up dramatically (to 2,500 yuan) and is beyond most people's reach. Manipulations of old customs surrounding births and adoption practices are employed to avoid detection and payment. Family planning is rejected by Uyghurs on moral grounds, but for villagers it is also an interference with their future labour supply, a vital resource. That coercion is equated by minority peasants with oppression by an alien state is perhaps illustrated by the fact that while urban intellectuals use the native word for fines (*järimanä*), Uyghur farmers in the Kashgar region prefer to use the Chinese equivalent (*pakän*).

Economic coercion through fines is now a pervasive theme in Uyghur life.[50] It deepens the gulf between the interests of peasant and state, and the strategies that peasants pursue to avoid fines (including feigning ignorance and lying) strengthen mutual trust and interdependence.

---

[50] Once I overheard small children chanting the Uyghur and Chinese words for 'fine' in unison for about two minutes, as part of their game.

The Agents of Enforcement

Peasants and state interact through local rural cadres who, like other intermediaries, (such as the colonial headmen studied by earlier anthropologists), play a crucial and ambiguous role. In the reform period, they have been endowed with more power to manoeuvre for their own benefit. As elsewhere in China, whether 'cadres' are government employees or other kinds of local officials, they are often seen simply as representatives of the state who frequently abuse their positions for their own ends. The lowest level of government administration is that of the township (the former commune), and below are the levels of village and team. While most township cadres are Uyghur, there are some Han Chinese in top positions. Lower level cadres, however, are all Uyghur, usually members of the village or team where they work. In one township where the top position was held by a Chinese cadre, the blame for misguided agricultural policies was put on him. In the other township, where the top position was occupied by a Uyghur cadre of humble origins, peasants' resentment was directed primarily against low-level cadres.

Production team and village leaders are the only officials with whom most villagers have regular contact. Commune officials are already perceived as remote, not seen by ordinary peasants (unless they happen to be residents of their neighbourhood). Low-level rural cadres are charged with announcing and implementing the often unpopular policies, collecting land rent and other debts, allocating communal work, organising grain procurement, and so on. They are often accused of fiddling with the accounts so as to minimise their own grain sales, while causing more to be extracted from others. It is also commonly believed that they do not perform as many compulsory labour days as they should, and that they make others work more instead. They are widely perceived as representatives of the state, who are supported by peasant labour. The lowest level village cadres (team and brigade leaders) are not salaried state employees but receive only a modest annual fee, which is indeed paid from villagers' contributions. Furthermore, since they are themselves land-cultivating peasants with rural residence, they are not entitled to any of the privileges enjoyed by urban residents and state employees resident in the village.

Low-level rural cadres receive bonuses if they implement a policy successfully, for example, meeting particular deadlines. If, however, their village performs badly in any area they too may be subjected to heavy fines, and perhaps the loss of their position. They are expected to set a good example in following regulations. If they do not comply, they risk losing their position. In one village this happened to the local representative of the All-China Women's Federation after she became pregnant with her fourth child and refused abortion. Low-level cadres' prestige and popularity as well as their economic position are perpetually in the balance. It seemed to me that some low-level cadres had very little room for manoeuvre, but many peasants perceived them as parasites. Many times I was told: 'the policies issued at the top are good, but they are not implemented as they should be'. Yet from the point of view of the county-level authorities, rural cadres are primarily peasants, whose interests and loyalties are with fellow villagers, and who are therefore potentially subversive and untrustworthy. Thus these cadres occupy a highly ambiguous position: as intermediaries they are constantly surrounded by resentment and by a measure of deference.[51] In effect, they are mediating buffers between the main actors of the rural scene: the state and the peasants. It also seems likely that since the highest levels of authority, where policies are formulated, cannot be criticised without severe punishment, the only way for peasants to voice their dissatisfaction is to praise the good intentions of the highest authority and blame the small officials, with their ambiguous position as both office holders and vulnerable individuals. This widespread and automatic scapegoating of low-level cadres can be understood as a weapon devised by peasants to express discontent without openly criticising higher authorities. Rural cadres' mediating role at the lowest level is unambiguous only in the matter of family planning, as noted earlier. Here they side with the local population, and regularly turn a blind eye to strategies employed by their fellow villagers to avoid being caught.

While government employed township cadres are openly appointed 'from above', low-level rural cadres supposedly are elected democratically by their neighbourhood and village. Many farmers, however, describe these elections as undemocratic: favouritism and corruption prevail, and the nominees of existing cadres at the same level are almost invariably elected. Information in this hierarchy seems to flow only in one direction: from top to bottom. Although I was assured by township cadres that villagers were regularly consulted, for example about decisions concerning production methods, peasants did not confirm this claim. They may, however, turn to the authorities with requests: on three occasions I was present when requests for social or material aid were made directly by ordinary peasants to village or township officials. On each occasion the addressed cadre declared that he or she was unable to help. Yet a great deal depends on them: when asking for a bank loan, trying to do business outside the village or even to get married, farmers need a reference letter from their local cadres.

---

[51] For a detailed analysis of cadres' ambiguous position see Oi (1989).

At the same time, somewhat paradoxically, Uyghur villagers generally do not distinguish between local authority in the village and higher levels of authority as far as the issue of land ownership is concerned. Although technically the land leased to peasants is owned collectively and the township has become the socialist landlord (Oi 1989: 189), Uyghur villagers typically consider their landlord to be the state (*dölät*). The state is equated with the government (*hökümät*) and the Communist Party (*partiyä*). This concept of authority implicitly includes that of the collective, but farmers never mention the collective as an authority. When asked about the collective's role in the reform era, they say that today the collective has no power and no property to speak of: it is regarded as a thing of the past. Villagers see themselves as dealing directly with the state.

In the two townships near Kashgar I found that the power of village committees remains limited. They are dominated by the township government, as has been reported elsewhere in China (Oi 1989: 178–80; Dearlove 1995: 123). Thus peasants are correct in their assessment of their position, which they conceptualise in terms of direct dealings with, and often opposition to, the state. In this situation, all cadres are primarily representatives of the state since their orders always come from higher levels. Peasants are also clear about cadres' abuses of power and resent them as individuals who use their position for manipulation; but as representatives of the higher state authority with a certain degree of control over peasants, even the most corrupt cadres command a measure of deference. I turn in the final section of this chapter to examine the wider social context of local ideas of authority and respect, which brings us necessarily to a discussion of religion.

The Two Authorities: State and Religion

Religious intolerance is another legacy of the Maoist era that has persisted strongly in this region.[52] Today Uyghur peasants are not banned from attending the mosque but are constantly reminded of the dangers of organising activities that are labelled illegal, such as participation in Sufi rituals or sending their children to religious instruction.[53] Muslim religious leaders who are perceived as collaborating with the authorities are not tolerated by radical Uyghurs: shortly after we arrived in Kashgar in the summer of 1996, one such leader was the victim of an assassination attempt.

---

[52] For a discussion of official attitudes towards Islam during the collectivised period see McMillen (1979: 113–29).

[53] Women's position remains ambiguous. Most women prefer to keep their religious practices confined to the privacy of their homes.

Given this general situation in Xinjiang, it would seem that religious and secular authorities are locked in open conflict. Yet I argue that in some respects they reinforce each other, since peasants' attitudes towards these two types of authority are ultimately similar.

My first interviews with villagers took place in highly formal circumstances with an array of cadres accompanying us, and not surprisingly informants felt that they had to toe the official line. The Communist Party was mentioned with great frequency and deference, and everyone told us how well things had been going for them since the launch of the reforms. One old lady repeated several times: 'Our Party has made us rich. With the help of our Party we have become successful and content'. Then she quickly corrected herself: 'With the help of God and our Party we have become successful'. Her idea of political correctness was clearly hierarchical, and even in a monitored conversation she decided that God had to come first, immediately followed by the Communist Party. A similar ordering was repeated in other households. I did not find this juxtaposition of religious and secular hierarchy surprising, since I had not expected that decades of severe religious repression would erode religious sentiments. But I was surprised when, in the course of many later interviews in more relaxed conditions, informants persistently made explicit comparisons between the workings of the religious and secular authorities. In their daily lives, Uyghur villagers confront two basic types of authority, religious and secular, and there is a high degree of congruence between the two.

Religious and secular authorities are often seen as reinforcing each other in the realm of morality: the idea of sin as discussed in the mosque is perceived as closely corresponding to what the secular authorities regard as crime. In both cases one is bound to be punished, in this world with imprisonment, in the other world with hell fire. This parallel was drawn explicitly by a man who said that all people (apart from those who die young and therefore in an innocent state) go to hell first after their death. Good Muslims will then be released and allowed to enter Paradise 'just as when a criminal has finished his punishment he will be set free again by the government'. Orthodox religious dignitaries forbid all practices recognised as superstitions incompatible with Islam, while the state condemns visiting shrines and resorting to the activities of traditional healers as outmoded feudal customs. The imams' teaching against gambling, drinking, drugs, and fistfights are echoed in the message of the secular authorities, which seek to curtail any kind of informal socialisation among Uyghur men for fear that these can take on political colouring. Although Sufism is widespread and clandestine meetings are regularly held in both villages and cities, officially they are condemned by both the religious and the secular authorities.

Villagers describe their obligations toward the state as their duty, responsibility, or task (*wäzipä*), or as their compulsion (*mäjburiyät*). The term *wäzipä* is used to describe a whole range of obligations: people talk about having a cotton duty, grain duty, family planning duty, duty to perform communal work, and so on. *Wäzipä* has a strong moral connotation: women's and men's daily activities are described in terms of *wäzipä*, and the individual's moral conduct is also conceived in similar terms. It is a man's duty to look after his wife and family; it is a woman's duty to keep house and care for her children. In this sense the concept of duty also has religious connotations. Villagers' moral discourse and to some extent daily lives are governed by the principles of sin (*guna*) and meritorious deed (*sawap*), which, according to some people, were written down by God himself. It is commonly believed that each person has two angels sitting on his shoulders. The one on the right shoulder records a person's good deeds, the one on the left shoulder takes notes of his sins. Thus each person has a book (*däptär*), and his or her fate after death will be decided according to what has been written in this book. This is called *hisaplash* or accounting. One informant explained this more explicitly: 'this is very similar to our position in the village: village leaders have our book (*däptär*) and they keep note of our duties and debts. Once a year, there is an accounting, *hisaplash*'. The image of the *däptär* is also present in an annual ritual which is frowned upon by Muslim religious leaders because it is regarded as non-Islamic, and by the state authorities because of its 'feudal' character.[54]

The image of each person having a book kept by a superior in the hierarchy, who notes the fulfilment or dereliction of duties to higher authority, is rich in irony. Both Chinese and Islamic cultures have had a long history of elite literacy. More recently compulsory education has become a somewhat painful issue to many rural families. They do not see the point in educating their children to the end of primary school, since further education is not considered as a real option for village kids. But if they do not send their children to school, they are fined. Many peasants, some of whom were rendered illiterate by the stroke of a pen in the early 1980s when the Uyghur alphabet was changed, have had to attend new literacy courses (Bellér-Hann 1991) and those who refused were fined. In spite of these efforts and the long tradition of literacy in their culture, government authorities continue to reach Uyghur peasants almost exclusively through oral means. This reinforces their feeling that literacy is useless for them. Being kept in the

---

[54] The Barat ritual involves one to three nights of vigil beginning on the fifteenth of the Islamic month of Sha'bān during which people pray incessantly for the pardoning of their sins. According to informants this vigil (*tünäk*), serves the purpose of washing away sins and opening a new page in one's book. For more details see chapter 8.

dark about most details of their finances is an integral part of this approach. Keeping a *däptär* is regarded as the prerogative of the higher authorities, and most farmers, even those with secondary education, do not keep track of their own accounts.

Parallels between the agents of religious and secular authority were drawn by a young peasant. When asked why he thought that low-level rural cadres showed little or no understanding of the plight of ordinary farmers, he smiled and answered with a proverb: 'When the priest's stomach is full, he does not want to know anything'.

Conclusion

Struggle for the harvest has remained an important theme of the reform era and the Chinese state insists on remaining firmly in control of farmers' lives. Uyghur peasants often say that 'the state keeps us under tight control' (*dölät bizni bäk jing tutidu*). For many Uyghurs, agricultural modernisation is a mixed blessing. They see a confrontation between traditional religious agriculture (*diniy dihqanjiliq*) and modern scientific agriculture (*pänniy dihqanjiliq*) (chapter 6). While they usually acknowledge that the introduction of new cultivation methods may yield more, many also point out that the widespread, compulsory use of pesticides and chemical fertilizers has led to a general decrease in young people's health. Health problems in humans and bad crops, especially the declining quality of local fruit, are frequently attributed to the nuclear tests regularly performed by the Chinese military in the Taklamakan Desert. I have argued that the economic reforms of the 1980s opened up new inequalities among Uyghur villagers, and that the responsibility system leaves little room for most of them to manoeuvre. Only those with substantial resources can avoid the tighter grip of the state by purchasing new freedoms, such as a city residence, higher education for their children, better health care, and exemption from corvée. In the socialist market economy, such freedoms have themselves become commodities: peasants with the means to pay the prescribed fines can acquire the right to control their entire crop, and make their own decisions over production, utilisation of time, and number of children. Although economic coercion dominates, Uyghur villagers also continue to fear other forms of punishment, imprisonment, or worse, if they are suspected of exercising freedoms which at the moment are not for sale, such as taking part in 'illegal religious activities'.

Uyghur farmers are seen by the Chinese state as a serious threat: they constitute the largest pool of subordinates in a region with a long history of antagonism towards the Han Chinese. These villagers resent Chinese rule, and their linguistic and cultural affinity to the peoples of the independent

Central Asian republics, in combination with their Islamic faith, helps them formulate repudiation of this alien state. But peasants' attitudes toward authority show some ambiguities. In their daily lives the state is represented by Uyghur cadres – villagers in their own communities – to whom deference is shown because of their position, but also resentment because of their perceived abuses of it. The conceptualisation of secular authority (in which the state, the government, and the party are subsumed together) shows some congruence with the conceptualisation of traditional religious authorities. Dependence on and submission to both guiding authorities is considered correct: both have a degree of legitimacy. But the actual manifestations of state control over the two most important resources of peasants – land and labour – and over the birth of new humans are strongly resented and provoke the many forms of everyday peasant resistance described above.

References

Bellér-Hann, I. 1991. Script Changes in Xinjiang. In S. Akiner (ed.), *Cultural Change and Continuity in Central Asia*, pp. 71–83. London: Kegan Paul.

Benewick, R.,and P. Wingrove (eds.). 1995. *China in the 1990s*. London: Macmillan.

Blecher, M. 1995. Collectivism, Contractualism and Crisis in the Chinese Countryside. In R. Benewick, and P. Wingrove (eds.), *China in the 1990s*, pp. 105–19. London: Macmillan.

Bramall, C., and M. Jones. 1993. Rural Income Inequality in China Since 1978. *Journal of Peasant Studies* 21 (1): 41–70.

Croll, E. 1988. The New Peasant Economy in China. In S. Feuchtwang, A. Hussain, and T. Pairault (eds.), *Transforming China's Economy in the Eighties*, pp. 77–100. London: Zed Press.

——. 1995. Family Strategies: Securing the Future. In R. Benewick, and P. Wingrove (eds.), *China in the 1990s*, pp. 204–15. London: Macmillan.

Croll, E., D. Davin, and P. Kane (eds.). 1985. *China's One-Child Family Policy*. London: Macmillan.

Davin, D. 1991. Women, Work and Property in the Chinese Peasant Household of the 1980s. In D. Elson (ed.), *Male Bias in the Development Process* (2nd ed.), pp. 29–50. Manchester: Manchester University Press.

Dearlove, J. 1995. Village Polities. In R. Benewick, and P. Wingrove (eds.), *China in the 1990s*, pp. 120–31. London: Macmillan.

Dillon, M. 1994. Muslim Communities in Contemporary China: The Resurgence of Islam after the Cultural Revolution. *Journal of Islamic Studies* 5 (1): 70–101.

——. 1995. Xinjiang: Ethnicity, Separatism and Control in Chinese Central Asia. *Durham East Asian Paper 1.* Durham: Department of East Asian Studies.

Feuchtwang, S., A. Hussain, and T. Pairault (eds.). 1988. *Transforming China's Economy in the Eighties.* 2 vols. London: Zed Press.

Gladney, D. 1994a. Ethnic Identity in China: The New Politics of Difference. In W. A. Joseph (ed.), *China Briefing*, pp. 171–92. Boulder: Westview Press.

——. 1994b. Representing Nationality in China: Refiguring Majority/ Minority Identities. *The Journal of Asian Studies* 53 (1): 92–123.

Hinton, W. 1972. *Turning Point in China: An Essay on the Cultural Revolution.* New York: Monthly Review Press.

——. 1990. *The Great Reversal: The Privatization of China 1978–1989.* New York: Monthly Review Press.

Hoppe, T. 1987. Observations on Uygur Land Use in Turpan County, Xinjiang – A Preliminary Report on Fieldwork in Summer 1985. *Central Asiatic Journal* 3 (1): 3–4, 224–51.

Kane, P. 1987. *The Second Billion: Population and Family Planning in China.* Harmondsworth: Penguin.

Kelliher, D. 1992. *Peasant Power in China: The Era of Rural Reform, 1979–1989.* New Haven: Yale University Press.

Lattimore, O. 1975 [1950]. *Pivot of Asia: Sinkiang and the Inner Asian Frontiers of China and Russia.* New York: AMS Press.

——. 1962. *Studies in Frontier History. Collected Papers 1928–1958.* Paris: Mouton & Co. La Haye.

Liu, M. 1994. Commune Responsibility System and China's Agriculture. In Q. Fan, and P. Nolan (eds.), *China's Economic Reforms: The Costs and Benefits of Incrementalism*, pp. 104–36. New York: St Martin Press.

Mackerras, C. 1995. *China's Minority Cultures: Identities and Integration since 1912.* New York: St. Martin's Press.

Madsen, R. 1991. The Countryside under Communism. In R. MacFarquhar, and J. Fairbank (eds.), *The Cambridge History of China* (Vol. 15): *The Peoples Republic* (Part 2): *Revolutions within the Chinese Revolution 1966–1982*, pp. 619–81. Cambridge: Cambridge University Press.

Mätrozi, M. 1996. Muhäbbät. *Tarim* 5: 23–61.

McKinley, T., and K. Griffin. 1993. The Distribution of Land in Rural China. *The Journal of Peasant Studies* 21 (1): 71–84.

McMillen, D. H. 1979. *Chinese Communist Power and Policy in Xinjiang, 1949–1977*. Boulder: Westview Press.

Nolan, P. 1988. *The Political Economy of Collective Farms: An Analysis of China's Post-Mao Rural Reforms*. Oxford: Polity Press.

Oi, J. C. 1989. *State and Peasant in Contemporary China: The Political Economy of Village Government*. Berkeley: University of California Press.

Potter, S. H., and J. M. Potter. 1990. *China's Peasants*. Cambridge: Cambridge University Press.

Rai, S. 1995. Gender in China. In R. Benewick, and P. Wingrove (eds.), *China in the 1990s*, pp. 181–92. London: Macmillan.

Riskin, C. 1987. *China's Political Economy: The Quest for Development since 1949*. Oxford: Oxford University Press.

Rudelson, J. J. 1997. *Oasis Identities. Uyghur Nationalism along China's Silk Road*. New York: Columbia University Press.

Scott, J. C. 1985. *Weapons of the Weak: Everyday Forms of Peasant Resistance*. New Haven: Yale University Press.

Selden, M. 1988. *The Political Economy of Chinese Socialism*. Armonk: M. E. Sharpe.

Shinjang Statistika Yilliq Toplimi (Xinjiang Statistical Yearbook). 1996. Ürümchi: XUAR Statistika Idarisi.

Siu, H. 1989. *Agents and Victims in South China: Accomplices in Rural Revolution*. New Haven: Yale University Press.

Tokhti, N. M. 1996. Khotändin khät. *Tarim* 1: 6–28.

Weggel, O. 1984. *Xinjiang/ Sinkiang: Das zentralasiatische China. Eine Landeskunde*. Hamburg: Institut für Asienkunde.

Zweig, D. 1990. Patrons, Clients and the Exploitation of the Chinese Peasantry: A Review Essay. *Peasant Studies* 18 (1): 39–51.

Chapter 2
Work and Gender among Uyghur Villagers in Southern Xinjiang[1]

As is widely known, the People's Republic of China has introduced extensive legislation to promote equality between the sexes (Croll 1980: 5). Admittedly, changes in this respect have been slow, and in some areas of social life the progress has been reversed since the beginning of the reform period in the early 1980s (Stacey 1983; Mackerras 1995: 158; Rai 1995). During the decades of collectivisation, minority areas experienced special treatment which facilitated the persistence of traditional values (Mackerras 1995: 159). This explains why, in spite of many radical social changes, basic assumptions about women's status and power relations within the household have persisted with great strength among the Uyghurs.

My research project has focused on changes and continuities in gender relations in Xinjiang throughout the twentieth century. This project could only be undertaken in cooperation with Han Chinese co-researchers, and it was often interesting to hear and observe how these local scholars broached the issues of work and gender. They repeatedly made the point that Uyghur women's present situation is a step backwards after the decades of col-lectivisation, arguing that once collective responsibility was largely aban-doned and control over farming handed back to households, women had fallen once again into the grip of Islamic patriarchy.[2] It is ironic, however, that the general situation reported elsewhere in rural China, where it is not possible to blame Islamic influence for the problems emerging since the onset of reforms, is not unlike the situation which I encountered in rural

[1] First published in *Cahiers d'Études sur la Méditerranée Orientale et le Monde Turco-Iranien* 1998, 25: 93–114.
[2] Elsewhere in China, problems concerning the persistence of traditional patterns of the sexual division of labour into the socialist period have been explained in terms of 'ideological conservatism' (Croll 1982: 240).

Xinjiang.[3] I shall show in this chapter that rural women's present position does indeed reflect strong and direct continuities with pre-socialist values, but contrary to the official rhetoric, I see these as persisting throughout the decades of collectivisation. A similar line of argument has been formulated by Delia Davin, who summed up the general situation in rural China as follows: 'I argue that the inequality of women is rooted in family structures, and that as these structures have been reinforced by recent economic policy, it is unrealistic to think that such inequality will be eliminated in the near future' (Davin 1995: 29). In the present situation rural women's economic contribution to the household in Southern Xinjiang remains hidden or devalued in ways common among women producers elsewhere.[4] Before exploring this theme with the aid of fieldwork data from 1996, it is important to sketch the main principles of work and society in Xinjiang in the pre-socialist period.

Men's and Women's Work before 1949

Informants' recollections of pre-1949 divisions of labour are far from uniform. This variety reflects the fact that the division of labour took different forms among different social groups. They also reveal a strong tendency to stress the value system prevailing at the time, rather than actual practice. Recollections have also been strongly influenced by socialist ideology dominating people's lives during the commune period (1958–78) which emphasised the 'feudal' nature of women's subordination in pre-1949 society.

Indigenous sources describing the daily life and work of men and women make a sharp distinction between male and female domains. Men engage primarily in agricultural production, while women are responsible for processing raw materials (i.e. preparing food, making clothes, and providing domestic services). An indigenous description of how men and women in the oasis of Guma disposed of their day reveals a set of assumptions and expectations concerning how people occupied themselves in the course of a normal day. According to this text, dating from the 1930s, a man would normally get up in the morning and proceed to the mosque to say his morning prayers. If the mosque were near his parents' tomb, he would also

---

[3] The explanation must be sought in the precise types of male dominance encountered in Chinese and Uyghur societies. For an understanding of the latter, Deniz Kandiyoti's sensitive analysis would provide a good starting point (Kandiyoti 1992).

[4] For example see Jenny White's study of Istanbul pieceworkers (1994: 4–6) and Ursula Sharma (1980: 126–27). Within the Chinese context, Elisabeth Croll has commented on the less visible nature of women's work (1988: 96–97). For a description of 'ideological bias' concerning women's work see Benería (1982).

go there to pay his respects. By the time he went home, his wife would have risen, prayed and prepared food, and the family would share a meal. Then the man would feed his animals and go to his fields. At lunchtime he returned home, ate and slept before bringing home fodder for his animals in the afternoon. Later he might go to his garden, eat grapes with his family, and in the evening he might entertain guests with whom he would perform the evening prayer. In the course of their day women had to take care of the house and children, prepare and serve meals, and carry out all the jobs that their husbands had set them. A woman was responsible for the welfare of the members of the household, including nutrition, sanitation, health and education of the children, the milking of the cow and cream preparation. Women also sewed clothes for their families (Jarring 1951: 83–91).

Another source dating from the first decade of the twentieth century describes how women made dough and bread (*nan*), and prepared all kinds of food. All women had to make clothes at home except for the wives of rich men who could employ the services of a professional dressmaker. The wives of common people spent their time sewing, sweeping the house, washing the laundry, picking lice, combing their hair, and making up. Some skilled women could make *doppa* (skull cap) and embroider headscarves, others could sew overcoats and dresses, and some could spin yarn for sale. Women in the countryside took part in agricultural work, did the weeding, and milked cows. Winnowing grain, sowing, harvesting, carrying water, looking after the animals, haircare, and self-decoration are also classified among women' daily occupations (Muhammad 'Ali Damolla 1905–10: 15).[5] Gunnar Jarring's informant pointed out that 'some bad women do not care for the welfare or harm of (their) houses. They stroll about embellishing themselves. But then the husbands of such wives either divorce these wives or they themselves take care of the keys of the boxes, having shown the household implements to those wives (i.e. their duties)' (Jarring 1951: 89).

References to women's work show them primarily not as cultivators but as domestic workers. Jobs such as keeping the domestic fire going or fetching water were also considered to be women's work. Fetching water used to be regarded as shameful for men, except when the woman of the house was ill; in those circumstances the man was prepared to take over and do her jobs (Katanov and Menges 1933, 1976: 1217). A late nineteenth century description of men and women's work by a native of the oasis of Qumul represented men as the main agricultural producers but allowed that

---

[5] This collection of essays was written by a local *molla* probably around 1905–10 in Kashgar, at the instigation of Gustaf Raquette, the Swedish missionary-surgeon. The unpublished manuscript is held at Lund University Library. For a discussion of source materials for social life in Xinjiang see Bellér-Hann (1996).

women too participated in working the land: 'Men cultivate cereals, they do the watering and harvesting. The reaped cereal is tied by the women. The horse doing the threshing can be led by either the man or the woman' (Katanov and Menges 1933, 1976: 1217).

My interlocutors, when recalling pre-socialist conditions, commonly claim that women did not work outside in the fields. That many women did in fact perform agricultural work has already been alluded to above. Confirmation comes from Gunnar Jarring's informant from Guma, who mentioned that 'some women, when they sow maize or wheat, follow behind their husbands and put the seed in the furrow' (Jarring 1951: 91). A similar situation was also observed and noted by another foreign visitor, George Sheriff, in 1928: 'A woman follows behind the plough, pouring seeds into the furrow. She keeps the seeds in a gourd. Then a few men and women just walk over the sown area and kick the sandy earth over the seed – a very easy business' (Sheriff 1928).

The formula which attributes land cultivation exclusively to men is probably a legacy of the pollution prohibition according to which sowing the seed of any cereals was a male prerogative. Ideally, women were not allowed to walk across a sown field or to go to a well in case their very presence might pollute the water and the field, the two vital resources of subsistence. Yet, as our sources confirm, women did perform agricultural work in pre-socialist times. Informants concede that this may have been the actual practice, but it was not the norm. The apparent contradiction between the written sources and contemporary ethnographic accounts that focus on women as domestic workers is a reflection of the upheld ideal which saw its expression in the lives of the richer strata whose women could withdraw from agricultural production. It is these women to whom linguist Édgem Rachimovič Tenishev's female informant must have alluded in 1956: '[Before] there used to be women who did not do any work. Today there are no such women' (Tenishev 1984: 137).

There was undoubtedly considerable variation according to age as well as social and economic position. Individuals' recollections imply that women of the richest strata were the most housebound. Wives and daughters of wealthy men performed tasks mainly within the domestic domain, since they had sufficient numbers of servants or day labourers to work on the land. Those representing the middle range (i.e. wives of small holders who themselves had to work their land) were likely to be found in the fields alongside their husbands.[6] These middle-income families also practised extensive inter-household labour cooperation. Many landless peasants

---

[6] A very similar pattern was found by fieldworkers in India, see Jeffery, Jeffery and Lyon (1989: 46–47).

worked as sharecroppers or day labourers, and their wives worked both as agricultural labourers and as domestic servants if they found such employment. Indigenous texts confirm a divergence between actual practice and values, and that elite behaviour established the norms for the entire community, even if their actual attainment remained beyond the reach of the majority.

Sources from the past also illuminate existing patterns of managing household finances. Gunnar Jarring's informant from the 1930s described a domestic situation in which the woman had full control over the domestic budget:

> If her husband has sold something belonging to the house and brings the money along his wife will spend it for a necessary purpose without asking her husband. Her husband will not ask, 'What have you done with the money?' Sometimes his wife (will say), 'I will invite some guests. Please give me ten or twenty *sar*!' she will say. Her husband will say, 'Ten or twenty *sar* is not sufficient. As you have the key in your own hand, why do you ask me! Take yourself from the box and spend as much as you like to spend!' he says. That wife (says), 'Why, (it is true that), even if I did not ask, it would do. But (I would rather) spend it with your permission', she says (Jarring 1951: 89).

The above paragraph presents an affluent household, where the wife had the leisure to invite her own guests and the husband not only allowed her to make free use of the common funds, but also encouraged his wife to spend more than she had intended for prestige reasons.[7] My informants' oral reminiscences in villages near Kashgar suggest that control of the household budget was usually the privilege of the male household head. This was especially true of poor households with little or no cash income. Gunnar Jarring's information from Guma, however, is valuable in implying an ideal pattern of gender relations and prosperity to which many poor families must have aspired. His evidence also reveals that variations existed in an era characterised today by modern Chinese propaganda as an inflexible feudal patriarchy.

Further insights into domestic budget arrangements might be gleaned from marriage and divorce documents and other lawsuits. Such data are mostly inaccessible to foreign researchers at present, but one published document from the late nineteenth century is revealing: 'a sum of thirty-three *tanga*s was lost from the house of Sufûrgi Baï from his bed, and afterwards Sufûrgi Baï said to (his) wife Aï Khan: "If you have put away this money,

---

[7] A reference to women's 'family status production work' is elaborated by Papanek (1989).

thirty-three *tanga*s, produce it, (and) I will add twenty-four *tanga*s, and will make a cloak after your heart's desire and give (it to you)'" (Shaw 1878: 86). Here the man kept the money in his bed and his wife was accused of stealing it from there.[8] Another document from the same period sheds partial light upon both domestic budgeting and conjugal obligations:

> Malaq, the son of Qabil Bai, made a legal agreement (as follows): that on account of contentions (with) my wife Aqlim Bibi, I, who now agree, having been unreasonable, henceforward have undertaken not to strike or beat (her) without reason; to give (her) the necessary cost of living at the (proper) time, and have undertaken not to take any strange man into the house where my said wife is and whenever it shall be known and proved that I have taken a strange man into my house into the presence of my wife, or have beaten her without just cause, my said wife shall be free, if she chooses, to give me the writer of this agreement, one bill of divorcement separating herself (Shaw 1878: 85).

This short document reveals several important aspects of domestic arrangements: that domestic violence was justified if the woman gave cause for it; that taking strange men into the presence of a wife was regarded as an offence (according to the prevailing modesty code [*namähräm*]; see chapter 4); and that in this particular family, although the man was holding the purse strings, he gave a regular cash allowance to his wife, not according to specific needs, but on a regular basis.[9]

It is noteworthy that in various life-cycle rituals, such as weddings, circumcision and mourning ceremonies, women were supposed to contribute food and clothing, while a monetary contribution may have been expected from men. Women's gifts were often products of their own domestic labour, the acquisition of which therefore did not necessarily require cash. This illustrates the general principle of gender relations before 'Liberation': men and women played complementary, symbiotic social roles. Certainly these were profoundly marked by Islam; but to conclude simply that men exploited and dominated women is a gross simplification not only of the social diversity, but also of the underpinning cultural constitution of male and female personhood.[10]

---

[8] Stealing money from the husband was one of the many illicit strategies to which, for example, American wives resorted in the early twentieth century to counteract their relative poverty (Zelizer 1989: 358).

[9] On the earmarking of domestic currencies see Zelizer (1994).

[10] Moreover, the incidence of high divorce rates indicates that even if Islamic cultures generally can be construed as patriarchal, the position of women in Xinjiang was markedly different from norms elsewhere in China. I have been unable to identify divorce rates for the period prior to socialism.

Men's and Women's Work during the Decades of Collectivisation

In this section I treat the first three decades of socialism as a unity, even though I am aware of the many swings and changes of emphasis in what can loosely be thought of as the Marxist period. One of its most radical changes was the mass mobilisation of women, thought to represent a huge 'reserve army of labour' (Croll 1980: 4). In the Xinjiang context this move was indeed a radical break with the past, not because it sent women to the fields for the first time, but because it openly defied the previously upheld normative idea that women should not work in the fields. In the public domain, the new official ideology held that in the name of progress and equality, women should take an equal part in production. This shift turned upside down the traditional modesty code regulating men's and women's everyday behaviour. It is possible that this factor contributed to the bitterness with which Uyghur men and women remember the socialist transformation of the sexual division of labour during the collectivised period.

The agrarian reforms of the 1950s which culminated in the setting up of the communes in 1958 had dramatic repercussions on all aspects of social life.[11] Collectivisation changed traditional property relations and inheritance patterns: once land passed into collective ownership it ceased to be the marker of wealth and status that it had been previously. Recurring themes in villagers' memories concern communal eating and the insufficiency of food, communal work, enforced communal childcare, and restrictions on artisans' private production. The establishment of communal canteens temporarily emptied household kitchens – some informants recall bitterly that not even a teapot was left in their homes. Communal cooking divested the peasant household of its role as a unit of consumption. One informant quoted his father, who apparently used to say: 'The big cooking pot was full, the little cooking pot was empty'. This short sentence is more than an ironic reference to the years of enforced communal eating during the Great Leap Forward which Uyghurs in Southern Xinjiang call the era of the Big Cooking Pot or Cauldron (*chong qazan*): it also confirms the widespread view concerning the unequal nature of distribution between the collective and the private sectors. Private property was retained in the form of houses and tiny plots which usually took the form of a back garden where villagers could grow small amounts of cereal. A maximum of two sheep could be kept at home, and those who overstepped this limit risked being subjected to public humiliation and other forms of punishment. Informants recall working in the

---

[11] On women's participation in production in the Chinese countryside see Davin (1976) and Croll (1980). Within the wider framework of memory and history, reference must be made to Watson (1994).

fields six days a week in all seasons. Some craftsmen were allowed to keep practising their trade in officially organised workshops (*karkhana*), but many more could not get employment in these establishments and were given tasks in the fields. Making money for private gain was not merely discouraged but also severely punished.[12]

Sending young women to do heavy work previously regarded as men's tasks flew in the face of traditional gender roles. My Chinese co-researchers quoted impressive figures to prove that women's equality was principally realised through their participation in production.[13] Thus in the county of Toqquzaq, 32 reservoirs (*su ambiri*), and 838 irrigation canals (*östäng*) were constructed by women's groups in 1958; 11,800 *mu* of uncultivated land were opened up by them, and an area of 36,000 *mu* was afforested by women. Many women took part in mining activities (*tagh dolquni*)[14], which provided coal for 'backyard' steel production in the autumn and winter of 1958, an experience that still looms large in the memories of both male and female villagers. What for my Chinese co-researchers represented a great advance for women was remembered with great bitterness by the people themselves. Many women attribute their present ill-health and backache to the communal work they were obliged to undertake during the years of collectivisation, even during late pregnancy and soon after giving birth. Several villagers claimed that 'women were used instead of draught animals'. Their testimony contradicts evidence from else-where in China according to which 'women were usually allocated lighter jobs', although the same author also allowed for cadres' miscarriages in this respect (Davin 1976: 133).[15] Inadequate diet and calorie intake were also perceived to be contributing factors for women's difficulties. In short, like elsewhere in China, participation in the domain of public production did not ease all aspects of women's domestic burden (Croll 1982).

People in the 1990s have generally scathing views about the efficiency and rationality of collective work during the years of collectivisation. Collective work included putting down fertilizer, gathering wood, and levelling out fields – a job which many people described as totally un-

---

[12] For an excellent summary and evaluation of this situation in rural China generally see Croll (1982).

[13] These figures were quoted to us orally, but we were denied access to written statistics of this kind.

[14] Literally, 'mountain wave', the expression is a socialist invention. The word *dolqun* was typically used during the years of collectivisation in a figurative sense to refer to the collective work effort. For example, *inqilap dolquni* meant 'revolutionary tide' (cf. Schwarz 1992: 271).

[15] Elisabeth Croll noted that 'lighter' jobs assigned to women were not physically less demanding (1986: 6). Both Croll and Delia Davin dealt with the general situation in China, and their data comes from outside Xinjiang.

necessary. As one man summed up: 'we were made to do many useless things, in order to keep us busy'. Local custom was maintained in some respects, in that men and women often worked in segregated groups and female work leaders were assigned to lead female working groups (cf. Davin 1976: 147).

Memories of collective childcare arrangements are particularly bitter.[16] In one commune, crèches were organised in private houses, while there was one public kindergarten in the same building which housed the headquarters of the production brigade. Small children were entrusted to the care of older women and to women who were exempted from work for 40 days after they had given birth. It could happen that one woman would take care of a large number of children, and this was particularly hard on frail and elderly women as well as on young mothers who were still weak after delivery. Several women recall how they were regularly harassed by the production team leader shortly after giving birth to return to communal work. One couple who had four small children during the early years of collectivisation recalled: 'It was hardest for families with young children. Each morning we would have to get up and carry the baby and his cradle to the crèche, and take the others to the kindergarten. At lunchtime we would rush home, and my wife would cook a quick meal and feed the baby who then had to be taken back to the crèche'.

Occasionally, when a crèche could not be opened because no one could be found to take care of the infants, working women had no choice but to take their babies with them to the fields. Of course experiences were not uniform, and not all women worked in the fields. Those engaged in communal cooking or sewing in the communal workshop have somewhat better memories than those who took part in the mining work in the mountains or in working the land. Easiest of all was the job of those who became cadres at a young age and were put in charge of supervising communal work. It seems that the main reasons why rural women have largely negative memories of the support services of the collective period, which were meant to ease their burden, were as follows: the obligatory nature of such provisions; the inadequacy of practical implementations; the largely negative effects of the collectivised period on the household economy (scarcity of food and fuel) as well as on social life (inadequate provisions to celebrate religious festivals and life-cycle rituals and to provide hospitality). The crèche system also entailed a further consequence: women often breastfed babies left in their care to keep them quiet and happy. This

---

[16] This is quite ironic, especially when rural women's complaints concern institutions which were originally introduced to reduce their household responsibilities. On such initiatives see Croll (1980).

meant that a great number of milk siblings (*emildash*) were created who, following Koranic edicts, were then not allowed to marry each other. As the children grew up, this practice limited the circle of available marriage partners in the neighbourhood and ran against accepted ideals. Nowadays most women report that if a mother cannot breastfeed her baby she should resort to cow's milk rather than let another woman feed her infant and create milk siblings.

For men, the major problem during the years of collectivisation was how to augment their families' meagre income since the daily food ration (*norma*) was never enough. This meant moonlighting for many craftsmen, who continued to practise their profession to make cash at home in secret (*mäkhpiy*) before and after the communal work. Others tried to raise sheep or grow fruit and wheat on their tiny plots for the black market.

As elsewhere in China, men's work was valued more highly than the same work performed by women. Although the maximum daily points (*nomur*) one could earn varied according to the nature of the job performed, the women's maximum was consistently kept lower than the men's. A typical example quoted to me was that for performing the same work, a man earned 25 *nomur*, while a woman earned 18 (cf. Croll 1980: 28; 1986: 6). It would seem that this officially sanctioned and public devaluing of women's work through unequal remuneration which remained under the control of the commune was fully in line with both Uyghur and Chinese patriarchic values. No major shift took place during the decades of collectivisation in the primary identification of Uyghur women as carers and nurturers despite women's large-scale mobilisation for communal work.

Since the decision-making power of the household was largely taken over by the collective, there is no evidence to assess the claim that the gender equality advocated by officials was actually achieved in the intra-household context. In the absence of regular cash income, decision making over a very limited family budget remained, by and large, in the hands of the male household head. In such circumstances, the management of the household budget had to be tightly controlled. Furthermore, the demands of organised communal work for all people limited women's movements. They were always struggling to find the time for household chores, childcare, and social obligations. Many found it more difficult to go to town, where in the past they could be involved in market interaction.[17] While pre-1949 patterns of budget allocation showed variation according to social class, as a result of the general economic 'levelling', the scarcity of cash, and the universal

---

[17] Many of my interview partners also commented on the absence of suitable vehicles: carts and draught animals were made available mainly to cadres, and common people had to walk many hours to reach town.

obligation to take part in production during collectivisation, the pattern of budgeting which privileged the male household head now appears to have become more widespread among Uyghur peasant families in Southern Xinjiang.

Men's and Women's Work in the Reform Period

The reform period is commonly dated from the end of 1978 and was effectively launched in Xinjiang from 1980 with the splitting of collectively farmed land and the distribution of plots on an egalitarian basis to rural households, not with full ownership rights but with long-term leases.[18] Work regarded as requiring considerable physical strength, such as ploughing, harvesting, irrigation, and construction remains identified as a man's job. Once again, most of women's daily movements take place within the space of the domestic sphere, which includes the home and the immediate neighbourhood. A typical day for a rural woman starts at dawn with prayer and the feeding of animals. This is followed by preparing tea and serving breakfast for the family, cleaning, cooking lunch and later on supper, and another session of animal feeding; twice a week she must wash; and once every ten days she must bake bread. There is usually more than one woman in a household, and the division of female labour is organised according to age and family status with the mother-in-law taking charge of the children and the daughter-in-law doing practically everything else. Details of such arrangements vary from family to family and periodic variations can be observed within the same household. For example, when the daughter-in-law is pregnant or shortly after childbirth, her mother-in-law may take over some of her household chores. Married daughters commonly visit their natal home once every eight or fifteen days (depending on the proximity of their natal home), and during such visits they often take on household chores, especially food preparation. The seasonal nature of some jobs women engage in, including agricultural work, as well as the varying pattern of men's activities, also require constant adjustment from women in organising their work. Taking care of a few sheep may involve trips to the field during the growing season to gather grass, which may take up to one or two hours a day. Cleaning involves sweeping and (in the summer) sprinkling water on the mud floors of the house and the courtyard. Meal preparation for the family remains time-consuming, since most meals are wheat-based and on each occasion fresh dough and vegetables have to be prepared just before cooking. Such procedures may take up to several hours per meal. Baking is

---

[18] For a general discussion of rural reforms see Croll (1988), Nolan (1988), and Kelliher (1992).

usually undertaken by two or three women together, sometimes on a neighbourhood basis, and it takes up to half a day and is performed every 10 days or so. Washing is also time-consuming since most households have no washing machine. During the time of agricultural work, many women go to the fields to work alongside men, and women participate equally with their husbands in harvesting and sowing.

In the present era women also continue to be regarded as primary carers of the young and the elderly. Men also verbalise their dependence on women. They insist that it is very important to have a woman in the house, and it is expected that elderly divorced men or widowers should try to remarry. As an old man whose third wife had just left him explained: 'We cannot do without a woman. We have to have someone to boil the kettle and make tea, to bake bread, wash our clothes, and take care of us when we are sick. My son could not care for me physically if the need arose, and my daughter or daughter-in-law should not do it because of the modesty code. A wife needs to be around. Besides, a man needs someone to sleep with'.

Although elderly women may also consider remarriage, and the practice is perfectly acceptable, they are not thought to need a husband to the same extent, especially if they have a son or another male relative close at hand. While women are considered to be weak (*ajiz*) and incapable of looking after themselves, and therefore in a constant need of male protection, such protection is not limited to the conjugal relationship. It is somewhat ironic that although women's physical weakness is constantly emphasised in popular lore, they are nonetheless perceived as physically more self-sufficient than men. A woman's value thus finds expression in terms of the services she can provide within the domestic domain, comprising social and sexual reproductive functions. This is underlined in marriage and divorce practices. Nowadays, even if a young couple has already acquired a house of their own, they stay with the husband's family for a number of years. The time of separation from the parental home must be agreed upon with the husband's parents, who require that their daughter-in-law perform some years of 'service to her mother-in-law' (*qeynana khizmiti*). Customary divorce settlements require that the possessions a woman can take away from her husband's household in case of divorce depend on the length of time she has served her mother-in-law, and therefore if the divorce takes place within a year after marriage she is not entitled to anything.

In the reform period beginning in the early 1980s, the gender specificity of certain jobs is again emphasised. Housework, childcare, care for the elderly, and piecework such as making the traditional Uyghur hat (*doppa*), are all identified as women's work. Agricultural work, business, and most other crafts are perceived as men's work. Communal work has survived into the post-reform era, and it is the obligation of landholding peasants to work for the township in the construction and maintenance of irrigation canals, roads and schools, and in opening up wasteland to cultivation. This communal work is popularly known by the pre-1949 term denoting feudal corvée obligation, *alwang*.[19] As has been noted in chapter 1, following the post-reform authorities' official appropriation of the indigenous term for voluntary work (*khalis ämgäk*) to denote communal work, another expression, *öz ikhtiyari bilän ämgäk*, meaning 'work done out of one's own free will' has been introduced by villagers to denote truly voluntary work.[20] Communal work, which during the decades of collectivisation had to be performed by both men and women, has once again become an exclusively male responsibility and no woman is ever expected to undertake such work.

Specialisations

The most successful households of the 1990s in the villages we studied appeared to be those which managed to engage in extra-agricultural business activities as soon as this became possible. Some households with traditions of a family craft were able in a short period to accumulate enough capital to become specialised households and build up lucrative animal stocks.[21] Others with a craft that generates a more modest income can still earn enough cash to ensure a comfortable living standard. Felt-making families (*kigizchi*) are a good example of the former, while the latter case can be illustrated by cobblers (*mozduz*) who buy up old shoes and sell the repaired and cleaned products on the second-hand market. During the years of collectivisation, open apprenticing was not possible although the trade could sometimes be learnt from a father who worked secretly at home. Such conditions limited the options of many young men who were brought up in the 1960s and 1970s. They typically started physical work at the age of 10 or 11 to earn workpoints which entitled them to grain for their families, and many have remained illiterate. These men, now in their thirties and forties, represent a lost generation. They and their nuclear families constitute some of the poorest households of the relatively well-endowed villages where we worked. Today their options are extremely limited; many make cash through

---

[19] An unpublished indigenous document dating from the 1930s from Yarkand calls forced labour *hashar* ('Abdul-Qadir: 2), a term also quoted by Schwarz (1992: 392).

[20] The pre-1949 equivalent of voluntary work is given by Ėdgem Rachimovič Tenishev as *özimiz chiqaghan* (Tenishev 1984: 30).

[21] On diversification and specialisation among rural households in China see Croll (1988).

working as hired labourers, competing with each other on the casual labour market (*medikar baziri*).

As part of the government's initiative to encourage rural specialisation, most villagers in one of the hamlets we studied specialise in intensive animal husbandry. Out of the 30 households we visited, most had between 30 and 70 sheep accommodated in the courtyard. Since most villagers have only a small amount of land to cultivate, agriculture is not perceived as an income-generating activity. Animal husbandry is therefore the major source of cash income to these families. The feeding and watering of these animals is exclusively done by women, and this job often takes up several hours of their day. Cleaning the pens is sometimes done by men, but often also by women. Men's main responsibility is to buy and sell the animals themselves and to buy animal feed from the market.[22] In these households women arguably contribute most of the total cash income of the household. Since the marketing is regularly done by men, the cash income generated by women's labour tends to remain in men's hands.

Felt-making, like other crafts, could be learnt either from one's father or acquired through informal apprenticeship. Traditionally, felt-makers have been men, and although many could not practise their trade during the years of collectivisation or could only carry on in secret, nowadays it is a legal and lucrative business. In felt-makers' homes, women often work alongside their husbands and carry out some stages of the work by themselves. Married women who have not learned the business from their own fathers pick it up from their husbands shortly after marriage. These women estimated that at least 50 per cent of the total labour input was theirs. Yet, when asked, these same women described themselves as unqualified with no skilled knowledge, while their husbands were considered to be specialised craftsmen. Since marketing is again the responsibility of men, the resulting cash income also remains under male control; women's role is reduced to that of unpaid family labour.

Somewhat similar is the situation in another hamlet which has been assigned the task of specialisation in making wedding chests (*sanduq*). Many local men are qualified carpenters (*yaghachchi*). In addition to making the wooden structure, they also decorate it with metal strips which they fix onto the surface of the chest with many small nails. Families with no expertise in carpentry buy the undecorated chests for decoration. In both settings, women learn the art of decorating and often they do as much or more of this work as their men. Among men, decorating is typically done by teenage boys and young men, for whom it is a way to make money; but because it entails

---

[22] In this village women only very occasionally went out to collect grass.

continuous banging and monotony, it is not considered a suitable career for an adult man and nobody perceives it as a long-term career. Decorating wedding chests is not a craft in its own right that one needs to learn as an apprentice, the necessary skills can be acquired informally in the course of a few weeks. The buying of raw materials and marketing of the finished product are again exclusively done by men, so that women's participation as cash earners is disguised.

Plate 4. Young men decorating wedding chests, Kashgar, Southern Xinjiang (Photo: Chris Hann).

The same pattern can be observed yet again in households where men engage in repairing and re-selling old shoes. The repair job and the cleaning of the shoes are often equally shared by women. But while men are the acknowledged cobblers, women are perceived merely as helpers.

Thus women's participation remains masked in virtually all areas of production which I could observe, including agricultural work and animal husbandry, crafts such as felt-making, decorating wedding chests, and shoe repair. It is referred to both by men and women as 'helping their husbands' or as an extension of daily domestic chores. Women have no direct access to the income they generate. Such families follow a traditional pattern of budgeting, which can be characterised as the 'doling' or 'asking' method and 'gift giving' patterns which express unequal, hierarchical relationships (cf. Zelizer 1994: 141).[23]

One particular activity that I could observe more closely in which Uyghur women's income-earning abilities cannot be disguised is *doppa*-making, an exclusively female craft where the buying of raw materials and selling of the finished product remain under female control.[24] Yet here too women's economic contribution is devalued. Unlike animal husbandry and agricultural work which constitute part of women's domestic chores (*öy ishi*), or the above-described engagement in crafts which is classified as 'helping their husbands', piecework is perceived by both men and women as leisure activity which women do in their 'spare time, leisure' (*bikar waqtida*). This is so even when women spend as much as six hours per day on the work. It is possible that this interpretation of handicrafts as leisure rather than work was common in pre-1949 peasant society and was applied to male crafts as well, as the primary occupation of men was with agriculture, and that of women with housekeeping. In 1956, Èdgem Rachimovič Tenishev's 73-year-old male carpet weaver from Khotan referred to weaving as a leisure activity done after he had finished his work (Tenishev 1984: 77). If this was the general situation, it is certainly changing in the post-reform era at least in those communities which derive most of their cash income from sideline occupations, which results in the higher valuation of men's crafts. However, even though *doppa*-making is officially classified as a recognised sideline, it continues to be perceived as leisure rather than work.

Very different is the position of *doppa*-makers who work in the Kashgar Craft Centre. These women, many of whom come from neighbouring villages are employed full-time by the state-run enterprise. They complete eight hours of work for six days per week and are paid by the piece. Like many village women working at home, they too specialise in specific stages of *doppa*-making. They prefer to be employed by this state-run enterprise mainly because of the fringe benefits they enjoy: meat allowances at the times of religious festivals; a secure income in the long term; subsidised health care; and other perks that their status of government employee offers. Being part of this stratum also gives these women enormous social prestige, much higher than that of rural or even urban housewives. In contrast to ordinary pieceworkers, these women perceive themselves, and are regarded by others, as income earners.

---

[23] This roughly corresponds to the 'pool pattern' or 'common fund' as described by Roldán (1988: 233).

[24] It is very likely that the situation of women who specialise in producing yoghurt and cream is similar, but I have no evidence to support this assumption.

In the local media, rural *doppa*-makers are hailed as examples of successful development planning, while women's agricultural work and participation in virtually all other income-generating activity are devalued. This is underlined by the fact that the All-China Women's Federation (ACWF) publicly acknowledges women's performance mainly within the domestic domain: on Women's Day some village women will be selected for praise as a good mother-in-law (*güzäl qeynana*) or a good daughter-in-law (*güzäl kelin*), but not for much of their economic performance.

Conclusion

In this chapter I have considered Uyghur villagers' perceptions of work in three periods, pre-1949, 1949–80, and post-1980. I have argued that their experience of the collectivised period was largely negative. This holds true for both men and women, even though official ideology in the 1990s, as represented by local research collaborators, insists that women have been the beneficiaries of socialist gender policies. Since 1980, most observers agree that women have withdrawn once again into the domestic sphere. I have argued that their participation in production and contribution to family income remain significant in the 1990s, but it continues to be masked and largely undervalued. Both men and women perform a wide variety of tasks throughout the year, and the nature of their daily work is far from immutable. Variation exists according to season, locality and opportunities to specialise, age, and household composition. In spite of the new opportunities that many households enjoy, the legacy of the collectivised period endures in the poverty of middle-aged men who were prevented from learning a craft during the Cultural Revolution. Whereas in the pre-socialist period there was a clear normative gendered division of labour which assigned different tasks to men and women but valued both, in the socialist period men and women were thrown together to carry out for the first time almost identical tasks, but even when doing the same work, men received the greater credit. After 1980, the socialist legacy has made it very difficult to recover the pre-1949 pattern of domestic relations. In spite of the official promotion of gender equality, in the 1990s rural women's subordination is perpetuated by the socialist authorities themselves. Villagers are under the firm control of the government, which means that their decision-making power remains extremely limited. Present government policies are fostering new inequalities in rural areas and this exaggerates women's subordinate position, especially among the poor.

In summary, the pre-socialist legacy prescribed clear-cut division of labour between men and women which, however, allowed for variations in women's participation in production and some degree of female control in the household. The norm was set by more affluent households but practice and values often diverged, especially in the middle- and lower-ranking groups. These traditional patterns reveal great similarities with Elisabeth Croll's description of traditional patterns of the division of labour and morality in rural Han Chinese households (Croll 1982: 224–25). Behind the ostensibly egalitarian policies, villagers' recollections reveal a drastic violation of local morality as well as the explicit subordination of women through enforced communal work and inadequate support services. In this, my informants echo Elisabeth Croll's comments on the uneven establishment of rural welfare facilities in China generally. Women's burden during these years increased greatly. This is again clearly formulated by Croll in her seminal analysis of rural women's position in China:

> Peasant women have thus been expected to enter the waged labor force and, at the same time, to continue to service and maintain the household. It seems that the establishment of the communes may not have reduced the demands on women's labor so much as they have led to an intensification of female labor. There has been some redefinition of the sexual division of labor in the public sphere, to the benefit of women, but despite numerous policies to reduce the content of domestic labor and equalize the distribution of the remainder between the sexes, there has been little correlative redefinition of labor within the domestic sphere (Croll 1982: 239–40).

Together, local customary and Maoist legacies combine in the new context of 'socialist commodity economy' to ensure that women's work remains undervalued. It is curious that local Han scholars in Xinjiang, echoing socialist ideology, continue to insist that patriarchy flows only from Islam, and to claim that the policies which the state has rejected since 1980 were actually the right policies for ameliorating the position of women.

References

'Abdul-Qadir. ca. 1930. *A Collection of Eastern Turki Folkloristic Texts.* Unpublished manuscript, Yarkand, Jarring Collection, Lund University Library. Prov. 464. (Turki).

Bellér-Hann, I. 1996. Narratives and Values: Source Materials for the Study of Popular Culture in Xinjiang. *Inner Asia Occasional Papers* 1 (1): 89–100. Cambridge: Mongolia and Inner Asia Studies Unit.

Benería, L. 1982. Accounting for Women's Work. In L. Benería (ed.), *Women and Development: The Sexual Division of Labor in Rural Societies*, pp. 119–47. New York: Praeger.

Croll, E. 1980. *Women in Rural Development: The People's Republic of China*. Geneva: International Labour Office.

——. 1982. The Sexual Division of Labor in Rural China. In L. Benería (ed.), *Women and Development. The Sexual Division of Labor in Rural Societies*, pp. 223–47. New York: Praeger.

——. 1986. *Chinese Women since Mao*. London: Zed Press.

——. 1988. The New Peasant Economy in China. In S. Feuchtwang, A. Hussain, and T. Pairault (eds.), *Transforming China's Economy in the Eighties*, pp. 77–100. Boulder: Westview Press.

Davin, D. 1976. *Woman-Work: Women and the Party in Revolutionary China*. Oxford: Clarendon Press.

——. 1995. Women, Work and Property in the Chinese Peasant Household of the 1980s. In D. Elson (ed.), *Male Bias in the Development Process*, pp. 29–50. Manchester: Manchester University Press.

Jarring, G. 1946–1951. *Materials to the Knowledge of Eastern Turki. Tales, Poetry, Proverbs, Riddles, Ethnological and Historical Texts from the Southern Parts of Eastern Turkestan*. Part IV: Ethnological and Historical Texts from Guma. In Lunds Universitets Ärsskrift N. F. Avd.1. Bd 47. Nr.4.

Jeffery, P., R. Jeffery, and A. Lyon. 1989. *Labour Pains and Labour Power: Women and Childbearing in India*. London and New Jersey: Zed Books Ltd.

Kandiyoti, D. 1992. Islam and Patriarchy: A Comparative Perspective. In N. R. Keddie, and B. Baron (eds.), *Women in Middle Eastern History: Shifting Boundaries in Sex and Gender*, pp. 23–42. New Haven: Yale University Press.

Katanov, N. T., and K. H. Menges. 1933, 1976. *Volkskundliche Texte aus Ost-Türkistan*. Proceedings of the Prussian Academy of Sciences, Section of Philology and History, 1933. Leipzig: Zentralantiquariat of the German Democratic Republic.

Kelliher, D. 1992. *Peasant Power in China: The Era of Rural Reform, 1979–1989*. New Haven: Yale University Press.

Mackerras, C. 1995. *China's Minority Cultures: Identities and Integration since 1912*. New York: St. Martin Press.

Muhammad 'Ali Damolla. ca. 1905–10. *A Collection of Essays on Life in Eastern Turkistan*. Unpublished manuscript, Kahsgar, Jarring Collection, Lund University Library. Prov. 207. I.–II. (Turki).

Nolan, P. 1988. *The Political Economy of Collective Farms: An Analysis of China's Post-Mao Rural Reforms.* Oxford: Polity Press.

Papanek, H. 1989. Family Status-Production Work: Women's Contribution to Social Mobility and Class Differentiation. In M. Krishnaraj, and K. Chanana (eds.), *Gender and the Household Domain: Social and Cultural Dimensions,* (Vol. 4) *Women and the Household in Asia,* pp. 97–116. New Delhi: Sage.

Rai, S. M. 1995. Gender in China. In R. Benewick, and P. Wingrove (eds.), *China in the 1990s,* pp. 181–92. London: Macmillan.

Roldán, M. 1988. Renegotiating the Marital Contract: Intrahousehold Patterns of Money Allocation and Women's Subordination among Domestic Outworkers in Mexico City. In D. Dwyer, and J. Bruce (eds.), *A Home Divided: Women and Income in the Third World,* pp. 229–247. Stanford: Stanford University Press.

Schwarz, H. G. 1992. *An Uyghur-English Dictionary.* Washington: Western Washington University.

Sharma, U. 1980. *Women, Work and Property in North-West India.* London and New York: Tavistock Publications.

Shaw, R. B. 1878. *A Sketch of the Turki Language as Spoken in Eastern Turkestan (Kashghar and Yarkand).* Calcutta: The Baptist Mission Press.

Sheriff, G. 1928. *Diaries.* Unpublished manuscript. London: Museum of Mankind.

Stacey, J. 1983. *Patriarch and Socialist Revolution in China.* Berkeley: University of California Press.

Tenishev, E. R. 1984. *Uigurskiie teksty.* Moscow: Nauka.

Watson, R. S. (ed.). 1994. *Memory, History, and Opposition under State Socialism.* Santa Fe: School of American Research Press.

White, J. B. 1994. *Money Makes Us Relatives: Women's Labor in Urban Turkey.* Austin: University of Texas Press.

Zelizer, V. A. 1989. The Social Meaning of Money: 'Special Monies'. *American Journal of Sociology* 95 (2): 342–77.

——. 1994. The Creation of Domestic Currencies. *The American Economic Review* 84 (2): 138–142.

Chapter 3
Crafts, Entrepreneurship, and Gendered Economic Relations in Southern Xinjiang in the Era of the 'Socialist Commodity Economy'[1]

In the oasis towns of Xinjiang in north-west China, permanent and periodic markets are among the most popular attractions of local life, both for local people and tourist marketing. The Sunday market of Kashgar is generally mentioned by Western guidebooks as the largest of Central Asia, but less well-known oasis towns receive similar treatment. The centrality of trade and market activity is illustrated in the following paragraph from a locally published English language travel brochure of Kucha:

> Kuqa has been a trading center frequented by merchants from all corners of the world ever since early ages. In the Song dynasties merchants traveled to the midland with their families on business. In the period of the Republic of China, large numbers of itinerant businessmen from Kuqa were often met with in Beijing, Tianjin and Shanghai. Since the foundation of the People's Republic of China, especially since the 3rd plenary Session of the Eleventh Central Committee of the Communist Party of China, the commerce of the country has grown still more prosperous and the market still more brisk both in the cities and in the rural areas (Pei 1993: 29).

Visitors to Kucha are assured that the colourfulness of the weekly Friday market is second only to that of Kashgar. This is the day rural producers and craftsmen come to town to sell their agricultural and other produce, and also to buy the products which the city and long-distance traders have to offer. The knowledge that oasis towns like Kucha, which today are open to foreign travellers, were once important commercial centres along the eastern stretch of the legendary caravan routes known as the Silk Roads, enhances the attractions of these markets for foreign tourists. Locals appreciate the relatively recent revival of large-scale markets for different reasons. They

---

[1] Published in *Central Asian Survey* 1998, 17 (4): 701–18.

enjoy not only a wide range of goods to purchase, but also the freedom to produce and to market their products, following the economic reforms implemented all over China from the early 1980s onwards. During the decades of collectivisation, especially during the late 1960s and most of the 1970s, many rural markets in Xinjiang were closed, while others, including large weekly markets in the oasis towns, were much restricted in range. During this period most agricultural and industrial produce was distributed through the bureaucratic channels of the commune, and for a number of years individual production for the market was branded as 'capitalist' and subject to punishment, especially if one were caught in black market trading.

The reforms dubbed 'the great reversal' by William Hinton (1990) have drastically changed the socio-economic relations of the decades of collectivisation.[2] The introduction of the 'responsibility system' was accompanied by the liberalisation of sideline activities and the expansion and development of rural markets.[3] Farmers can sell some if not all of their agricultural surplus on the free market, and most rural families living close enough to large markets respond positively to government encouragement to pursue sideline production such as intensive animal husbandry, dairy production, and engagement in various crafts. But informal economic relations, which dominated the market during the decades of collectivisation, have not disappeared altogether: other continuities in exchange practices have persisted. Using material based on fieldwork in Beijing during the late 1980s, Frank Pieke made the following observation:

> Before the reforms, personal transactions made possible market-type exchanges in a situation in which no real market existed. These transactions provided an essential channel for individuals and work units seeking to correct the inefficiencies of the planned economy, thereby preventing the system's collapse. The growth of the market sphere under the reforms has, however, not led to a decline in these kinds of transactions. On the contrary, the relaxation of central control has increased their scope and facility. Personal relations provide an arena for social action in which actors can trade and convert the resources obtained in the bureaucratic and market spheres (Pieke 1995: 501).

In this new era of free markets, Uyghur villagers too continue to make use of a variety of informal relationships to assist them in getting away from poverty. Alongside increasing reliance on institutionalised credit and

---

[2] For a general overview of the economic reforms in China see Blecher (1986); Feuchtwang, Hussain and Pairault (1988); Nolan (1988). For changes in minority regions see Mackerras (1995).
[3] For a good summary of the content of these reforms, see Perry and Wang (1985).

investment facilities, informal transactions acted out away from the actual marketplaces remain an important characteristic of their economic activities. In what follows I shall explore male and female economic activities outside agriculture in order to identify patterns of the organisation of work and their cultural underpinnings. I will argue that, although in popular lore Uyghur women's participation in the market is minimal, in fact their economic activities are merely invisible rather than non-existent. In some areas women are in full charge of production and marketing, and they follow diverse strategies to gain profit. Although the male and female domains appear to be strictly separated, in practice the ostensibly male domain of work often relies on female participation.[4]

The majority of the population of Southern Xinjiang are primarily agricultural producers and their main crops are wheat and maize. Because of the scarcity of arable land and government regulations which require the obligatory sale of a percentage of the harvest, the grain produced by households is hardly enough to meet subsistence needs (chapter 1). Villagers have been given rights to use the land, but have no right of ownership. In these circumstances almost all villagers living in the vicinity of markets and larger centres try to engage in economic activities outside agriculture. The two townships in which we were allowed to carry out interviews are situated in the vicinity of Kashgar and their per capita income is higher than the average in the county. Both boast high levels of household specialisation in various crafts.[5] Although most households have mixed sources of income, interview partners tend to describe themselves primarily as peasants (*dihqan*): crafts, business and other activities are typically seen as additional (*qoshumjä käsp*).

Economic Activities: *Doppa*-Makers

The local folk model of work is dichotomous: village women's central job is housekeeping and childcare, as summed up in the expression *öy tutush* (house keeping), while men's job is to earn money (*pul täpish*). A number of activities in which women engage are not regarded as 'work' according to the locally accepted folk concept. As a point of departure I follow the model

---

[4] See chapter 2. For example, Thomas Hoppe assumed a strict division of labour between men and women: while the woman takes care of the household, the kitchen, the children, and now and then works in the vegetable garden, the man takes over the hard physical work in the fields, including irrigation, and he is also active as a trader and craftsman. Although Hoppe acknowledged that women too take part in carpet knotting and in business, he primarily identified Uyghur women as domestic workers who do not participate in production (Hoppe 1995: 131–32).

[5] For a discussion of domestic sidelines in China see Croll (1986, 1988).

of work formulated by Cato Wadel. In addition to folk models, this model also considers all kinds of informal activities, which may not be recognised locally as work but 'include the mutual activities that go into maintaining personal and private relations and the collective activities that have to do with the maintenance of community, democracy and other valued social institutions' (Wadel 1979: 382).

Agricultural work and other types of wage earning jobs, like working in a factory or the work undertaken by a craftsman or day labourer, are described as *ämgäk* and are regarded as male prerogatives, while women's jobs are designated with the more general term *ish*.[6] The ideology behind this often verbalised distinction is the inherently weak (*ajiz*) nature of women and the traditional modesty code (*namähräm*) which places women firmly in the domestic sphere (chapter 4). According to commonly held beliefs, village women hardly ever attend the markets, either as buyers or as sellers. That these sentiments express ideals rather than actual practice is supported by textual evidence from the past as well as fieldwork observations.[7]

Elsewhere I have argued that although village women take part in a great variety of income-generating activities, their work remains hidden, unrecognised, or undervalued (chapter 2). Although female participation in agricultural work in this region has a long history, in popular perception this is reduced to an auxiliary status, be it in felt-making, shoe repair, animal husbandry, or the production of wedding-chests.[8] But there are some areas of production which are strongly associated with women to the extent that even marketing remains under female control. One such area is the making of the

---

[6] For an elaboration of the association of women with the domestic sphere and men with non-domestic activities see, for example, Benería (1979).

[7] See, for example, an indigenous essay by Muhammad 'Ali Damolla (1905–10) in which female traders on the Kashgar market are mentioned. A few decades earlier, Thomas Forsyth found in Yarkand that many grocer's and baker's shops were kept by women (1875: 89). The same author also noted that on market day in Kashgar 250 stalls selling thread were occupied by women, 150 women were selling cotton, and 60 women traded in bits of silk and ornaments. Altogether he estimated that out of a total of 27,520 people circulating in town on a market day one-fourth was women (1875: 501–02). Fernand Grenard also mentioned women's active participation in selling and buying (1898: 125). Percy and Ella Sykes noted that some 'farmers' wives ... haggled with the men in the bazaar ... transacting business with their veils thrown back!' (1920: 61).

[8] Female participation in agriculture has traditionally been determined by financial status and social prestige. In this respect the decades of collectivised agriculture were exceptional in that employment of women in agriculture for the first time became universal (cf. Croll 1986: 1–19). Elisabeth Croll also noted about the situation in China in general, that where both sexes work in the fields, women's work remains less visible (Croll 1986: 97). On the obscurity and underestimation of women's work, see Benería (1982: 119–47).

traditional Uyghur hat, the *doppa*. *Doppa*-making is not conceptualised as work (*ish ämäs*)[9], instead, it is considered a leisure activity done in one's spare time (*bikar waqtida qilidu*), even if some women spend as much as six hours or more daily doing it.[10] *Doppa*-making is a skill which is learnt informally from a relative or neighbour. This differentiates it from most 'male' crafts which can be acquired through apprenticeship, have a patron saint (*pir*), and in the past also had a written code of conduct (*risalä*) (Häbibulla 1993: 313–15).[11] *Doppa*s can be sewn at home, in the courtyard, in the neighbour's house, or by the nearby irrigation channel; in other words anywhere in the neighbourhood (*mähällä*) where women can move around freely. There are many varieties of *doppa*. They are produced primarily for local consumption and as such their production belongs to what Stan Toops has termed 'ethnic crafts' (Toops 1993).

In rural Kashgar, most women produce the currently most popular *kök chimän doppa*, but even this can vary according to the quality of materials and the execution of the embroidery. *Doppa*-makers identify five stages of the work: embroidering by hand, patterning with a sewing machine, stitching the embroidered material and the lining together, finishing the edges, and shaping. The most time-consuming and skilful job is embroidering by hand.[12]

*Doppa*s may become a currency in informal exchanges among women. For example, Nigar, a young married woman, does *doppa* embroidery for her mother-in-law – apparently free of charge. Yet the mother-in-law regularly bakes bread from her own flour for her son, Nigar, and the couple's three children. Many women regularly contribute to female relatives' *doppa*-making as part of similarly open-ended, long-term exchanges.

---

[9] This does not apply to the *doppa*-makers employed by the Kashgar Craft Centre. As regular government employees who work away from home, their *doppa*-making is considered work and they enjoy higher social prestige than ordinary village women in spite of the fact that some have rural residence and also work in agriculture (chapter 2).

[10] This situation closely resembles the position of the lacemakers of Narsapur (Mies 1982).

[11] Of course, many 'male' crafts can also be learnt informally within the family. Cobblers tend to pass on their knowledge informally, although they have a patron saint. No apprenticing is needed for decorating wedding chests. This job, however, often done by women, is not regarded as suitable for mature men (chapter 2).

[12] That these stages of work really follow age-old traditions is confirmed in an indigenous description of hat makers' work dating from the first decade of the twentieth century (Jarring 1992).

Plate 5. *Doppa*-maker, Kashgar, Southern Xinjiang (Photo: Chris Hann).

But many other women produce directly for the market. Some buy the materials and do all the stages of the work themselves before selling the finished product to a male merchant who has a permanent stall in the bazaar, or perhaps directly to the customer. Many others, however, only do stages of the work, and there is scope for a division of labour. These women are effectively pieceworkers whose labour is organised by the female equivalent of the middleman. These are usually local women from the same neighbourhood, who formerly made *doppa* themselves, but who now specialise in organising others' work. They are usually referred to as the 'neighbourhood woman' or 'neighbourhood merchant' (*mähällä ayal, mähällä sodigär*).[13] In some cases, they provide squares of cotton and other necessary materials which they have bought and prepared. They distribute these among the women who do the embroidery, before passing the product on to others who can do the next stages. The final stages of the work, which are simple and quick, are usually done by the agent herself or a younger member of her family, her daughter or daughter-in-law, as unpaid family labour. Money is sometimes paid to a pieceworker upon collection, but

---

[13] These are locally used terms which do not necessarily conform to the literary standard.

payment may be delayed by weeks. In other cases, a male merchant with a stall in the market visits the agent's home at regular intervals and pays her for the goods he accepts.

Women may opt for other strategies. Those who have no skill, time, or intention to make whole *doppa*s themselves, but wish to avoid the mediation of the neighbourhood agent may resort to the weekly *doppa* market. Very early every Sunday, before the famous weekly Kashgar market gets into full swing, *doppa*-makers meet from inside and outside Kashgar to buy and sell their half-finished products. The women's *doppa* market is far removed from the permanent *doppa* bazaar of male merchants. In early 1996, *doppa*-makers met under the bridge over the river. When the local authorities decided to plant flowers on this spot, the market moved a few hundred metres away, along the road. Business is brisk and the *doppa* market dissolves within a few hours. Of course, such exchanges could also be arranged in the neighbourhood, with neighbours and relatives. But the *doppa* market has a strong appeal: within the neighbourhood, women feel that they have to make allowances in both buying and selling when they are dealing with relatives, neighbours, and friends. The relative anonymity of the *doppa* market allows them to bargain, buying and selling as profitably as the market will allow. Women who regularly attend the *doppa* market pass on information about current prices to pieceworkers in the village. In this way prices paid to pieceworkers are gradually adjusted, although some variations may remain. This knowledge can induce some pieceworkers to ask for a price increase from their agent, or perhaps to switch from one agent to another who is willing to pay more.

Most pieceworkers are aware that they work cheaply, and that the neighbourhood agents make large profits with less work. Although in principle anybody can become a neighbourhood agent, in practice options for the majority are limited. To be able to leave her house regularly and spend a great deal of time with neighbours, or to talk to male merchants, a woman needs a great deal of freedom. This mobility is unlikely to be open to many, on account of age, health problems, the presence of small children, obligation to participate in a husband's craft, or expectations to strictly adhere to the modesty code. Agents also need a small amount of capital with which to start up their business. All agreements are verbal and informal, payments may be delayed, sometimes by weeks, and occasionally advances are required. Therefore trust among the partners is essential. Only those agents who have other sources of prestige can generate the confidence necessary for running a profitable business. In one neighbourhood, the most successful such agent was 65-year-old Zibiräm, whose merchant husband had just returned from the pilgrimage to Mecca. This trip increased his and his family's pious reputation and has been good for Zibiräm's business. Another successful agent is Tursunkhan, who is a few years younger than Zibiräm and happens to be the wife of the *dadüy jang* (village headman, still referred to with the socialist terminology as production brigade leader). The *dadüy jang* himself is a cadre who in the collectivised period used to be the *shaodüy jang* (head of the production team). Although his conduct during those years provoked dislike, and his present successful economic position may stimulate envy, the fact that he is still an office holder and remains influential automatically invests him with prestige which facilitates his wife's position as neighbourhood agent.[14] Less successful is Baharkhan, whose household boasts neither a successful businessman husband, nor an influential cadre, nor any reserves of 'cultural capital' from either the religious or the secular realms. Although she has been trying to establish herself as a neighbourhood agent for several years, initially aided by a modest grant from UNICEF, her business remains on a much smaller scale than that of the other two women.

Economic Activities: Some 'Male' Crafts

As it does for *doppa*-making, accumulated 'cultural capital' plays an important part in the development of other crafts too. Such capital may simply consist of the successful transmission of a family skill throughout the years of repression, as has been the case with felt-makers, cobblers, and carpenters. In these crafts, as in *doppa*-making, skills may be transmitted informally. Even in crafts where apprenticing is the norm, informal transmission within the family is considered a quicker and cheaper way of acquiring specialised knowledge. Informal transmission became the norm in the years of collectivisation, when the practising of any crafts for private gain (including *doppa*-making) was forbidden.[15] Informal marketing and secret production flourished and business relationships established during that period often form the basis of continued cooperation in the reform period.

---

[14] Similarly, the two successful female entrepreneurs I came across in another neighbourhood were the wives of the present production team leader and brigade leader. The two women, who were not related through kinship, received some money as starting capital from their husbands in 1995. They bought up apricots in the village which would normally be marketed at the village bazaar. They dried them in their courtyards and then sold the dried products. In the course of one month, they made 5,000 yuan profit which they divided equally between themselves. This money was then largely used by their husbands to invest in livestock.

[15] For an overview of the debate concerning the compatibility of small-scale commodity production and socialist principles see Croll (1986: 31).

Like *doppa*-making, which is dependent upon other household occupations and obligations, male crafts are not pursued with the same intensity throughout the year. All crafts are neglected during the weeks of most intensive agricultural work. Felt-making and the manufacture of wooden ceilings are outdoor occupations which cannot be practised during the winter months. Wedding chests and *doppa*s sell better during the late summer and autumn months when most weddings are held, while a cobbler may easily find a market for his goods throughout the whole year.

In the post-reform period, informal social relations continue to play an important part in economic transactions. For example, Adil is a 34-year-old carpenter who makes wedding chests. He buys material from his first cousin. He claims that he pays his cousin enough to make sure that the latter makes a small profit for himself, but for Adil the wood is still cheaper than if he were buying it from a stranger. The elaborate ornamentation of the chest is done by his wife, and Adil sells the finished product to a merchant whom he knows well. This ensures that he can get an advance when needed, but sometimes Adil has to be prepared to wait for his money if the merchant is unable to pay him.

Yüsüpjan is a cobbler who repairs second-hand shoes that he buys from his brother, who regularly travels to the interior of China and brings them back by the thousand. After his wife has cleaned them, Yüsüpjan will sell the end product to a merchant with whom his father previously dealt. For Yüsüpjan, all of these transactions may be considered as driven by considerations of economising and profit maximising. For his brother, selling Yüsüpjan the old shoes at a low price might be seen as altruistic aid to a relative who is less successful than himself. However, interviews with both brothers revealed that there is a more complicated web of mutual indebtedness: Yüsüpjan and his wife had given a baby in adoption to the childless elder brother.

The presence of middlemen (*dällal*) is of particular significance in the exclusively male domain of animal sales acted out in the market, but this mediation contrasts conspicuously with the female neighbourhood agents in the *doppa* market, whose activities mostly take place away from the actual bazaar. However, a closer look reveals that such 'invisible' transactions are not unknown in the male domain. Many butchers avoid middlemen by establishing reliable contacts with villagers whose houses they visit regularly to buy sheep. Some well-established cobblers rely on seasoned relationships with merchants who visit their homes to inspect and select goods. Often such relationships originate in the market place: producers who in the past took their goods to the market built up trustworthy contacts over the years. The transaction gradually moved away from the bazaar to the village.

Family cooperation could also facilitate the accumulation of substantial capital during the years of collectivisation. The most successful merchants in one neighbourhood are two brothers who spent years away from their village after 1968. Although they worked as farmers, they also became involved in illegal animal marketing with Kazakh herdsmen in the vicinity of the provincial capital Ürümchi. From this business they accumulated a small amount of capital by the time they returned to the village in 1980. Using this money they established a chicken farm. After three years, they sold the business and used the profit to set up a carpet-weaving workshop. To operate it they employed six permanent weavers from the famous weaving centre of Khotan. In turn, the profits derived from the weaving workshop were invested into buying the lease on a brick factory in the village, which the brothers run by employing poor Han migrant workers.[16] In the meantime, their eldest brother has bought a nail factory in Kashgar, part of which has been transformed into a new weaving workshop for the six weavers.

Investment and Credit

Land reform in the 1950s was followed by collectivisation and land ceased to be a significant object of household investment.[17] This situation has not changed with the implementation of the economic reforms since the early 1980s. Villagers now exercise the right of land use and they pass this right to their sons, but the actual ownership over land is still held by the collective. Some entrepreneurs are able to lease larger holdings from the collective and occasionally from other individuals. In some cases with large areas of wasteland, wealthier individuals are also in the position of being able to buy land cheaply and invest to bring it under cultivation. However this is very exceptional. Most households have only enough arable land to meet their household's subsistence needs and the state's demands in terms of cereal and cotton quotas.[18] Many of my interlocutors agreed that agricultural production itself is not an income-generating activity.

In contrast to land, houses are regarded as a form of long-term investment since, unlike land, they have remained private property, even throughout the years of collectivisation. Following the introduction of reforms, a feverish construction of new houses began in the more affluent

---

[16] The employment of cheap labour from the interior of China is becoming more common as the number of impoverished Han migrants in Xinjiang increases. On Han immigration into Xinjiang see Hoppe (1995: 308–35).

[17] For a brief overview of the land reform in Xinjiang see Hoppe (1995: 117–18).

[18] For an analysis of the present situation of Uyghur peasants see chapter 1.

villages. Traditional small peasant houses have been demolished and re-placed by more spacious buildings, by all those who could afford it. On such occasions the traditional wooden ceiling of the guest-room was often saved and carried over to the new house. This made economic sense, since the wooden structures make up more than half of the total expenses of the building of a new house. However, when older farmers proudly pointed to such ceilings in their new homes and explained that this used to belong to the paternal home, there seemed also to be a strong sense of sentimental attachment to the most permanent form of private property. Although they are expensive, I never heard of anyone selling this part of the paternal inheritance. Wealth is also indicated by the building materials used: modern brick is valued more highly than traditional mud brick and the use of the former at least by the main entrance is a source of prestige and pride. Houses can be sold and rented, although more commonly they form the most important part of inheritance. Wealth is also invested into household furnishings, particularly knotted carpets and felts, which continue to figure prominently in dowry, inheritance, and divorce settlements.

In addition to houses, Uyghur farmers in the Kashgar region use livestock, usually sheep, as deposits of wealth. In one township, in a hamlet where households did not specialise in animal husbandry, most families owned approximately 6–10 sheep. Surplus money is usually invested in sheep rather than banked. In fact some of my interview partners said that 'these sheep are our bank' – they are kept as a security in case of an emergency such as illness or death. Although banks are used by successful merchants and entrepreneurs, for middle- and low-income families investing money in sheep is the safest option. Money may also be invested in draught animals and a cart: transporting people and goods for cash is one of the few options of sideline activity open to a poor farmer who lives near an urban centre. Alternatively, more well-to-do families may invest in a tractor, which can also be used for transport and hired out for work on the land.

An important aspect of the economic reforms has been the active encouragement of specialisation. In principle, bank loans are available for villagers wishing to start a sideline. In practice, many peasants are discouraged from taking out a loan by the interest demanded by banks.[19] In the villages, bank loans were cautiously taken by some men to expand animal husbandry or a craft.[20] In obtaining credit, informal arrangements

---

[19] In 1996 the interest required by banks was 180 yuan for every 1,000 yuan loaned.

[20] One man took out 5,000 yuan to buy sheep. Another used a mixture of strategies to buy the empty house next door to his own for 10,000 yuan; he obtained 6,000 yuan through selling a large number of sheep and he borrowed 4,000 yuan from the bank. The house is now used as

avoiding the official bureaucracy altogether are preferred. Many regard the interest charged by banks as excessive, and for poorer families a bank loan may not be an option at all. For substantial loans, one needs a reference letter from local cadres and only those whose financial position is already relatively strong will qualify. Furthermore, a certain degree of suspicion surrounds most dealings with officialdom, and peasants who are illiterate or semi-literate may be discouraged by the necessary paperwork required.[21] If banks are avoided by many for both investment and credit, other informal arrangements are called for.[22] Families which are unable to grow enough cereal to satisfy their subsistence needs may typically ask for a grain loan from the few farmers who have a surplus. The grain loan must be repaid at the next harvest in grain and often some interest is also charged. Grain loans are said to be extremely common in poor villages, but they were also present among some low-income families in the relatively rich villages where our interviews were carried out. This type of transaction was well known in pre-1949 Xinjiang, when high interests on loaned grain could reduce free peasants to the state of dependent serfs (Hoppe 1995: 111).

Cash loans can also be obtained through informal contacts, for example from one's family members, a strategy that both peasants and urban residents employ if they can. Such a loan is typically interest-free and can be paid back over a longer period of time. Furthermore, it creates open-ended relations of mutual obligation from which the lender may also benefit, for example in the form of generous wedding presents for his children. Within the village context Ärkin bought his tractor from interest-free loans provided by members of his extended family. He then started using it for transporting goods. From the money he earned in this way he could pay the loan back within two years.

Another source of credit for at least some people is the *mäshräp*, a traditional male leisure activity, which has been revived in some neighbourhoods since the reforms (Häbibulla 1993: 448–59). In one township over the last few years groups of men have started regular get-togethers that involve communal eating, singing, and discussion and double as rotating savings and credit associations. The *mäshräp* was a popular form of voluntary association before the communist takeover, although according

---

a felt-making atelier, although in the future it is envisaged that one of his married sons will move there with his wife.

[21] This attitude has also been found in other peasant societies (e.g. Bailey 1964: 128).

[22] Pawnshops used to be an important feature of local life prior to 'Liberation', but they were outlawed by the socialist authorities in the 1950s. See Millward (1993: 297–82) and Muhammad 'Ali Damolla (1905–10: 45). On pre-1949 banking customs see Muhammad 'Ali Damolla (1905–10: 46).

to elderly people it did not then function as a credit association. Throughout the commune period, the institution seems to have experienced decline, only to be revived in the wake of the reforms. My interlocutors insist that even in the mid-1980s the *mäshräp* was not a credit association and that its traditional aspects were foregrounded. In general the exclusively male meetings take place during the late autumn and winter months, between November and February, when there is no agricultural work. Membership of such a group is typically between 10–20 people. They meet once a week or once every two weeks, usually on a Saturday evening, and the party may continue into the small hours. The meetings take place in the houses of members, who take it in turns to host the party. At the introductory meeting lots are drawn to decide who should start. It is also on this occasion that the amount of money to be contributed on each occasion is fixed. In the summer of 1996 this amount was typically in the range of 50–100 yuan. The age of members was between 20 and 50, but the traditional rule of avoidance prevents fathers and sons from attending the same *mäshräp*. The money contributed by the members on each occasion is given to the person who hosts the party (who is exempt from making a contribution). This money is widely regarded as interest-free credit (*ösümsiz ötnä*). It is used by members for investment in sheep or for securing money for other economic initiatives, but informants agreed that this is seldom discussed between members and that wives also remain ignorant of how this money is spent. In fact, wives normally do not even know the level of their husbands' contribution. Informants tend to emphasise the social and entertainment value of the *mäshräp*. The meetings are marked by a communal meal cooked by the female members of the host's household. The dishes served are plentiful and represent festive food associated with life-cycle and religious rituals. Jokes are told and games are played. Some play music on traditional instruments and others dance the *usul*, which is also considered an important component of Uyghur identity. There is a strong emphasis on the tradition-bearing function of the *mäshräp*: these are the occasions when young people are taught by older males about proper behaviour, discipline, respect, and tradition. In one village, members of a recently established *mäshräp* were accused of abusing the institution to justify alcohol consumption, which flies in the face of Islamic teachings. As a response to these accusations members of this group invited some village elders, including religious personages such as the imam and the muezzin, to take part. This invitation was accepted, and the elders approved of what they saw. Invitations can always be extended to people who are not members of the credit association, who may take part in the meal and at the meeting without contributing to the common fund. A lot of information of local concern is exchanged, and such discussions may form the starting point of new economic cooperation between individuals or of marriage alliances.

The *mäshräp* may also be used as a framework for other types of alliances. Among some circles of Uyghur refugees living outside China, the institution is consciously used to organise young people for political action: in this respect the *mäshräp* serves as a means to disguise political content and as a suitable framework through which to mobilise the young. That this potential is also recognised, if not necessarily realised, among the Uyghurs living in China is indicated by the unwillingness of some men to take part on the grounds that such participation might potentially be dangerous and lead to trouble.

It is also possible to speculate that the *mäshräp* may further multiply its functions to include a stronger religious orientation. It is well documented that before 1949 one of the central functions of the *mäshräp* was the communal reading and explanation of religious texts, usually of the Sufi tradition (Pantusov 1907: 5). Some *mäshräp*, at least in the towns, were based on professional loyalties and the Sufi orientation of Central Asian guilds also point to the possible religious dimensions of this institution. There is therefore reason to believe that, in spite of the modern representation of the *mäshräp* both by Uyghur ethnographers and villagers as a secular organisation with an educational, entertainment, and in some instances economic function, in its revived form the *mäshräp* may potentially foster other types of loyalties too.

Membership is usually village or neighbourhood-based, although some *mäshräp* are based on professional loyalties. Sometimes the demands of membership may prove too much: the economic reforms may turn some members into successful businessmen, but others may become visibly impoverished. The recognition that turning the *mäshräp* into a rotating savings and credit association can lead to an accentuation of economic inequality among villagers, and therefore to the exclusion of some members, led in one instance to the elimination of the function of the *mäshräp* as a credit association. For other groups, however, the credit association continues to ensure access to large sums of money at regular intervals.

In the same township, some women tried to organise their own equivalent of a credit association, popularly known as *olturush* (sitting). However, although such associations among Uyghur women are mushrooming in the cities, in the villages only female cadres seem able to sustain an association. When other village women tried to organise a similar enterprise, they failed. Their first meetings became the subject of male gossip and criticism, and they quickly abandoned the idea. Even women in high powered jobs (such as the deputy secretary of the township's

Communist Party) agree that, while the financial details of men's credit associations remain hidden to them, all women would need their husbands' permission to participate in an *olturush*. Husbands must have full knowledge of women's contributions, even if women use their own earnings for this purpose. In the county seat of Kucha, credit associations were said to be common among female government employees, but I have no data to suggest that they have spread to other groups either among the urban or rural populations. It seems reasonable to assume that at present women's credit associations are less likely to develop a religious-political character.

However, like the male *mäshräp*, the female *olturush* too serves multiple functions. The communal consumption of what are considered traditional Uyghur foods, music, and dancing are important in strengthening ethnic belonging, while the relative social and occupational homogeneity of the groups observed also fosters professional and class identities. When the female cadres of one township started their first credit association, they contributed one-sixth of their monthly salary per month (20 yuan out of a salary of 120 yuan). The amount of the contribution increased in the later cycles as salaries became higher. In 1996 interest in joining credit associations among women cadres was high, such that with meetings held only once a month (with the exception of the month of Ramadan), the potential membership would have made it impossible to complete a cycle within a year. Younger women therefore decided to organise a separate group. Such meetings tend to take place on Saturdays during the day while the men are out of the house. The women draw lots each time to decide where the next meeting should be held, and the money collected on each occasion is given to the hostess. This arrangement was considered satisfactory and fundamentally equal, and in this respect comparable to the situation documented in many other countries (March and Taqqu 1982; Bellér-Hann 1996). The credit earned in this way is used for expensive clothes, which are important markers of social status, although in some families women discuss with their husbands how best to use the money jointly. These women, who all had jobs and their own salaries, agree that the husband's permission for participating is indispensable.[23]

---

[23] Materials concerning credit associations and their institutional framework among Uyghur refugees living in Kazakhstan reveal further variations in organisational patterns. For example, among young, unmarried women, separate groups were formed by first generation migrants as opposed to the so-called local (*yärlik*) Uyghur whose ancestors had migrated from Xinjiang prior to the latest large wave in the early 1960s. There was also some possibility of membership in multiple associations. Some forms of the *mäshräp* among the Uyghur in Almaty, who mainly originate from the northern part of Xinjiang, also appear to function as a charity providing emergency aid to its members according to need (e.g. in case of weddings,

In one township, an additional and atypical source of potential credit has been provided by a UNICEF development project aimed at the alleviation of poverty in China. In the implementation of this project, UNICEF has been relying largely on the All-China Women's Federation. According to an unpublished document, 'UNICEF assists ACWF to implement revolving credit programmes. These schemes give poor women access to the capital required to start small businesses and, in so doing, provide them with an opportunity to lift themselves and their families out of poverty' (UNICEF Cooperation in China: 1). The credit programme, which was introduced in this village in 1992, was designed, among other objectives, to make seed money available to poor rural women. The UNICEF document quoted above confirms the message I was given in interviews with village-, township-, and county-level cadres: all reported that the first three years of the project were very successful. All loans had been repaid and in 1996 a new three-year-cycle of loaning seed money was launched.

Discussion of the administration of the UNICEF programme was not part of my original project, but it came up regularly in conversations with both officials and villagers. The latter complained about the inadequacy of the dissemination of information about this credit source. They were convinced that local officials were partial to their kin and friends when money was allocated, and that most poor families did not benefit. This allegation was confirmed by the officials, who claimed that the very poor were indeed not considered because they would be unable to repay the debt. To qualify for the UNICEF credit, a deposit (*amanät puli*) of 1 yuan for every 8 yuan borrowed had to be put in the bank. This amount was later to be deducted from the repayment of the debt. During the first three years, *doppa*-makers were the prime target of the scheme and many small grants were distributed. Some women were aware that decision making concerning the distribution of grants was influenced by the successful neighbourhood agents who had been invited to the village administrative centres and consulted as to who should receive a loan. Of course, they themselves were also eligible. Most people assumed that the loan was interest-free, but officials admitted that interest was charged and the profits were paid into the township's charity fund. County-level officials claimed that the money was given to women alone, and that the recipients had to have their own bank account. However, village cadres confirmed that in practice the general financial position of a woman's household was taken into account when deciding the distribution of UNICEF credit. The income of the male

---

deaths, or financial difficulties), but a detailed discussion of this situation does not belong here.

household head guaranteed the deposit, and money was often paid out to him rather than to his wife. The grassroots-level consideration of households, rather than individuals, for the loans automatically disqualified some young married women, unmarried daughters, and divorced single mothers sheltering in the parental home because only one woman per household was eligible to receive a loan. Women who wished to apply for the credit had to take part in a two-day course organised for them by cadres of the county-level ACWF, at which they were taught simple accounting and book-keeping; recipients of the grant were then expected to keep detailed accounts of how they used the money. In practice, no such accounting took place. It turned out that small loans given for *doppa*-making were often used by the family to buy sheep. I do not wish to suggest that the money was accepted with improper intentions. In some cases a family crisis dictated the diversion of its use. In other cases a simple calculation of how it could be best utilised determined the direction of the investment.[24] Poorer families who never received the UNICEF credit admitted that if such money had been given to them, they too would have invested it into sheep. My interview partners had only the vaguest ideas about the long-term rationale of the scheme and the principles of its distribution. Most were convinced that the money should have been given primarily to poorer families, and were disappointed to see that very few of the recipients in fact belonged to this category.[25]

The Concepts of Obligation and Voluntariness

For both men and women, definitions of daily activities revolve around the complementary concepts of obligation and voluntariness, concepts equally important in the religious sphere and in dealings with secular authority, the state and its representatives.[26] *Wäzipä* (duty) and *mäjburiyät* (obligation) are often contrasted with the term *khalis* (voluntary, altruistic), and here I wish to argue that these same definitions underpin definitions of work. *Wäzipä* is used in a more general sense, covering both the secular and the religious spheres. *Mäjburiyät* is more often used to refer to family obligations and duties towards the state. However, in practice these terms are often used interchangeably. In Islamic terminology, religious obligations are summed

---

[24] See Frederick Bailey's description of the use of government loans by farmers in India (1964: 127).

[25] The comments of both ordinary peasants and local cadres confirm the need to consider intra-household dynamics in projects which aim at self-sustained economic development, as elaborated by Dwyer and Bruce (1988) and Rogers (1990).

[26] The identification of domestic work as women's duty by women themselves has been documented in many contexts all over the world (e.g. Croll 1986: 6; Jeffery, Jeffery and Lyon 1989: 126; White 1994).

up as *pärz* (mandatory duty) and the equivalent of *khalis* is *sawap* (meritorious deed). One needs to perform one's religious obligations to avoid committing a sin. However, the performance of a meritorious deed is not obligatory, it comes from one's heart; it is performed voluntarily; and therefore it counts as additional to the fulfilment of one's obligations. In practice, relatively few villagers know the word *pärz*, and the concepts of religious obligation and meritorious deed are usually merged in *sawap*. The terms *wäzipä* and *mäjburiyät* were often used when villagers tried to explain religious concepts to me, together with the adjective *khalis*.[27] I suggest that the obligatory-voluntary opposition provides important underpinnings of people's daily actions. The pursuit of crafts by men is perceived as income-generating activity and as such an integral part of their obligations. To maintain the fiction that men are the exclusive breadwinners in a household, *doppa*-making and other forms of female engagement with crafts is relegate to the sphere of *khalis ish*, that is 'voluntary work'.[28] While all aspects of women's work performed as part of their obligations are closely controlled by men who are in charge of the acquisition of materials, marketing, and the allocation of the resulting income, work outside such close control is classified as voluntary. Even for voluntary work, however, male permission (*rukhsät*) is needed.[29] Similarly, permission is required from the male household head for participation in ritual activities which are considered as being beyond a woman's obligations or in the meeting of a rotating credit association. Meeting one's obligations is ensured by communal and religious sanctions while voluntary actions, always a positive concept, are expected to entail reward.

Patterns in the allocation of women's earnings from *doppa*-making also illustrate the importance of the underlying concepts of obligation and voluntariness. In poor families where the husband has little or no cash income, *doppa* money, regardless of its quantity, is spent on household necessities such as food, books and pens for school-age children, or medical treatment.[30] In these circumstances, *doppa*-making becomes an obligation, since without it the family's basic needs cannot be met. In such a family, a woman who cannot sew is mocked and ridiculed by her husband. At the other extreme, are well-to-do families in which women engage in the *doppa*

---

[27] See chapters 1 and 2.

[28] Obligation and voluntariness may come into conflict with each other. If a woman is called upon to play a supporting role in her husband's enterprise, her own wish to carry on *khalis* work such as sewing *doppa* must give way to *mäjburiyät*.

[29] This concept of *rukhsät* is not unlike the concept of *izin* in rural Turkey as elaborated by Carol Delaney (1993).

[30] In one case it was put aside for the couple's fertility treatment.

business as organisers. Their often substantial earnings are also pooled, and they may be invested in sheep or other business ventures managed by the male household head. In both these groups *doppa* money is of importance: in the first case, because the family is so poor that even relatively small amounts of cash matter a great deal, in the second, because the *doppa* income is conspicuously high. Within low-income families the woman's control over her income may be nominal since the basic needs of her household must be met.[31] In middle-income families where the man's cash income is sufficient to ensure at least the basic necessities, *doppa* money is generally considered as pin money, dismissed as unimportant. Women are typically allowed to keep this income under their control and are more likely to spend it on themselves, and in particular on materials and dressmaking, since clothes are important status markers in Uyghur society.[32] However, only part of the materials bought from *doppa* money will be spent by women on themselves. An important proportion is used to allow women (in all social categories) to help fulfil their ritual obligations. Custom requires that women take gifts, typically cloth, to weddings, circumcision ceremonies, and commemorations of the dead. Since such presents are becoming expensive, rural women in Southern Xinjiang have recently come under increasing pressure from both the religious and the secular authorities to cut down on such gifts or even give up the practice altogether. While the bearing of such gifts has traditionally been in the women's domain, material provisions for buying them have been part of men's duties. By allowing women to spend their *doppa* earnings on such gifts and on dresses for themselves, men are at least partially relieved from their customary obligations. The perpetuation of the fiction that *doppa* money is unimportant is therefore in the interests of both men and women: as long as the money is regarded as irrelevant, women can keep and even increase their income without losing control over it, while men escape some of their obligations without openly admitting to doing so.

---

[31] As Ursula Sharma remarked about the income allocation patterns of low-income families in another context, 'this is less a case of greater personal freedom than of there being less scope' (Sharma 1980: 110). Lourdes Benería and Martha Roldán too asked to what an extent 'a wife's role in handling a very limited fund of money, already committed to necessary basics, should be considered a manifestation of control' (1987: 120).

[32] After marriage, a man is obliged to meet his wife's needs; these are generally taken to include providing two sets of clothes annually, to be given to the wife at the two major religious holidays. Beyond these minimal requirements, many women want such gifts more frequently. A man's failure to meet these demands is often said to be the cause of family arguments and even divorce.

Conclusion

In this chapter I have tried to explore some of the economic transactions in the reform period which are played out away from the marketplace in rural Kashgar. A multitude of commercial transactions may at first sight appear to be the direct result of the principles of the socialist market economy. However, many of these trends are acted out within the framework of traditional social relations which have survived the decades of col-lectivisation. Liberalisation of the market has not led to the massive commoditisation of all economic relations, but has rather activated a multitude of forms of private, informal production and trading. Verbalised ideas concerning the sexual division of labour mask female contributions to household income in a number of ways. Women participate actively in 'male' jobs, and the organisation of work and marketing in the exclusively female craft of *doppa*-making follows strategies familiar from the male domain. Successful male entrepreneurs and female *doppa* agents all rely on forms of cultural capital, which often date back to the decades of collectivisation. Villagers talk about a recent tendency for commercialism to be superseding communalism, but in all areas of rural production informal contacts based on kinship, friendship, neighbourliness, familiarity, and trust remain important components of transactions.[33] I have argued that ideas of work and the strategies followed by craftsmen in exchange demonstrate the fine balancing of an old cultural schema of voluntariness and obligation. The organisation of men's rotating credit association is an example of how, taking advantage of new liberties, an informal credit source can be established on the basis of voluntariness, yet remain fully embedded in a traditional institution. The *mäshräp* has not been reduced to a commercial transaction, but retains its potential to strengthen different types of loyalties, including ethnic, residential, professional, peer group, and religious iden-tities. The commercial aspect adds a secular veneer to this form of socialisation which may both be welcome to participants and render it more acceptable to the state. One may also speculate that the *mäshräp* may also promote class loyalties and render such differences more visible, since membership assumes a level of economic capability which leads to the exclusion of some. There is an important tension, which in some groups is resolved by giving up the credit function, seen as incompatible with ideas of communalism based on mutual obligations.

A similar cultural schema underpins attitudes to women's production and marketing of *doppa*s, and the allocation of the proceeds. As a result of

---

[33] This is also the case in the informal transactions of agricultural produce, although these are not discussed in this chapter.

globalisation and standardisation, peasants in one of the villages studied have become eligible for a completely new and atypical credit source. This originates from an international organisation, UNICEF, but is administered by local bureaucrats. While other economic transactions acted out away from the marketplace are embedded in traditional notions of solidarity, kinship, and friendship, in this case there is an expectation that international funds should be distributed impartially among the poor. This reflects a recognition and admission of increasing inequalities and a desire to level them out. In all economic activities acted out away from the marketplace we can see that accelerating commoditisation has not led to an impoverishment of traditional social ties. Rather, new forms of wealth and economic activity must be situated within traditional patterns of social relations even while adding to their complexity.

References

Bailey, F. G. 1964. Capital Saving and Credit in Highland Orissa (India). In R. Firth, and B. S. Yamey (eds.), *Capital, Saving and Credit in Peasant Societies*, pp. 104–132. London: George Allen & Unwin Ltd.

Bellér-Hann, I. 1996. Informal Associations among Women in North-East Turkey. In G. Rasuly-Paleczek (ed.), *Turkish Families in Transition*, pp. 114–138. Frankfurt am Main: Peter Lang.

Benería, L. 1979. Reproduction, Production and the Sexual Division of Labour. *Cambridge Journal of Economics* 3 (3): 203–225.

——. 1982. Accounting for Women's Work. In L. Benería (ed.), *Women and Development: The Sexual Division of Labor in Rural Societies*, pp. 119–147. New York: Praeger.

Benería, L., and M. Roldán. 1987. *The Crossroads of Class and Gender: Industrial Homework, Subcontracting, and Household Dynamics in Mexico City*. Chicago: University of Chicago Press.

Blecher, M. 1986. *China, Politics, Economics and Society*. London: Frances Pinter.

Croll, E. 1986. *Chinese Women since Mao*. London: Zed Books.

——. 1988. The New Peasant Economy in China. In S. Feuchtwang, A. Hussain, and T. Pairault (eds.), *Transforming China's Economy in the Eighties*, pp. 77–400. Boulder: Westview Press.

Delaney, C. 1993. Traditional Modes of Authority and Cooperation. In P. Stirling (ed.), *Culture and Economy: Changes in Turkish Villages*, pp. 140–155. Huntingdon: Eothen Press.

Dwyer, D., and J. Bruce. 1988. Introduction. In D. Dwyer, and J. Bruce (eds.), *A Home Divided: Women and Income in the Third World*, pp. 1–19. Stanford: Stanford University Press.

Feuchtwang, S., A. Hussain, and T. Pairault (eds.). 1988. *Transforming China's Economy in the Eighties*. London: Zed Press.

Forsyth, Th. D. 1875. *Report of a Mission to Yarkund in 1873*. Calcutta: Foreign Departments Press.

Grenard, F. 1898. *Le Turkestan et le Tiber. Étude éthnographique et sociologique*. (J.-L. Dutreuil de Rhins: *Mission Scientifique dans la Haute Asie 1890–1895*). Paris: Ernest Leroux.

Häbibulla, A. 1993. *Uyghur Etnografiyisi*. Ürümchi: Shinjang Khälq Näshriyati.

Hinton, W. 1990. *The Great Reversal: The Privatization of China 1978–1989*. New York: Monthly Review Press.

Hoppe, Th. 1995. *Die ethnischen Gruppen Xijiangs: Kulturunterschiede und interethnische Beziehungen*. Hamburg: Institut für Asienkunde.

Jarring, G. 1992. *Garments from Top to Toe: Eastern Turki Texts Relating to Articles of Clothing*. Stockholm: Almquist & Wiksell International.

Jeffery, P., R. Jeffery, and A. Lyon. 1989. *Labour Pain and Labour Power: Women and Childbearing in India*. London: Zed Books.

Mackerras, C. 1995. *China's Minority Cultures: Identities and Integration Since 1912*. New York: St Martin's Press.

March, K., and R. L. Taqqu (eds.). 1982. *Women's Informal Associations in Developing Countries. Catalysts for Change? Women in Cross-Cultural Perspective*. Boulder: Westview Press.

Mies, M. 1982. The Dynamics of the Sexual Division of Labor and Integration of Women into the World Market. In L. Beneria (ed.), *Women and Development: The Sexual Division of Labour in Rural Societies*, pp. 1–28. New York: Praeger.

Millward, J. 1993. *Beyond the Pass: Commerce, Ethnicity and the Qing Empire in Xinjiang, 1759–1864*. Ph.D. dissertation. Stanford: Stanford University.

Muhammad 'Ali Damolla. ca. 1905–10. *A Collection of Essays on Life in Eastern Turkistan*. Unpublished manuscript. Kahsgar, Jarring Collection, Lund University Library. Prov. 207. I.–II. (Turki).

Nolan, P. 1988. *The Political Economy of Collective Farms. An Analysis of China's Post-Mao Rural Reforms*. Oxford: Polity Press.

Pantusov, N. N. 1907. *Material k' izucheniiu narechiia taranchei iliiskago okruga. IX. Igry taranchiniskikh' detei i muzhchin*. Kazan: Tipo-Litografiya Imperatorskago Universiteta.

Pei X. 1993. *A Tourist Guidebook to Kucha*. Ürümchi: Xinjiang Fine Arts and Printing Press.

Perry, E. J., and C. Wang. 1985. Introduction. In E. J. Perry, and C. Wang (eds.), *The Political Economy of Reform in Post-Mao China*, pp. 10–21. Cambridge: Harvard Council on East Asian Studies.

Pieke, F. N. 1995. Bureaucracy, Friends and Money: The Growth of Capital Socialism in China. *Comparative Study of Society and History* 37 (3): 494–518.

Rogers, B. L. 1990. The Internal Dynamic of Households: A Critical Factor in Development Policy. In B. L. Rogers, and N. P. Schlossman (eds.), *Intra-Household Resource Allocation: Issues and Methods for Development Policy and Planning*, pp. 1–19. Tokyo: United Nations University Press.

Sharma, U. 1980. *Women, Work and Property in North-West India*. London: Tavistock Publications.

Sykes, E., and P. Sykes. 1920. *Through Deserts and Oases of Central Asia*. London: Macmillan & Co. Ltd.

Toops, S. 1993. Xinjiang's Handicraft Industry. *Annals of Tourism Research* 20 (1): 88–106.

UNICEF Cooperation in China. *Women in Development*. Unpublished document.

Wadel, C. 1979. The Hidden Work of Everyday Life. In S. Wallman (ed.), *Social Anthropology of Work*, pp. 365–384. London: Academic Press.

White, J. B. 1994. *Money Makes Us Relatives: Women's Labor in Urban Turkey*. Austin: University of Texas Press.

Chapter 4
Women, Work, and Procreation Beliefs in Two Muslim Communities[1]

This chapter is based on data collected in the course of two fieldwork projects in two different regions of the Muslim world. Among Lazi villagers in north-east Turkey my exploration of ideas concerning procreation started with the accidental discovery of an illuminating folk metaphor. During more recent research among the Turkic-speaking Uyghurs in Xinjiang I was more consciously looking for beliefs concerning human procreation. In considering these issues I have found Carol Delaney's exploration and analysis of the 'seed and soil' metaphor of human procreation among Anatolian villagers inspiring (Delaney 1986, 1991). Delaney's rural interlocutors attributed the primary, active role in the creation of children to men as 'seed-givers', while women are relegated to a secondary, passive role as 'fields'. In her analysis, Delaney applied a hierarchically ordered monogenetic view of human procreation to virtually all details of social organisation in an Anatolian village. She claimed that this monogenetic view of procreation is linked to monotheistic religions and presents one large tidy system of beliefs. In her words: 'paternity is embedded in an entire matrix of beliefs about the world and the way it is constructed .... From the most intimate to ultimate contexts, from physical to metaphysical realities, an entire world is constructed and systematically interrelated' (Delaney 1986: 510).

Leela Dube's study of the symbolism of biological reproduction in India complements that of Delaney in so far as it pays special attention to the correspondence between procreation ideology and the ideologies and realities of women's role in agricultural production. She argued that 'man's rights over the woman do not relate only to her sexuality and reproductive capacity, but encompass her productive capacities and labour power also.

---

[1] Published in P. Loizos and P. Heady (eds.), *Conceiving Persons: Ethnographies of Procreation, Substance and Personhood*, pp. 113–37. London: Athlone, 1999.

Just as he is entitled to have control over her sexuality and over the product of her sexuality, he is entitled to have control over her labour and also the proceeds of her labour' (Dube 1986: 43–44). From this Leela Dube concluded that women's role in cultivation is devalued to a merely supportive role and that the under-recognition of women's economic contribution matches the asymmetrical ideology of human procreation. The unequal contribution of the two sexes to human reproduction, as expressed through the symbolism of 'seed and earth', provides the rationalisation for a system in which women stand alienated from productive resources, have no control over their own labour power, and are denied rights over their offspring (Dube 1986). Similar conclusions about labour are reached in the north Indian context by Patricia and Roger Jeffery, who pointed out that 'women's work is ... trivialized and brings them little credit' (Jeffery and Jeffery 1993: 12).

My findings in two Muslim communities show that procreation beliefs similar to the 'seed and soil' metaphor are sometimes articulated in modified forms, tailored to local conditions. At other times, although encapsulated in language itself, they are not given full conscious expression. I shall argue that, as Leela Dube suggested, there is indeed a correspondence between procreation beliefs and the evaluation of women's participation in production, but that these two domains do not always parallel each other. In the case of the Lazi, a well-articulated procreation metaphor projects women as subordinate and passive in human procreation, but at the same time it implicitly recognises women's role as primary agricultural producers. Among the Uyghurs, 'seed and soil' type procreation ideas are implicit in kinship vocabulary and some commonly held beliefs, but contemporary informants may not have explicit knowledge of the metaphor. Within a patriarchal setting, man and woman are attributed an equal role in the creation of a child, but this symmetry accompanies a conspicuous underplaying of women's role as economic producers. The two cases lead us to the tentative conclusion that ideological recognition of women's productive or reproductive roles may be linked to variations in social organisation, such as a new migration pattern or changed assumptions about the nature of marriage. In such situations it is as if the necessity to maintain the ideological fiction of male supremacy requires the accentuation of gender asymmetry in at least one of the two domains.

Baskets among the Lazi

Among both the Lazi and the Uyghurs, information was collected from several villages in one large region rather than from one small, bounded community. Both groups have been settled agriculturalists for a long time, albeit in very different natural environments, and both societies are characterised by patriarchy and virilocal residence patterns. In addition, both are Sunni Muslims, and form ethnically and linguistically small minorities in states dominated by much larger ethno-linguistic majorities, though in the case of the Lazi they are not differentiated from the majority by religion. Speaking a language of Caucasian origin, the Lazi occupy a strip of the Black Sea coast in the north-eastern corner of Turkey.[2] Although they were converted to Islam about 400 years ago, their pre-Islamic Christian past has been completely erased from their collective memory. Their strong identification with Islam is a reflection of their high level of integration into the Turkish state. Their distinctive accents when they speak Turkish and a number of stereotypical characteristics mark them out when away from home. The biggest change within living memory was the introduction of tea as a cash crop in the mid-1950s, which quickly replaced what had been predominantly a subsistence economy.[3]

The Lazi region borders on the district of Of, where the American anthropologist Michael Meeker carried out fieldwork in the 1970s. An important ethnographic detail in Delaney's 'seed and soil' argument, in fact the strongest factual support for her theory, is quoted from Meeker's fieldwork: 'If you plant wheat, you get wheat. If you plant barley, you get barley. It is the seed which determines the kind of plant which will grow, while the field nourishes the plant but does not determine the kind. The man gives the seed, and the woman is like the field' (Meeker 1970: 157; quoted in Delaney 1986: 497).

During many conversations with Lazi, Turkish, and Hemşinli[4] men and women in the region I came across a metaphor which likens women not to a field but to a basket. Lazi women are closely associated with the carrying of baskets and other weights. This is often one of the first points people make when evaluating women's position in this region. Although

---

[2] The term 'Laz' as an ethnic marker is highly ambiguous. In general it is used to designate regional identity, in which sense it covers all the coastal people living east of the Black Sea city of Samsun, most of whom today, regardless of their ethnogenetic history, are monolingual Turkic speakers. Even in this broad sense, the term is a shifting one. Only a small group in the far eastern corner of Turkey's Black Sea region, who today number approximately 200,000 people, identify themselves as 'real' Laz. In addition to Turkish they speak their own Caucasian language called Lazuri. Since my data were collected among the Lazuri speakers, to distinguish them from the wider category of Laz, I shall refer to them as the Lazi, their own self-designation. On shifting Laz and Lazi identities and stereotypes, see Meeker (1971); Benninghaus (1989); Bellér-Hann (1995); and Hann (1997).

[3] On the development of the tea economy, see Hann (1990).

[4] The Hemşinli are a heterogeneous group of Armenian origin who traditionally inhabited more upland villages of the Kaçkar Mountains, while the villages situated closer to the coast were mainly occupied by the Lazi.

many locals are eager to point out that the lot of the Lazi woman has improved dramatically in recent decades, they also agree that the number of women to be seen carrying heavy weights along steep paths and roads far outstrips the number of such men.

Baskets and Material Culture

Basket-making has a long tradition among the Lazi. The four main types have been described as unique to the Lazi by Wolfgang Feurstein (1983: 53–60) who considers two types, *kalati* and *tikina*, a kind of 'ethnic marker' (Feurstein 1983: 56). These baskets have been described by Turkish folklorists as 'the ingenious invention of the people of the Eastern Black Sea coast', and as an inseparable part of women's life in this region (*Rize'de el sanatları* 1991: 22). The stereotype of the Lazi woman, well-known through-out the rest of Turkey, depicts her carrying an enormous loaded basket on her back. Young girls start carrying a miniature version at an early age. Baskets are an adaptation to the geographical conditions of the traditional Lazi settlements, which are scattered across steep valleys where narrow mountain paths limited transportation options until very recent times. Women in their seventies recall how in their youth, before the introduction of tea, they used to go to market carrying their produce in their baskets, which were then filled with shopping for the return journey. In his excellent work on the material culture of the Lazi, Wolfgang Feurstein noted that the largest basket has associations with human living quarters. In the Fındıklı Lazuri dialect, such a basket is called a 'woven hut', and Feurstein pointed out that its shape is indeed that of a round hut turned upside down. Furthermore, he added, this large basket was exclusively carried by women, and it was mainly employed for carrying grass in mountain villages, where animal husbandry was of particular importance (Feurstein 1983: 55).

As far as the *tikina* and the *kalati* are concerned, Feurstein drew a parallel between them and humans on the basis that these baskets have little 'feet'. This parallel seems to be confirmed by the fact that in Georgian, to which Lazuri is closely related, the word *iina*, itself a derivative of *tikina*/*kalati*, also means 'baby' (Feurstein 1983: 58). In the past, large baskets were used for carrying ferns, leaves, and hay and the smaller type for collecting fruit (Feurstein 1983: 54). Nowadays baskets are used for carrying tea, wood, grass and fodder for animals, and shopping. Although most villages now have at least a single-track dirt road, Lazi women still frequently carry heavy burdens on their backs in baskets.

Baskets and Symbolic Culture

Most informants, regardless of ethnic affiliation, are also familiar with the basket as symbol and metaphor and associate it with the Lazi. The metaphor exists in several versions in the Lazuri language.[5] Usually Lazi men were thoroughly embarrassed when asked about it, but Lazi women's reaction was – most of the time – a hearty laughter.

In Pazar and Ardeşen, the two western, politically more conservative districts of the Lazi region, the metaphor sounds something like this: 'A woman is a basket: you empty it and then fill it again (Turk. *Kadın sepettür. Boşaltıyorsun, sonra yine dolduruyorsun)*'.[6] I first heard this metaphor from a 25-year-old village girl, who was telling me about her own difficult position. She had been proposed to by a young man from another Lazi village, and although she knew that she should accept because she had reached the age beyond which she would be regarded as a spinster whose fate was 'closed' (Turk. *kısmeti kapanmış*), she nevertheless declined. Her main reason was that she did not want to carry on living in a village, not even married to a good husband: 'The work is too hard here for women. And then they have to give birth to many children and they are ruined in no time. Women here age quickly. But what shall we do? A woman is a basket, and her fate is to be filled and emptied again'. She said this with a grave face.[7] Her use of the metaphor brought together two of the most important aspects of women's life: biological reproduction and economic production.[8] After this incidental discovery of the metaphor, I began to ask about baskets more systematically in and around ethnically mixed Pazar. All women who were familiar with it agreed that it was a Lazi metaphor which the Hemşinli and ethnic Turks did not endorse: it was said to be an expression of Lazi women's degraded position. Lazi villagers usually stated that the basket metaphor emphasised two aspects of women's life: their heavy workload and

---

[5] Fieldwork among the Lazi was carried out in Turkish as I have no competence in Lazuri; but, whenever possible, informants were asked to name and write down the Lazuri equivalent of a phrase or a sentence. This was often difficult, because knowledge of Lazuri is uneven and varies according to village, age, gender, and education, and because it is not a written language. Lazuri speakers are literate only in Turkish. For one man's extraordinary attempt to give the Lazi a script, see Feurstein (1984).

[6] My rendering of Turkish utterances follows local pronunciation rather than standard Turkish.

[7] This is a quotation from my field diary in 1992. The woman later married a Lazi man in a nearby village.

[8] As is clear from my interview partners' interpretations, the metaphor is understood as expressing both similarity (in its procreational sense) and an interaction (in its productive sense) between the objects involved. See John Searle's criticism of the two schools of metaphor theory (1979: 99).

their reproductive function. A full basket is like a pregnant woman, an empty one is like a woman before getting pregnant, after giving birth, or between two pregnancies. Alternatively, an empty basket may also stand for barrenness. An empty basket is seen as one which can and should be filled. Just as the purpose of a basket is to be filled, the function of a woman is to reproduce. This idea is consistent with the underlying Islamic view that children are a gift of God, and that getting married and having children is the only acceptable course of life for a woman.

Some interpretations of the basket metaphor appeared to emphasise the passive role of the Lazi woman in reproduction. She is said to be the mere recipient of others' (men's) actions: filling the basket is under the exclusive control of the male. I was told that one can, if one wishes, dispose of a basket if it proves to be useless, replacing it with a new one. One woman unambiguously voiced the fears of many: 'A woman is a basket. You throw the old one away and replace it with a new one (Turk. *Kadın sepettir. Eskisini atarsın, yenisini alırsın*)'. A woman who stays empty for too long (a sign of barrenness) can be sent back to her father's home and another woman found in her place. Most people agree that the most frequent reason for a second, polygamous marriage is the first wife's inability to produce a male heir.[9] This kind of interpretation, though often stated in humorous fashion by the villagers themselves, is no joke at all. Male offspring are a must and women have to keep trying for a son, even after the birth of as many as seven or eight daughters. Divorce cases are often initiated as a result of the woman's alleged barrenness or her 'inability' to produce a son. Divorcees, especially those whose previous marriage was childless, find it hard to remarry and have lower social status in their fathers' or brothers' household, where they return after divorce, than the status of married mothers and widows with children in the same household. The stigma of barrenness is exclusively carried by the woman. Although under social pressure to become mothers and to produce sons, Lazi women are painfully aware that bearing many children and their heavy workload combine to affect their health and beauty. They often say that they age quickly and that this, too, may cause them to lose their men to other, younger women.

My interlocutors explain the basket metaphor in terms which point to a complete lack of agency for women, in a context of virilocal residence patterns and the basically temporary nature of their stay with their natal family. In contrast to women, who are viewed as temporary and potentially ready to move on or rather to be moved on, men are seen as permanent. This idea is expressed in a simile, which was told to me by Lazi girls when

---

[9] Polygamous marriages are illegal in secular Turkey, but they still take place unofficially.

interpreting the basket metaphor: 'A man is like a lake, a woman is like a stream (Turk. *Erkek göl gibi, kadın dere gibi*)'. In spite of this representation of women as temporary, in a community where long-term labour migration has become part and parcel of many families' lives, the incoming women may yet come to be more settled and permanent in their husbands' homes than the men themselves. This attitude may be detected when women give an account of the size of a household: they usually start by counting the number of daughters-in-law (Turk. *gelin*).

A variation of the 'seed and soil' metaphor can also be heard among the Lazi: 'Whatever you sow will grow (Turk. *Ne ekersen, o biter*)'. The explanation may continue: 'if you plant cabbages, you grow cabbages and not carrots'. This saying can be conflated with the basket metaphor to result in something like: 'whatever you put into the basket is what will come out of it'. I only ever heard the pure seed and soil metaphor explicitly mentioned by one Lazi, a man of exceptional knowledge himself engaged in local ethnographic research: 'A woman is like a field, whatever you sow will grow' (Laz. *Oxorca ontules nugams. Mu xackare heya yulun*; Turk. *Kadın tarlaya benzer. Ne ekersen o biter*). A very similar proverb was repeatedly quoted by Lazi villagers: 'A nettle produces a nettle' (Laz. *Tutucik tuci eligams*; Turk. *Isırgan otu ısırgan otu yapar*). The popularity of such sayings suggests that the Lazi, like Carol Delaney's (1991) villagers elsewhere in Central Anatolia, and those close by studied by Michael Meeker (1970), believe that men play the predominant role in human procreation. Informants readily confirm the gender asymmetry which gets articulated in the basket metaphor. One young, educated government clerk of Lazi origins claimed that 75 per cent of a child's characteristics are determined by the father.

The carrying of heavy weights also figures in speech about female bodily functions. Because of the lack of sex education, either at home or at school, young village girls are often taken by surprise at the onset of the menarche and attribute it to their having carried heavy weights. People also say that it is easy for a woman to resume work after she has given birth because she has been relieved of her heavy load. A local midwife related that miscarriage during the early stages of pregnancy used to be prevented by tying belts around the woman's abdomen to stop the baby from 'falling' (Turk. *düşmesin*) in the same way that heavy weights may be tied to a woman's back to prevent them from falling off.

Reproduction, Patriarchy, and the Value of Work

The basket metaphor may be less widespread than the metaphors discussed by Carol Delaney (1991) and Leela Dube (1986), and possibly the exclusive property of a region in which the geography has dictated the use of baskets in shifting goods. I think it is significant that in this metaphor, which draws attention to women's central role in production, it is women's reproductive function rather than their sexuality that gets the major emphasis, which contrasts with Carol Delaney's account (1991: 97). The basket metaphor is often quoted in connection with mothers: 'The mother is a basket. She has emptied (Laz. *Nana alation. Mocodinu)*'. This emphasis may also be noticed in a Black Sea joke which I was told by a man from the district of Ardeşen: 'A man from the Black Sea region is asked, "What is a woman?" "A woman is someone with a baby on her lap", he answers (Turk. *Karadenizliden sorarlar: "Kadın nedir?" "Kucağında bebektir")*'.[10] Commenting on the basket metaphor, locals also said that it expresses the idea that a woman is a tool, both for work and for childbearing, and that she has no value in herself.

The strong association of baskets and women's reproductive functions is clarified in the gender specificity of basket carrying. Wolfgang Feurstein stated that Lazi men have traditionally refused to carry baskets (Feurstein 1983: 36). A local solicitor told me that when he was a student on holiday he once tried to help out in his village by carrying a heavy basket. His female relatives were appalled and objected by saying that his behaviour was shameful (Turk. *ayıp*), and it would be their shame if their men were seen performing such a task. When pressed for an explanation of this attitude on the women's part, some women rationalised it in relation to the long-term migration that has prevailed among the Lazi for a long time. Since at least the nineteenth century, many Lazi men have gone to Russia to work as long-term migrant labourers and thereby to escape poverty, a trend which has continued in the Republican period, though its direction has largely shifted to the big cities of Turkey, Germany, and Saudi Arabia (Marr 1910: 618; Toumarkine 1995: 85). During the men's absence, women have managed the farms alone. Not only has male labour migration remained an important component of the local economy, but the cultivation of tea from the 1950s has also become primarily identified as female work. Women say that since their men are often absent for longer periods of time and work hard for their families, it would be unfair to make them perform hard work when they come back. Some men say that it is this attitude on the women's part which has made them spoilt, and less likely to offer help with carrying. Today it is possible to see men with baskets on their backs, but often these are Kurdish sharecroppers or ethnic Turks from neighbouring regions, who are unfamiliar with the local gender associations of the basket.

The social context within which the basket metaphor has become articulated is characterised by stable marriages and very low divorce rates.

---

[10] The Black Sea joke or *Karadenizli fıkra* is a well-known genre of local oral tradition.

Polygamy, though illegal in the state's eyes, is still practised but is becoming increasingly rare. But great emphasis is laid upon women's conformity to the modesty code, and community sanctions for women and men who do not conform are harsh. The great importance placed on virginity at marriage and the relatively low status of divorcees upon return to their natal home are part of a pattern which values women's chastity and guarantees paternity rights in circumstances where husbands are often absent through long-term labour migration.[11] In cases of divorce, local custom asserts the father's right to his children. Nowadays children may remain with the mother, who may have little choice but to retreat to her natal home.[12] Control over the product of female labour is usually in male hands, if men are present at all, although there are significant variations in this respect between the different valleys. Overall this can reasonably be labelled a patriarchal society.

If a child turns out to be particularly difficult, or perhaps retarded, it is the mother's side which gets the blame. It is said that 'the child takes after his maternal uncle; you have inherited this fault from your maternal uncle (Turk. *çocuk dayıdan çeker; sen dayıdan bozuksun*)'. This is clearly a way of putting the blame on the woman's side, while at the same time reinforcing man's primary role in procreation.[13] In fact the woman herself is victimised by her husband when children turn out badly. In Turkish, the maternal uncle (*dayı*) is meticulously distinguished from the paternal uncle (*amca*), and the same designations are used in Lazuri. In a rapidly disappearing part of the local wedding ceremony, when the groom and his party go to fetch the bride, sums of money are requested by her family for 'milk right' (Turk. *süt hakkı*) payable to the mother, 'brother's right' (Turk. *kardeş hakkı*) payable to one of the girl's brothers, and the 'maternal uncle's right' (Turk. *dayı hakkı*) payable to her maternal uncle. Explanations of these ritualised payments turn on the exceptional proximity of the maternal uncle to his sister and to her children. They are from the same womb, and he therefore has special responsibilities towards his sister's family. The paternal uncle is not considered close enough to have the same rights.

Controversy concerning the biological proximity of the paternal and maternal uncles finds expression in local definitions of the modesty code articulated in the concept of *namahram*.[14] The term, which is widely used to

---

[11] Golden jewellery is obligatorily given to the bride by the groom's family and is customarily kept by the woman upon divorce regardless of which party was considered to be at fault or the length of the marriage. The gold is said to be the price paid to the woman for her virginity.

[12] Decisions about the children after divorce are usually made by courts.

[13] Such references to the maternal uncle are missing from Delaney's argument.

[14] In modern Turkish, the correct spelling of this word derived from an Arabic stem and a Persian prefix is *namahrem*. The concept will also be mentioned in the second part of this

govern women's everyday behaviour in relation to men, categorises all men from the female ego's point of view as those covered by the incest taboo (with whom a woman can be more socially intimate) and those who are exempt from the taboo, and therefore potential marriage partners for her. In the presence of all those who fall into this latter category, referred to as *namahram* (lit. 'a canonical stranger'), a woman must at all times maintain spatial distance and observe the rules of modesty such as keeping her hair, arms, and legs fully covered. With non-*namahram* males such as her father, son, or brother, a woman is free to relax the modesty rules, since marriage and sexual relations are strongly prohibited between herself and such men.[15] About half of those asked considered that the maternal uncle was so close to a woman that he could not be considered *namahram* to her because he and her mother had come from the same womb, while there was general agreement that the paternal uncle was *namahram*. Others argued that both were *namahram* and therefore there was no difference in proximity between them as regards their niece. These beliefs deviate from the Koranic view which makes no distinction between the maternal and paternal uncles, and they would seem to go against the bias in favour of the male side, as expressed in the 'seed and soil' theory. However, ideas surrounding first cousin marriage reinforce the bias. First cousin marriages are said to have been common in this region for a long time, and even today, despite large-scale government campaigns, the practice continues. Most of my interview partners agree that ideal marriage partners from the point of view of the male ego, listed in order of biological proximity include: 1. father's brother's daughter (FBD) (Turk. *amca kızı*); 2. mother's brother's daughter (MBD) (Turk. *dayı kızı*); 3. father's sister's daughter (FZD) (Turk. *hala kızı*); 4. mother's sister's daughter (MZD) (Turk. *teyze kızı*). There is general consensus that two brothers' children are the most closely related among cousins (through the father's blood), while the biological link between the children of two sisters is the loosest.[16] The contradiction in these examples, between the proximity created by the maternal link in some instances and the priority given to the paternal side in others, is more apparent than real. As Leela Dube has pointed out for India, the mother's contribution can be recognised and emphasised in the moral context of obligations, while the

---

chapter since it is also well-known among the Uyghur. The correct transliteration of the Uyghur form is *namähräm*. To avoid alternative forms in the same chapter I have chosen the form *namahram* throughout which more closely follows the Arabic-Persian usage.

[15] My present definition of the concept does not cover all aspects of its usage and understanding in the local context. An excellent elaboration on the concept, albeit within the Shi'ite context, is that of Khatib-Chahidi (1981).

[16] On cousin marriages in Turkey, see Stirling and Incirlioğlu (1996).

father's contribution is nonetheless articulated in terms of his right over the child (Dube 1986: 36). The somewhat enigmatic role of the Lazi maternal uncle may similarly be seen as an expression of the moral obligation transmitted through the female line.

In everyday life, the basket as an implement is mainly associated with women's work. In the metaphor the woman becomes what in daily life she is most closely and visibly associated with during her outdoor activities. There is a clear visual parallel between carrying a heavy basket and being pregnant, and the walk of a pregnant woman is not unlike the walk of someone carrying a large load on her back. Local newspapers actively promote the stereotype of the basket-carrying Lazi woman as a symbol of the eastern Black Sea coast. In contrast to Carol Delaney's observations (1991: 115), work has enormous prestige in the Lazi region, both for the Lazi and for neighbouring ethnic groups.[17]

The ability to carry heavy loads enhances the attractions of a girl as a potential wife, and is a source of pride among women, just like pregnancy. The implication is that one who is capable of carrying heavy loads is strong and healthy, and will also be capable of coping with numerous pregnancies. In opposition to the commonly held Islamic idea that women are weak and vulnerable, the image and self-perception of Lazi women show them as strong agents, who are capable of heavy work and of looking after the household during their husbands' long absences.

We may therefore interpret the basket metaphor in two very different ways. It is an encapsulation of women's subordinate position, passivity, lack of agency, and substitutability. For many informants the metaphor is also an assertion of women's primary role as workers and agricultural producers. The attribution of lack of agency is valid enough as far as human reproduction is concerned, but women as producers and labourers have an extremely positive image in the whole eastern Black Sea region, and their self-perceptions underline this. 'There is no work in the village that a woman does not do', said one young Lazi girl. In the absence of historical sources it is impossible to tell whether the basket metaphor and the meanings

---

[17] When questioned about the division of labour, most Lazi men maintain that their women work harder than they themselves do. Many say they want to see this changed, but few actually take action in this direction. As if in self-defence, many add that women perform these tasks willingly without being forced to do so (Turk. *zorlama yok*). Others point out that in former times women had to use baskets because animals could not be used on the dangerously steep narrow paths. Women usually give a similar account. They do not describe men as lazy: although most men do not participate in carrying loads, they work as lorry drivers, as workers in local tea factories, or they have a business in town. Husbands who are away as migrant workers are mostly perceived as hard workers.

associated with it emerged as a result of large-scale migration, or whether
the present combination of elements has even older roots in Lazi culture.

The Uyghurs: No Metaphor, No Asymmetry?

My second set of data comes from fieldwork carried out among the Turkic-
speaking Uyghurs in north-west China. The Uyghurs changed from a
nomadic way of life to a settled agricultural economy over one thousand
years ago. Their ancestors embraced a variety of world views and religions
before they were converted to Islam, a process which was completed by the
end of the sixteenth century. Perhaps the most dramatic changes in Uyghur
peasants' lives started in 1949 with 'Liberation' (i.e. the beginning of
Chinese communist rule). This was soon followed by the collectivisation of
agriculture, which persisted until the early 1980s. Since then, in another
dramatic turn, economic reform and decollectivisation have once again
transformed life in the countryside.[18]

The Seed of a Metaphor

In what follows I shall discuss procreation beliefs in the context of two sets
of ideas, the first reflecting Islamic ontology, the second consisting of folk
theories focused on the human body. Various sources make references to
God's creation of the first man, the Prophet Adam, from earth, and to his
marriage with Eve, the first woman (Katanov and Menges 1933, 1976:
1206–07; Häbibulla 1993: 389; Rakhman, Hämdulla and Khushtar 1996:
172). But even the mythical beginnings of humankind are not entirely free of
bodily images. A story (*hikayä*) collected by Gunnar Jarring from a farmer
and *molla* from Southern Xinjiang in 1935 stresses the bodily aspects of
sexual intercourse between the first couple. The description, an example of
the discursive intermingling of the sacred and the profane, makes no use of
metaphor. Instead of resulting in a description of human procreation, the
story focuses on a miracle, the creation of the jade stone:

---

[18] All interviews were conducted in Uyghur. Asking Uyghurs about procreation metaphors in
China is complicated by the fact that any topic which could possibly be related to sexuality
among Muslims has been highly politicised by the Chinese authorities ever since the so-called
Chinese Salman Rushdie Affair in 1989 (Gladney 1991: 293; 1992). Since I was always
accompanied by a male Chinese academic, and occasionally by Uyghur cadres as well, the
shyness of Muslim women was particularly hard to overcome. Ideas and practices
surrounding birth and birth control are also sensitive issues because of the implementation of
the government's unpopular family planning policies.

The holy Adam – peace be upon him – and mother Eve were separated from each other for seven years. One day the holy Adam – peace be upon him – and mother Eve met each other on a glacier. ... They had coition at this place. The seminal fluid flowed out on the glacier. The seminal fluid froze. From this the jade stone has its origin. That is the miracle of the holy Adam – peace be upon him. That women feel cold on their rump and men on their knees has remained from this time (Jarring 1951: III 64).

Metaphors are also absent from other native descriptions of birth and connected practices. In an indigenous essay dating from the 1930s, Muhammad 'Ali Damolla described the power of God by saying that humans 'pass from the loins of the father to the womb of the mother. When at a certain period of time they receive soul (*jan*), their mother's menstruation stops and [the baby] feeds on the mother's blood' (Muhammad 'Ali Damolla 1905–10: l. 22).

I found that contemporary informants also had no explicit knowledge of a procreation metaphor comparable to the basket metaphor or that of the seed and the soil. However, language and some beliefs surrounding procreation point to an implicit familiarity with the seed and soil beliefs. The word for seminal fluid used by the storyteller quoted by Jarring above is *mäni*, which is associated by informants primarily with male blood. Synonymous with this is *uruq*, which also means 'seed' and 'species' (Schwarz 1992: 582, 894). The generic word for 'relative' is *uruq-tuqqan*, the first element meaning seed, and the second a past participle derived from the verb *tugh-* which carries the meanings of 'to give birth to [a child]' (*bala tugh-*) and 'to lay an egg' (*tukhum tugh*) (Schwarz 1992: 226). However, even older people could not elaborate on such clues encoded in the language.[19] One elderly woman said that a newborn baby is like the growing wheat plant which never grows alone but is always surrounded by plants of a similar kind, thereby emphasising the social aspect of birth: human beings are surrounded by relatives from the second they are born.

In spite of more than 30 years of socialist collectivisation, the old belief that women should not go to the fields because 'if they were to go, so would fertility' is still well remembered although rarely adhered to literally. However, the rule that under no circumstances should women sow the seeds of wheat or corn is more rigorously observed. The exclusive association of

---

[19] Of the numerous expressions for becoming pregnant, the most commonly used among peasants are *qosaqta qal-* ('it remains in the stomach/belly', referring to the seed) and *qosaq kötär-* ('to raise the stomach/belly'). The first makes implicit reference to the seed, the second focuses on the transformation of the female body only.

the sowing of grain seed with men may be seen as another implicit manifestation of the seed and soil beliefs.

The term *uruq-tuqqan* means all types of relatives, both maternal and paternal. Another term, *qandash* – derived from *qan* (blood) and *-dash* (a suffix expressing companionship) – is also used to denote close relatives related by blood. The term *qerindash*, derived from *qarin* (belly, stomach), is usually used in conjunction with *qandash* in the form *qan-qerindash*, the dictionary meaning of which is given as 'blood brother' (Schwarz 1992: 627). The main substance provided by the mother to the child is milk (*süt*) while the father contributes blood (*qan*). The quotation above from the indigenous author, Muhammad 'Ali Damolla, indicates that during pregnancy the baby is supposed to feed on its mother's blood and milk, as female substance becomes prominent only after the birth. But milk and the womb remain intimately connected in the popular imagination: milk siblings (*emildashlar*), though otherwise unrelated, are considered to be 'of the same womb' (*qerindash*) and are prohibited from marrying each other in line with Koranic edict. One informant insisted that *qandash* refers to the children of two full brothers, while *qerindashlar* stands for the children of two sisters. Most, however, maintained that *qandash* are all those sharing a father, *qerindash* are children sharing a mother, and *qan-qerindashlar* originally referred to full siblings by the same father and mother. Children of the same father are believed to share the same blood group.

This explanation makes sense within the given social context. For at least the past hundred years there has been a very high incidence of divorce and remarriage among the Uyghurs.[20] Unlike the situation in India described by Leela Dube (1986: 42) and in many other Muslim societies, among the Uyghurs it is not considered shameful for a woman to leave her children with their biological father and to remarry while she is young; it is, instead, normal practice. Customarily, 'social ownership' of the child has been assigned to the father's side. It is also the father's side which exercises the right to choose a name for the newborn. Giving up their children is usually interpreted by women as a practice which is necessary for them to be able to remarry. Distinguishing between siblings who shared a father but not a mother and those who shared a mother but not a father was important in determining rights over children and property. As among the Lazi, entitlement to property through inheritance in customary law reveals gender asymmetry. In accordance with Islamic values, women are regarded as lawful heirs of their biological father's property, but their share is supposed to be half or less than that of their brothers ('Abdul-Qadir 1930: 40v;

---

[20] It appears to have been more common among the poor (Benson 1993; Mackerras 1995: 72–73). See also chapter 2.

Muhammad 'Ali Damolla 1905–10: I.5). In practice, land is usually divided among male heirs only and women inherit land only if they have no brothers.[21]

A Symmetrical Model of Biological Procreation

Although one may be implicitly found in the language and some social practices, neither historical nor contemporary sources reveal a fully developed procreation metaphor of seed and soil, even though some alternative metaphoric allusions to sexual relations and human procreation are known. Gunnar Jarring recorded the following indigenous description of a Muslim shrine (*mazar*) in Yarkand. 'Every Sunday a number of women go to that shrine [saying] "Oh, ghodja of the shrine! Give me a husband who can take care of his house! Give me a man who can put a ladle into the kettle" ... thus they pray crying' (Jarring 1951: 174). Jarring explained that 'the women are praying for children: "ladle" and "kettle" probably allude to the sexual organs of man and woman' (ibid.). This description of women's prayers at the shrine of a female saint corresponds closely to another person's account of this same ritual, also practised by childless women wishing for a child: 'Unmarried women made a cooking pot out of two pieces of clay, put two more pieces of clay, firewood and some bran in it. This meant that they asked, "we have put up a pot, we have put a ladle in it – we wish for a good husband, lord of the shrine!"' (Tenishev 1984: 65–66).[22] Both references concern the shrine of the saint known as Süt Padishahim or 'Lady Milk' (see Baldick 1993: 191–92). Milk is, of course, the female substance par excellence. However, it is hard to tell to what an extent such a form of prayer was widespread or known outside Yarkand.

In contrast to the gender asymmetry implicit in the seed and soil or basket metaphors, data from Xinjiang support a binary, symmetrical model of procreation. Some of my Uyghur interlocutors said that the child may look like his mother, but usually inherits his father's humoural disposition

---

[21] In the wake of the PRC's economic reforms, many farmers have started to pass on land use rights (if not legal ownership) to their offspring as part of their patrimony. However, since fertile land in the oases situated along the fringes of the Taklamakan Desert is scarce, the plots in question tend to be very small, a factor which further fosters and reinforces gender asymmetry in matters of inheritance. On the economic conditions of Uyghur peasants in the reform era, see chapter 1.

[22] It is worth noting that Jarring's information was collected in the late 1920s, while Ėdgem Rachimovič Tenishev's data were collected in 1956. Food as sexual symbol is also used elsewhere: according to an indigenous description from the end of the nineteenth century, if a newly married bride turned out not to be a virgin on her wedding night, a flat bread with a whole in its middle was prepared and shown to the bride's parents (Katanov and Menges 1933, 1976: 1206–07).

(*mijäz*).[23] Most agree that, like the sex of the unborn child, its disposition too depends upon God's will (although several people claimed that the sex of the child depends on the degree of love and passion between the parents at the time of conception).[24]

In Uyghur society getting married and having children is regarded as the most desirable course of life for a woman. Women unable to conceive resort to a variety of traditional practices to ensure pregnancy.[25] Barrenness is sometimes blamed on the woman, but more often it is acknowledged that either party can be 'at fault'. A divorcée is not stigmatised, and even if her previous marriage was childless, she can remarry without difficulty. My interview partners confirmed that young divorcées who already had children in a previous marriage are often considered more desirable marriage partners than unmarried girls.[26]

Some beliefs surrounding menstruation and childbearing attribute positive outcomes (i.e. the birth of a beautiful child) to the workings of the female body, while negative outcomes may be blamed on male action. Menstruation (*häyiz, adät, khun*) is considered an illness (*käsäl*). Some rural women insist that this is the way women's bodies are regularly cleansed of their sins because, as men and women agree, women have a great many sins by nature. Although the absence of menstruation is often a sign of pregnancy, they also know of cases when women continue to bleed during pregnancy. If this is the case, the woman is likely to have a particularly beautiful child, since her body continues to purify itself. Menstruation is a state of pollution during which no sexual intercourse should take place. But

---

[23] This is also closely connected to assumptions about the influence of food on the human body (see chapter 7).

[24] If the woman is more passionate at the time the baby is conceived, she will have a girl; if her husband is more passionate, a boy will be conceived.

[25] Although some village women have heard of fertility treatments available in Ürümchi, these remain beyond the reach of all but a few. The locally available family planning organisations aim at reducing family size, and therefore seek to prevent and interrupt unplanned pregnancies.

[26] The value placed on virginity is shown in the fact that the marriage payment (*toyluq*) required for a virgin is higher than that asked at subsequent marriages. However, in cases of divorce, the amount of movable property a woman can take from her husband's house has nothing to do with her sexual status before marriage. It is measured instead in terms of the length of the marriage, which is taken as an indicator of how much work she has put into her husband's household. If the divorce takes place shortly after the wedding, she is likely to get nothing because she has not rendered enough services to her husband's family.

some men do break the prohibition, and children conceived during this time
are said to be deformed as a result of God's punishment.[27]

In contrast to the Lazi, Uyghur kinship terminology makes no
distinction between the maternal and paternal uncles (both are called *tagha*)
or maternal and paternal aunts (both are called *hamma*). Close-kin marriages
continue to be common despite government ban, but local people do not
differentiate degrees of proximity between the various possibilities on the
paternal and maternal sides. Qing images of the peoples of Xinjiang dating
from the second half of the eighteenth century also noted that among the
Uyghurs (known then as Turkis) a man's children by various wives were
considered of equal rank (apart from birth order seniority), and a woman's
children by different husbands were regarded as consanguineous (Millward
1993: 266).

In addition to an egalitarian, symmetrical view of procreation some
persistent traditions emphasise the close links maintained through the female
line, and the celebration of fertility. Villagers say that at least the first two
children must be born in the woman's natal house with her mother's
assistance, though subsequent births may take place at the husband's house.
This tradition persists today in rural areas and even among urban intellectuals. Rural women express their preference for giving birth in their
natal home by saying that their own mothers are the best ones to look after
them; ideally they would like to return home for each subsequent birth, but
their husband may not give consent after the second occasion. This practice
has been described as common 'in societies where marriages tend to be
unstable, where there is not a great deal of trust and cooperation between
husband and wife, or where the matrifocal family is common' (MacCormack
1982: 13).

Uyghur language textual material from the first half of the twentieth
century reveals that when a baby was born to a middle-income or rich
family, they called together the midwives (*toghutchi khotun, toghut anisi*) to
help with the birth. As soon as the baby was born, the umbilical cord (*kindik*)
was to be cut by a close female relative of the mother, such as her
grandmother or her mother, or by any other woman with a good disposition
(*khuy*) and morality (*äkhlaq*). It was thought that the child's temper and
habits would be similar to those of the person who cut the cord; in other
words, a woman is held responsible for the qualities of a child (Nur Luke
1950: 2–3). The term *toghut anisi* (lit. mother of birth) was synonymous
with the term *kindik anisi* (lit. mother of the umbilical cord) which implies

---

[27] The breaking of pollution taboos by the woman can also have negative effects. If a lactating
mother fails to take a full ablution following intercourse and feeds her baby in a polluted state,
her baby is likely to become sick and even die.

that the cutting of the cord was often done by the midwife herself. Contemporary informants confirm that after the birth the placenta (*äsh, yoldash*) must be buried in the mud floor of the house where the birth took place. If this is not done, the baby will be unlucky, may become sick, or even die (Muhammad 'Ali Damolla 1905–10: II.12.1). Rumour has it that, following deliveries in modern hospitals, only the male child's placenta is preserved to be used for making medicine. Women assume that female babies' placentas are thrown away as rubbish, and some are extremely unhappy about this. However, this equal concern for babies of both sexes is not necessarily reflected in all areas of childcare: female children are usually breastfed for shorter periods of time than male children because the latter are considered more vulnerable. Besides, the birth of a male child was said to be celebrated more elaborately in the past (Nur Luke 1950: 7). However, some of my interlocutors confirmed that the 'cradle ritual', a large celebration, is more likely to be held for a girl than for a boy. It is viewed by some as a compensation for girls since their brother will have celebrations following circumcision.

Plate 6. Village women visiting a young mother and her new baby, Southern Xinjiang (Photo: Ildikó Bellér-Hann).

Before the incorporation of Xinjiang into the People's Republic of China in 1949, a common practice among well-to-do and rich families was the 'hair-tying ritual' (*chachwaq toyi, chach qoshaq toyi*), also known as the 'ritual of the young married woman' (*juwan toyi*) (Jarring 1992: 29–32). Local people say that this ritual was always organised either during a woman's first or later pregnancy, or shortly after she gave birth to her first or second baby. Following customary norms, it typically took place in the woman's natal home and involved a great many presents for the woman from her natal family, and from her husband and his family. Her hairstyle was permanently changed, and minor alterations were made to the ornamentation of her dress. These changes marked her transition from the status of *chokan* (young married woman without children) to the status of *juwan* (young married woman with children). That this was a rite of passage for the woman (sometimes described as grander and more important than the actual wedding) and not a celebration of the baby is clear from the fact that this ritual could only be performed once in a woman's lifetime; it could not be repeated, even if none of her babies survived.

In line with these traditions, relationships with the mother and through the female side are very important among contemporary Uyghurs. The anthropologist Justin Rudelson (1997: 126) described how in Ürümchi, the provincial capital of Xinjiang, he found that young married couples maintained closest ties with the wife's sister and her husband; these were much closer than, for example, ties between couples related through two brothers. One explanation for the phenomenon may be the prevalence of avoidance rules between males. A young man feels more relaxed (e.g. he can smoke and drink) in the company of his wife's sister's husband than in the presence of his elder brothers.

The Devaluing of Women's Work

The relative freedom and power of women in this region in comparison with adjacent Muslim lands was remarked upon by many travellers visiting the region in the nineteenth and early twentieth centuries, as well as by Chinese sources (Warikoo 1985; Mackerras 1995: 78). The French traveller Fernand Grenard went to great lengths to elaborate on the historical antecedents of such practices, which he connected to social customs rooted in pre-Islamic times (Grenard 1898: 123–24). Although these remain speculations, they cannot be dismissed as completely without foundation. The brand of Islam developed in Xinjiang has allowed women to give birth in their natal home, the fertility ritual of 'hair-tying', frequent divorce, and a symmetrical folk theory of procreation. Women's reproductive role has thus been given enormous emphasis. However, in contrast to the Lazi, Uyghur women's contribution to production seems to have been consistently downplayed. Traditionally, women are regarded as weak and vulnerable (*ajiz*). Their activities are ideally restricted to the home: rural women are not associated with cash earning.[28] Old people sometimes assert that before 1949 no woman worked in the fields because of the modesty code expressed in the concept of *namahram*. Closer questioning reveals that this was an ideal rather than an absolute rule, and that poorer women did work in the fields. As in other peasant societies, Uyghur women's participation in agricultural work depended on their social standing and showed a great deal of variation. But the value system prevailing prior to 1949, nevertheless saw women as home-makers and mothers rather than as agricultural producers. This state of affairs changed drastically after 'Liberation' when women became active contributors to agricultural and even industrial production and construction, and the working woman was vigorously promoted by the state (Davin 1976; Croll 1979). The 30 years between 1950 and 1980 were extremely disruptive and affected every aspect of Uyghur villagers' lives. While some officials today maintain that it was during this period that Uyghur women became liberated from the yoke of Islamic patriarchy, villagers' own accounts tell a different story. By ordering women into the fields, the socialist authorities violated the rule of *namahram* and flouted traditional norms, if not necessarily traditional practice.

Since the economic reforms of the early 1980s, the old value system seems to have been revived among Uyghur villagers, though with important modifications. A woman's place is seen once more as being in the home. Although some deny that *namahram* rules still apply, in practice most women do observe them in everyday life. At the same time, women are visibly present in the fields. As in the past, they play the primary role in cotton production. They also work alongside men in the wheat and corn fields. All this work outside the home is described as 'helping their husbands'. Women's participation in sideline production – whether in animal husbandry, felt-making, or the decoration of wedding chests – is seen as auxiliary to that of men. When women engage in embroidering and marketing *doppa*, they maintain that this is a leisure activity, even when they spend a considerable amount of time doing it (chapters 2, 3).

Conclusion

The two groups discussed in this chapter both belong to regions which have been characterised by their dominant agricultural practices which include male farming systems (Boserup 1970) and the Eurasian model of plough agriculture (Goody 1976), and which have been associated with hierarchical

---

[28] This is the prevalent view in the Kashgar region but there is considerable regional variation: women in the Aqsu and Kucha oases are said to have much more freedom to engage in money-earning activities.

social systems and relatively restricted roles for women (Jeffery and Jeffery 1993: 8). However, in spite of the differences in climate and surroundings, the traditional, largely subsistence economies of both the Lazi and the Uyghurs were in fact hoe-based. The plough, though known to both groups, was never adopted by either, which may explain why an artefact prominent in the seed and soil beliefs depicted by Leela Dube and Carol Delaney does not figure in the procreation beliefs of these peoples (Dube 1986: 41; Delaney 1991: 49). Among the Lazi, it is baskets – implements primarily associated with women – that are considered the symbol of agricultural work. In contrast, among the Uyghurs it is the hoe (*kätmän*) – associated with male work – which has achieved this symbolic status.[29]

But both sets of data exhibit important elements of the monogenetic theory of procreation, although neither is without complications and contradictions. This is only to be expected once we accept that there is no such thing as a static, fully developed Islamic world view. Local ideas and traditions, the uneven penetration of scientific thought and the state, contacts with other ethnic groups, and the pace of modernisation must all be considered. The data presented here suggest that there is a close relationship between ideas about women's presumed participation in biological reproduction and their perceived role in production. Among the Lazi, women's primary role in agricultural production is publicly recognised, but their role in biological reproduction is downplayed. These two aspects of women's roles are expressed in the basket metaphor. A woman's pregnancy and subordination to men have been likened to her most conspicuous work, carrying agricultural produce and shifting goods. Uyghur society is just as patriarchal as that of the Lazi, yet women's reproductive function has traditionally been emphasised. Here the seed and soil metaphor, though present in traces, is overshadowed by a more balanced idea of human reproduction. However, women's considerable economic role has been devalued and this has not changed in spite of the drastic changes enforced by the communist government over the past 40 years.

These two Muslim communities, remote from each other, have had very different social, political, and economic histories. The monogenetic theory identified by Carol Delaney as shaping decisively the overarching world view of peoples with monotheistic religions is admirably clear in her account, but hardly borne out by other ethnographic realities. Real communities have never existed in isolation, free of changes from internal and external sources, imposing the same views on all community members. The social context may in some places evoke fully elaborated metaphors, while

---

[29] In addition to land cultivation, the hoe is also important in the male jobs of digging and operating irrigation canals which are of primary importance in Xinjiang's oasis agriculture.

in other circumstances these remain latent. Patriarchy can be maintained regardless of the extent to which women's role in production or biological reproduction is recognised. I suggest that in such cases, even if there is positive recognition of the role of women in one domain, it tends to be negated or underrepresented in the other domain.

References

'Abdul-Qadir. ca. 1930. *A Collection of Eastern Turki Folkloristic Texts.* Unpublished manuscript. Yarkand, Jarring Collection, Lund University Library. Prov. 464. (Turki).

Baldick, J. 1993. *Imaginary Muslims: The Uwaysi Sufis of Central Asia.* London & New York: I. B. Tauris.

Bellér-Hann, I. 1995. Myth and History on the Eastern Black Sea Coast. *Central Asian Survey* 14 (4): 487–508.

Benninghaus, R. 1989. The Laz: An Example of Multiple Identification. In P. A. Andrews (ed.), *Ethnic Groups in the Republic of Turkey*, pp. 497–502. Wiesbaden: Otto Harrassowitz.

Benson, L. 1993b. A Much-Married Woman: Marriage and Divorce in Xinjiang 1850–1950. *Muslim World* 83 (3–4): 227–247.

Boserup, E. 1970. *Woman's Role in Economic Development.* New York: Saint Martin's Press.

Croll, E. 1979. *Women in Rural Development: The People's Republic of China.* Geneva: International Labour Office.

Davin, D. 1976. *Woman-Work: Women and the Party in Revolutionary China.* Oxford: Clarendon Press.

Delaney, C. 1986. The Meaning of Paternity and the Virgin Birth Debate. *Man* 21 (3): 494–513.

——. 1991. *The Seed and the Soil: Gender and Cosmology in Turkish Village Society.* Berkeley: University of California Press.

Dube, L. 1986. Seed and Earth: The Symbolism of Biological Reproduction and Sexual Relations of Production. In L. Dube, E. Leacock, and S. Ardener (eds.), *Visibility and Power: Essays on Women in Society and Development*, pp. 22–53. Delhi: Oxford University Press.

Feurstein, W. 1983. *Untersuchungen zur materiellen Kultur der Lazen.* Magister Dissertation. Freiburg: Albert-Ludwigs-Universität.

——. 1984. *Lazuri Alfabe: lazca alfabe: Entwurf eines lazischen Alphabets* (Parpali 1). Gundelfingen: Lazebura.

Gladney, D. 1991. *Muslim Chinese: Ethnic Nationalism in the People's Republic.* Cambridge: Harvard Council on East Asian Studies.

——. 1992. Transnational Islam and Uighur National Identity: Salman Rushdie, Sino-Muslim Missile Deals, and the Trans-Eurasian Railway. *Central Asian Survey* 11 (3): 1–18.

Goody, J. 1976. *Production and Reproduction: A Comparative Study of the Domestic Domain.* Cambridge: Cambridge University Press.

Grenard, F. 1898. *Le Turkestan et le Tiber. Étude éthnographique et sociologique.* (J.-L. Dutreuil de Rhins: *Mission Scientifique dans la Haute Asie 1890–1895*). Paris: Ernest Leroux.

Häbibulla, A. 1993. *Uyghur Etnografiyisi.* Ürümchi: Shinjang Khälq Näshriyati.

Hann, C. 1990. *Tea and the Domestication of the Turkish State.* Huntingdon: Eothen Press.

——. 1997. Ethnicity, Language and Politics in North-east Turkey. In C. Govers, and H. Vermeulen (eds.), *The Politics of Ethnic Consciousness*, pp. 121–156. London: Macmillan.

Jarring, G. 1946–1951. *Materials to the Knowledge of Eastern Turki. Tales, Poetry, Proverbs, Riddles, Ethnological and Historical Texts from the Southern Parts of Eastern Turkestan.* Part IV: Ethnological and Historical Texts from Guma. In Lunds Universitets Ärsskrift N. F. Avd.1. Bd 47. Nr.4.

Jarring, G. 1992. *Garments from Top to Toe: Eastern Turki Texts Relating to Articles of Clothing.* Stockholm: Almquist & Wiksell International.

Jeffery, R., and P. Jeffery. 1993. Traditional Birth Attendants in Rural North India: The Social Organization of Childbearing. In S. Lindenbaum, and M. Lock (eds.), *Knowledge, Power and Practice: The Anthropology of Medicine and Everyday Life*, pp. 7–31. Berkeley: University of California Press.

Katanov, N. T., and K. H. Menges. 1933, 1976. *Volkskundliche Texte aus Ost-Türkistan.* Proceedings of the Prussian Academy of Sciences, Section of Philology and History, 1933. Leipzig: Zentralantiquariat of the German Democratic Republic.

Khatib-Chahidi, J. 1981. Sexual Prohibitions, Shared Space and Fictive Marriages in Shi'ite Iran. In S. Ardener (ed.), *Women and Space: Ground Rules and Social Maps*, pp. 112–134. London: Croom Helm.

MacCormack, C. P. 1982. Biological, Cultural and Social Adaptation in Human Fertility and Birth: A Synthesis. In C. MacCormack (ed.), *Ethnography of Fertility and Birth*, pp. 1–13. London: Academic Press.

Mackerras, C. 1995. *China's Minority Cultures: Identities and Integration since 1912.* New York: St Martin's Press.

Marr, N. 1910. Iz poezdki v tureckij Lazistan. *Bulletin de L'Academie Imperiale des Sciences de St.-Petersbourg* 4 (7–8): 547–632.

Meeker, M. 1970. *The Black Sea Turks: A Study of Honor, Descent and Marriage*. Ph.D. dissertation. Chicago: University of Chicago.

——. 1971. The Black Sea Turks: Some Aspects of their Ethnic and Cultural Background. *International Journal of Middle Eastern Studies* 2 (4): 318–345.

Millward, J. A. 1993. *Beyond the Pass: Commerce, Ethnicity and the Qing Empire in Xinjiang, 1759–1864*. Ph.D. dissertation. Stanford: University of Stanford.

Muhammad 'Ali Damolla. ca. 1905–10. *A Collection of Essays on Life in Eastern Turkistan*. Unpublished manuscript. Kahsgar, Jarring Collection, Lund University Library. Prov. 207. I.–II. (Turki).

Nur Luke. ca. 1950s. *A Collection of Essays on the Habits and Customs of Eastern Turkestan*. Unpublished manuscript. Jarring Collection, Lund University Library. Prov. 212. (Turki).

Rakhman, A., R. Hämdulla, and S. Khushtar. 1996. *Uyghur Örp-Adätliri*. Ürümchi: Shinjang Yashlar-Ösmürlär Näshriyati.

Rize'de El Sanatları. 1991. Rize: Halk Eğitim Müdürlüğü.

Rudelson, J. J. 1997. *Oasis Identities: Uyghur Nationalism along China's Silk Road*. New York: Columbia University Press.

Schwarz, H. G. 1992. *An Uyghur-English Dictionary*. Bellingham: Western Washington University.

Searle, J. R. 1979. Metaphor. In A. Ortony (ed.), *Metaphor and Thought*, pp. 92–123. Cambridge: Cambridge University Press.

Stirling, P., and Emine O. Incirlioğlu. 1996. Choosing Spouses: Villagers, Migrants, Kinship and Time. In G. Rasuly-Paleczek (ed.), *Turkish Villagers in Transition*, pp. 61–82. Frankfurt am Main: Peter Lang.

Tenishev, E. R. 1984. *Uigurskie teksty*. Moscow: Nauka.

Toumarkine, A. 1991. *Les Lazes en Turquie (XIXe-XXe siècle)*. Istanbul: Isis.

Warikoo, K. B. 1985. Chinese Turkestan during the Nineteenth Century: A Socio-Economic Study. *Central Asian Survey* 4 (3): 75–114.

Chapter 5
Law and Custom among the Uyghur in Xinjiang[1]

Historians of Xinjiang present pre-socialist dispute management as essentially controlled and informed by two normative systems: state law (imperial and later Republican) and Islamic law (Fletcher 1978: 77; Millward 1998: 121–24). There is some evidence that the number of cases tried in imperial courts was not small. However, to date we know very little about the activities of these courts.[2] Similarly, the functioning of Islamic courts in Xinjiang also awaits research.[3] Although there is sporadic evidence that suggests that the opening up of local archives could shed light on these issues, given the present limitations of archival research in the region, such a study is not yet feasible.[4] In this chapter I argue that the historians' binary model is insufficient. Codified normative systems representing state and Islamic law undoubtedly played an important role in the past in managing social life, but there were also alternative mechanisms at work. Conflicts were often settled informally and social relations were regulated by a number of unwritten rules that aimed at containing conflict. The enforcement of many of these rules took place within the immediate mosque community, using informal but powerful mechanisms of social control. In this respect, the socialist period shows some continuity with the past, in that the dominant codified legal system continues to be challenged by a set of normative rules.

Following the definition proposed by legal anthropologists, I suggest that this set of rules should be categorised under 'customary law' or 'local law' (Benda-Beckmann and Benda-Beckmann 1988). Although definitions vary in detail, they agree on the point that legal systems are essentially

---

[1] Published in W. Johnson and I. F. Popova (eds.), *Central Asian Law: An Historical Overview. A Festschrift for the Ninetieth Birthday of Herbert Franke*, pp. 173–94. Topeka: Society for Asian Legal History, the University of Kansas, 2004.

[2] Laura Newby, oral communication.

[3] Recently I have learned about the accidental discovery of hundreds of *qazi* documents (documents bearing the seal of the Muslim judge) in Kashgar by the Japanese historian Sugawara Jun.

[4] See the examples cited by Bellér-Hann (2000: 14–15).

'bodies of norms', and they recognise the existence of normative orders outside of state law in many societies. Legal anthropologists depart from the narrow, étatist definition of law which acknowledges only those systems that are directly bound to, created by, and appropriated by the state. Instead, they propose a broader definition that goes beyond state-legal systems to include 'non-state normative orders' (Woodman 1999: 11). This approach assumes that most societies display a degree of legal pluralism and conceive of law as a contested field in which state-based and non-state based normative systems exist side by side and are often in competition with each other.

Local or customary law is defined here in a broad sense as a set of normative rules that lacks codification, jurisdiction, and organised executive force, is subject to change, and has fuzzy boundaries. It has been argued that customary law cannot be separated from other normative frameworks such as ethics, morals, and good manners, since it is 'concerned not only with what is permitted and prohibited, but also with the ethical world in which actions and relationships take place. It has a strong moral component that passes judgment on how people ought to behave. "Customary law" is very much a moral system' (Benda-Beckmann 2001: 48). This broad definition is particularly useful in discussing aspects of social life among the sedentary Muslim population in Xinjiang because indigenous discourse often interprets the concepts of rights and obligations as religious and moral categories rather than as legally defined ones (chapter 3).

This chapter is a preliminary attempt to understand some aspects of managing social relations in pre-socialist and socialist Xinjiang from the point of view of legal pluralism, paying special attention to the re-interpretation of the complicated interplay between codified and uncodified norms in changing political contexts. It has emerged as a by-product of more general research into continuities and changes in Xinjiang between the pre-socialist and socialist periods (Ambler 2001: 43). The empirical research was carried out over a longer period in 1995 and 1996 in the Kucha and Kashgar oases. In Kucha, the research was mostly conducted in the market centre and took the form of informal conversations and participant observation, while in Kashgar the acquisition of an official research permit meant more restricted research conditions. I conducted long, open-ended interviews in peasant households in villages situated in the vicinity of the city, which were usually monitored by a Uyghur-speaking Chinese colleague.

The Pre-Socialist Period[5]

Following the gradual Islamisation of the region from the tenth century onwards, the oases had a two-tier normative system: Islamic law was enforced through Islamic courts and legal scholars, while customary law continued to regulate social relations through informal mechanisms. With the Qing conquest, a third normative system – that of the empire – was superimposed over the pre-existing frameworks. Of the three realms, the Islamic and the imperial legal systems were codified, institutionalised, and had trained specialists. These two systems in some respects operated parallel to each other, and observed a certain division of labour. Often this division of labour between the two systems ran along ethnic lines, but there were also cases when the two overlapped. The pattern was that civil disputes between local Muslims were tried in the Sharī'a courts, while those concerning the 'Chinese' (i.e. imperial subjects who were foreign to the region, including Chinese Muslims) were taken to the Chinese magistrates. There are some indications that at least during the early Qing, civil disputes involving Muslims and non-Muslims could also be tried at the Islamic courts. Serious criminal cases such as murder had to be, at least theoretically, referred to the imperial courts, including those that involved local Muslims, although even in such cases the choice of courts could vary (Fletcher 1978: 77; Millward 1998: 121–24). These instances illustrate that throughout the Qing period religious law was subordinated to imperial law. This pattern was temporarily broken during Ya'qūb Bek's Islamic theocracy (1864–77), when Islamic law became the only acknowledged codified legal system.[6] However, after the demise of Ya'qūb Bek's short-lived power, Chinese rule and imperial law were restored. After this, in spite of the ensuing political upheavals and the gradual transformations in economic and social life, the legal status quo in which state law dominated but Islamic law retained its salience in local society, persisted until 1949.

In the pre-socialist period (especially following the Ya'qūb Bek episode), state law insisted on its superior position but was content to share space with other forms of normative systems. State law observed a certain division of labour with Islamic law and tolerated customary law inasmuch as it did not interfere with the management of everyday social relations among

---

[5] In describing pre-socialist conditions I mostly consider the situation from the late nineteenth century (i.e. post-Ya'qūb Bek) to the middle of the twentieth century, unless indicated otherwise. For the period after 1884, the terms Eastern Turkestan and Xinjiang will be used interchangeably.

[6] On this period, see Kim Ho-Dong (1986).

the indigenous population. In what follows, I shall consider some areas of social life to demonstrate instances of legal pluralism.

Land and Water

In Xinjiang, as in many other regions of Central Asia, oasis agriculture was dependent on the simultaneous availability of land and water. It was and has remained a truism that through the construction of new irrigation canals, land could be reclaimed from the desert and brought under cultivation, and conversely, whenever irrigation canals were abandoned or neglected, cultivation would decline. The state of the irrigation system was a reliable indicator of the political situation. Political unrest usually entailed the neglect of irrigation works through which large cultivated areas were lost to the desert. Their recovery was only made possible through years of hard work and could be guaranteed only by a measure of political stability.

   Throughout most of the Islamic centuries, feudal landlordism prevailed in Eastern Turkestan with many peasants reduced to the state of quasi serfs, while others owned the land they cultivated. Following the Qing occupation, land in Northern Xinjiang became the theoretical property of the emperor who could confiscate it if he wished. This happened only rarely, typically as punishment for criminal acts, especially for treason and for taking part in anti-government rebellions. Confiscated land and that of war victims were given to Chinese settlers, a practice characteristic of Zungharia in the north but never introduced in the Tarim Basin south of the Tian Shan Mountains. Here, village communities had a relatively high level of autonomy in organising the sharing of water and irrigation, while in Zungharia the state assumed some organising role. This arrangement was reminiscent of the situation in Transoxania and East Iran prior to the Mongol conquest, where the state interfered in the organising of irrigation only in the so-called imperial oases, and otherwise communities treated irrigation as an internal affair (Paul 1996: 61).

   Given the similarities in the conditions of ecology and agricultural production, resource management and the accompanying local customary norms were probably not entirely dissimilar from the situation in Russian Turkestan. There too, water and land rights were closely intertwined with each other, and as a written formulation of an official report from 1908 testifies, customary law and Islamic law could be mobilised simultaneously to legitimise prevailing practice. The report begins with the statement that according to both Islamic and customary law (*adat*), water is a gift of God for which reason it cannot be owned by anyone. Water can neither be sold nor bought, and those who want to use water for irrigation are obliged to take part in the construction and maintenance works of the canals. Moreover, water cannot be sold without land. The use rights of water that flows over a field are transferred to the proprietor of the land (Busse 1915: 55–56). It is important that the written source simultaneously drew on the authority of Islamic and customary law, thus acknowledging the force of both.

How uniformly these regulations were observed in adjacent regions awaits future research. But the above formulation itself contains some contradictions: it stipulates that water can neither be sold nor bought, but also that it cannot be sold without land. In fact, there are indications that in parts of Central Asia, water and water rights could constitute private property. For example, when several persons together invested in land reclamation by building irrigation canals, only these persons could exercise water rights (Paul 1996: 61). There are also tentative indications that prior to the Chinese conquest some religious authorities such as the Kucha khojas[7] may have enjoyed special water rights and responsibilities concerning irrigation. Arshad al-Dīn, the founder of a saintly lineage, married and settled in the oasis of Kucha. There he built three irrigation canals and conferred them on to the people. His son had a dam built, and with this he saved the people of Aqsu during a drought (Hamada 1978: 84). Thereafter the Kucha khojas had special water privileges that may explain why the khojas' estates were considered 'models of neatness and thrift', and why their apples, pears, and pomegranates enjoyed particular fame (Forsyth 1875: 44). These rights derived from the khojas' construction activities and were sanctioned by custom.

In the late nineteenth and early twentieth centuries, the provincial government in Northern Xinjiang had a vested interest in the construction of irrigation works not only because it contributed to the public welfare, but also because land reclamation opened up new sources of tax revenue. The governor discussed such plans with his immediate subordinates and eventually authorised the work, but the central authorities typically failed to supply financial or any other assistance for the carrying out of the project. Village headmen and irrigation officials organised the work, estimating how many draft animals and labourers were to be contributed by each settlement benefiting from the new canal. In this respect, no conceptual distinction was made between urban and rural populations. Farmers' labour contribution was determined according to the size of their property, but craftsmen were also mobilised to take part in the construction works. Even merchants had to contribute, on the understanding that indirectly they also benefited, but their contributions could also take the form of monetary payment (Golab 1951: 196).

---

[7] Khoja is an honourific title of Persian origin. The khojas of Eastern Turkestan claimed to be the descendants of the Prophet Muhammad.

As was the case in Russian Turkestan, in Eastern Turkestan access to water was not determined by written laws. Sources emphasise that the Republican legal system introduced in 1911 was little observed; instead, old customary law prevailed (Busse 1915: 50; Golomb 1959: 30).[8] Even in the northern part of Xinjiang, where government control tended to be stricter, customary law was said to have such force that no Chinese or local officials dared violate it, since they would have risked being killed, as reportedly did happen on occasion (Golab 1951: 198). The missionary Ludwig Goląb, who lived in Xinjiang between 1922 and 1939, gave the following account of the allocation of water rights in the north, not merely as an outsider, but as a participant observer, since he also owned a garden plot and fields:

> The main rule for the portioning out the water is this: He who can show a duly processed title to his land, and has paid the taxes due on it (payment is made in wheat) has a right to water. If an owner is unable to till a portion of his field because not enough water is available, he need not pay taxes on the uncultivated part. On the other hand, he who cannot or will not pay taxes on his property receives no water.... The quantity of water allotted to each [cultivator] is determined by the total amount of water at hand and by the area of the fields to be irrigated. A certain definite time is fixed for each *mo* [i.e. *mu*] of land. In the oasis of Hutupi ... a period of four to five minutes was allowed for each *mo* of land. Since very few people in that locality owned clocks ... the time for watering was reckoned by walking at a slow pace around an area of one *mo*. That would be four or five minutes (Golab 1951: 198).

The same author explains that the days for irrigation were also strictly regulated. As with the rules prevailing in Russian Turkestan, the fields situated closest to the head of the irrigation canal had priority access. If there were a dozen average-sized farms for a small canal, each the size of 50–100 *mu*, then each farm had access to irrigation water every 10 to 14 days. Other users of water, who themselves did not consume it, but needed it as a source of energy were also subject to regulations: owners of water mills had special rights to lead water over their wheel after which it was returned to the canal (Lattimore 1975 [1950]: 164).

The official locally in charge of distributing water was the *mirab*. In the early twentieth century, the *mirab*'s responsibilities continued to be

---

[8] The Golab and Golomb mentioned in this section as two separate authors are almost certainly the same person. Not only do their initials coincide, but there is a great deal of overlap between long sections of Golab's English text (1951) and Golomb's German text (1959). The two forms of the name may be explained by divergent transliterations of the Polish letter 'ą'.

manifold. His permission was needed to open an irrigation canal. When a person needed water, he had to go and ask the *mirab* first (Muhammad 'Ali Damolla 1905–10: I.42). There were basically two periods when the oases would enjoy a relatively abundant supply of water: first in the spring, when snow melted on the lower mountains, and later in the summer, when snow started to melt on the higher peaks. Especially in the summertime when it was crucial to have sufficient water supply to ensure a good crop, the *mirab*'s power could temporarily supersede that of other government officials ('Abdul-Qadir 1930: 44V).

In spite of official controls, disputes over access to water often flared up seasonally. Such conflicts were common both between individuals – over who would water his land first – and between upstream and downstream communities (Lattimore 1975 [1950]: 164). On one occasion when a quarrel over water broke out in the Kashgar region, many people were wounded in the ensuing fight. After this, the local *molla*s decided to act as guardians of order: they went to every house and broke the points of all knives to prevent further violence (Sykes and Sykes 1920: 173). Like other local officials, the *mirab* too, was likely to abuse his power. He could withhold water from the peasants until his demands for payment were met, and he extracted labour services from individuals who were dependent on him for their water supply (Warikoo 1985: 81). From the end of the nineteenth century we learn that 'the Beg of Tazgun received an annual sum of one thousand tenges from the inhabitants of the Tarim and Yupugay oases in the Maralbashi district for allowing the water to flow through their lands. He cut off the required water supply after the natives withheld the payment of bribes to him for about two years. Their complaints made to the Tao-t'ai of Kashgar against the arbitrary action of the Beg produced no result' (Warikoo 1985: 110, quoting Deasy 1901: 286). But because the *mirab*'s power, prestige, and influence were considerable during the irrigation seasons, he might also be called upon to settle minor disputes (Muhammad 'Ali Damolla 1905–10: I.42). The *mirab*'s exceptional power during irrigation periods, the inability or unwillingness of the Chinese authorities to curtail the *mirab*'s power, and the *molla*s' communal action to prevent violence, all support the supposition that local authority backed up by custom could on occasion supersede state authority.

As we have seen, old customary law gave water rights to those who individually or collectively invested in land reclamation by building irrigation canals. A similar principle seems to have regulated mining in the late nineteenth century. The ownership rights of the original workers of a jade mine were acknowledged and 'scrupulously respected' by other prospectors even many years after the first digging (Stein 1904: 235–36).

Throughout the late imperial period, even in Zungharia individuals could retain their ownership rights over their houses and courtyards. Following the end of the Qing dynasty in 1911, Zungharian peasants became legal owners of the land they cultivated. From this time, at least in theory, Republican laws applied which stipulated that undisputed ownership of property had to be verified by obtaining a sealed document from the authorities. Since few people had such a document, a new title could be drawn up, provided that the claimant could prove with witnesses that he had either bought or inherited the property. In disputed cases, land was given to the person who had cultivated it in the previous year, which was the customary practice (Golomb 1959: 56).

Family Law and Civil Disputes

If Islamic law had little impact on the regulation of the most important resources in pre-socialist times, it nevertheless seems to have dominated civil disputes and family law. Similarly to many other parts of the Islamic world, Muslim legal experts in Xinjiang also resorted to the handbooks of the Hanafite legal school (Hooker 1997). General accounts of the operation of Islamic courts written by local religious dignitaries reveal that their organisation and vocabulary followed patterns elsewhere in the Islamic world. Court settlement of various disputes took the form of a written agreement (*razinamä*), while divorce cases were concluded with the drawing up of a written document (*talaqnamä* or *talaq khät*). Civil court cases such as inheritance and alimony were recorded, giving the date, the names of the adversaries, the nature of their dispute, the names of witnesses, and the final decision. An example of such court records, comprising cases from the late nineteenth century, was obtained by the German orientalist Martin Hartmann in Kashgar in 1902.[9] Other documents also acquired by Hartmann include deeds of a house sale, an inheritance document in which a person called Bay Khojam transfers land, money, a hoe, a coat, a sack, and a bed to his younger brother from the paternal inheritance and a lawsuit in which several sisters demand their share of the paternal inheritance from their brother.[10] These documents seem to be representative of the civil cases brought to Islamic courts, which mostly dealt with aspects of family law, endowments, and property rights (Hooker 1997: 321–28).

---

[9] Hartmann Sammlung, Staatsbibliothek zu Berlin, 2 3296. I am grateful to Mr. Sugawara Jun for drawing my attention to this document.

[10] These are housed in the Hartmann Collection, Deutsche Morgenländische Gesellschaft in Halle, Germany (items unnumbered).

There is some evidence that the separation of Islamic courts and local secular authorities was not complete. Representatives of the secular authorities could also perform legal functions. For example, legal documents had to be obtained before contracting a marriage (Forsyth 1875: 84). Such written permission to marry could be obtained from the local *bek*, who issued it for a small fee, but a certificate from the imam of the neighbourhood was also needed to prove that the woman was free to marry (Sykes and Sykes 1920: 311). In such instances the legal and religious authorities were fulfilling complementary functions that were unconnected with the courts.

Since a judgment derived from Islamic legal books was considered to be of divine origin, any judgments that contradicted the written authority of the books on Hanafi jurisprudence (*fiqh*) were regarded as unjust. But many people disregarded Islamic courts altogether, and, instead of resorting to them, they directly approached a high officeholder (*bek*) who sometimes conducted the investigation himself and sometimes delegated it to lower ranking officials who were prone to accept bribes. Fair settlement of a dispute was therefore not always granted, since cases were often decided according to the adversaries' respective ability to bribe the judges (Muhammad 'Ali Damolla 1905–10: I. 48).[11]

The above source written by a native of the area and its assertion that local officeholders often acted as legal authority is corroborated by an eyewitness account describing such proceedings in the southern part of the Tarim Basin in the late nineteenth century. Riyaz Bek, the richest man in Merket, held court in his own yard every day. Seated on his veranda, he was assisted by a scribe as well as a number of other clients and servants. The first case witnessed concerned a man who had five wives. One of them, a young woman, had run away from her husband with another man all the way to Kashgar. The *bek* notified the Kashgari authorities who found the woman and duly sent her back to Merket. After it was concluded that she was indeed guilty of adultery, she was slapped on the cheeks by the *bek*. Then she was sent first to live in the house of the local *molla* before being finally forced to return home to her husband. The second case tried by Riyaz Bek involved domestic violence. A young woman who had a badly scratched face was brought to the court by her husband. Like the first woman, she had also left her husband, who upon finding her mistreated her badly. Witnesses claimed that he also had a razor in his hands while abusing his wife, although he

---

[11] Describing the legal situation in Xinjiang as a dual system, James Millward noted that Islamic law was administered by the *bek*s and religious functionaries, but attributed no particular significance to this ostensible participation of secular officials in the religious legal system (Millward 1998: 122).

denied this accusation. To prod his memory, the *bek* had him hanged from a column by his hands that had been tied together on his back. After a short while he confessed, upon which he was taken down and was given a severe beating of 40 strokes on his buttocks. He then claimed that his wife had also beaten him on the back, but as no sign of such abuse was found on him, another beating was meted out to him for lying in court (Hedin 2001: 187–88).

Evidently the *bek*'s authority did not derive from his religious learning and there is no mention of his using any *fiqh* books or any other written aid in passing judgment. What is not clear is whether the *bek*'s court could simply be seen as an imitation of the Islamic court, or as a customary court. It is more likely that the *bek*'s decisions were determined by his second-hand knowledge of Islamic law, though he may have been advised by religious office holders in the mosque community. But his judgments were also inevitably influenced by local opinion rooted in customary practice. If this was the case, then the *bek*'s court merged Muslim and customary normative orders.

The dubious reputation of many of the judges and the payment of bribes may also have contributed to the persistence of informal forms of dispute settlement, which, however, rarely get mentioned in the sources. These alternative methods of dispute settlement derived their force entirely from customary law. As reported by Fernand Grenard (1898), in Khotan, in cases of serious disputes during which one of the parties was hit, injured, or otherwise hurt, the adversaries went to the street, accompanied by their wives and children, where a 'Homeric exchange of mutual verbal abuse' took place in public. The curious onlookers from the neighbourhood interfered only when physical violence was used. At this point, the person who had struck harder asked his adversary to acknowledge that he had done wrong and apologise. The offender was expected to offer his pipe to his adversary; the acceptance of the pipe concluded the affair. Although people who had some social standing made efforts to avoid the public scene, they too, resorted to the 'pipe ceremony' that was mediated by respected members of the mosque community (Grenard 1898: 145). To what extent the verbal exchange and violence acted out in public could be considered as a premeditated and orchestrated ritual action is impossible to tell. But resorting to communal mediation and public reconciliation which had to be concluded with ritualised smoking or other forms of commensality did have the backing of the force of custom. Other sources also speak of reconciliation ceremonies that were concluded with the person who had been forced to give way in the dispute inviting the other party to tea. In Yarkand, lesser disputes were concluded with the communal smoking of the water pipe (*chilim tutmaq*)

(Jarring 1975: 18). Throughout the first half of the twentieth century, the water pipe and the teacup continued to play a symbolic role in dispute settlement: 'One of the two had to be made available for such purposes: the person who had been wronged had to be offered tea or a pipe by the offender (his opponent). The ensuing reconciliation apparently had much more force than a written agreement and many solemn words' (Nur Luke 1950: 64–68). And in the first half of the twentieth century in Khotan, customary law also stipulated that at the time of dispute between two parties, if the instigator of the dispute offered a cup of black tea to his opponent in the assembly, it was accepted as a symbolic act indicating that he gave up his claim (Nur Luke 1950: 64–68). In other words, symbols of communal consumption (tea and pipe) were used to settle disputes without resorting to the provisions of formal legal systems.

Another area of civil law was inheritance. In Kashgar, inheritance had a predominantly Islamic and Turkic legal vocabulary; an heir was called *waris* and the person who left the inheritance was called *mawrus*. The inheritance was known as *miras, tärkä,* or *mal äshya.* When it was divided up, the different portions were known as *oq,* a term inherited from the nomadic Turkic-Mongolian vocabulary. Muhammad 'Ali Damolla refers to the authority of the Koran to justify prevailing inheritance practices, according to which a man was entitled to inherit twice the amount that a woman might get. In Kashgar, in the early twentieth century when a married couple had no children and the woman died, her husband received half her possessions. If, however, the man died, the woman's entitlement was only one-fourth of his estate. The remainder went to their respective families and relatives. If they had children, the man's share was one-fourth and the woman's one-eighth (Muhammad 'Ali Damolla 1905–10: I.5). The description indicates Islamic legal solutions. However, my interlocutors in the 1990s maintained that women in pre-socialist society did not inherit and therefore did not possess real estate. They were aware that this practice contradicted Islamic law that granted a woman half the amount of her brother's entitlement. Thus, informants pointed out contradictions between Islamic law and customary practice in property rights, and emphasised (retrospectively) the primacy of the latter. At the same time, some sources suggest more complicated patterns of property relations.

In late nineteenth century Khotan, if a woman had no children, the income from her property went to her parents. If she was married with children, the income of her property went to her husband's family. In case of divorce, she was also said to be able to retain control over her own property, and in addition she was also entitled to the value of everything that had been spent from it on her husband's family. Her sole responsibility was to bring up her children to the age of seven, during which time it was her husband's responsibility to pay for the children's upkeep (Grenard 1898: 125). What is not clear in these examples is to what extent they represent the judgment expected from Islamic courts or actual practice. But the source confirms that women did have ownership rights to real estate.

The implications of the following case are similar. At the end of the nineteenth century, the wife of Muhammad Bek, a major functionary in the district of Keriya, petitioned for and was granted a divorce on the grounds that her husband was too old for her. The case is interesting because the property relations were unusually complicated. The land – which she must have brought into the marriage from her natal family or perhaps from a previous marriage – belonged to her, but the buildings on it (including the family house) had been erected by her husband. Both parties were now pursuing their rights; the woman insisted on keeping her land, the husband refused to give up his house. In the end the woman won. The *bek* saw no other solution but to pull down the buildings and transport them elsewhere (Grenard 1898: 167). Although we have no direct indication as to whether the conflict was settled by an Islamic court (although the judgement was in accordance with Islamic law) or by self-appointed representatives of customary law, the woman's victory demonstrates that customary law rooted in patriarchal values could sometimes be subverted. The case also demonstrates that women could own property, even if inheritance from the parents had to be established through resorting to a Sharī'a court, as one of the Hartmann documents mentioned above also suggests.

We have somewhat more information about Turki women's ownership and control of property in cases of ethnically mixed marriages, where ethno-religious differences made a legal difference. These cases at least partially explain how Turki women could get hold of property through marriage. Apparently, if a Turki woman married a Chinese or Hindu, her husband had no legal rights over her. If she ran away, the Muslim *molla*s did nothing for him; what is more, he was obliged to pay up. Such a wife could 'hold over him the threat of returning to her family, and tap his money-bags with confidence for herself and her relations' (Skrine 1971 [1926]: 103). Upon his death she usually got some or all of his property. Although considered an infidel throughout her life, such a woman usually decided to use her wealth to purchase the right to an Islamic burial. This she could do by settling in another town and by giving liberal donations to Muslim shrines, or by dedicating some or all of her land as a pious foundation to a mosque. The Muslim judge then prescribed certain prayers and observances for the donor and later she could be buried with full Islamic ceremony

(Skrine 1971 [1926]: 203).[12] This could only happen among strangers, in a place where her marital history may have been suspected but was not known with certainty. No matter how generous her donations to the local mosque or shrine would have been, the religious representatives of her earlier place of residence would have had to excommunicate her under communal pressure. In excommunicating Muslim women who married non-Muslims, local law seems to have integrated Islamic norms.

Neither Islamic nor customary law considered husband and wife as a legal unit whose interests always coincided. Conflict between husband and wife was rife, and two published legal documents dating from the late nineteenth century, from the time of Ya'qūb Bek's rule, indicate that court cases were determined by local notions of gender relations, which simultaneously contained elements of patriarchal values and their partial subversion:

> (Whereas) by his statement (it appears) that, as was pre-ordained, a sum of thirty-three *tanga*s was lost from the house of Sufúrgi Baï from his bed, and afterwards Sufúrgi Baï said to (his) wife Aï Khan: 'If you have put away this money, thirty-three *tanga*s, produce it, (and) I will add twenty-four *tanga*s, and will make a cloak after your heart's desire and give (it to you) ... (and) if (when) you have produced the money, I should not add the (other) money and give you the cloak, and should not stand to my promise, (then) be you thrice divorced.' Thus he made conditions (Shaw 1878: 86).

The case was taken to the Islamic court in Kashgar and there is an accompanying legal opinion attached, but it is more important for us to consider the case itself, which allows us a glimpse into the nature of the conflict that was taken to court. The incident evidently occurred in an affluent household, which is indicated partly by the honourific title of the household head, partly by the fact that he kept substantial sums of cash in his bed. He must have had some grounds for suspecting his wife of stealing the money, perhaps because she had before been caught helping herself to some cash without asking him, or because this was common practice in families where financial decisions were made exclusively by men. It is remarkable that although in this case the husband is the plaintiff, all he expects from his wife is admission of the theft. He declares himself prepared not only to let her keep this sum; he also offers to augment it to enable her to buy herself a new cloak. Rather than threatening his wife with divorce or other forms of

---

[12] Nevertheless, at least the Turki wife of a Hindu trader was likely to lose her children to the husband upon divorce. In case he died, her children could be and often were claimed by his relatives. The Hindu husband's (and his family's) rights over the children of such a mixed union were apparently not contested by the *molla*s (Skrine 1971 [1926]: 203).

punishment, the husband favours a conciliatory settlement of the case. That domestic budgeting and conjugal obligations were intimately connected is also illustrated by another court case:

> Malaq, the son of Qabil Bai, made a legal agreement (as follows): that on account of contentions (with) my wife Aqlim Bibi, I, who now agree, having been unreasonable, henceforward have undertaken not to strike or beat (her) without reason; to give (her) the necessary cost of living at the (proper) time, and have undertaken not to take any strange man into the house where my said wife is and whenever it shall be known and proved that I have taken a strange man into my house into the presence of my wife, or have beaten her without just cause, my said wife shall be free, if she chooses, to give me the writer of this agreement, one bill of divorcement separating herself (Shaw 1878: 85).

In this legal agreement, which reveals several aspects of conjugal rights and obligations, another husband of an affluent household promised to fulfil his obligation to pay his wife regular cash allowance to run the household. Although the husband was controlling the purse strings, his wife clearly did not refrain from exercising her legal rights to put pressure on him to pay her household allowance regularly.

Both cases illustrate underlying tensions in gender relations implied in customary expectations, the husband's ostensible right to control household income and the wife's claims to a regular household allowance (chapter 2). The promise of the cloak also refers to women's customary rights (*häq*) to regularly receive items of clothing from their husbands, at least twice a year at the times of the major Islamic holidays. The husband's promise not to take a stranger to the house in his wife's presence refers to the locally salient gendered division of space encapsulated in the concept of *namähräm* (chapter 4).

If the divorcing couple had children, the woman was expected to look after them until they reached the age of seven. If the children were older, then sons were supposed to stay with their father and daughters with the mother (Sykes and Sykes 1920: 64).[13]

Some aspects of gender relations were practically under the exclusive control of customary law, one example being elopement (*apqashqan toy*) (Katanov and Menges 1933, 1976: 1204–07). This was resorted to when the girl's parents refused to agree to a marriage, or when the young man, some-times in agreement with his family, wished to avoid making a marriage

---

[13] But modern ethnographic data suggest a pragmatic approach. To enable her to remarry, the woman typically leaves her children with their father, which in practice means that they are cared for by their paternal grandmother or aunts.

payment (*toyluq*). Towards the end of the late nineteenth century in Qarakhoja, following an elopement, the girl's fiancé and the girl's parents pursued the lovers separately.[14] Custom dictated that if the young man found the lovers within three days, he could marry the girl without paying the *toyluq*. However, if the girl's parents found the lovers, the seducer had to pay the fiancé the amount of the *toyluq*. In case the couple could not be found within three days, the seducer made full preparations for the wedding and, accompanied by his parents and members of his mosque community, he begged the girl's parents for forgiveness (Katanov and Menges 1933, 1976: 1202–05). Corroborating the indigenous report, a European account states that it was quite common for young people who failed to get their parents' approval to elope. They stayed in another place for several months, after which time they returned to their native oasis, invited their parents to a communal meal and concluded the affair with reconciliation (Hedin 2001: 189).

This example takes us to the question of marriage payment, which displays a certain convergence of customary and Islamic law. The most frequently used term for marriage payment mentioned by most accounts was the *toyluq*. *Toyluq* referred to the gifts given to the young couple by the bridegroom's family. Its size and quality were determined during repeated negotiations between the two sides. In the early nineteenth century in Qumul, the *toyluq* presented by a wealthy groom to the bride comprised 10 to 20 sheep, and a great deal of cloth which sometimes also included expensive Chinese silk. Following the wedding, the *toyluq* typically stayed with the bride (Katanov and Menges 1933, 1976: 1190–93). In the 1870s, the most important items comprising the *toyluq* of a wealthy bride included hats, beads, a string of pearls, earrings, bracelets, charms, boots, socks, pyjamas, a shawl, a chemise, and an overcoat. The groom's party took all this to the bride's house together with some sheep, rice, and sheep fat, and they remained as guests in the bride's house for three days. The bride's family met all the other expenses for feasting, dancing, and singing (Forsyth 1875: 85). Such generosity could only be expected from rich families and on the occasion of a girl's first wedding.

In the southern oases, the bridegroom's parents sent the bride's parents a large bag containing a quilt, a hat, coat, trousers, comb, mirror, a long coat, and one piece of Chinese silk for the bride's dress. Ordinary smallholders' and poor families' contributions were less extravagant. As a

---

[14] This example assumes that the girl was forcibly engaged to another man which, however, was not the only cause for elopement. Marriage by elopement could be chosen because of the girls' parents' refusal to agree to the marriage, but it was also an attractive option for poor men since such circumstances automatically entailed a reduction of the marriage payment.

rule, the basic foodstuffs for the wedding feast (e.g. mutton and rice) were purchased by the bridegroom's parents, and their presents comprised a cloak, a pair of cotton trousers, a hat, a pair of shoes, and leather stockings for the bride (Dunmore 1893: 333–34).[15] In the late 1920s and early 1930s in Southern Xinjiang, the betrothal gifts to the bride marrying into an affluent family included a pair of golden earrings, two gold bracelets, two coral bracelets, one silver buckle, two pairs of shoes, two garments (one of them silk), a small cap and a big one with otter-skin trimmings, many carpets, cushions, and counterpanes (Jarring 1975: 24).

Sources suggest that *toyluq* was a flexible, almost elastic concept. It included the wedding presents received by the bride and her family, but it is uncertain whether it also included the gifts received by the groom from the girl's side, as well as the other provisions for the wedding feast contributed by the respective sides. In trying to understand the nature of *toyluq*, it is perhaps advisable to discard the straightjacket of western analytical categories such as bridewealth, dowry, indirect dowry and the like, and consider *toyluq* as a local category, which was an important device in creating mutuality between groups of people. Its quality and quantity were negotiated by the participating families and local dignitaries, whose decisions were informed both by pragmatic considerations and by normative rules.

There are indications that pre-1949 Eastern Turkestani society also recognised another type of marriage payment, that of the Islamic *mahr* (Uyghur *mähr*). In Islamic law the quantity of *mahr* had to be decided at the time of the marriage.[16] This term was included in Dr. Bellew's Eastern Turki *Comparative Vocabulary* and translated as 'dowry' (Forsyth 1875: 554–55), and Thomas Forsyth mentioned that in the case of first marriages arranged for young people by their immediate families, the bridegroom's parents fixed the 'dower or mahr' for the girl (Forsyth 1875: 84). A few decades later, Fernand Grenard specifically commented on the absence of the *mahr* payment in Eastern Turkestan, in contrast to other Islamic lands, which 'deprived the woman of any guarantee against her husband's whims' (Grenard 1898: 119). Sir Clarmont Skrine considered this statement 'correct so far as it goes', but added that its existence was nevertheless universally recognised 'if only as a legal fiction', which constituted the 'only liability (and that merely a nominal one) incurred by the bridegroom', but was not to be confused with the maintenance payable for 100 days by a husband to his wife whom he divorced against her will (Skrine 1971 [1926]: 194). In the early twentieth century, the amount of the *mähr* was fixed verbally, ideally

---

[15] For the situation in Merket see Hedin (2001: 189).

[16] For a general introduction see Spies (1991: 78–80) and Bakhtiar (1996: 438–44).

in the presence of the community elders, and it was regarded as a debt that –
in theory – could be claimed by the wife at any time throughout the
marriage. But in practice, such claims were hardly ever made if the marriage
lasted. If it was claimed by the wife following divorce, it was typically
waived since the husband could simply declare that his wife had let him off
the *mähr* at the wedding. At this point, the wife could challenge him to prove
it with witnesses. When no agreement could be reached, such disputes could
be taken to the Islamic court.[17] Since witnesses could be bribed, such
disputes were usually decided by the financial position of the respective
parties. Poor women were more likely to lose their case and had to find a
new husband to support them. A local author, the learned *molla* 'Abdul
Qadir, specified the amount of *mähr*, but he did not say whether these sums
were ever actually paid or remained a formality ('Abdul-Qadir 1930: 15R,
24V). Another indigenous author, Nur Luke, used the expression *toyluq-
mähr* when making the point that the sum had to be twice as much at the
time of a girl's first marriage than at subsequent marriages (Nur Luke 1950:
34–36). Compared to other sources, Nur Luke's description is relatively late,
describing customary practices in the Republican era. It suggests that by the
mid-twentieth century, *mähr* lived on only in name and was treated as
synonymous with *toyluq*. At the same time, the author mentions the
possibility that the woman may not have received all the marriage payment
that had been fixed. The promise of further payments could perhaps be
interpreted as a residue of *mähr*. A similar meaning was suggested by
Mäqsut Haji from Guma in a narrative dating from 1935: 'with *nika*: [it] is
meant that on the side of the girl three or four of the very important people
and on the boy's side three or four people act as witnesses and having fixed
the marriage portion [*mähr*] of the girl at four or five hundred *sar* he gives
clothes to the amount of two or three hundred *sar*' (Jarring 1951: 115).[18]

The fact that the amount of the *mähr* was fixed by the witnesses at the
time of the religious wedding suggests that it was a provisional agreement
rather than an actual payment. But Mäqsut Haji's reference immediately
afterwards to the gifts of clothes given by the man's side to the woman raises
the possibility that the notions of *mähr* and *toyluq* were inextricably
intertwined. One part of this general betrothal gift was paid to the girl in the

---

[17] Having listened to the evidence, the Muslim judge (*qazi*) either passed judgment at once or
ordered one of the adversaries to take an oath. Usually, the party who was ordered to take an
oath refused to do so, and thus lost his case. The reason was that it was considered a disgrace
to swear on the Koran. The term *qäsämkhor* (oath-eater, a frequent oath-maker) was a term of
abuse, meaning a greedy and unscrupulous person (Skrine: 1971 [1926]: 196; Schwarz 1992:
633).

[18] *Sär* was a weight measure equalling 35 grammes (Schwarz 1992: 469).

form of clothes to her immediate relatives, and another part was verbally promised but not actually given.

Although we have no conclusive evidence concerning the Islamic *mähr* payment in Eastern Turkestan, it is clear that the term was known and used primarily to refer to a bridal gift payable by the groom's side. There remain two possibilities: that the term was used in its original sense and thus referred to payment, part of which or perhaps the whole of which could be deferred and actually paid in case of divorce. However, given the very high incidence of divorce in Eastern Turkestan (chapter 2), the rigorous observance of this payment would certainly have rendered divorce more expensive and therefore less desirable. The ease and frequency of divorce makes it likely that the term *mähr* was adopted from the Islamic legal vocabulary. But by the late nineteenth century it had merged with the *toyluq*[19], which indicates a convergence of customary and Islamic institutions.

The Socialist Period

Following the incorporation of the region into the People's Republic of China, Islamic courts were officially abolished, ostensibly leaving the Muslims of Xinjiang with a single, secular legal system. At the same time, the previously dominant non-interference policy was also abandoned. This was particularly true during periods of extreme social control, such as the Great Leap Forward and the Cultural Revolution. Although customary law has never been recognised explicitly as a legal system in its own right, aspects of it have come under repeated attack during socialism. Through various campaigns, the state legal apparatus claims an absolute monopoly over the regulation of social life at the expense of both Islamic and customary institutions.

The boundaries between permitted religious activities and forbidden feudal customs and superstitions remain open to alternative interpretations. The official lumping together of the strands of Islamic values and custom has contributed to their further merging.[20] The permitted standards are known as *örp-adät*. Originally referring to pre-Islamic norms and practices, these terms are commonly used in many Islamic lands to denote custom and customary law.[21] In this respect, *örp-adät* implicitly but accurately encapsulates the fusion of customary and Islamic norms. This local definition

---

[19] Several westerners explicitly mentioned the absence of bridewealth in Eastern Turkestan (Grenard 1898: 119; Skrine 1971 [1926]: 195).

[20] For a good overview of legal changes in minority areas see Mackerras (1995).

[21] On these terms see Lokhandwalla (1986).

is also likely to be increasingly enriched by Islamic values partially derived from the Islamic legal system – at least among farmers in Southern Xinjiang – which lived on following the abolition of Islamic courts in the early 1950s. It seems that knowledge of some of its elements is perpetuated today as part of what I term the 'bundle of customs'. We cannot exclude the possibility that informal transmission of such legal knowledge and even books has been taking place among religious scholars and through their sermons. In addition, in being used in participation in informal attempts at dispute settlement, the permitted standards of *örp-adät* contribute to the trickling down of Islamic legal knowledge into customary practice. Insistence on the observance of the three months of waiting period for women between divorce and remarriage is one such example. Another is the awareness of the contradiction between the customary expectation of daughters to give up their claim to land from the paternal inheritance and the provisions of Islamic law.

The standard usage of *örp-adät* in official rhetoric and in folklore publications reduces it to a sanitised concept that includes the permitted elements of religion and omits 'feudal superstitions' conceived as backward and reactionary. In official rhetoric and publications, *örp-adät* refers merely to a loosely connected bundle of social norms that forms the basis for the definition of the Uyghur as a national minority. However, it seems that such officially promoted understandings of *örp-adät* do not coincide entirely with local usage, and that local understandings have retained 'superstitious' and 'feudal' elements. A good example of this appears in the persistence of pre-socialist ideas of honour and shame that are encapsulated in the concept of *namähräm* (chapter 4). Local people, no doubt familiar with state rhetoric and especially its hostile attitude towards feudal superstition, successfully avoid definitional contradictions by making pragmatic use of selected elements of *namähräm* on the normative, discursive level and in actual practice.

In what follows, I shall discuss some areas where the force of customary law has retained its salience. I use the concept of customary or local law to include cases that: 1. are explicitly discussed in codified legal systems; 2. contradict the regulations of the dominant legal system; 3. are defined as 'right' in local normative discourse.

Family Law

Contradictions with secular law emerge when new regulations are introduced for those areas of social behaviour that previously had been under the exclusive control of custom. For example, the Marriage Law introduced a minimal age of marriage for both men and women which is considerably higher than those sanctioned by custom (Mackerras 1995). Compliance with custom can also be achieved through manipulating the age of children born from earlier marriages. Endogamous tendencies in pre-socialist times included close-kin and cousin marriages. The Chinese authorities have tried to curb the practice by launching vigorous campaigns against it. My own observations indicate that the practice persists and that the proximity of kinship between bride and bridegroom is simply denied when the marriage is registered (chapter 4).

During fieldwork, I noted a conspicuous discrepancy between the different legal systems in matters of inheritance. It is well known that collectivisation drastically interrupted the previously dominant practice controlled by patriarchal ideology. As contracts granting land to villagers for private use have become extended, it is to be expected that such land will continue to be passed down to sons (but not daughters) as de facto inheritance in line with customary practice (chapter 1).

Custom dictates that at the time of major religious holidays married women should receive gifts of clothing from their husbands (chapter 3). It would be a mistake to dismiss this claim as trivial; together with food and money, clothing (materials and dresses) has continued to persist as one of the most important means of social exchange. It is used as payment for social services as well as for gifts given and received at all life-cycle rituals. Giving, receiving, and possessing such goods are also important markers of social standing and prestige. At life-cycle rituals, such gift giving is the exclusive province of women. In the present period of the 'socialist market economy' that has granted more freedom to individuals and has allowed for the re-emergence of pre-socialist practices, the financial value of such gifts has increased greatly. In order to mask the ever-increasing gap between successful rural entrepreneurs and poor farmers, the government launches rigorous campaigns against such ritual displays of wealth. In this, it is also supported by those Islamic religious institutions that function under state control. Women continue to perpetuate this customary practice, justifying it with their own emotional need to give, and resorting to semi-secret measures to circumvent state intervention. Women therefore simultaneously insist on their customary rights (*häq*) both to receive and to give.

A married woman's claim to be allowed to visit her natal home 'once every eight days' is similarly defined, provided it is situated reasonably near her husband's residence. So too is defined a woman's right to return to her natal home to give birth to her first two children (chapter 4). To do this for her third and perhaps fourth confinement, she is dependent on her husband's goodwill and approval. But on the first two occasions, the husband risks communal disapproval and criticism if he objects. Each time I asked what happens when a husband denies his wife such rights, I received the standard answer 'it is not done' (*bolmaydu*). Evidently, customary law is just as often violated as the regulations of other legal systems, and such generalised statements should be interpreted as normative prohibitions. These customary practices may become mobilised nowadays to avoid or even subvert family planning policies. On occasion, it may happen that the woman's right to give birth to her first two children (in her natal home) is now actively supported by her husband if the children are born without the authorities' expressed permission. Particularly helpful is if this house happens to be in a different administrative area because in such cases both pregnancy and birth may be more easily kept secret, due to the lack of communication between administrative units. Similarly, women's visiting rights may be exploited to the same end, especially at times of official inspections; in this way, pregnant women, breastfeeding mothers, and babies can be temporarily kept out of sight. It remains to be seen whether family planning policies inadvertently encourage exogamous marriage tendencies, since it is convenient to have in-laws in a different administrative unit if one wishes to avoid the detection of unauthorised pregnancies and births.

In pre-socialist times, women also had the right to claim their dowry from their in-laws in case of divorce. More importantly, they were further entitled to claim additional items from the household possessions in compensation for their invested labour. The longer a woman had lived and worked in her husband's family, the more she could claim in compensation for her labour. It seems that this practice, also defined as *örp-adät*, has persisted into the present day and it has such force that modern secular courts also take account of it.

Following divorce, which is no infrequent occurrence in Uyghur society, customary law grants the patrilineal group the right over the children. In Islamic law, this right is valid when the child is seven years of age or older, but customary law allows the patrilineage full ownership even in the case of very young children. Typically, the paternal grandparents look after the children, an arrangement which allows the mother to remarry. During the socialist period, secular law deciding residence status contradicted the patriarchal principles controlling these customary rules (chapter 4).

Informal adoption that had been practised among families in pre-socialist times is also influenced by family planning policies. Unplanned children are registered under the name of a childless brother or sister. New patterns of adoption that cut across ethnic boundaries are also emerging. There are indications that before 'Liberation', Chinese couples occasionally adopted Muslim children. In the 1990s, one heard stories of Muslim parents adopting the 'unauthorised' children of Han couples, sometimes from the local orphanage. Customary ideology supports such interethnic adoption; it holds that, although a person's temperament is inborn, it may be influenced and even drastically altered through socialisation (chapter 7).

Similar problems emerge in connection with legal definitions of citizenship and ethnicity. Locals subscribe to the view that all states comprise a number of different ethnic groups but a person can only have a single ethnic affiliation. This latter argument is often explained in terms of the 'right of blood' (i.e. the paternal line). An important role is ascribed to the concept of 'temperament', so that children of interethnic marriages are attributed either the father's or the mother's ethnicity (e.g. Chinese or Uyghur), but not a hybrid form (chapter 7). The choice seems to depend entirely on the socialisation of the child. This assumption is at odds with pre-socialist assumptions, which found expression in a number of different terms used to describe the offspring of ethnically mixed marriages. This may indicate some change within the body of customary law. The official recognition of the Uyghur as an ethnic group by the Chinese socialist state has promoted ethnic awareness among the Uyghur. This ethnic identity may have become so strong that it no longer tolerates the recognition of hybrid ethnic affiliation. The unambiguous classification of a person's ethnicity on the everyday level exerts a profound influence upon his or her social life; given the tense political atmosphere dominating the region today, an anomalous position would mean social exclusion from both groups.

Further Examples

There are a number of further examples that serve as illustrations for the conflict between the various legal realms. The anti-religious policies of the socialist state that continue to keep Islam under tight control are often directed against practices sanctioned by custom. Thus ritual payment for taking over the sins of the dead at the burial is forbidden, but people continue to practise it in secret (chapter 8). The situation is similar with regard to the informal transmission of religious knowledge in the household. Although the 'green revolution' is also gaining adherents in Xinjiang, many farmers see contradictions between the new scientific farming methods and the old 'religious' agriculture, which can be interpreted as a clash of two diagonally opposed normative systems.

Conclusion

This chapter has presented some ethnographic materials from pre-socialist and socialist Xinjiang to demonstrate both the persistence and the changing constellations of legal pluralism. I have used the term 'customary law' in the widest possible sense, and my point of departure was that it cannot be defined as a homogenous system, but rather as a collection of ideas and regulations concerning social relations which is always susceptible to changes. I have shown that the concept of *örp-adät* may often be mobilised to counter state campaigns, laws, and regulations that influence people's daily life but it is also used by state authorities to put forward a reductionist, folklorised view of ethno-religious identity. During various phases of socialism, a number of customary practices have been forbidden or discouraged. Such prohibitions may often politicise these elements of custom and enhance their legal character. One could argue that as long as customary law remains uncodified, it continues to be more susceptible to constant change, and that local custom emerges as customary law most visibly in direct confrontation with a codified legal system.

References

'Abdul-Qadir. ca. 1930. *A Collection of Eastern Turki Folkloristic Texts.* Unpublished manuscript. Yarkand, Jarring Collection, Lund University Library. Prov. 464. (Turki).

Ambler, J. 2001. Customary Law and Natural Resources Management: Implications for Integrating State and Local Law in Asia. *Tai Culture: International Review on Tai Cultural Studies* 6 (1–2): 41–62.

Bakhtiar, L. 1996. *Encyclopedia of Islamic Law: A Compendium of the Views of the Major Schools.* Chicago: ABC International Group, Inc.

Bellér-Hann, I. 2000. *The Spoken and the Written: Oral and Written Transmission of Knowledge among the Uyghur.* Berlin/ Halle: Das arabische Buch.

von Benda-Beckmann, F., and K. von Benda-Beckmann. 1988. Adat and Religion in Minangkabau and Ambon. In H. J. M. Claessen, and David S. Moyer (eds.), *Time Past, Time Present, Time Future: Perspectives on Indonesian Culture*, pp. 195–212. Dordrecht: Foris Publications.

von Benda-Beckmann, F. 2001. Legal Pluralism and Social Justice in Economic and Political Development. *IDS Bulletin (Making Law Matter: Rules, Rights and Security in the Lives of the Poor)* 32 (1): 46–56.

Busse, W. 1915. *Bewässerungswirtschaft in Turan und Ihre Anwendung in der Landeskultur.* Jena: Verlag von Gustav Fische.

Deasy, H. H. P. 1901. *In Tibet and Chinese Turkestan*. London: Fisher Unwin.

Dunmore, C. A. M. 1893. *The Pamirs; Being a Narrative of a Year's Expedition on Horseback and on Foot through Kashmir, Western Tibet, Chinese Tartary, and Russian Central Asia*, Vol. I. New Delhi: Vintage Books.

Fletcher, J. F. 1978. Ch'ing Inner Asia c. 1800. In D. Twitchett, and J. K. Fairbank (eds.), *The Cambridge History of China* (10), *Late Ch'ing 1800–1911*, Part I, pp. 35–106. Cambridge: Cambridge University Press.

Forsyth, T. D. et al. 1875. *Report of a Mission to Yarkund in 1873, under Command of Sir T.D. Forsyth ... with Historical and Geographical Information regarding the Possessions of the Ameer of Yarkund*. Calcutta: Foreign Department Press.

Golab, L. W. 1951. A Study of Irrigation in East Turkestan. *Anthropos* 46 (1–2): 187–199.

Golomb, L. 1959. *Die Bodenkultur in Ost-Turkestan. Oasenwirtschaft und Nomadentum*. Freiburg: Verlag des Anthropos-Instituts.

Grenard, F. 1898. *Le Turkestan et le Tibet: étude ethongraphique et sociologique* (J.-L. Dutrueil de Rhins: *Mission Scientifique dans la Haute Asie 1890–1895*). Paris: Ernest Leroux.

Hamada, M. 1978. Supplement: Islamic Saints and their Mausoleums. *Acta Asiatica* 34: 79–98.

Hedin, S. 2001. *Durch Asiens Wüsten. Von Stockholm nach Kaschgar 1893–1895*. Stuttgart: Erdmann.

Hooker, M. B. 1997. Sharī'a. *Encyclopaedia of Islam*, pp. 321–328. Leiden: Brill

Jarring, G. 1946–1951. *Materials to the Knowledge of Eastern Turki*. Tales, Poetry, Proverbs, Riddles, Ethnological and Historical Texts from the Southern Parts of Eastern Turkestan. Part IV: Ethnological and Historical Texts from Guma. In Lunds Universitets Ärsskrift N. F. Avd.1. Bd 47. Nr.4.

Jarring, G. (ed.). 1975. *Gustav Raquette and Qasim Akhun's letters to Kamil Efendi. Ethnological and Folkloristic Materials from Southern Sinkiang*. Lund: CWK Gleerup.

Katanov, N. T., and K. H. Menges. 1933, 1976. *Volkskundliche Texte aus Ost-Türkistan*. Proceedings of the Prussian Academy of Sciences, Section of Philology and History, 1933. Leipzig: Zentralantiquariat of the German Democratic Republic.

Kim H.-D. 1986. *The Muslim Rebellion and the Kashghar Emirate in Chinese Central Asia 1864–1877*. Ph.D. dissertation. Cambridge: Harvard University.

Lattimore, O. 1975 [1950]. *Pivot of Asia. Sinkiang and the Inner Asian Frontiers of China and Russia*. New York: AMS Press.

Lokhandwalla, S. T. 1986. '`Àda'. *Encyclopaedia of Islam*, Vol. 5, Uhe-Madi (2nd ed.), pp. 170–173. Leiden: E. J. Brill.

Mackerras, C. 1995. *China's Minority Cultures: Identities and Integration since 1912*. New York: St. Martin's Press.

Millward, J. A. 1998. *Beyond the Pass: Economy, Ethnicity, and Empire in Qing Central Asia, 1759–1864*. Stanford: Stanford University Press.

Muhammad 'Ali Damolla. ca. 1905–10. *A Collection of Essays on Life in Eastern Turkistan*. Unpublished manuscript. Kahsgar, Jarring Collection, Lund University Library. Prov. 207. I.–II. (Turki).

Nur Luke. ca. 1950s. *A Collection of Essays on the Habits and Customs of Eastern Turkestan*. Unpublished manuscript. Jarring Collection, Lund University Library. Prov. 212. (Turki).

Paul, J. 1996. *Herrscher, Gemeinwesen, Vermittler. Ostiran und Transoxanien in vormongolischer Zeit*. Beirut: Orient-Institut der DMG.

Schwarz, H. G. 1992. *An Uyghur-English Dictionary*. Bellingham: Western Washington University.

Shaw, R. B. 1878. *A Sketch of the Turki Language as Spoken in Eastern Turkistan (Káshghar and Yarkand)*. Calcutta: The Baptist Mission Press.

Skrine, C. P. 1971 [1926]. *Chinese Central Asia*. New York: Barnes & Noble.

Spies, O. 1991. Mahr. *Encyclopaedia of Islam*, Vol. 6, Mahk-Mid (2nd ed.), pp. 78–80. Leiden: Brill.

Stein, M. A. 1904. *Sand-buried Ruins of Khotan: Personal Narrative of a Journey of Archaeological and Geographical Exploration in Chinese Turkestan*. London: Hurst and Blackett.

Sykes, E., and P. Sykes. 1920. *Through Deserts and Oases of Central Asia*. London: Macmillan and Co. Limited.

Warikoo, K. B. 1985. Chinese Turkestan during the Nineteenth Century: A Socio-Economic Study. *Central Asian Survey* 4 (3): 75–114.

Woodman, G. R. 1999. The Idea of Legal Pluralism. In B. Dupret, M. Berger, and L. al-Zwaini (eds.), *Legal Pluralism in the Arab World*, pp. 3–20. The Hague: Kluwer Law International.

Zelizer, V. A. 1997. *The Social Meaning of Money*. Princeton: Princeton University Press.

Chapter 6
The Mobilisation of Tradition: Localism and Identity among the Uyghur of Xinjiang[1]

While there is a respectable body of literature concerning the history and anthropology of Xinjiang[2], little attention has been paid to the conceptualisation of place by its inhabitants, in spite of the fact that, like time, place matters for the simple reason that human existence is constrained by it. Following Martin Heidegger's concept of dwelling, Keith Basso suggested that 'dwelling is said to consist in the multiple "lived relationships" that people maintain with places, for it is solely by virtue of these relationships that space acquires meaning' (Basso 1996: 54).

Many authors have studied aspects of the emergence and shaping of modern Uyghur ethnic identity among Uyghurs who are tied to one particular place, that is the political entity today known as the Xinjiang Uyghur Autonomous Region (Gladney 1990, 1994, 1998; Rudelson 1997; Smith 1999, 2000; Cesàro 2000, 2002). This chapter is a preliminary attempt to consider more mundane expressions of localism in the sentiments expressed toward people's more immediate environment, the oases, natural settlements, and specific places where they live and work, notably the land and the house.[3]

My point of departure is that spaces become bounded, definable places through the symbolic meanings humans attach to them, be it geographical features, urban centres, villages, administrative units, or human dwellings. In this sense, all places are constructed as they become invested with meanings and associations, which in turn are capable of evoking

---

[1] Published in R. L. Canfield and G. Rasuly-Paleczek (eds.), *Ethnicity, Authority, and Power in Central Asia: New Games, Great and Small*, pp. 39–57. London: Routledge, 2011.

[2] For a summary of the diverse research see Starr (2004) which also provides a useful bibliographic guidance.

[3] My enquiry is limited to social groups which define themselves primarily as peasants (*dihqan*) and I pay no attention to urban elites.

emotions of all sorts. Emotional reactions to places, such as attachment or a sense of belonging, can be summed up under the concept of 'localism'.

Plate 7. Village in Southern Xinjiang (Photo: Chris Hann).

The central argument of the chapter is as follows. In the wake of major interruptions of social life during the era of collectivisation by the state, the reform period which followed the end of the Cultural Revolution ushered in the introduction of the market economy. Due to the special position of Xinjiang within China, where the government fears Muslim separatism, liberalisation has, to a great extent, remained restricted. Thus, in spite of the undeniable changes and improvements to the repressive policies which characterised the Cultural Revolution, the state today continues to make its powerful presence felt in many areas of life, including production, family planning, and political and religious freedoms. Since the second half of the 1990s, religious repression and the fight against separatism have been stepped up; and in the aftermath of 9/11, political tension has once again gained momentum. But all these developments have done little to erode the localism characteristic of traditional society; parallel to the search for ethnic and regional identification, claims to locality may take on more specific and tangible forms, which also perpetuate important links to pre-socialist social practices. Among farmers, one of the side effects of state policies has been the partial loss of the security provided by local networks and knowledge of how things work. Formerly unquestioned security has become challenged, and in an atmosphere of sustained political tension and religious repression, an ostensibly benign ethnic policy is incapable of filling the ensuing gap. As a result, old attachments are perpetuated and have merged with new levels of attachment in order to stress belonging to a particular place. Access to and symbolic appropriation of local space continues to be a contested field in which asymmetrical power relations between alien power holders and indigenous populations are played out. Places are conceptualised in this chapter as 'sites of power struggles' and 'histories of annexation, absorption, and resistance' (Feld and Basso 1996: 5). In what follows, I shall first look at the history of instances of interference by powerholders in the daily life and traditional practices of the inhabitants in the pre-socialist and socialist periods. This sets the historical scene which necessitated both the perpetuation of old and the emergence of new forms of localism. The following sections consider examples of symbolic identifications with locality, ranging from naming places to attachments to land and house.

Interference with Local Practices: A Historical Overview

Largely concentrated in the Xinjiang Uyghur Autonomous Region (XUAR), the Uyghur are a Turkic-speaking group who profess Sunni Islam. With an area of approximately 1.65 million square kilometres, the XUAR covers one-sixth of the total area of the PRC and constitutes its largest province-level administrative unit. The total population of the region in 2000 was over 18 million. According to the 1990 population census, 47 per cent of the total population was ethnically Uyghur, 38 per cent Han, 7 per cent Kazakh, 4.5 per cent Hui, and 1 per cent Kyrgyz (Toops 2004: 247–48). Continuous immigration into the region from the interior of China, which since the mid-1990s has been encouraged as part of the government's efforts to develop the region as quickly as possible, may soon reverse the present demographic proportions, leaving the Uyghur a minority in their autonomous region. Although often a battleground of internal factionalism and wars, it was only with the Qing conquest in the middle of the eighteenth century that the region became part of a large empire on a more permanent basis. While the policies of the centre towards Xinjiang were modified in response to the Muslim revolts of the nineteenth century, in general Manchu rule resorted to indirect forms of administration and there was little state interference in the daily practices of villagers and townspeople as long as taxes and revenues were collected and relative political stability was maintained (Fletcher 1978; Millward 1998; Millward and Perdue 2004: 57–62).

The political entity of Xinjiang was created in 1884, in the wake of the Muslim rebellions. This formal incorporation of the region into imperial China was an important step towards the imposition of a larger regional identity from above, which also contributed to the emergence of the modern Uyghur identity in an ethnic and political sense. Following the demise of the Qing dynasty, the Republican period (1912–49) was marked by the turbulent rule of local warlords before the region became part of the PRC (Forbes 1986). In an overview of the political history of Xinjiang, James Millward and Nabijan Tursun pointed to important continuities between Qing policies and developments in the socialist period, which include the increasingly tighter control of the Chinese centre over the region, the permanent settlement of large numbers of loyal Chinese, and relative economic development. These authors also emphasised that, ever since the Qing conquest in the mid-eighteenth century the region has been governed by the centre through contrasting policies which alternated between integrationist attitudes and more liberal tendencies; the liberal policies favoured a greater measure of regional autonomy and tolerated local ways (Millward and Tursun 2004: 64). While the alternation of these contrasting policies has persisted up to the present day, to understand their impact it is insufficient to look at shifts in policy-making alone. An event-based historical view 'from above' should be supplemented by looking at local understandings of both continuities and change.

In the pre-socialist era there were occasional attempts to interfere with local traditions. For example, following the Manchu conquest in the mid-eighteenth century, restrictive measures were introduced which included forbidding conversion to Islam; prohibiting Muslims from leaving their villages for prayer services; barring preachers from preaching outside their localities; banning the construction of new mosques; and forbidding Muslims to adopt non-Muslim babies (Fletcher 1995: xi). In an attempt to control the pilgrimage to Mecca in the first half of the twentieth century, Governor Yang Zengxin (1912–28) withheld passports, using the First World War as an excuse. Those who received a passport were charged a high price for it, and were given the explanation that the money would be used to promote mosque construction and Islamic education. (Wei-Yin 2002: 149–50). Toward the end of the 1920s, the Chinese *tao-yin*[4] made efforts to curb Soviet influence in the region and implemented corresponding measures, one of which was the imposition of a heavy tax on Muslims from Southern Xinjiang who decided to travel through the Soviet Union on their way to Mecca (Forbes 1986: 66). The Jin Shuren administration (1928–33)

---

[4] The term (also known as *tao-tai*), referred to the Chinese circuit administrator or intendant in Xinjiang whose power superseded that of the county or district magistrates.

antagonised its Muslim subjects by introducing two regulations. One was the levying of a tax on butchering animals, the other the prohibition for Muslims to perform the pilgrimage to Mecca (Forbes 1986: 42). In the early 1930s, to prevent a mass out-migration, the local authorities once again refused to issue passports to prospective pilgrims (Forbes 1986: 96). Although these restrictions were harsh, they were generally motivated by short-term political considerations, and their implementation was always short-lived.

Ironically, the most dramatic interference with daily practices came not from the non-Muslim overlords, but from the leader of the biggest Muslim rebellion of the nineteenth century, Ya'qūb Bek (1864–77). He attempted to impose a much tighter observance of the tenets of Islam than was prescribed by local practice, and his policies were not always welcome. His attempts to restore some 60 shrines and mosques which had been neglected under Chinese rule and his support of pious foundations may have met the approval of some sections of the local population (Bellew 1875: 324; Shaw 1984 [1871]: 465–66), but his religious policy, which launched a strong attack on lax morality blamed on infidel rule, was controversial and often resented by the subject population. In his attempts to promote Islamic law, he enforced the veiling of women in public and the active participation of men in communal prayers. He attacked wine drinking and gambling, which he considered incompatible with an Islamic way of life; and drunkards, brawlers, disorderly behaviour, and neglect of prayers were all severely punished. At the same time, he persecuted prominent Sufi leaders – even though they enforced his policies – since these represented regional loci of power and posed potential danger as rivals to his rule (Kim 2004: 129–31).

Following the turbulent years of the Republican period – which was characterised by the nominal sovereignty of the centre and Muslim insurgences – and the annexation of the region into the PRC, the socialist period of Xinjiang closely follows the national events of China.[5] The first years of socialism saw the reorientation of the region towards the centre, as well as major restructuring. Attempts were made to abolish the traditional class system by changing property relations. The years 1958 through 1961 marked the notorious period of the Great Leap Forward. Some of the excessive measures introduced at this time were later abolished, but the communes continued to function as autocratic units of production and consumption. Although periods of political excess were followed by more moderate policies, campaigns aiming at the cultural and political education of the masses and the elimination of traditional class structures and

---

[5] John Fairbank's periodisation is, by and large, applicable to local conditions (Fairbank 1989).

ideologies were repeatedly launched. The leadership, consistently dominated by ethnic Han, was committed to modernising the economy and society and to destroying local nationalism. These were to be achieved through eliminating the pre-socialist class structure and fighting illiteracy and the feudal legacy which also included Islam (McMillen 1979: 79–81, 85).

In Xinjiang, as elsewhere in the People's Republic of China, the period between 1966 and 1976 also represented ten lost years. Although officially the Great Proletarian Cultural Revolution only lasted for three and one half years (1966–69), the terror it initiated continued until 1976. In Xinjiang, this meant disturbances, anarchy, and a power struggle between the regional leadership and the political faction in Beijing. In the name of ideological campaigns against the Four Olds (old ideas, old culture, old customs, and old habits), intellectuals were attacked (McMillen 1979: 185). Mao's death in 1976 marked the end of the Cultural Revolution and the beginning of a new era, characterised by the reforms of Deng Xiaoping. The party was rebuilt, many victims of the Cultural Revolution were rehabilitated, and the household responsibility system was introduced into the economy.[6] In a full reversal of previous policies, economic production for private gain became encouraged and agriculture was decollectivised. These measures marked the beginning of the most recent era in China's history, that of the 'socialist market economy' (Fairbank 1989; Madsen 1991; Soucek 2000: 263–74).

In spite of the persistence of alternating policies between tighter control and greater regional autonomy between the pre-socialist and socialist eras, 1949 represents a watershed. In an almost unbroken continuity, periodic restrictions notwithstanding, imperial and Republican policies generally allowed for the unimpeded persistence of local practices sanctioned by tradition and custom.[7] After 1949, the socialist state subjected local people to unprecedented intrusions into their daily lives and practices which had a much wider scope and made a much deeper impact than any of the previous restrictions. The implementation of these intrusions oscillated with changes in the political climate, but they were almost continually backed up by an ideology that declared war on feudal customs.[8]

---

[6] For a brief summary of these changes in China in general see Hinton (1990), Kelliher (1992), Seitz (2002: 221–35); for the situation in Xinjiang see chapter 1.

[7] Continuities in ritual and daily practice may be seen when considering the evidence of indigenous and foreign testimonies dating from the late imperial and republican times. See Bellér-Hann (2008: 217–302).

[8] This trend was still in force at the time of fieldwork in the 1990s, as the general liberalisation of the economy elsewhere in China has remained more restrictive in Xinjiang.

As far as collective identity is concerned, two important counter-trends can be observed as a result of these processes. Collectivisation and other drastic measures under Mao could entail persecution and the confiscation of private property. And, previously unquestioned identifications rooted in local practice and custom (which could be subsumed under the label 'traditions') were challenged. Although one's locality continued to offer familiarity, the security provided by local knowledge, networks, practice, and 'tradition' was shattered. Custom and religion became condemned as feudal practices by representatives of the centralising state and branded as expressions of backwardness. This partial loss of security prompted a search for new forms of identification. The recognition of the Uyghur and other groups as ethnic groups (Ch. *minzu*) by the state has certainly contributed to the emergence and strengthening of a modern Uyghur ethnic identity which had its roots in pre-socialist history and social practice. This has also increased people's consciousness of a regional identity which went beyond local oasis-based identifications. The Uyghurs' homeland became the Xinjiang Uyghur Autonomous Region. At this level, claims are made to the homeland as an imagined symbolic space circumscribed by foreign occupation. But parallel to these processes, other forms of attachment have also been perpetuated or reworked, as we shall see in the following sections.

Naming Places

The act of naming always has an (often unintentional) political dimension and may play a critical part in ongoing struggles over ownership and the symbolic expressions of religious, ethnic, or national identity. In Xinjiang, naming places has been a contested field for a long time: oasis names and larger settlements have both a local and a Sinicised name (e.g. Kashgar is the Uyghur name for the place called Kashi by its Han residents). Referring to a place by its local name is a clear statement of a person's ethnic affiliation or at least his sympathies. In other instances, however, the equivalence between an individual's ethnicity and his naming of places is complicated by other considerations.

In addition to investing places with proper names, settlements and administrative units also have generic names which may be changed according to political circumstances. Uyghur terms for the units of pre-socialist social organisation were *yeza*, *känt*, and *mähällä* respectively, which were replaced during the commune period with the distinctive terminology of Chinese socialism: the largest unit, the *yeza* became the commune (*gongshe*), *känt* became the production brigade (*dadüiy*), and the *mähällä* became the production team (*shaodüiy*). It seems that, in many places, when these new administrative units were introduced, they often closely followed pre-socialist boundaries. In the post-reform period, among a number of other liberalising moves, the administrative units were renamed again with the traditional, local terminology without essentially changing the unit boundaries. But in the mid-1990s, 16 years after the introduction of the first reforms, Maoist terminology doggedly persisted among Uyghur peasants in the vicinity of Kashgar. The re-instated pre-socialist Uyghur terms started appearing in official documents, but the vernacular insisted on the Chinese socialist vocabulary. This apparent conservatism in language use may be explained by the congruence of a number of factors. Specifically, even though for many villagers memories of the Maoist period were far from positive, such negative historical experiences may also reinforce a sense of belonging. Besides, even during periods of severe repression and economic hardship, individuals do experience personal happiness, which may also promote attachment. Finally, in spite of the dramatic changes which were introduced with the reforms, there remained enough continuity with the past that also encouraged this conservatism in language use.

The contrast between local people's insistence on the perpetuation of indigenous place names and their simultaneous readiness to adopt and keep Chinese socialist administrative terminology instead of reverting to the old indigenous names warns us against simplistic assumptions that linguistic strategies of the powerless always follow the straightforward logic of promoting native terminology: various forces may influence language use on different levels and with very different outcomes.

Attachment to locality has been long embedded in religious sentiment: in much of Xinjiang the landscape and places are inextricably linked to Islam. Neither the generic nor proper names used for the region by its inhabitants and outsiders do justice to its cultural diversity. Rather, the names tend to project an image of the region as a more or less unified and bounded political entity. As is well known, the name 'Xinjiang' was imposed by the Manchus, reflecting the imperial perspective. The designation of 'Eastern Turkestan', on the other hand, represented European views, which emphasised continuities with the Turkic-speaking regions of Central Asia, while the alternate 'Chinese Turkestan' implied recognition of Manchu supremacy. Oasis names must have dominated the territorial self-perception of those segments of the indigenous population which frequently travelled long distances before the middle of the twentieth century. Foreign observers used these names in both restricted and extended senses, referring either to an oasis or a wider region (e.g. Kashgar and Kashgaria). Prior to the Manchu occupation, the oases had no unifying political structure. This state of affairs continued to be reflected for quite some time in locally used terminology, following the formal incorporation of the region as a fully fledged province into the Qing Empire in 1884. Indigenous sources dating from the late nineteenth and early twentieth centuries used the designation of the 'Six Cities' (Altä Shähär) to refer to the oasis settlements south of the Tian Shan Mountains. This reflected a loose sense of shared features as well as the fragmented nature of the region as a whole. In practice, Altä Shähär seems never to have meant a definite number of cities, although indigenous people and foreigners from time to time attempted to identify the six in question. The German archaeologist Albert von Le Coq gave two possible lists of the six cities: Aqsu, Maralbashi, Kashgar, Yangi Hisar, Yarkand, and Khotan formed one list; in his alternate list Aqsu was replaced by Qarghaliq (Le Coq 1928: 107). Chokan Valikhanov named the six cities as Ush Turpan, Kashgar, Yangi Hisar, Aqsu, Yarkand, and Khotan (Valikhanov 1961: 325). Others evidently gave other combinations, sometimes making references to seven rather than six cities (Le Coq 1911: 55). The actual reference to the 'Seven Cities' apparently came into use after Ya'qūb Bek had occupied Turpan, and also included Kashgar, Yarkand, Khotan, Aqsu, Ush-Turpan, and Kucha (Hamada 1978: 79; Millward 1998). The fluctuation and uncertainty concerning the identity of the Six Cities in local usage reflected the use of the term in a general territorial sense, and simultaneously the fluid nature of these connections, the relative autonomy of the cities, and their lack of fixed political ranking.

A late nineteenth century indigenous source names the Six Cities with their epithets. Kashgar is *Azizanä* (the City of the Saints; Yarkand is *Piranä* (the City of Patron Saints); Khotan is *Shähidanä* (the City of the Martyrs because of the great number of martyrs buried there); Aqsu is *Ghaziyanä* (the City of the Ghazis, the Triumphant ones, in reference to the Muslim fighters who victoriously fought against the infidels); Kucha is *Güli-ullanä* (the City of God's Governors, after the Muslim governors buried there); and Turpan is *Ghäribanä* (the City of Strangers, after the many Muslim pilgrims to the numerous saintly shrines) (Katanov and Menges 1933, 1976: 1220–21).[9] The toponyms themselves were designations of whole oasis complexes, which included both urban settlements and villages; but it was the epithets which symbolically turned them from a dot on the map into three-dimensional localities by evoking a ritual landscape. Evoking images of an essentially Islamic landscape with shrines, mausoleums, tombs, and cemeteries, all being continually visited by Muslim pilgrims, these epithets simultaneously imply the local and transregional character of the oases. The

---

[9] About Turpan, see also Jarring (1933: 16). Yarkand, Kashgar, Aqsu, and Khotan are also mentioned with the same epithets by a Central Asian author, Nushirvan Yavshef, in an early twentieth century Tatar language publication, as cited by Zarcone (2001: 138–39).

fact that the epithets were all of Arabic and Persian derivatives connected them to the Islamic *umma* and the Islamic West. This naming made implicit claims to religious traditions, exclusively Islamic in nature, and disclaimed the pre-Islamic past and the non-Islamic presence as alien. This extended toponymy already encapsulates the symbolic appropriation of social space. Passed down as oral tradition and still remembered today by many in both urban and rural areas, the epithets emphasise the specific features common to these various localities which are unified by a shared religion.[10] This example illustrates that the perpetuation of old place names may also serve as a metaphorical re-assertion of religious identity. At the same time, the acceptance and transmission of recent innovations, such as the Chinese names of administrative units and the rejection of pre-socialist indigenous terminology, suggest that there are more complex forces at play in naming processes. Naming preferences are not marked merely by a simplistic asymmetry which always privileges native terms over Chinese equivalents.

The Land

Today, some young educated Uyghurs reject precisely the aspects of localism which constitute part of the 'tradition' package. For them, the Islamic legacy, also encapsulated in strategies for naming places, is associated with backwardness. They see their homeland as peripheral to the Chinese centre, to the Islamic community, and to the modern world with its multiple centres in Japan, the United States, and Western Europe. Nevertheless, among most social groups, this potential self-perception as marginal is overridden on the more mundane levels of daily life by the central position of locality, which continues to be experienced as positive, as something inherently 'ours'.

Claims to locality can be made in many different ways and may assume diverse forms: naming places is only one of the many possibilities. In traditional agricultural societies claiming place could be done naturally through claims to land. However, in my experience in the 1990s, claims to specific pieces of ancestral land by peasant families were rarely part of the prevalent discourse. When the economic reforms were introduced in the early 1980s, as elsewhere in China, collectivised land was redistributed among Uyghur farmers in Xinjiang and they were given long term rights to land use, but not its legal ownership. In villages near Kashgar, the redistribution of land rarely corresponded to pre-socialist ownership patterns,

---

[10] The extended oasis names ritualise and appropriate localities, as do many names of saintly shrines, which often double as place names (Dawut 2001).

and few families received plots which had belonged to their forefathers.[11] Only the descendants of landowners with at least a sizeable land property stood some chance of receiving a plot which had been cultivated by their ancestors. In the beginning of the reform period, land was distributed among farming families in Southern Xinjiang according to egalitarian principles (chapter 1).[12] The implementation of such principles left little or no room for claims made on the basis of emotional attachment. In fact we cannot even be certain to what extent such attachment was present in pre-modern society.[13]

In the 1990s I found no signs of close emotional attachment to specific plots. People's attitudes to land were shaped by a number of factors, such as the ratio of producers and consumers determined by the number of workers and dependents in the household at the time of my interviews; patterns of non-agricultural employment of household members; and patterns of mutual help and exchange with members of other related or non-related households. If the overall constellation was favourable, then the allotted plots catered to the family's basic subsistence and the household's grain needs, and cash was earned through employment in the non-agricultural sector. Others, lacking the necessary labour force or skills to market were entirely dependent on their landholdings. The small plots were seen as a basic guarantor of minimal levels of security, but this cannot necessarily be interpreted as emotional attachment. Instead, many such producers regarded land as a mixed blessing, and some of the younger farmers expressed their preparedness to give up their land altogether and take a job in industry or services in a city, if only they had the choice. Very few people were able to amass large holdings through renting from the collective or from individuals. For them, land was a source of wealth.

In contrast, I noted a strong attachment to land in a more general sense, that is a strong identification of Uyghur farmers with their peasant status and modes of cultivation. People generally described themselves as *dihqan* (peasants), even in cases when agriculture was no longer their only or primary source of livelihood. Insistence on a basically peasant identity

---

[11] Given the unequal patterns of pre-socialist property relations, the majority of rural families had owned little or no land, instead they had worked the land of others as tenant farmers or serfs (Hoppe 1998: 107); such families could not have made claims on their forefathers' land property in any case.

[12] See also Nolan (1988).

[13] Hann (1999). In the late nineteenth century, Fernand Grenard noted the presence of a certain pragmatic detachment rather than strong emotional attachment of peasants to their land in the area (Grenard 1898: 158). We can only speculate as to this perceived lack of attachment to specific pieces of land; perhaps it can be explained with the observation that in traditional society, land itself was only a guarantee of wealth when there was also enough water available to irrigate it.

among families in the vicinity of Kashgar whose households had multiple sources of income could be explained by a strong desire to meet the household's subsistence needs. This was articulated through the frequent use of the adjective *yärlik* (local) in everyday discourse, which seemed to encapsulate attachment to a notion of land which was below the abstract idea of the regionally defined homeland, Xinjiang, but above the attachment to specific pieces of ancestral land. Among producers, the adjective clearly had acquired a highly positive connotation. This mid-level attachment was expressed through positive, often nostalgic evaluations of the means and end results of agricultural production. For example, the so-called red wheat was still talked about as a local variety in the 1990s, though it had been by and large replaced by modern hybrids which produce higher yields. Farmers generally acknowledged that, from a practical point of view, the new wheat varieties introduced 'from above' have indeed increased yield, and they like the taste of the bread made out of it. The higher yields of the modern variety ensure that, in contrast to pre-modern times when wheat bread could only be consumed by a privileged minority and maize constituted the staple for most people, today wheat bread and wheat-based dishes make up about 80 per cent of the local diet (Hoppe 1987).

Old men and women also reminisced about the local variety of cotton which used to be grown before 'Liberation'. In contrast to the new variety, it was smaller and greyish in colour. Those remembering the old cotton did not deny that the introduction of the new variety was a success, but reminiscences of the old type also evoked memories of the home-spun cotton cloth (*kham*) made by women. This in turn conjured up romantic images of the traditional, pre-socialist division of labour between the sexes which assigned women to housework and men to agricultural production and crafts (chapters 2, 3). Although in the pre-socialist period such ideals were rarely fully upheld in reality, they conformed to normative notions of morality rooted in Islam, and contrasted sharply to the socialist ideology of the commune period, which violated the traditional division of labour and therefore the moral code (chapter 2).[14]

The adjective *yärlik* is prefixed to the traditional, so-called white maize (*aq qonaq*) which is being substituted (under external pressure) by a modern hybrid of yellow maize (*serik qonaq*). Although the new maize indeed produces higher yields, in local discourse preference is given to the old variety. It produces less maize but more leaves, and is therefore more suitable for feeding animals. In wealthy villages, maize has been supplanted completely by wheat as a staple in human diet. Although in earlier historical

---

[14] Both male and female behaviour is and was regulated by local concepts of morality (chapter 4).

periods (including the era of collectivisation) maize bread was associated with poverty while wheat bread and noodles have for long been regarded as prestige food, nowadays corn bread (*zaghra*) is occasionally referred to as a token gesture to perpetuate tradition. It is in this context that people argue that only the local variety is suitable for making maize bread because of its more distinctive, sweeter flavour.

There is much talk about the harmful consequences of the widespread use of chemicals on the land for human health, against which emotionally loaded arguments in favour of the forefathers' cultivating methods weigh heavily. Today, when a great deal of chemical fertilizer is employed, farmers who still try to use as much natural fertilizer as possible refer to the latter as *yärlik oghut* (local fertilizer). Local fertilizer mostly consisted of animal manure, but remnants of old adobe houses, namely the floor and the heated platform of the living room could also be added to it (Häbibulla 1993: 96). In this way a natural recycling of the ancestral houses and re-incorporation of them into an established local cycle of production and consumption takes place, which under government pressure in the mid-1990s had to be abandoned for the sake of chemicals.

Not directly related to agricultural production, but fitting in well with the discourse on local produce representing the 'traditional' way of life was the distinction made between local and factory-produced salt. The distinction was a very real one and referred to the origin of the salt and to the method of its manufacture. Factory-produced salt came from the regional capital, though one could also buy packet salt made in Kashgar factories. Unadulterated local salt was sold on the weekly markets in its natural form: large slabs. The slabs were bought by housewives who distilled and prepared it for human consumption at home. Local natural salt was considered to have healing qualities, as opposed to the factory-produced salt.

New cultivating methods introduced by the township authorities may entail more expense and more labour than the old ones. In the 1990s, planting the new maize seeds in regular rows and covering them with plastic film was expensive and seemed like drastic innovations in the face of traditional methods. In spite of this, new methods were not automatically rejected by all as undesirable, and old methods were not universally hailed as the best: local discourse often went beyond such simplistic 'peasant conservatism'. Adopting the vocabulary of the authorities and internalising a great deal of the new campaigns, many cultivators acknowledged the need to improve their economic status, and that development (*täräqqiyat*) was best achieved through embracing the principles and methods of modern agriculture. Nevertheless, they also insisted on positive images of a largely idealised past when life was subordinated only to God's will and remained free from other forms of interference. Some producers saw a confrontation between the traditional religious agriculture (*diniy dihqanjiliq*) characteristic of the pre-socialist period, which followed the rhythm of the seasons and was based on local knowledge, and top-down scientific agriculture (*pänniy dihqanjiliq*), which had been gaining ground throughout the socialist period. Cultivators readily acknowledged that new cultivation methods might bring quantitative changes – in yields, for example. But many were quick to point out the shadowy sides of the Green Revolution, such as the negative effects of the compulsory use of pesticides and chemical fertilizers on people's health. Health problems, bad crops, and the declining quality of local fruit were also frequently attributed to the nuclear tests performed regularly by the Chinese military in the Taklamakan Desert. For all these reasons, cultivators did their best to ignore or subvert state regulations which promoted scientific agriculture, using peasants' traditional weapons of resistance in the face of state interference (Scott 1985). The concept of 'local' in this discourse became an implicit symbol of resisting and subverting state control. The positive glosses of locality, not in terms of land but in terms of its produce and cultivation methods, were an accurate reflection of the adjustment to altered property relations: as has been mentioned above, in the post-reform period, the exact terms of landownership for most farmers remain unclear and the future uncertain, but the right to some of their agricultural produce renders it suitable for symbolic expressions of attachment to locality.

The House

If there is little evidence for attachment to specific plots of land property, one may ask if living quarters may ever become a primary focus of emotional attachment (Carsten and Hugh-Jones 1995). The reforms introduced in the early 1980s liberalised the market and opened up numerous possibilities for private accumulation. These changes, however, have not diluted the central place of the house as the focus of family life and basic attachment; rather, they have re-enforced the role of the house as a site of economic and ritual production as well as of human reproduction.

The traditional scattered settlement pattern almost everywhere in Xinjiang was dramatically altered in the 1970s by major road building programmes, which turned many, if not all, villages into almost geometrically arranged, orderly settlements. Many houses fell victim to these programmes, while others were transformed from ordinary living quarters to public buildings. During the excessive periods of socialist transformation, some buildings were temporarily turned into communal buildings, such as party offices, kindergartens, and workshops. Some of these were later returned to the original owners and turned back into living quarters; in some cases, socialist slogans painted on the outer walls remain as reminders of the building's history. In contrast to land, houses, courtyards, and the tiny garden plots attached to them remained in private use throughout the Maoist period. It is perhaps thanks to this, that in spite of the changes in both settlement pattern and the function of some individual houses, living quarters never ceased to form the focus of attachment. During collectivisation, houses remained the focus of family life and constituted the only remaining form of private property, which could be legally passed down as inheritance. At times of heightened repression houses also become the site of forbidden activities, such as illegal production for the black market or banned religious rituals (chapters 2 and 8).

The reforms have made peasants de facto landowners, and in spite of the legal uncertainties they pass down their land to the next generation. Details of how this is done and which principles guide farmers still require detailed research. As far as traditional (i.e. pre-socialist) patterns of dividing inherited land are concerned, farmers gave a surprisingly uniform description of the basic principle, which made the primary distinction between the sexes: the general verdict was that daughters did not inherit land, only sons (chapter 4). Farmers were aware that this contradicted the principles of Islamic law, but insisted on the prevalence of this practice in pre-socialist property relations. Clearly, this rather unified description encapsulated ideals rather than actual behaviour, as did similar references concerning the traditional gendered division of labour. Nevertheless, it contrasts strikingly with people's generalised formulation of the ideal way to dividing the house equally between their children. In the division of the parental house, daughters and sons should receive an equal share of the house's contents. If a couple has two daughters and two sons, and the house consists of four rooms, then each child should receive the furniture (or the value of the furniture) of one room. The actual house will become the property of the son who takes care of his aging parents, usually the youngest. Although more ethnographic data is needed to determine how houses are passed down to the next generation, the contrast in normative ideals between house and land is clear. Land inheritance seems to be governed by hierarchical ideas, while the house by principles of equality. There is some uncertainty as to the time of the emergence of the inheritance ideals concerning the house: most people did not date it firmly to the pre-socialist period. One could tentatively suggest that this ideal is a relatively new development, which emerged during the collectivised period, as a partial response to the new ideology of gender equality as well as to the many uncertainties caused by the restrictions of property ownership. If this was so, then it could support the supposition that the house gained in importance during this period because other types of private property became redundant.

Following the re-instatement of de facto land ownership of small parcels, continuous state interference with cultivation, production, and marketing have made the producers dependent on other income sources (chapter 1). In these circumstances, many people who lived close enough to a market started to follow the government's encouragement to engage in sideline production (chapter 3). In this context, it was the authorities that appealed to the emotional pull of 'tradition' and 'localism'. Production for the market was encouraged in crafts traditionally practised in certain localities. On occasion, even financial incentives were made available, for example through offering cheap credits. These policies, aimed at progress and modernisation, also opened up ways which led to a reconfirmation of the house as the primary site of traditional practices. By the mid-1990s, many households in the vicinity of Kashgar had started responding positively to these initiatives, and engaged in production for the market. Many cultivators were participating in crafts such as shoe-making, shoe repair, carpentry, felt-making, intensive animal husbandry, and tailoring. The site of such production was typically the craftsman's house and its courtyard where pre-socialist ideals of the division of labour along the lines of gender and generational ranking were re-activated.

The economic reforms also had further repercussions which re-enforced such trends. Following the restrictive years of the Maoist period, reforms once again encouraged the informal transmission of local knowledge, which often took the form of apprenticeship. Pre-socialist rituals with very strong religious connotations, the passing down of the names of the Islamic patron saints of a particular trade, and Sufi texts teaching codes of conduct (*risalä*) were all parts of this 'modernising package', which ran counter to the government's continued and persistent struggle against feudal customs and religion. These may have been conducive to the re-emergence of traditional forms of socialisation in new garb. Thus the expansion of local markets entails the reclaiming of the house as ritual space. The return to domestic production restored the house as the locus of economic production and of related rituals which had receded during the commune period, but which continue to stand for those 'traditional' and 'feudal' values that continue to attract the government's disapproval.

Elsewhere I have shown that the domestic cult forms the backbone of popular religion among the Uyghur (chapter 8). This focuses on the veneration of the spirits of dead relatives (rather than mythical ancestors of the lineage) for whose appeasement food sacrifice has to be performed to ensure their benevolence and support. In pre-socialist society, the domestic cult was primarily but not exclusively centred on the house: rituals pertaining to the dead were multi-focal and could also be performed outside the house, in the cemetery, and – during major religious holidays – the celebrations could even spill out into the streets. During the decades of socialism, due to repressive policies against feudal superstitions, customs, and religion, communal worship in the mosques and in the Sufi cloisters was seriously curbed. The domestic cult withdrew into the confines of the household and underwent a certain feminisation. This was apparent in the fact that in the mid-1990s, house-centred rituals, such as the *Barat* (chapter 8) and healing rituals, which in pre-socialist times had a mixed audience, were said to rely on a predominantly female audience. Once again, houses became the sites of women's informal religious and social meetings. Participation in meetings with a religious character may have been tolerated tacitly by the authorities but subverted the official stance on practices condemned as feudal superstition.

The close associations of houses, women, and ritual were further promoted by the introduction of compulsory family planning policies in the early 1990s among the minorities of Xinjiang (chapter 4). This had several repercussions on practices surrounding birth. In comparison to pre-socialist conditions, medical care and the availability of health centres had improved in most places, but because women feared that by giving birth in hospital they might risk being sterilised against their will and without their knowledge, they preferred to stay at home and give birth without professional medical help. This in itself confirmed the role of the house as a site of human reproduction underlined by practices surrounding birth. In both peasant and urban households, custom grants a woman the right to give birth to her first two children in her natal house. After delivery the child's umbilical cord is buried in the house's mud floor. This act symbolically confirms the child and the mother's close relationship with her father's house (i.e. with the matrilateral patriline). New ties with her husband's house can be cemented only after subsequent births take place there.

Conclusion

Attachment to and identification with locality may assume many forms, as do the definitions of places to which humans develop emotional attachments, such as the idea of a homeland, traditional settlements, or administrative units. The object of identification may also be a small piece of land one cultivates, or the house or street where one lives and which offers familiarity and a sense of security. One sort of attachment does not necessarily exclude others: even people who have experienced limited or no significant mobility or displacement throughout their lives can name several places as foci of belonging.

Uyghur ethnic identity is nurtured by many sources of localism, and oasis-based attachment is only one of the numerous possibilities. Localism may also be inextricably linked to Islam, which is also expressed through the handing down of extended place names which emphasise the unranked and essentially equal nature of places as abodes of Islamic saints and martyrs and as loci of pilgrimages.

The frequent mentioning of the adjective 'local' in the daily discourse of cultivators in the Kashgar region in the 1990s can be interpreted as a reaction to the abrupt changes and interventions introduced by the government: without these the attribute would be meaningless. Among villagers in the Kashgar region this term has become an encapsulated way of referring to the ideal and romanticised pre-socialist past which is often perceived or projected as unadulterated, more natural, and in many ways therefore preferable. Although we have little evidence concerning pre-modern sentiments of attachment to land and house, locality in modern discourse takes on positive glosses. Locality encapsulates more than the symbolic appropriation of a piece of land: it also claims one's own past and tradition as opposed to the forces coming from outside. Thus, emphasising the virtues of things 'local' has an element of at least discursively devaluing or resisting top-down innovation.

In face of the ongoing penetration of local social space by the state, indigenous strategies sanctioned by tradition are frequently mobilised. Such efforts are increasingly focusing on the house. Its function as an important focus of emotional attachment among farmers has been reinforced by a combination of factors: the introduction of the market economy, which has led to the partial domestication of the local economy; religious repression, which has confined the previously multi-focal domestic cult to the house; and family planning, which reinforces the role of the house as the site of biological reproduction. The increasing privacy and multi-functionality of the house in itself evokes memories of pre-socialist practice and constitutes a reaction to the painful memories of the periods of socialist excesses when the household was deprived of its elementary functions of commensality and social reproduction. Farmers are reclaiming the house and notions of locality in search of some degree of security which, however, remains compatible with ideas of broader identifications on an oasis or regional level. In these discourses, locality becomes a symbolic space where relations of domination are acted out and it can become the locus of strategies of passive resistance to unpopular state policies.

References

Basso, K. 1996. *Wisdom Sits in Places: Landscape and Language among the Western Apache*. Albuquerque: University of New Mexico Press.

Bellér-Hann, I. 2008. *Community Matters in Xinjiang 1880–1949. Towards a Historical Anthropology of the Uyghur*. Leiden: Brill.

Bellew, H. W. 1875. *Kashmir and Kashgar: A Narrative of the Journey of the Embassy to Kashgar in 1873–1877*. London: Tübner & Co.

Carsten, J., and S. Hugh-Jones (eds.). 1995. *About the House: Lévi-Strauss and Beyond*. Cambridge: Cambridge University Press.

Cesàro, C. 2000. Consuming Identities: Food and Resistance among the Uyghur in Contemporary Xinjiang. *Inner Asia* 2 (2): 225–238.

——. 2002. *Consuming Identities: The Culture and Politics of Food among the Uyghur in Contemporary Xinjiang*. Ph.D. dissertation, Canterbury: University of Kent at Canterbury.

Dawut, R. 2001. *Uyghur Mazarliri*. Ürümchi: Shinjang Khälq Näshriyati.

Fairbank, J. K. 1989. *Geschichte des modernen China 1800–1985*. (trans. Walter Meimer). München: Deutscher Taschenbuchverlag.

Feld, S., and K. H. Basso. 1996. Introduction. In S. Feld, and K. H. Basso (eds.), *Senses of Place*, pp. 3–11. Santa Fe: School of American Research Press.

Fletcher, J. F. 1978. Ch'ing Inner Asia c. 1800. In D. Twitchett, and J. K. Fairbank (eds.), *The Cambridge History of China* (Vol. 10), *Late Ch'ing 1800–1911*, Part I, pp. 35–106. Cambridge: Cambridge University Press.

——. 1995. *Studies on Chinese and Islamic Inner Asia*. (ed. Beatrice Forbes). Aldershot: Variorum.

Forbes, A. D. W. 1986. *Warlords and Muslims in Chinese Central Asia: A Political History of Republican Sinkiang 1911–1949*. Cambridge: Cambridge University Press.

Gladney, D. 1990. The Ethnogenesis of the Uighur. *Central Asian Survey* 9 (1): 1–28.

——. 1994. Representing Nationality in China: Refiguring Majority/ Minority Identities. *The Journal of Asian Studies* 53 (1): 92–123.

——. 1998. Internal Colonialism and the Uyghur Nationality: Chinese Nationalism and its Subaltern Subject. *Cahiers d'études sur la Méditerranée orientale et le monde turco-iranien* 25: 47–61.

Grenard, F. 1898. *Le Turkestan et le Tibet: Étude Ethnographique et Sociologique*. (J.-L. Dutreuil De Rhins: *Mission Scientifique dans la Haute Asie 1890–1895*). Paris: Ernest Leroux.

Hamada, M. 1978. Supplement: Islamic Saints and their Mausoleums. *Acta Asiatica* 34: 79–98.

Hann, C. 1999. Peasants in an Era of Freedom: Property and Market Economy in Southern Xinjiang. *Inner Asia* 1 (2): 195–219.

Häbibulla, A. 1993. *Uyghur Etnografiyisi*. Ürümchi: Shinjang Khälq Näshriyati.

Hinton, W. 1990. *The Great Reversal: The Privatization of China 1978–1989*. New York: Monthly Review Press.

Hoppe, Th. 1987. Observations on Uygur Land Use in Turpan County, Xinjiang – A Preliminary Report on Fieldwork in Summer 1985. *Central Asiatic Journal* 31 (3–4): 224–251.

——. 1998. *Die ethnischen Gruppen Xinjiangs: Kulturunterschiede und interethnische Beziehungen*. Hamburg: Institut für Asienkunde.

Jarring, G. 1933. *Studien zu einer osttürkischen Lautlehre*. Leipzig: Harrassowitz.

Kane, P. 1987. *The Second Billion: Population and Family Planning in China*. Harmondsworth: Penguin.

Katanov, N. T., and K. H. Menges. 1933, 1976. *Volkskundliche Texte aus Ost-Türkistan*. Proceedings of the Prussian Academy of Sciences, Section of Philology and History, 1933. Leipzig: Zentralantiquariat of the German Democratic Republic.

Kelliher, D. 1992. *Peasant Power in China: The Era of Rural Reform, 1979–1989*. New Haven: Yale University Press.

Kim, H.-D. 2004. *Holy War in China: The Muslim Rebellion and State in Chinese Central Asia 1864–1877*. Stanford: Stanford University Press.

von Le Coq, A. 1911. *Sprichwörter und Lieder aus der Gegend von Turfan*. (Baessler-Archiv Beiheft 1–8, 1910–17). Leipzig and Berlin: Teubner.

——. 1928. *Von Land und Leuten in Ostturkistan. Berichte und Abenteuer der 4. Deutschen Turfanexpedition*. Leipzig: Verlag der J. C. Hinrichs'schen Buchhandlung.

Madsen, R. 1991. The Countryside under Communism. In R. Macfarquhar, and J. Fairbank (eds.), *The Cambridge History of China* (Vol. 15). *The People's Republic*, Part 2: *Revolutions within the Chinese Revolution 1966–1982*, pp. 619–681. Cambridge: Cambridge University Press.

Mcmillen, D. H. 1979. *Chinese Communist Power and Policy in Xinjiang, 1949–1977*. Boulder: Westview.

Millward, J. A. 1998. *Beyond the Pass: Economy, Ethnicity, and Empire in Qing Central Asia, 1759–1864*. Stanford: Stanford University Press.

——., and P. C. Perdue. 2004. Political and Cultural History of the Xinjiang Region through the Late Nineteenth Century. In S. F. Starr (ed.),

Xinjiang: China's Muslim Borderland, pp. 27–62. Armonk: M.E. Sharpe.

——., and Nabijan Tursun. 2004. Political History and Strategies of Control, 1884–1978. In S. F. Starr (ed.), *Xinjiang: China's Muslim Borderland*, pp. 63–98. Armonk: M. E. Sharpe.

Nolan, P. 1988. *The Political Economy of Collective Farms: An Analysis of China's Post-Mao Rural Reforms*. Oxford: Polity Press.

Rudelson, J. 1997. *Oasis Identities: Uyghur Nationalism along China's Silk Road*. New York: Columbia University Press.

Scott, J. C. 1985. *Weapons of the Weak: Everyday Forms of Peasant Resistance*. New Haven: Yale University Press.

Seitz, K. 2002. *China. Eine Weltmacht kehrt zurück*. Berlin: Berliner Taschenbuch Verlags Gmbh.

Shaw, R. B. 1984 [1871]. *Visits to High Tartary, Yarkand and Kashgar*. Hong Kong: Oxford University Press.

Smith, J. N. 1999. *Changing Uyghur Identities in Xinjiang in the 1990s*. Ph.D. dissertation. Leeds: University of Leeds.

——. 2000. Four Generations of Uyghurs: The Shift towards Ethno-Political Ideologies among Xinjiang's Youth. *Inner Asia* 2 (2): 195–224.

Soucek, S. 2000. *A History of Inner Asia*. Cambridge: Cambridge University Press.

Starr, F. S. (ed.). 2004. *Xinjiang: China's Muslim Borderland*. Armonk, London: M. E. Sharpe.

Toops, S. W. 2004. The Demography of Xinjiang. In S. F. Starr (ed.), *Xinjiang: China's Muslim Borderland*, pp. 241–275. Armonk: M.E. Sharpe.

Valikhanov, Ch. V. 1961. *Sobranie Sochinenii, Vol. I*. Alma-Ata: Akademii Nauk Kazakhskom SSR.

Wei-Yin T. 2002. *Junggo Musulmanlirining Häj Pa'aliyätliri*. Ürümchi: Shinjang Khälq Näshriyati.

Whyte, T. 2000. Domination, Resistance, and Accommodation in China's One-Child Campaign. In E. J. Perry, and M. Selden (eds.), *Chinese Society: Change, Conflict and Resistance*, pp. 102–118. London: Routledge.

Zarcone, Th. 2001. Le Culte des Saints au Xinjiang de 1949 á Nos Jours. *Journal of the History of Sufism* 3: 133–172.

Chapter 7
Temperamental Neighbours: Uyghur-Han Relations in Xinjiang[1]

The geographical focus of this chapter is the north-western province of the People's Republic of China (PRC) nowadays known as Xinjiang, where, behind a façade of socialist multiculturalism, Han Chinese effectively still rule over non-Han minorities. The region which incorporates a long stretch of the ancient Silk Roads has had a long history of Chinese presence, going back to the times of the Han dynasty. It has been officially part of China since 1884, although the effective incorporation of the area into the Qing Empire dates back to the second half of the eighteenth century. The largest administrative unit of the PRC, the Xinjiang Uyghur Autonomous Region (XUAR) is home to 13 officially recognised ethnic groups, 6 of whom are Muslim and speak Turkic languages.[2] The largest of these groups, the Uyghurs, have been the titular majority of the region since the foundation of the XUAR in 1955. There has been ethnic tension in the province throughout this period, and preceding eras are also often perceived in terms of ethnic conflict and violence.

This chapter is largely based on a stay of two months in the oasis town of Kucha in Southern Xinjiang in 1995.[3] Kucha is the administrative centre of a county (*nahiyä*) of 400,000 people, 92 per cent of whom are Uyghur. The rural townships (*yeza*) it governs have an almost exclusively Uyghur settled agricultural population, but the town, with a population of 50,000, has a nearly 40 per cent Han Chinese presence, a percentage which is rapidly increasing. Few of the Han speak even basic Uyghur, while few Uyghur

---

[1] Published in G. Schlee (ed.), *Imagined Difference: Hatred and the Construction of Identity*, pp. 57–81. Münster: LIT Verlag, 2002.
[2] This figure is based on Dawamat (1993: 78). For data on the officially recognised minorities in China see Gladney (1994b: 172–73).
[3] In the original article I used the pseudonym Ürükzar for the oasis of Kucha; such anonymity is no longer necessary.

have more than a rudimentary knowledge of Chinese.[4] The choice of this particular town for research was not mine. It was suggested by Han Chinese partners in Ürümchi who thought that the oasis I had originally suggested was not a feasible choice: it was too poor, and it had a reputation for being a stronghold of Islamic mysticism always closely associated with anti-Han sentiments.[5] Kucha, on the other hand, had appeared prosperous and stable, hence the suggestion that it would be a suitable fieldsite.[6] In fact this oasis too can look back on a history chequered with protests and uprisings, but the approval of the authorities for an extended stay led me to expect stability, equilibrium, and peaceful co-existence rather than conflict, hatred, and violence.[7]

---

[4] The perspective of this chapter is one-sided: it focuses on interethnic relations from the point of view of Uyghur identity. My data come primarily from direct interactions with Uyghur people in their mother tongue. My command of Uyghur and lack of Chinese occasionally led to suspicious reactions from Han residents and prevented me from studying Han perceptions of the Uyghur and indeed their self-perceptions.

[5] Joanne Smith and I carried out fieldwork in Xinjiang at the same time independently from each other, and wrote our respective pieces on the subject of ethnic relations unaware of each other's work. I consider similarities between our approaches as mutual confirmation of our evaluation of the ethnic situation in Xinjiang, and regard her article (2002) as complementary to this chapter, as her ethnographic material comes mostly from Ürümchi.

[6] In spite of its ancient history and prominence throughout the later Islamic centuries as a religious and trading centre, Kucha has received little attention in works of modern political history (unlike Kashgar, Ghulja, and Ürümchi). Unlike some of the other oasis towns of the region, it has little prominence in foreign travel writing, except for descriptions of its ancient pre-Islamic sites. In contrast to other locations, western missionary presence in the twentieth century has also been negligible here. Since the town was opened to foreign visitors only in the early 1990s, in 1995 individual tourists were still a novelty. As the town boasts no institution of higher education, foreign missionaries – who elsewhere register as students or work as English teachers – had not established themselves by 1995.

[7] For an introduction to the Uyghur and Chinese in Xinjiang see Hoppe (1998: 56–170, 308–40).

Plate 8. Kucha in 1996 (Photo: Chris Hann).

The emergence of the Uyghur as a modern ethnic group is essentially a twentieth century phenomenon, comparable to developments among the Uzbek and other Turkic groups in the former Soviet Union. After 1949 China followed the Soviet model in many respects, including collectivisation and the economic exploitation of its peripheral regions. Policies towards national minorities comprised an attempt to control rather than to integrate them (Bergère 1979; Gladney 1991: 66). Justin Rudelson, who has studied the dynamics of ethnic consciousness among Uyghur intellectuals (1997), has shown how competing self-definitions of intellectuals of different oasis backgrounds combine with class differentiations to work against the emergence of a united Uyghur ethnic group. Through a detailed study of the Chinese Muslims, Dru Gladney has demonstrated how the intricate, dynamic interplay between self-perception and state interference shapes ethnic identity in the PRC (1991). He has addressed both general aspects of ethnicity within the PRC (1991, 1994b) and the case of the Uyghur of Xinjiang in particular, including their ethnogenesis and the role adopted by the state in the process (1990; 1991; 1994a). He has also discussed ethnic identities in a transnational perspective and, developing a model of 're-lational alterity', has argued that essentialised attempts at final definitions of the meanings of identities (such as a Uyghur, Muslim, Turk, dweller in a particular oasis, or citizen of the PRC) should give way to an examination of the circumstances which temporarily foreground some identities and background others (Gladney 1996).

In contrast to Gladney's focus, in this chapter I shall examine lower levels of identity in a town that qualifies as one of the more remote ones of the Silk Roads. I shall consider the different strategies employed by the Uyghur of Xinjiang to reproduce and reinforce ethnic boundaries vis-à-vis the Han, efforts which are also instrumental in promoting the 'amorphous, invented' identity of the latter, both nationally and within Xinjiang (Grobe-Hagel 1991: 14; Gladney 1994a: 112).

It is not surprising that while clear-cut rules are frequently articulated, ethnic boundaries are sometimes crossed. But it may appear paradoxical that, in spite of the dominance of the Han in what can be characterised as a ranked hierarchical relationship between the two groups (Horowitz 1985: 22), in some aspects of daily interaction the rules are sometimes dictated by the lower-ranking group, the Uyghur.[8] Such interaction may take a variety of forms. The markers of difference most often articulated are language and religion, but a host of other distinguishing features augment the repertoire of boundary markers to emphasise real or imagined differences. I am especially interested in how various traits that are evoked as ethnic boundary markers serve also as intra-group markers of difference. Ideas concerning the body, diet, temperament, and other more visible symbols, some of which are easily overlooked or dismissed as trivial, such as women's fashion sense, may all become subtle expressions of ethnic identity while remaining markers of intra-group difference between the generations, the sexes, the sophisticated city dweller and the villager, or other, hierarchically ordered groups within Uyghur society. They become markers of ethnicity only in the close physical or symbolic presence of another group. Hence an oasis town in which Uyghur and Han co-exist and have to interact regularly is a good location for observing how such symbols double up and operate as markers of ethnicity.

Some of these symbols and ideas which in the context of the oasis town may become ethnic boundary markers also develop this second meaning within villages where the population is almost exclusively Uyghur. Here the presence of the other group may be restricted to a few Han government officials working in the township leadership, or a handful of recent settlers, but the force of this presence is still considerable. Even in the now increasingly rare 'pure' Uyghur villages, Han hegemony over what is perceived as Uyghur land has been imprinted on people's minds by past experience. This imprint is constantly renewed in the representations of the media, through continuous rumours of ethnic violence and anti-Han protests

---

[8] A similar observation was made by Gladney concerning asymmetrical hospitality patterns between Han and Chinese Muslims (1991: 120–22).

throughout the province, and through the direct impact of policies associated with the Han, such as birth control or religious policies. In these conditions, no aspect of culture is innocent of ethnic implications: a subtle change in female fashion may be an expression of a desire to mark social distance between peasants and cadres, but such a declaration remains within certain parameters which make it plain that the wearer is Uyghur rather than Han. Thus various expressions of intra-group identities may simultaneously acquire meanings as markers of religious, regional, or ethnic belonging. The multiplicity of meanings may not be obvious to all observers: a particular dress style may reveal to a Han only that the wearer is a Uyghur, but Uyghur women may recognise the cut and know that the material of the dress is of the most expensive sort which only cadres or the wives of rich merchants can afford. External identity markers which double as internal shapers of identity are neither uniform nor unchangeable. Uyghurs often emphasise the importance of external aspects in confirming and perpetuating their group identity, and may insist on their uniformity and continuity over long periods of time. However, they may also acknowledge, albeit implicitly, that less visible components of identity, such as a person's temperament (*mijäz*), are susceptible not only to personal variation within the group but also to social construction and may therefore change in the course of further social interaction.

Time and Space

One of the most fundamental dichotomies between the two major ethnic groups in Kucha (and the rest of Xinjiang) lies in the keeping of time. The Han observe the official time known throughout the PRC as Beijing time. This is the time displayed on clocks in public places, including all government offices. Beijing time determines bus and flight departures and arrivals. However, the Uyghur live by local Xinjiang time which is two hours behind Beijing time. If a foreign visitor fails to identify a person's ethnic affiliation from physical features and other attributes, a glance at the person's watch can usually provide a decisive clue.

Yet it would be a mistake to imagine that Han and Uyghur maintain rigid temporal apartheid. In reality, many accommodations are reached. Office workers who in eastern China would begin work at eight o'clock in the morning turn up for work at ten o'clock in Kucha: the rhythm of their day is basically in harmony with that of the sun and of the Uyghur. Uyghurs who work alongside Han may have to use Beijing time for some formal purposes. Such people may as a matter of course add the phrase 'Xinjiang time' or 'Beijing time' to every time specification they have to make, but in most social interaction it will be obvious from the context which is being used.

Like many other Central Asian urban settlements, Kucha gives a first impression of sharp spatial segregation. The new colonial town sharply contrasts with the old Muslim town situated by the river. This segregation has antecedents which pre-date socialism. In a historical study of Qing policies in Xinjiang, James Millward pointed out that the cautious policies of the Qing to segregate the Han from the local Muslim population – aimed at preventing conflict and violence – were seldom rigidly imposed. Segregated communities developed only following the first wave of Muslim rebellions in the early nineteenth century. In Kucha, the spatial segregation is well documented from the late nineteenth century, by which time there existed separate Chinese and Muslim garrisons (Millward 1998: 140). Today the visible sense of apartheid is confirmed by the local Uyghur guide, who tells western visitors that the Old Town is 'pure' Uyghur, while the New Town is overwhelmingly Han. Such separation of new and old towns is a common feature of cities in Xinjiang. Although today there is no specific boundary marker between the two, Uyghur cart-drivers point to a stretch of major road which they regard as the border. The physical appearance of the two parts presents striking differences: the Old Town with its adobe houses has a Middle Eastern atmosphere that contrasts sharply with the wide, geometrically designed asphalt roads and modern blocks of the New Town. All the major government buildings, as well as the main post office, central bus and taxi stations, court, prison, Communist Party and police headquarters, western style hospital, some small factories, the main library, banks, and larger shops are located in the New Town. So too are the major sites of entertainment – the two dance halls and the theatre. The Old Town has most of the characteristics of a Muslim city, inward-looking houses protected with walls from curious passers-by, the Friday mosque, a central square around which the weekly Friday bazaar is held, and a permanent covered bazaar. Most of the roads in this section are still dirt roads where carts pulled by donkeys, mules, or horses compete chaotically with pedestrians, buses, and bicycles.[9] Street peddlers and beggars are numerous. The Old Town boasts a number of schools, a local history museum, a small library, and some banks. It also has a large hospital but this is a 'minority national hospital' where traditional Uyghur medicine is practised rather than biomedicine. Cheap private hotels catering for Muslim traders still bear more resemblance to old style caravansarais than to modern hotels. In the heart of the Old Town, where the major bridge runs into the central square,

---

[9] On the juxtaposition of the traditional old town and the colonial town see Brown (1984) and Eickelman (1981: 273–77). On the Muslim city, see Eickelman (1981: 266–73).

unemployed unskilled labourers and potential employers meet at dawn every day on what is known as the 'day labourers' market' (*medikar baziri*).

But the sense of spatial apartheid is also deceptive. Although the modern buildings and asphalt streets of the New Town present a façade of Han rule, behind them we find the landmarks of Muslim quarters. These neighbourhoods in the New Town may remain undetected by the short-term visitor. They are tight-knit communities with most of the attributes of the Muslim quarters of the Old Town. Their small mosques are invisible to the passers-by on the main streets. The call to prayer is recited without a loudspeaker, and so is unheard outside the immediate neighbourhood. This is a reminder of the limits within which Islam is tolerated: as much as possible, it must remain invisible and muted to the outside world.[10] In contrast, loudspeakers remain in use along the major roads of the New Town, transmitting Chinese language news, music and policy, and other public announcements. Although the central mosque, a cultural monument, and another important Friday mosque are both located in the Old Town, the town's most important shrine is only five minutes' walk from the inter-section of the main asphalt roads of the New Town. In the Old Town there is a Chinese school, surrounded by Muslim neighbourhoods.

Thus the spatial organisation of the town exhibits both segregation and subtle patterns of intermingling. While whole neighbourhoods appear at first sight to be ethnically homogenous communities, and are sometimes presented as such by local residents, behind the apparent spatial segregation lies a more complex reality of shared spheres and interaction. Han in government employment occupy modern blocks in the New Town, but these work units are shared with Uyghur employees and their families. Shared public spaces, particularly in the marketplace and street stalls, are frequently the scenes of open conflict. When the arguing parties involve a Han and a Uyghur, differences in opinion over faulty merchandise, high prices, mis-taken calculations, or wrong change will invariably be expressed in ethnic terms. Such scenes may quickly become a source of violence as more people join in on both sides.

Ethnic boundaries are occasionally straddled in leisure activities. In theory, the clienteles of the two dance halls, situated along the same main road in the New Town, are separated along ethnic lines. The Uyghur dance hall is indeed frequented by Uyghur only, but the Chinese dance hall has a mixed group of customers. Educated young Uyghur sometimes take their female partners there because it is said to be a clean, safe, and civilised place in contrast to the Uyghur dance hall, which is known for heavy drinking,

---

[10] On the religious policies of the Chinese state see Dillon (1995: 17–26) and Grobe-Hagel (1991: 31–67).

brawls, and prostitution. In this context the Han are clearly marked as the bearers of civilisation.[11] Although Han men are said to be keen on establishing contact with Uyghur women, they avoid the Uyghur dance hall since it is perceived as highly dangerous for them, in part due to excessive alcohol consumption but also because their presence would imply a sexual interest in Uyghur women likely to provoke extreme reactions from Uyghur men. Educated Uyghur may also criticise the culture of the dance hall, but they may suggest that its abuses are the fault of the Han, who have made cheap alcohol widely available. This is consistent with the more general tendency to attribute social evils to Han influence (e.g. various forms of gambling).

Occupation and Education

Occupational segregation in Kucha mirrors both the basic ethnic dichotomy and the fuzziness of boundaries in the town. Uyghur catering is primarily based on the dietary observances of the Muslims, who meticulously avoid eating pork, a prime ingredient in Han cuisine. Other services too, such as tailoring, hairdressing, certain branches of trading and local education, reflect duality: Uyghur traders attract Uyghur customers, Han cater for Han customers.[12] The ethnic division of labour has a strong symbolic colouring: the drivers of carts drawn by draught animals – which primarily carry associations with the Old Town, traditionalism, and backwardness – are exclusively Uyghur, while rickshaws in the New Town are operated exclusively by Han men. Blacksmiths, goldsmiths, and other indigenous craft workers are all Uyghur, while street peddlers selling ice cream and yoghurt tend to be Han or Chinese Muslims.

---

[11] Civilised or cultured (*mädäniy*) behaviour appear as key concepts in contemporary Uyghur language journals and magazines, which criticise the backwardness of some Uyghur practices. Instead of explicitly holding up the Han as a positive model to emulate, 'bad' habits are condemned as recent deviations from the old national norms of Uyghur culture (Hüsäyin 1995a, 1995b, 1995c; Tahir 1995; Tokhti 1995).

[12] The Chinese Muslims in Kucha, like elsewhere in Xinjiang, occupy a somewhat ambiguous position between the two groups. Their groceries, hairdressing salons, and restaurants may be frequented by members of both groups. On the complex interplay between food and ethnicity, see Cesàro (2000).

Plate 9. Animal market in the dry river-bed, Kucha, Southern Xinjiang (Photo: Chris Hann).

However, the divisions are far from complete. For example, the permanent marketplace in the New Town is divided into a Uyghur and a Chinese section; each section sells clothing, shoes, vegetables, and meat, and customers tend to visit one section or the other according to ethnic affiliation. But some customers straddle this line, especially in the clothes market. Typical Uyghur products such as flat bread or dried apricots are normally sold by Uyghur, but their customers may include Han who are keen consumers of most Uyghur delicacies. Employment in areas such as construction work may also be multi-ethnic, though in practice specific gangs of labourers may remain ethnically homogenous. A higher degree of mixing can be observed in government offices because of regulations which require the presence of a certain percentage of minority cadres. The duties as well as the boredom of office work are shared by members of the two groups, and this common experience may foster a certain degree of com-radeship, usually along gender lines. Han and Uyghur male colleagues occasionally may be seen drinking together at street stalls. This apparent comradeship can easily give way to ethnic stereotyping and can become a source of conflict. On one such occasion that I witnessed, two Han members of the party fell off their chairs and lay on the pavement unconscious for a few minutes. After the fall of the third and last Han, one Uyghur – himself on the verge of collapsing – said repeatedly: 'look at the Han! They do not

even know how to drink properly! We Uyghur manage better than them!'.
This was a relatively rare scene in which members of the two groups
displayed a high degree of physical proximity, sharing the same table in the
street and even drinking from the same glass. Yet it is precisely this kind of
contact which has a high potential for conflict. In other examples of friendly
interethnic socialisation, such as the participation of Han guests at a Uyghur
wedding, interaction remains on a more formal level and a relatively high
degree of physical distance is consciously maintained.[13]

Occupational segregation and mixing are both encouraged by the
state. On the one hand, certain types of jobs are filled exclusively by Han.
On the other hand, by law government offices must employ a certain
percentage of minorities (the exact figure varies at different levels of
administration). However, the appointment of a Uyghur to a relatively senior
position may still in practice prove to be nominal, if real power is exercised
by a Han deputy.[14] This appeared to be the situation with the county
leadership, where the chief party boss was a Uyghur but power was clearly
concentrated in the hands of his Han deputy who had a superior education.
This was also the case with the leadership of the county branch of the All-
China Women's Federation, in practice under the tight control of the
Communist Party. All township representatives of this organisation were
Uyghur, and the county-level leadership too was headed by a Uyghur lady.
She had been an ordinary village woman before becoming a cadre and
receiving training at short party courses. Literate in her mother tongue and
highly intelligent, she had no knowledge of the Chinese language, and
whenever she spoke at a conference she looked constantly for the approval
of her Han deputy. County-level government organisations all employ
official interpreters whose job is to translate between Uyghur and Chinese,
but in this case there was no need for such mediation. Unusually, the Han
deputy, born and brought up in Kucha, spoke fluent Uyghur and so the
communication around the conference table was entirely in that language.
When my Han research partners met her on a brief visit to me, they were
convinced that she must be a Chinese Muslim rather than a Han. Their
assumption rested on the widely known phenomenon that among Chinese
Muslims in Xinjiang it is quite common to be bilingual in Chinese and
Uyghur, while bilinguilism is rare among Han.[15]

---

[13] A further example of ethnically mixed socialisation is birthday parties, a recent fashion
among urban youth.

[14] Gladney confirms that this tends to be the general pattern in minority areas all over China
(Gladney 1994b: 185).

[15] The bilinguilism of the Chinese Muslims is not met with universal approval among the
Uyghur. Chinese Muslims are surrounded by Uyghur suspicion and mistrust. This has much

Other leading Uyghur cadres in the leadership of Kucha are generally well-educated and have enough knowledge of spoken Chinese to be promoted to the highest levels of government organs in the provincial capital. Members of ethnic minorities receive favourable treatment at the university entrance examination, one of the many privileges granted to urban residents of state-recognised minority groups which renders minority status desirable (Gladney 1991: 219–20). Nevertheless, few young people from a town such as Kucha can ever hope to gain admittance to higher education establishments. Students who have a history of exclusively Uyghur primary and secondary education are not equipped with sufficient knowledge of Chinese to succeed in what is basically a Chinese higher education programme. Many secondary school graduates from minority schools in Kucha were facing unemployment in 1995. Some opted for the local equivalent of the Open University, which they could pursue through correspondence courses, but others were bitter and complained of pro-Han discrimination in certain prestigious public sector jobs, such as banks and the army.[16]

The Uyghur resent the well-known fact that the developing oil industry of the province tends to employ only Han brought in from overpopulated areas elsewhere in China. Not only are there no skilled Uyghur in higher level jobs, but even unskilled jobs are offered to Han migrant labourers, some of whom occasionally visited Kucha to attend the dance halls and relax. Such apartheid in certain employment sectors is particularly resented by the Uyghur, and is among the most frequently mentioned reasons for hostile feelings against the Han.

For most office jobs, a good command of at least spoken Chinese is usually a precondition. It is Chinese education which paves the way to such jobs, and Justin Rudelson's analysis of the dilemma faced by Uyghur intellectuals concerning the education of their children is also valid for urban parents in virtually all occupations (1997: 115). Uyghur housewives, cleaning ladies, traders, and primary school teachers with young children may all consider the possibility of sending their children to the Chinese schools rather than to the Uyghur minority schools. The majority of Uyghur children attend the latter but some Uyghur families do choose to educate

---

to do with memories of bloody conflicts between the two groups. For centuries, the Chinese Muslims have occupied an anomalous position between the Uyghur and the Han, frequently changing alliances at times of conflict. As one Uyghur summed it up: 'The Chinese Muslims are worse than the Han. They share their language with the Han and religion with us. They belong to neither group'.

[16] By 1997 unemployment of young Uyghur secondary school graduates in the town became a source of general concern and the local government made an effort to create employment opportunities for them in two libraries, at hotel receptions, and in other white collar jobs.

some of their children in Han schools to give them better career opportunities. Such minority children educated in Uyghur schools (Ch. *minkaohan*) although fluent in Uyghur, speak excellent Chinese and tend to consume more of the products of Han culture. Their ability to read and write Uyghur is limited. They belong to a group of their own, sarcastically referred to in Uyghur as the fourteenth nationality of Xinjiang (*on tötinji millät*). They are singled out by their Uyghur peers on the basis of their different education and are treated as Uyghur with 'Han temperament' (*mijäzi khänzu*). In Uyghurs' perceptions, developing this ambiguous attribute is also possible through informal socialisation. It is for this reason that some local Uyghur officials sharing residential quarters with their Han colleagues discourage their children from playing with their Han peers. They believe that this would result in Uyghur children becoming Sinicised in temperament. Such attitudes lead to a conscious reproduction of social distance between families of different ethnicity living in the closest proximity.

The emergence of this group within the younger generation has provoked conflicting sentiments among the Uyghur themselves. Resentment stems from their having become a little less than 'real' or 'true' Uyghur. They are seen as only half (*chala*) Uyghur, and as such they constitute a social anomaly.[17] But their good command of Chinese and their familiarity with the ways of the dominant group gives them enviable resources. Their education may become their most significant asset among the peer group already at an early age which explains why Chinese-educated Uyghur do not become socially isolated. They are considered to be desirable marriage partners for Uyghurs educated in minority schools. In Kucha, as in the provincial capital, young Uyghur men educated in Uyghur schools (*minkaomin*) are said to be particularly keen to marry Chinese-educated Uyghur women, clearly seeing such an alliance as 'marrying up'. The rationalisation for such a preference is that owing to their Chinese ways, these girls are more modern, easy-going, straightforward, and 'less complicated' than Uyghur girls educated in minority schools. However, this also means that they are more likely to ignore Uyghur traditions. There is general consensus that, due to different socialisation patterns, there are frequent arguments between *minkaohan-minkaomin* partners and that many such marriages are likely to end in divorce. Arguments in such mixed

---

[17] The 'half Uyghur' who have been tamed is not a new phenomenon in Xinjiang. Using the local elite for governing multi-ethnic Xinjiang is an old device inherited from imperial China, as is well documented in Fernand Grenard's description at the end of the nineteenth century when the term *chala* was already in use to describe indigenous people with a Chinese education (Grenard 1898: 273–74). For modem Chinese usage, see Rudelson (1997: 127).

marriages are potentially explosive and may turn particularly bitter when the partner with a Uyghur education accuses the other with Chinese schooling of having become Han. One of the explanations for this is that traditional gender relations cannot countenance the wife enjoying much better career prospects than her husband. An ideal marriage partner for such a girl would, to the contrary, be a Chinese-educated Uyghur husband. That such girls nevertheless marry men with Uyghur educations can be explained by their own (or their families') wish to reinforce the ties to their own people that have been seriously loosened. The children of such marriages are often sent to Chinese schools, although the parents may try to counterbalance this by sending them to an after-school club to learn traditional Uyghur dance or music. In Kucha, such courses for schoolchildren were typically available during the summer holidays over a three-week period. The Uyghur dance course, attended exclusively by girls, was hugely popular among Uyghur families, regardless of educational background.[18]

Additional social difficulties encountered through such a marriage are exemplified by the following case. A young Uyghur housewife who had finished a Chinese secondary school looked down upon her primary school teacher husband, a graduate of a minority school. The husband humbly accepted and often joked about his inferiority. Although she seemed to be habitually bad-tempered with her neighbours, the wife could always be relied on to help Uyghur school children with their Chinese homework (Chinese language is compulsory in all minority schools), and therefore people tried to humour her, and good relations were maintained in spite of her arrogance.

The anomalous position of urban Chinese-educated Uyghur is shared by many Uyghur government officials and township and party leaders, regardless of their educational background. They have close working relationships with Han officials, and the policies they execute are often met with disapproval by local residents. Any suspicion of pro-Han sympathies may also provoke angry reactions against Muslim religious leaders.[19] When anger is turned directly against other Uyghur, the ensuing incidents are classified by the authorities as criminal cases rather than ethnic conflict. The

---

[18] The fact that many young girls hope to pursue careers as folk dancers is perhaps another indication that the stereotype promoted by the Chinese authorities of the colourful exotic minorities who dance and sing is not a pure Chinese invention: the Uyghur themselves regard this as an important expression of their identity and a possible career path.

[19] In the late spring of 1996, the *damolla* (main religious leader) of Kashgar was the victim of an assassination attempt. Rumours were also circulating in 1996 of the assassination of a village imam near Kucha.

Uyghur, however, invariably perceive such situations in terms of ethnic antagonism.

Many urban Uyghur do have a basic knowledge of spoken Chinese and a more limited knowledge of its written form. Han residents, though perceived as monolingual Mandarin speakers, may understand more of everyday Uyghur conversation than they like to admit, but many do remain completely ignorant. Linguistically, it would seem that many urban Uyghur have penetrated the Chinese arena more in line with the wishes of the authorities: the acquisition of the language of the dominant group is an important step towards acculturation. However, Uyghurs may rationalise this imbalance in the linguistic situation in terms of favourable self-stereotyping. They interpret it as proof of the Uyghurs' higher intelligence. As one Uyghur street peddler with only a limited knowledge of Chinese summed it up: 'we Uyghur all know some Chinese, look at the Han, they have been living among us for a long time and are still incapable of learning our language – surely a sign of their stupidity!' My Uyghur interview partners in Kucha were sure that the linguistic situation in some other oases was different. Some people were convinced that in Kashgar more Han could speak Uyghur, but even this assumption was explained in unfavourable terms for the Han: there the Han were said to be under more pressure to learn Uyghur for demographic reasons, and to do it out of fear and necessity. Lack of knowledge of the majority language in Kashgar, a traditional stronghold of Uyghur culture as well as anti-Han sentiments, could result in difficulties with shopkeepers, a potential source of violent interethnic conflict. In Kucha, the Uyghur complain of a reverse situation. They say that they are often ignored by Han shopkeepers if they do not address them in Chinese.

Just as the Uyghur must be seen as a socially and regionally heterogeneous group whose ethnic identity has been shaped by a subtle interplay of official policies and self-perception (Gladney 1990), it would be equally mistaken to consider the Han living in Xinjiang as a homogenous group with a static group identity. In fact, they have arrived in Xinjiang at different times and in very different circumstances (Lattimore 1950: 140; Dillon 1995: 31). They too are socially divided. Recent economic trends have further encouraged Chinese labour migration into Xinjiang. Many of these newcomers constitute part of the enormous floating population of China, on the move in order to find employment and escape poverty, residence registration, and thereby family planning restrictions.[20] While officially registered Han government employees, traders, and workers tend to be concentrated in the New Town, unregistered migrant Han families

---

[20] On the increase of the floating population brought about by the economic reforms, see Kane (1995: 199) and Hoppe (1998: 308).

from the most overpopulated provinces of the interior of China often set up temporary accommodation in the Muslim quarters of the Old Town. These men do construction work and other temporary jobs. Their very presence here is a form of rebellion against the state; they often live in extreme poverty with numerous children in makeshift accommodation and take on work the Uyghur would not be happy to perform. In these circumstances the Uyghur do not feel threatened by them, and make no attempt to increase social distance. Han migrant families are accepted as temporary residents in the Muslim neighbourhoods and interethnic relations seem to be peaceful. Their children mix freely with local Uyghur children on the streets, and Uyghur parents do not worry that such contacts might result in a 'contaminated' Sinicised temperament in their children. On the contrary, Uyghur adults may comment favourably on the ability of the migrants' children to pick up Uyghur very quickly.

Dress Code and Fashion

Stereotypes continue to be formulated on the basis of more formalised hierarchical power relations between the Uyghur and their Han overlords. Since some mixing within the urban context is inevitable, physical distance may prove ineffective as a boundary marker and symbols connected to the body may take on particular relevance. Both Uyghur and Han Chinese are usually confident in being able to distinguish a Uyghur from a Han. However, it is not just bodily features which facilitate distinction: the observer has a whole set of other clues simultaneously available (cf. Horowitz 1985: 46–47). These include preferences concerning styles of body decoration and clothing which are instrumental in drawing the boundary of the self. In both men's and women's worlds, the Uyghur have symbols which distinguish them from their Han neighbours. Skin colour is viewed as a continuous scale with white/European at one extreme and yellow/Asiatic at the other. Uyghur children at school are taught that, like the Han, they are 'yellow'. Following this classification, many Uyghur describe themselves as yellow-skinned and therefore members of the 'Asiatic race' (as they put it), but they also notice the numerous deviations from the constructed stereotype. They say about other Uyghur with a paler countenance that they 'look as if they could not possibly be Uyghur', which is meant as a positive assessment. That the ideal skin colour for the Uyghur is the one which contrasts most sharply with the colour associated with the Han is best illustrated by the trouble that some young Uyghur townswomen take in applying white powder thickly to their faces. This fashion is meticulously observed by Uyghur brides at the wedding ceremony.

Dress code also provides a set of clues for both stating and recognising ethnic affiliation. Uyghur standard male attire nowadays is more 'modern' and therefore close to the Chinese pattern, in both villages and towns. Yet they are quick to point out that Han office workers wear differently cut suits. The most important external marker of ethnic difference between Han and Uyghur men is the headgear. Uyghur men usually cover their heads, either with a traditional skullcap (*doppa*), a cap (*shäpkä*), or a straw hat (*shiläpä*) decorated with a ribbon with the inscription 'World Cup', which has become fashionable among cadres since 1994. A few village men still wear their *tumaq* (fur cap), even in the summer. In relation to the Han, these various items of headgear are important symbols of ethnic affiliation, but the same items also serve to separate generations of Uyghur men, and some versions of the skullcap are indicative of regional belonging. Changing fashions in skullcap also appear to mark class membership among Uyghur men. In the 1950s poorer peasants adopted the skullcap previously exclusively worn by rich peasants, while the style worn by government cadres in the 1980s is being appropriated and imitated by peasants in the 1990s. Uyghur male headgear is thus loaded with meaning. Although the skullcap is more or less obligatory in the mosque and a white turban complemented with a white belt over black clothes constitutes Uyghur male funerary costume, these markers of religious affiliation do not blur the difference between the co-religionist Uyghur and the Hui or Chinese Muslims: the many varieties of skullcaps worn by Uyghur men are all easily distinguishable from the Hui skullcap.[21]

As Uyghur men themselves point out, in addition to headgear a number of other obvious clues facilitate ethnic recognition. Many Uyghur men over the age of 40 sport a beard, which contrasts them both with the Han, who have less facial hair, and also with younger Uyghur men. Young Uyghur males in town tend to grow their hair longer and to wear a cap.

Fashion and body decoration are also prominent in women's self-presentation. Many urban women have unpleasant memories of the days of the Cultural Revolution, when they had to wear the unfeminine Maoist uniforms. Nowadays Uyghur women use many items which the Han do not (headscarf, henna on nails, earrings with native designs, and further items of golden jewellery). Among the Han, items of clothing are highly varied and may reflect differences in seniority, occupation, and social class. Fashion-conscious, young Han women tend to dress in western-style clothes, including tailored trousers and jeans, in pastel or plain colours; elderly ladies

---

[21] The Chinese authorities classified items of Uyghur male headgear into the more dangerous and controversial 'religious' category during the Cultural Revolution, when both the skullcap and the turban were banned (Rudelson 1997: 104).

put on navy blue trouser suits reminiscent of the Maoist period. In contrast, Uyghur women tend to don bright colours and their clothes allow different patterns of tailoring. Women's fashion reveals much variation, but these variations remain within parameters circumscribed by unwritten rules which allow for little overlapping between the two groups. Older Uyghur village women, who frequent the town on market days, wear a baggy dress; in summer their feet are bare, but covered by thick nylon stockings in winter. These thick stockings have become available and fashionable over the last 20 years, and are fast replacing the traditional baggy trousers. More sophisticated urban women wear a more transparent and thinner version of dress than peasant and lower class women. Waistless dresses meet the requirements of the Islamic modesty code, and even though Uyghur female cadres' clothes are often designed to display a waistline, most avoid wearing a belt. The sporting of belts, and especially trousers, by Chinese women are features which Uyghur cite as significant differences between the two groups. As elsewhere, so too among the Uyghur: clothes are invested with numerous symbolic meanings. Implicitly they are regarded as an extension of the body which can influence essential bodily features. Uyghur women told me that the flat nose – a characteristic bodily feature of the Han which the Uyghur consider unattractive and even ugly – is the result of Han women's habit of wearing a belt or trousers. During the first months of pregnancy, the baby's nose is flattened by the tight waist of the mother's clothing. I was also told that in Shanghai, where such customs are being abandoned by the Han, their children are growing up more handsome, with 'natural' facial features resembling those of the Uyghur.

Uyghur women's clothes are not merely markers of ethnic affiliation: like male headgear, they too indicate numerous intra-ethnic alliances as well as boundaries. For young girls wearing identical dresses is a symbolic expression of an especially close friendship. Material, cut, and the number of dresses a woman possesses are all indicative of her own and her family's social prestige. Female cadres, who stand at the top of modern Uyghur urban society, are constantly introducing new ideas to distinguish themselves from the lower groups. The latter, like their male counterparts, continue to subvert these efforts at differentiation by imitating the style of the higher social group as fast as they can. It may seem ironic that the types of material and other fashion ideas taken up by the Uyghur elite are said to originate mostly in the interior of China, especially in Shanghai. Long-distance traders, often Uyghur, choose colourful prints which are then further adjusted to local requirements by refined ways of tailoring and accepted as typically Uyghur. Some of the meanings expressed in clothes are decipherable only to other close female relatives, neighbours, and friends. A Uyghur housewife's wardrobe is perceived by some as a reflection of her marital relations with her husband, since one of the husband's conjugal obligations consists of presenting his wife with clothes at regular intervals.[22] The distinctive style of Uyghur women's clothes, perceived by most as more feminine than Han styles, contributes to the representation of them as a colourful minority, distinctive from the Han and against whom the Han can define themselves (cf. Gladney 1994a).

Traditional Uyghur female headgear has as many varieties as male headgear. Nowadays only elderly women wear a fur hat on top of a long white scarf. The white scarf is worn by many others, but only at mourning and other death-related rituals. The numerous female versions of the skullcap are rarely worn today, except by young girls and children. Instead, at about the same time as nylon stockings appeared, brightly coloured synthetic headscarves were introduced from Russia, and these have had a major impact on Uyghur female headgear. In line with Islamic traditions, hair must not be shown to strange men and village etiquette requires the wearing of the headscarf from puberty onwards. The custom is less diligently observed by township cadres, but in Kucha the headscarf is more ubiquitous than its alternative, a brown veil (*chümbäl*) covering the whole head, including the face. This is only worn by women from particularly pious families who are often labelled as 'fanatics'.

My interlocutors often told me of the great esteem Uyghurs hold for the upper part of the human body, the head in particular, which explains why they place so much emphasis upon headgear. Headgear preserves its symbolic function as a marker of gender until the very last ritual of the life-cycle: a white skullcap placed on the coffin as it is carried to the cemetery indicates that the deceased was a man, while women's coffins are decorated with a white scarf covered by a colourful female skullcap. All people, including the poorest, try to avoid wearing second-hand caps and hats. In contrast, all town and village markets have an extensive and thriving second-hand shoe section. Uyghur merchants bring cheap second-hand shoes from the interior of China, which are then repaired and cleaned by Uyghur craftsmen and resold on the local market, mostly to Uyghur customers. The great care with which headgear is chosen, and the insistence that it must never be second-hand, contrasts conspicuously with the free association of Chinese shoes with the inferior, lower parts of the body. Nevertheless, shoe styles also reflect ethnic affiliation. Uyghur townswomen insist on wearing colourful high heels, and even village women do the same when attending

---

[22] Alongside homemade bread and food, cloth has long been the most important gift presented at life-cycle rituals, religious festivals, and rituals connected to apprenticeship. Like bread, such gifts are usually presented by women (chapter 5).

weddings or visiting town. Fashion-conscious Han women tend to wear similar types, but more opt for what Europeans might call 'sensible' shoes; in contrast, no Uyghur woman can be seen in the flat black espadrilles typically worn by elderly Chinese ladies.

In Uyghur society, hair too is loaded with symbolic meanings. Ideally, a Uyghur woman should grow her hair as long as possible. Long hair symbolising femininity is traditionally associated with good luck. In the past women often used artificial or natural extensions to make their hair look longer. The most important ritual in women's life in pre-modern Uyghur society was the hair-tying ritual (*chachwaq toyi*) usually performed during the last stages of a first pregnancy or shortly after giving birth.[23] Regional variations exist as to the exact timing of the ritual (in some locations it was only performed after the birth of the third or fourth baby), but it is certain that it was a significant rite of passage for woman, more important than a wedding. The new status of the woman was marked by the adoption of a different number of braids, the cutting of the hair at the temples, and a change in the pattern of the front of her clothing. Today most Uyghur townswomen continue to have long hair usually worn in a bun, regardless of their age. Although the Uyghur, like the Han, mostly have straight black hair, Uyghur townswomen who frequent hairdressers tend to insist on waves which they say are unpopular among the Han Chinese. Short haircuts are also associated with the Han. In Kucha, only a handful of young unmarried Uyghur girls were brave enough to experiment with short hairstyles and also with trousers. Although in some cases their families tolerated such deviations, these girls were often the butt of jokes and even hostile reprimands from strangers and friends alike for their 'Chinese ways'. On one occasion a young Uyghur man started teasing a Uyghur girl because of her new 'Chinese haircut'. This took place on a street corner among other young people, and what started as mild teasing ended with the boy trying to hit the girl after she defended her right to keep up with fashion. At home, however, she took to wearing a headscarf for several days after her visit to the hairdresser's because she feared the reaction of her father and brothers. These young girls who deviated from the accepted dress code found it particularly hurtful when their appearance caused them to be addressed in Chinese by Uyghur shopkeepers, who had genuinely mistaken them for Han, in spite of their 'typical' Uyghur bodily features. Comparing a Uyghur to the Han may be used as a serious allegation (when a Uyghur-educated husband

---

[23] Alternate terms such as *juwan toyi* and *chach qoshaq toyi* are used in other oases. On the ritual, see Bellér-Hann (2002). For native descriptions of traditional Uyghur clothes with special reference to the hair-tying ritual, see Jarring (1992) and Rakhman, Hämdulla and Khushtar (1996: 131–32).

accuses his Chinese-educated wife), or a relatively mild form of disapproval (when a Uyghur mother says that her daughter is as stubborn as a Han). Behavioural stereotypes which project the Han negatively are paralleled by unflattering assumptions about what are perceived as typically Chinese facial features: one Uyghur woman commented that her young nephew unfortunately looked 'as unattractive as a Han'.

Temperament and Diet

As mentioned in the preceding section, items of clothing such as a belt may be seen as influencing bodily features and perceived as indications of an individual's change of temperament. I now wish to explore this idea further. I have indicated the common Uyghur belief that a Han temperament may be acquired either through formal education or through informal socialisation. The latter possibility is only considered where stereotypical power hierarchies dominate (e.g. among children of Han and Uyghur officials in the New Town where the former are dominant) and ignored in a reverse situation (e.g. among children from the Han 'floating population' in Muslim neighbourhoods). Temperament (*mijäz*) is a central component of Uyghur personhood and identity. It has a strong material, bodily aspect. Each person, male or female, is said to be born with a fundamentally hot (*issiq*) or cold (*soghaq*) temperament. Cold temperament is associated with pale skin while darker skinned people are said to have a hot disposition. According to some informants, more women tend to be white-skinned and therefore of a cold disposition, while more men fall into the dark-skinned, hot disposition category.[24] Some argue that an excessive consumption of 'cold' foods before conception and during pregnancy is conducive to the birth of a girl while lots of 'hot' food leads to the birth of a boy. Although babies are believed to be born with a specific disposition, either hot or cold, this basic nature may be modified and transformed by nurturing and lifestyle. An indigenous source dating from the first half of the twentieth century describes beliefs about the long-term nature of a craftsman's temperament: if his job involves constant exposure to heat, as in the case of a blacksmith or a baker, he will develop a cold disposition, while exposure to materials associated with cold such as water will result in a hot disposition (Muhammad 'Ali Damolla 1905–10: I. 25).[25] My interview partners confirm the evidence of Uyghur written sources that most foods have an essentially hot or cold nature. To have a well-

---

[24] This is also explained with the traditional patterns of the gendered division of labour: men tend to have more exposure to the sun since they are in charge of agricultural work.

[25] Ideas concerning temperament among the Uyghur are based upon my fieldwork data. For further references see Grenard (1898: 111).

balanced, healthy body is to be neither cold nor hot, but to maintain a
moderate temperature (*mötidil*). In order to achieve this one needs to eat
foods which counterbalance one's original disposition. Hot or cold
disposition is said to determine a person's reactions to different foods and
sleeping patterns, which in turn may affect general well-being as well as
character: people with a hot disposition are considered hot-tempered, while
those with a cold disposition are said to be of a calmer nature.

The diet of the Han is viewed with considerable suspicion by the
Uyghur, not only because of their inclusion of pork but also because of their
ignorance of this required balance.[26] But the main rationalisation for the
pronounced asymmetry of Uyghur-Han hospitality (the Uyghur dictate the
rules, entertaining Han colleagues when they wish to but denying them the
right to reciprocate) remains focused on the issue of pork consumption and
its contaminating effects on other foodstuffs. In addition, there are other,
more complex, hidden dimensions in the suspicion surrounding the Han,
whose disregard of the rules governing hot and cold temperament produces
people with uncontrolled dispositions. Han *mijäz* can appear as the sum of
out-of-control bodily processes. Fear of pollution may focus on pork
consumption and on the consumption of foods which may possibly have
been in contact with pork, but beneath this rationalisation for shunning Han
hospitality there is a more general anxiety of contamination of organisms

---

[26] This may come as a surprise for those familiar with the principles of traditional Chinese
medicine which pays attention to hot, cold, wet, and dry. While mutual influences between
the traditional Uyghur and Chinese medical systems cannot be excluded and certainly deserve
further study, it needs to be pointed out that traditional Uyghur medicine cannot be considered
a mere offshoot of traditional Chinese medicine. It has its roots in the Graeco-Arabic tradition
and it has also been influenced by traditions coming from South Asia. The two traditional
systems have developed side by side. Today in Xinjiang traditional Uyghur medicine is
practised in specialised hospitals, has its own training and pharmaceutical centres, while
traditional Chinese medicine can also be practised within bio-medical hospitals. Folk ideas
concerning the hot and cold nature of foods and the effect their consumption has on the
human body can be found in many parts of the world. In Uyghur folk concepts hot and cold
associations are different from Chinese ones. Not only are dry and wet irrelevant in this folk
system, but Uyghurs also meticulously observe the avoidance of pork and pork products in
their diet. For this reason interethnic commensality in Xinjiang has always been
underdeveloped. Much attention is paid by Uyghurs to the binary concepts of *halal* (legally
allowed) and *haram* (legally forbidden), Arabic concepts of Islamic law which typically
assume great significance among Muslims living under non-Muslim rule. *Mijäz*, the Uyghur
concept of temperament around which much of the hot and cold discussions revolve is also of
Arabic origin.

which are not controlled according to the main organising principles of hot and cold.[27]

One extreme illustration of this point was provided by an elderly lady whom I visited in her village with her grandchild. As a small gift, I gave her a packet of tea which I had bought in a local shop. It was brick tea, widely consumed by the Uyghur, but the lady refused to accept it, saying with evident disgust that it was only suitable for Han. Since she was illiterate, she could not read the Uyghur text (in Arabic script) on the packet which assured the consumer that it was suitable for Muslim consumption. It was clear that it was my own anomalous position, neither Uyghur nor Han, but definitely a stranger (and the first foreigner she had ever met) which bothered her, but she articulated her anxiety in the more familiar terms of anti-Han sentiments. Her granddaughter's efforts to convince her of the appropriateness of my gift failed to persuade her, and she insisted that the tea was likely to be contaminated by the touch of the Han Chinese harvesters. Back in town my young Uyghur friends were very pleased to take the tea home to their families. Fear of contamination and also of potential hostilities, not just between patients but also their visitors, lies behind Uyghur informants' disapproval of the inclusion of Han and Uyghur patients in the same wards of the town's modern biomedical hospital. Similar ideas may also lurk behind references to Uyghur villages or neighbourhoods without any Han residents as 'clean' (*pakiz*).

Uyghur avoidance of food touched by Han does not prevent them from taking considerable pride in the hospitality they may offer to the latter. Although ethnically mixed parties are rare, Han guests are occasionally invited to Uyghur weddings. On one occasion which I witnessed, the groom, a medical doctor, invited his Han colleague together with his family. They were offered the seat of honour among the wedding guests, although, unlike the rest of the guests, they had a separate table and individual plates.[28] Their partaking in the meal pleased the hosts. The symbolic incorporation of the Han into the wedding party through consumption of their food temporarily reduced the differences between them.[29] Hosting the Han and the latter's enthusiasm for Uyghur foods both serve to increase Uyghur self-esteem.[30]

---

[27] For the Uyghur folk taxonomy introduced here the closest equivalents can be found in neighbouring Afghanistan and Pakistan. For an elaboration of such ideas in Afghanistan see Penkala (1980), who also discusses possible historical antecedents.

[28] At weddings two or more guests share trays of food from which they eat by hand.

[29] But Uyghur hospitality to the Han is limited: the latter are not invited to religious celebrations or to rituals pertaining to death which also have marked religious connotations.

[30] Justin Rudelson emphasised how pejorative Han views of the Uyghur can lead to a considerable loss of self-esteem among Uyghur intellectuals (1997: 125). Although I too

Some Uyghur go as far as to say that as a result of close contacts and the adoption of a few Uyghur dishes, the Han of Xinjiang are different and better than other Han of the interior.[31]Nevertheless such views are not shared by all, and Uyghur are eager to exploit differences in Han tastes to their own advantage. Dried apricots in the orchards of the suburbs and townships are produced exclusively by indigenous farmers. Orange coloured dried apricots which look appetising but have been chemically treated by the producer are marketed at higher prices for Han consumers who believe them to be cleaner and of better quality than the naturally sun-dried brown ones primarily consumed by native producers. The Uyghur are aware that the latter are more natural, and mock the Han for this misguided preference.

Boundary Crossing and Intermarriage

Adopting the food habits of the other group can be considered an example of ethnic boundary crossing by the Han which results in a more general reinforcement of Uyghur self-esteem. Other adaptations have the same effect. Some Uyghur women related with unconcealed pride that nowadays there are local Han families who have their sons circumcised in the hospital because they have realised the health benefits of this Muslim custom. One Uyghur woman made positive comments about a Han child living in a predominantly Uyghur village, who looked charming when dressed in Uyghur clothes. I also came across cases of Uyghur couples adopting Han children from an orphanage. The parents insisted that this was a meritorious deed (sawap) and they were determined to raise the children as Uyghur. Such situations were regarded as straightforward, since socialisation in these instances was believed to be determinant for the disposition of the child.[32]

Day-to-day interaction between the two groups inevitably raises issues of the degree to which ethnic mixing is acceptable, and how far it is possible to tolerate departures from the ideals which are supposed to ensure group

---

came across such views, many of my interlocutors, who were not intellectuals by occupation, managed to find grounds for increased self-esteem in day-to-day interaction with the Han.

[31] In this connection it must be noted that a number of dishes which today are considered typically Uyghur are most likely of Chinese origin, as their Chinese names imply, the best example being the popular noodle dish known as *läghmän*.

[32] Direct contact between members of the two groups outside well-established office situations is always potentially ambiguous, as has been mentioned above. This is also illustrated by the following story which I heard from a woman in Kucha. One day her husband came back from the fields where he had been working and asked his wife to go there quickly because a strange young woman was in labour among the trees nearby. As she explained, her immediate reaction was to ask if the person in need of help was Han or Uyghur. Following her husband's reprimands she felt ashamed, and hurried out to assist with the birth.

cohesion (Banton 1994: 11). Intermarriage constitutes one extreme of group interaction (Smith 1981: 37). In Xinjiang it appears to be somewhat more common in the bigger cities, but in Kucha it is said to be almost non-existent because of the sanctions that the Uyghur community imposes on the parties involved. People explain these sanctions by telling stories of deviations from the articulated value system. Such stories fall into two main categories. One type is the hopeless love between a Han Chinese youth and a Uyghur girl, related within the context of the provincial capital. The other type involves tales of mixed marriages. I personally knew one such case which involved a Uyghur man married to a half-Han, half-Uyghur lady born and raised in Kucha. This case illustrates to what an extent deviation from the ideal may occur and become accepted. The lady appears to have been fully integrated into local Uyghur society in spite of her mixed parentage. Although she was educated in a Chinese secondary school, from a very young age she was brought up and socialised as a Uyghur. Her Uyghur husband, also a local man, was a former classmate. Since she was raised as Uyghur at home, the woman observed the Uyghur dress code in every detail. She also spoke fluent Uyghur and was perceived as no different from other local Chinese-educated Uyghurs; she was a popular member of local society, took part in Uyghur women's social visiting, and was better liked by many than her husband who was widely perceived as a shifty businessman and a womaniser. Their only child, a lively six-year-old girl, spoke Uyghur as her mother tongue, mixed with Uyghur children, and was typically Uyghur in every detail of her appearance. Her mother received a great deal of sympathy and was visited by Uyghur friends when she was admitted to hospital with a tumour. Her temperament was not regarded by anybody as 'Han', confirmation that temperament is implicitly viewed as a social construct rather than determined by descent. Another example of intermarriage between a half-Han and a Uyghur ended in violence and divorce. In this case, a Uyghur man married a woman he believed to be 'pure' Uyghur. Since she originated from a different oasis, she was able to persuade her fiancé that because her mother had died and her father was in prison it was impossible for her family to attend the wedding. Only half of her story turned out to be true. Apparently when the husband returned home one day, he found a strange Han man eating at his table. He understood this to be his father-in-law, who had just left prison. What made the husband realise that this man was Han was not his physical appearance, but his way of eating. It was not his use of chopsticks because the Uyghur have been using chopsticks for most dishes for several decades as one of their many adaptations to Han culture. It was rather that he ate *läghmän* from two plates rather than one. There is a small but rigorously observed difference between the way Uyghur and Han serve this dish. A favourite food of modern Uyghurs and also well-liked by the Han in northern China, *läghmän* is a noodle dish served with a meat and vegetable sauce. Whereas the Uyghur have the sauce poured over the noodles, Han have the two parts of the dish served on separate plates. This clue revealed the father-in-law to be Han, before he even said a word. Divorce followed almost immediately. This case illustrates that finding a Uyghur marriage partner for a woman of mixed parentage may be problematic, hence the woman's attempt to deceive. According to my interview partner, the woman in the story was born and brought up in a Uyghur environment; having been socialised entirely into Uyghur-Muslim culture it was 'impossible for her to wish to marry a Han'.

Stereotypical representations in both groups focus on the Han male from the point of view of the Uyghur woman. Han men are said to make more desirable husbands because they help more with children and housework and treat their wives more gently and with greater consideration than Uyghur males. However, even this positive stereotype has a negative edge, since the traits recognised in the stereotypical Han husband are considered unmanly by most Uyghur, including women. I never came across parallel representations comparing the advantages or disadvantages of the Han bride from the point of view of the Uyghur man, although such mixed marriages clearly occur. These lopsided stereotypes point to the Uyghur's group anxiety concerning situations when Han men may wish to marry Uyghur women, which is also consistent with Uyghur men's wish to exercise control over their women. Like the imbalance in dietary relations, this anxiety indicates attitudes to forms of ethnic boundary crossing which the dominated group tries to control.

Conclusion and Epilogue

In this chapter I have focused on Uyghur attitudes towards the Han in Xinjiang as I saw it exemplified in the oasis of Kucha. In the background there is a living historical memory of oppression and atrocities suffered by local people during ethnic conflict in the past, which I have not discussed here. To this are added more recent memories of humiliation and worse during the Maoist period, which are again inevitably associated with Chinese rule. Today, accelerating Han immigration into the region and the better job opportunities which they enjoy, enforced birth control policies, and religious oppression are listed as major factors contributing to the deterioration of Han-Uyghur relations.[33]

---

[33] For an evaluation of the recent political and economic situation in Xinjiang see Bovingdon and Gladney (2000).

The colonial nature of Han rule in Xinjiang, the long history of group conflict, and the Uyghurs' repeated attempts at independence (in the 1930s and 1940s) all point to the pattern which Donald Horowitz called a ranked system (1985: 22). As this model predicts, members of the Uyghur elite have ambivalent feelings: both pride in their own superior habits, and resentment over the backwardness of their own people. Chinese presence gives rise to conflicting desires, and to distancing as well as close contact and emulation (Horowitz 1985: 166–84). A certain degree of cautious, positive stereotyping of the Han may be found among some Uyghur intellectuals, who may distance themselves from the less educated and poorer members of their own group and invoke the ideals of more cultured behaviour to be found among the Han. But such attitudes remain limited to small sections of society, and even here they do not preclude a strong commitment to the actor's own group.

Official policies, which recognise minority rights as part of a strategy of control, encourage the fragmentation of minorities and the acculturation of elite urban groups and even small town residents with medium-level education. I have demonstrated how local perceptions dichotomise life in an oasis town, and how boundary maintenance by Uyghurs reinforces the duality imposed by the state. Instead of concentrating on the most obvious manifestations of difference, religion, script, and language, I have argued that numerous other, seemingly trivial visible symbols as well as ideas concerning the body and personhood are used to exaggerate real and imagined differences between the two groups. These ethnic markers largely overlap with strategies which have been employed for centuries to mark internal status and identity in Uyghur society. As Ceri Peach observed in another context, 'the language, values, religion, culture and dress of ethnic minorities are not simply badges of degradation imposed by more powerful groups to imprison, confine and divide those whom they dominate. They are elements of group and personal identity, fostered from within the group' (1981: 31). Although actors themselves are sometimes inclined to essentialise these elements of group and personal identity as static and given, constant changes of these components may be discerned. People recognise the dynamic elements. Both the idea that Uyghur children might acquire a Han temperament through interaction, and the idea of the fourteenth nationality consisting of Chinese educated Uyghur are ways in which social actors themselves implicitly acknowledge the constructed and therefore shifting nature of the ostensibly given traits which are supposed to form the core of Uyghurness. Components of ethnic identity are closely connected to the varied ways through which personhood, status, and other social roles are constructed. They may double as markers of ethnicity in relation to another group, but they also retain their multiple meanings as markers of intra-group social relations. Their constant reformulation is dependent on the social relations which they stand for, and which they in turn help to shape. This is truly a dialogical relationship in capturing these traits, and in their conscious and unconscious applications we see 'constantly shifting relations and multiplicities of perceived identities that mask many levels of social simultaneity' (Gladney 1996: 456).

Most of the materials that I have discussed were collected during a two-month stay in Kucha in 1995. In the following year, a projected five months' stay in the same location was interrupted after only two weeks because of violence. It was difficult to ascertain exactly what happened. Local media announcements asserted that nine Uyghurs died due to 'criminal activity', but my interlocutors spoke of revenge taken by Uyghur villagers upon corrupt Uyghur officials who were perceived as overstepping the boundary of acceptable collaboration with the Han. According to other rumours at the time, the incident was followed by the arrest of 600 Uyghurs in the county. This incident was one relatively minor episode in the general unrest characteristic of Xinjiang in the mid-1990s, a period during which the authorities were attempting to clamp down on separatists (i.e. splittists) and on religious extremists (i.e. fundamentalists). The apparent tranquillity of Kucha thus turned out to be an illusion, as underlying tensions spilled over into violence. Yet this had little or no impact on daily patterns of interaction in the town, since it merely reconfirmed the fundamental structuring aspects that were partially disguised during the relatively tranquil period of my initial stay.

References

Banton, M. 1994. Modelling Ethnic and National Relations. *Ethnic and Racial Studies* 17 (1): 1–19.

Bellér-Hann, I. 2002. The Hairbraiding ritual. In A. Kamalov (ed.), *Aktualniye problem sovremennogo Uigurovedeniya*, pp. 180–192. Almaty: Gylym Press.

Bergère, M.-C. 1979. L'influence du modèle Sovietique sur la politique des minorités nationales en Chine. Le cas du Sinkiang (1949–1962). *Revue Française de Science Politique* 29 (3): 402–425.

Bovingdon, G., and D. Gladney (eds.). 2000. *Inner Asia* 2 (2). Special Issue: *Xinjiang*.

Brown, K. 1984. The Uses of a Concept: 'The Muslim City'. In K. Brown et al. (eds.), *Middle Eastern Cities in Comparative Perspective: Points de vue sur les villes du Maghreb et du Machrek*, pp. 73–81. London: Ithaca Press.

Cesàro, M. C. 2000. Consuming Identities: Food and Resistance among the Uyghur in Contemporary Xinjiang. *Inner Asia* 2 (2): 225–238.

Dawamat, T. 1993. *Xinjiang – My Beloved Home*. Ürümchi: Xinjiang People's Publishing House.

Dillon, M. 1995. *Xinjiang: Ethnicity, Separatism and Control in Chinese Central Asia. Durham East Asian Papers*, Vol. 1. Durham: Department of East Asian Studies, Durham University.

Eickelman, D. F. 1981. The *Middle East: An Anthropological Approach*. Englewood Cliffs: Prentice-Hall.

Gladney, D. C. 1990. The Ethnogenesis of the Uighur. *Central Asian Survey* 9 (1): 1–28.

——. 1991. *Muslim Chinese: Ethnic Nationalism in the People's Republic*. Cambridge: Harvard Council on East Asia Studies.

——. 1994a. Representing Nationality in China: Refiguring Majority/ Minority Identities. *The Journal of Asian Studies* 53 (1): 92–123.

——. 1994b. Ethnic Identity in China: The New Politics of Difference. In W. A. Joseph (ed.), *China Briefing*, pp. 171–192. Boulder: Westview Press.

——. 1996. Relational Alterity: Constructing Dungan (Hui), Uygur, and Kazakh Identities Across China, Central Asia and Turkey. *History and Anthropology* 9 (4): 445–477.

Grenard, F. 1898. *Le Turkestan et le Tibet: étude ethongraphique et sociologique* (J.-L. Dutrueil de Rhins: *Mission Scientifique dans la Haute Asie 1890–1895*). Paris: Ernest Leroux.

Grobe-Hagel, K. 1991. *Hinter der Großen Mauer. Religionen und Nationalitäten in China*. Frankfurt am Main: Eichborn Verlag.

Hoppe, Th. 1998. *Die ethnischen Gruppen Xinjiangs: Kulturunterschiede und interethnische Beziehungen*. Hamburg: Institut für Asienkunde.

Horowitz, D. L. 1985. *Ethnic Groups in Conflict*. Berkeley: University of California Press.

Hüsäyin, N. 1995a. Bizdiki illätlär. *Shinjang Mädäniyiti* 1: 61–79.

——. 1995b. Bizdiki illätlär. *Shinjang Mädäniyiti* 2: 61–72.

——. 1995c. Bizdiki khotun – qizlar dishwarchiliqi. *Shinjang Mädäniyiti* 3: 76–79.

Jarring, G. 1992. *Garments from Top to Toe. Eastern Turki Texts Relating to Articles of Clothing*. Stockholm: Almquist & Wiksell International.

Kane, P. 1995. Population and Family Policies. In R. Benewick, and P. Wingrove (eds.), *China in the 1990s*, pp. 193–203. London: Macmillan.

Lattimore, O. 1950. *Pivot of Asia: Sinkiang and the Inner Asian Frontiers of China and Russia*. Boston: Little, Brown & Company.

Millward. J. 1998. *Beyond the Pass: Economy, Ethnicity and Empire in Qing Central Asia 1759–1864*. Stanford: Stanford University Press.

Muhammad 'Ali Damolla. ca. 1905–10. *A Collection of Essays on Life in Eastern Turkistan*. Unpublished manuscript. Kahsgar, Jarring Collection, Lund University Library. Prov. 207. I.–II. (Turki).

Peach, C. 1981. Conflicting Interpretations of Segregation. In P. Jackson, and S. J. Smith (eds.), *Social Interaction and Ethnic Segregation*, pp. 19–33. London: Academic Press.

Penkala, D. 1980. 'Hot' and 'Cold' in the Traditional Medicine of Afghanistan. *Ethnomedizin* 6 (1–4): 201–228.

Rakhman, A., R. Hämdulla, and Sh. Khushtar. 1996. *Uyghur örp-adätliri*. Ürümchi: Shinjang Yashlar-Ösmürlär Näshriyati.

Rudelson. J. 1997. *Oasis Identities: Uyghur Nationalism along China's Silk Road*. New York: Columbia University Press.

Smith. S. J. 1981. Negative Interaction: Crime in the Inner City. In P. Jackson, and S. J. Smith (eds.), *Social Interaction and Ethnic Segregation*, pp. 35–58. London: Academic Press.

Smith, J. N. 2002. 'Making Culture Matter': Symbolic, Spatial, and Social Boundaries between Uyghurs and Han Chinese. *Asian Ethnicity* (3) 2: 153–174.

Tahir, M. Y. 1995. Tughulghan kün'gä tughulghan qarashlirim. *Shinjang Ayalliri* 5: 28–31.

Tokhti, S. 1995. Hazirqi däwr Uyghur ayallarining oyliship körüshigä tegishlik bir qanchä mäsilä. *Shinjang Ayalliri* 7: 7–8.

Chapter 8
'Making the Oil Fragrant': Dealings with the Supernatural among the Uyghurs in Xinjiang[1]

Anyone interested in Xinjiang today must take account of the long-term cultural continuities which manifest themselves in many areas of life beneath the practices and institutions of the modern social formation. In this chapter, I shall deal with some aspects of traditional modes of dealing with the supernatural, concentrating on rituals and daily practices which link the world of the living to the world of the dead. Indigenous and other sources from before 1949 confirm that veneration of the dead has long been at the heart of popular religious practices among the Turki and modern Uyghurs. Fieldwork data from the 1990s point to the remarkable persistence of these practices throughout the socialist period, though they have not remained untouched by the dramatic social and political changes.

Approaches to the study of social life and religion in the region are best described as problematic. Official Chinese scholarship distinguishes some manifestations of local traditions (örp-adät) from religious practices. It defines the former as acceptable and even positive, since they contribute to the making of a colourful ethnic group within the People's Republic of China. Official scholarship tolerates some religious practices, but denounces many others as backward and negative, intimately connected to the legacy of feudalism which socialism seeks to overcome.[2] The suspicion and often contradictory attitude of the government towards Islam is partly due to its basic incompatibility with socialist doctrine, and partly to its close association with separatist movements (Reetz 1999). This negative view was often drawn to my attention by my Chinese co-researchers, who argued that Islam functioned as a conservative force among the Muslim minorities of the

---

[1] Published in *Asian Ethnicity* 2001, 2 (1): 9–23.
[2] See Mackerras (1995: 111); Rakhman, Hämdulla and Khushtar (1996: 1–3); Rudelson (1997: 129). For an analysis of the objectification and commodification of minorities in China on the basis of local traditions see Gladney (1994).

region.[3] At the same time, they endorsed the maintenance of diversity at the level of 'positive customs' as expressed, for example, in wedding rituals, music, and food culture. In other words, those cultural traditions which appear harmless to the dominant Han population are encouraged and occasionally even romanticised. These become constituents of what might be termed the folklorisation of local culture, a process induced from outside the group to define Uyghur ethnic identity. This approach even allows the encouragement of a small number of Uyghur intellectuals to take part in the pilgrimage to Mecca, but condemns or limits practices which concern large sections of the population, are inseparably intertwined with Islamic belief, and represent close links to the rest of the Islamic world.

Over the last century, many foreign observers have commented on the superficiality or inadequacy of Islamic observance among the settled oasis dwellers in Xinjiang.[4] Modern scholarship does not subscribe either to the artificial division of customs and religion, or to the typically Orientalist views of foreign observers. Nevertheless, some authors remain inclined to view religious practices in the region as a cultural mosaic in which Islamic and pre-Islamic folk traditions persist side by side and are discernible. In his discussion of popular Islam in Central Asia and Kazakhstan, following Ol'ga Sukhareva, the late Soviet scholar Vladimir Basilov argued that by the nineteenth century Sufism had degenerated into Ishanism which in essence manifested itself in a spectacular mingling of shamanistic and Sufi tradition (Sukhareva 1960; Basilov 1987). Basilov proceeded to offer an account of the influences exerted by shamanism and Sufism on each other and gave numerous examples of equivalencies which both enabled and followed from their interactions. Such an analysis implicitly assumes a dualistic, two-tier structure of popular currents in Central Asian religious practices for which the shorthand labels are shamanism and Sufism.

In the context of Xinjiang, the imposition of such dichotomies impedes recognition of the actual syntheses that have been worked out in beliefs and their manifestations in rituals and daily practices. Against such an approach, I prefer to search for an indigenous (emic) understanding of negotiations with the spirit world as expressed in ritual practices, but also in everyday symbols and their gendered appropriation. This perspective insists on the deeply Islamic character of local practices, but at the same time recognises the syncretic and hybrid nature of this Islam. I argue that, one hundred years ago, the integration of Islamic and non-Islamic practices was

---

[3] This negative view of Islam is also shared by some Uyghur intellectuals (Rudelson 1997: 129).

[4] For a summary see Warikoo (1985).

already deep enough to be indiscernible for practitioners.[5] Instead of contrasting local beliefs in a peripheral region with the idealised 'pure' or 'high' Islam of the centre (i.e. the local Little Tradition with a central Great Tradition), I am more impressed by the similarities of many small details in ritual and daily practice between regions situated far apart geographically; that is, with the similarities shared by the Uyghur and other Turkic and Iranian speakers of the former Soviet Central Asian republics, the Middle East, and South Asia. I hope to show that popular practices in Xinjiang over the last century cannot be viewed as an insufficiently developed, parochial version of the Islam of the centre, or as merely a curious, accidental juxta-position of pre-Islamic beliefs with Islam.[6] Instead, I argue that many aspects of popular beliefs and practices show a high level of integration of various traditions. While it is sometimes possible to trace the origins of specific elements of the fusion, such a deconstruction has little justification from the point of view of local understandings and interpretations.[7]

A very similar approach characterises Devin DeWeese's work on Inner Asian religion. He argued that the survivals of pre-Islamic features in Inner Asian Islam as discerned by (especially Soviet) ethnographers are part and parcel of normative religious practices of the community (DeWeese 1994: 54). He noted that:

> in much of the scholarship dealing with Inner Asian religion, and indeed in most incidental surveys of Inner Asian religion by nonspecialists, the role of the shaman has been emphasised to such an extent that it has become commonplace to refer to the religious life of Inner Asian peoples prior to their adoption of, say, Buddhism or Islam (and even after their 'conversion' as well) as 'shamanism', as if the term could designate something akin to the other religious '-isms' that entered Inner Asia (DeWeese 1994: 33).

He then elaborated that the undue emphasis on the shaman's figure diverts attention from and obscures the importance of domestic rites which have relevance to the daily life of most people. Instead, the focus of Inner Asian religious life is communality, which is expressed in the domestic cult of

---

[5] This is not to deny the efforts made by some local people to contrast mysticism and orthodoxy, folk tradition and the assumed traditions of the centre; but a discussion of this would take us further into the politics of syncretism than I have space to pursue in this chapter. For further examples of my approach, see Stewart and Shaw (1994).

[6] For recent works on Uyghur ethnography see for example Häbibulla (1993); Rakhman, Hämdulla and Khushtar (1996); Rudelson (1997). Among others, Gunnar Jarring's numerous publications (1980, 1986a, 1986b, 1987); Pantusov (1890); Grenard (1898); and Katanov and Menges (1933, 1976) give valuable insights into aspects of social life and religion.

[7] See Stewart and Shaw (1994). Of course local customs must also be conceived as composite and not as a homogenous, pure block of pre-Islamic relics.

ancestors (DeWeese 1994: 32–50). DeWeese's observations pertain to the Golden Horde, and his work is primarily a study into historical and epic tradition. Nevertheless, my sources and ethnographic field materials concerning Eastern Turkestan also point in a similar direction. In what follows, I shall look at ritual practices which are directly or indirectly connected to death, and argue for the centrality of the veneration of the dead in Uyghur popular beliefs and practices.

Rituals Pertaining to the Dead

The ideas that the well-being of the living is intimately connected to the well-being of the dead, and that the dead can influence the living, are widespread among the Uyghurs.[8] The persistence of these ideas through specific rituals is undoubtedly due to their compatibility with inspirational traditions. Visits to shrines to ask for the mediation of a saint buried there are not so far removed from the healing seance in which a *dakhan*, *bakhshi*, or *perikhan* (healer, shaman) calls for the help of good spirits in the form of Muslim saints and their helping or ancestral spirits against harmful spirits.[9] Most dealings with the supernatural are conceived in terms of encounters with the spirits of the dead, either as potential helpers or – when angered or neglected – as potential wrong-doers who need to be pacified and appeased. The manifestations of fearing, remembering, respecting, and evoking the help of the dead are central to funerary rites as well as to the rituals of the *näzir* and the *tünäk/Barat*. These practices closely resemble popular practices elsewhere in the Islamic world, even though they are not founded on the explicit teachings of the Koran (Welch 1977).

According to an indigenous account (Yarkand, c. 1930), after a dead man has been buried and the mourners have left, two angels – one beautiful, the other ugly, known as Munkir and Näkir respectively – enter the grave.[10]

---

[8] Perhaps it is worth pointing out that the ancestor cult among the Han Chinese and its manifestations are very different from Uyghur practice, which shows closer affinity to practices among the Turkic- and Iranian-speaking peoples of Muslim Central Asia. Ancestor cults are well documented in many parts of the world, from Africa to Japan and among Australian aborigines. In most cases, people revere specific deceased relatives going back two or three generations rather than the distant, perhaps mythical ancestors of a clan unknown to them personally. At the same time, a number of practices point to the wider significance of beliefs in the power of the dead, so that perhaps 'veneration of the dead' is the best broad designation.

[9] For a summary of materials concerning such Turki/Uyghur healing rituals see Basilow (1995: 205–15).

[10] The two angels are an integral part of Hanafite creed, but in contrast to the cited source, they are both normally considered to be black with blue eyes (i.e. ugly). See Wensinck and Tritto (1960).

Their entrance is quite dreadful, and they interrogate the dead person in Arabic. If he gives the right answer (i.e. that he is a believer and belongs to the Hanafi school) then they tell him to continue sleeping, and they leave him alone. But if he does not reply thus, they torture him ('Abdul-Qadir 1930: 41). Seven days later the spirit (*roh*) of the dead man comes to visit the body. The *roh* looks at the body (*tän*) and says: 'Oh, body, have I not always been your companion? Why have I separated from you?'; it says this and cries. The *roh* comes again 11 days later to visit the body. On seeing the body, the *roh* says: 'Oh, body, I used to be together with you, you used to be fragrant, now after our separation you smell bad. Such a fine figure that smells bad', it cries. The *roh* comes again to see the body 20 days later, and when it sees the decomposing body it weeps very sadly ('Abdul-Qadir 1930: 41).

Popular beliefs hold that all persons who died as adults remain accountable for their actions during their lifetime. The dead will face a period in hell in proportion to the sins they have committed; once they have been punished, Muslims will be admitted to Paradise. Consequently, the most important concern of the living during the funerary and commemorative rituals is to eliminate or at least ease the sins of the dead. My informants agree that members of the neighbourhood are under considerable social pressure to take part in the communal prayer for the dead (*jinaza namizi*), as the more who take part, the easier the burdens of the dead will be.

A similar end is served by the payment of *isqat*, a practice which has survived the Maoist years. A detailed description of *isqat* before 1949 is offered by a Khotanese author. According to him, when a person dies, the first 14 years of his life, which are regarded as the years of immaturity, are deducted from his age. It is assumed that during this time he lived innocently, and could not have committed a sin. For each remaining year, one or two *tängä*s are disbursed to strangers. The value of a single year is given to each person. So if a man lived to the age of 94, 80 or 160 *tängä*s will be distributed among 80 or 160 people. This is done in the following way:

> After the corpse had been put into the grave the money is collected and placed on its right hand side. A *molla* standing there takes an amount dedicated to one year [of the dead man's life] in his hands. A stranger comes and stands on the left of the dead, and stretches out his hand for the money. The person who is to give the money puts a copy of the Koran or alternatively the reins of a horse in his hands and asks him:

'Oh, brother', or 'oh, person, as a matter of fact know that the dead person lying here is burdened with many sins, because, although he had kept and realized some of God's commandments, being unable to keep some others he abandoned them. In gratitude for his fulfilment of many obligations and for the blasphemy of his neglected duties, holding the Koran or the reins of this horse, accepting the sins and ingratitude of this [dead] man, will you ask for forgiveness on his behalf?'

After this if the stranger says 'I agree to this', then the person who had given him the Koran or horse reins takes this back and says: 'now this Koran or horse has become yours, but are you willing to sell it to me for one or two *tängä*s?'. He gives the stranger one or two *tängä*s who says: 'I am willing to do this' (Nur Luke 1950: 104–06).

The same ceremony is repeated as many times as necessary (depending on the age of the dead person). This paying of money is called *isqat tasaduq* (the confirmation of *isqat*), which in effect means the annulment of sins. In other words, it is regarded as a type of alms which eliminates the dead person's sins (Nur Luke 1950: 106–08).

Although the above description concerns the death of a man, informants confirm that *isqat* is also paid for the expiation of sins upon the death of women. Regardless of whether the deceased was a man or a woman, the communal prayer for the dead in the mosque and the funeral service in the cemetery can only be attended by men, and therefore the payment of *isqat* has been an exclusively male obligation. During this time, women mourn at home in the company of visiting female relatives and friends.

Some modern ethnographers equate *isqat* with paying off the dead person's debts. In this view, money or matches are given for men's *isqat*, while cotton, needle, or a comb is given for women's. The imam asks the dead person's relatives if she or he has left any debts behind, and if the answer is yes, the relatives must pay off these debts. This is organised in many different ways. In some places, it takes place in the cemetery by the tomb; in others, in the courtyard of the dead man's house, or in any large space outside. In the Kashgar region, a horse is kept on a long tether and 41 mourners take it in turns to hold the ends of the rope. The price of the horse is then estimated and the imam shares out the equivalent of this money among the 41 persons. In addition, each person who has gone to the tomb gets a *nan* (flat wheat bread), and perhaps matches worth one *nan* (Häbibulla 1993: 323). This description obscures the difference between paying off the dead person's material debts to other people and securing his redemption.

A report from 1891 from Turfan confirms that the actual debts of the dead person were paid, but it does not equate these payments with *isqat*. According to this source, when a woman dies, before the ritual prayer (*namaz*) is performed, the household head brings three packets of sewing needles and gives two or three to each woman, the reason being that during her lifetime needles had been much used by the dead woman. These needles are given away in case the dead woman had borrowed some without being able to pay back her debt (*ötnä häqqi qalghan bolsa, ölükning gädänidä qalmasun dep*) (Katanov and Menges 1933, 1976: 1178–81).[11] On the day of the death, no meal is given to the mourners; instead they get a Koran and some fabric in order to eliminate the dead person's sins (*ölükning gunalarini kötärsün*). Children are given some raisins; women get needles and cotton to replace the money which the dead person may have left unpaid (*ölükning ötnägä alghan pulining ornigha*). Men receive raisins and bread on the day of death or at the funeral (Katanov and Menges 1933, 1976: 1184–85).[12] Another report confirms that, on the day of death, alms in cash and a piece of soap were distributed among beggars (Skrine 1971 [1926]: 204).

Other ethnographers confirm that participants (members of the mosque community) at the communal prayer for the dead receive *namaz häqqi* (their due for the prayer), while strangers who participate receive the *isqat*. Those receiving *isqat* say a *khalisanä namaz* (selfless, voluntary prayer) for the dead (Rakhman, Hämdulla and Khushtar 1996: 134).

Like all life-cycle rituals, the death ritual involves a transitional state – that is 'liminality' in the sense of Arnold van Gennep (1960 [1909]) and Victor Turner (1974) – between two very different social statuses, and it requires behaviour very different from normal daily practice. Close relatives and friends of the deceased must not cut their hair, beard, moustache, or eyebrows for 40 days after the death, nor should they wear new or colourful clothes. Instead, they wear white or black garments, and men tie a white belt around their waist. They do not hold any sort of entertainment in their homes. Women do not plait their hair during this time: rather it is tossed back, but one part of their hair is tied with a white ribbon. All these practices are summed up in the expression *qara tutush*, and people in this state of mourning are called *qaraliq kishi*. When such a person enters a meeting, those present avoid making jokes in his presence and even strangers try to show compassion and help him or her.

On the fortieth day after the death, when invited guests arrive to take part in the commemoration meal (*näzir-chiragh*), men have their hair and

---

[11] My interview partners in villages near Kashgar have confirmed the persistence of such paying of the dead person's debts, but also did not equate it with *isqat*.

[12] For a contemporary description of funerary rites in Turfan see Rudelson (1997: 84–85).

facial hair shaved by barbers invited specially by the 'owner of the dead' (ölükning igisi), a close male relative who organises and pays for the funeral (Nur Luke 1950: 90–98). This takes place in the courtyard of the house where death occurred. Although this area belongs to the domestic space, for the duration of this communal act it acquires a public character. Even men who were not mourning turn up to have their hair cut free of charge, since all the barbers' expenses are met by the owner of the dead. With this ceremony, the mourning is broken. After this, the mourners can again join parties, celebrations, and entertainment. Although the mourning is observed equally by men and women, the end of the mourning is recognised ritually only in the communal action for men. According to a widespread assumption, the spirit of the dead remains in or near the tomb until the Day of Judgement. Nur Luke, a native of Khotan who recorded conditions before 1949, reported that for 40 days or sometimes a whole year after the death of a well-to-do person, a tent or other white construction is erected by his tomb. During this time, two or three people take it in turns to stay in the tent day and night, burning a lamp to be able to continuously read the Koran. The purpose of the practice is to ensure that the dead person is not left alone. During this period, the spirit of the dead meets up with the old spirits of the cemetery, after which he is not so lonely. Engaging *molla*s to keep vigil by the graveside is supposed to ease the integration of the spirit of the deceased into the social world of the dead. The reciting of the Koran during this period counts as a meritorious deed (*sawap*) which is credited to the spirit of the dead person (Nur Luke 1950: 98–102). The expression *chiraq yandurush* (the burning of the lamp) could also refer to the burning of the light in the house of the dead person at night, normally observed for a minimum of three or seven nights. All these acts are symbolic sacrifices which only the well-off could afford, since one had to pay for the lamp oil as well as for the *molla*s' recitation. Occasionally the living are concerned that the dead person might feel lonely, even years later. The purpose of scattering wheat or maize on the graves, as I observed in oases such as Yarkand and Kucha in the mid-1990s, is to attract birds to keep the dead company.

Näzir-chiragh

According to local explanations, the original meaning of the word *näzir* in Uyghur is a meal offered for no returns, thus expressing the sacrificial nature of the occasion. *Näzir-chiragh* has the more specific meaning of the ritual held to commemorate the dead. Memorial services are organised on the third, the seventh, and the fortieth day following the death. An additional service is held one year later. At the heart of these commemorations is the communal meal prepared by women and consumed separately by men in the morning and then by women later in the day. During a *näzir*, the usual ceremonial foods of sweets, mutton, and rice are served; in addition the special pancakes fried in oil and known as *quymaq/poshkal/chälpäk/zhit* are also offered. Women attending the *näzir* also take gifts in the form of cooked food and bread as well as pieces of textile to their hosts.

Ritual visiting of the grave and praying by the graveside on these days is an exclusively male prerogative, as it is on the major religious holidays, the *Roza* and the *Qurban*. My interview partners' insistence that women should not go to the cemetery is closely connected to their expressed preference for at least one son, which is explained in terms of a daughter's inability to pray for her dead parents at the graveside (Grenard 1898: 129). However, actual practice reveals not only that many women visit their dead relatives' graves on a more regular basis than men outside the major rituals, but also that women play a central role in the veneration of the dead by nourishing the spirits, as shall be described below. However, like women's participation in production, their participation in the veneration of the dead is not articulated and thus remains 'muted' or invisible (Ardener 1975; chapters 2 and 3). Women's role in the rituals is nonetheless essential, not only because it is they who prepare the ceremonial food but also because it is they who must offer ceremonial gifts in the form of food and fabric to the family of the deceased.

Barat

I turn next to another ritual which is closely connected to death rituals. Sha'bān is the name of the eighth month of the Islamic lunar year, which was of special importance in early Arabia. In the early Arabian solar year, Sha'bān fell in the summer. Probably the weeks preceding and following the summer solstice had a religious significance which gave rise to propitiatory rites such as fasting. This period had the middle of the month of Sha'bān as its focus. Following conversion to Islam, this day must have preserved its New Year's day character in many regions. According to popular belief in the Middle East, in the night preceding the fifteenth of the Islamic month of Sha'bān, the tree of life on the leaves of which are written the names of all living persons is shaken. The names written on the leaves which fall down indicate those who are to die in the coming year. According to one tradition, during this night 'God descends to the lowest heaven; from there he calls the mortals in order to grant them forgiveness of sins' (Wensinck 1997: 154).[13]

---

[13] A handwritten manuscript, *Ölüklärning qomaqining bäyani* (A Description of Burials), copied for a Swedish missionary in Yarkand in the 1920s describes the tree of life in very similar terms, although it does not connect it directly to the Barat (*Ölüklärning* n.d.: 29).

The night of the fourteenth of Sha'bān has long been regarded as a venerable day in many parts of the Muslim world.[14] In modern Turkey, it is known under the name *Berat kandili*. In Pakistan and India, on the night of the fourteenth people pray for the dead, distribute food among the poor, eat sweetmeats, prepare illuminations, and organise fireworks (Gibb and Kramers 1974: 508; Wensinck 1997).

According to a native description from Kashgar from about 1905–10, people visited shrines and cemeteries this night or nights (some say that the vigil should be extended to three nights), taking with them torches and the ceremonial pancakes known as *quymaq*, which they presented to the person who recited the Koran for them. On this night, people also visited the graves of their parents, relatives, and friends; recited verses from the Koran; and prayed for God's forgiveness (*mäghpirät*). Then they returned home and lit a candle for each dead relative and friend. Alternatively, they wrapped pieces of cotton around some wood soaked in vegetable oil and lit this torch. They held a vigil (*tünäk*) until dawn and spent this time praying for the dead and the living (*ölük wä tiriklär üchün*) and reciting the Koran. Young people went out into the streets and walked around with their torches reciting Koranic verses. Many people greeted the dawn with music. The communal aspect of the vigil was emphasised throughout. Men and women of the neighbourhood would gather in separate houses and consume a sacrificial meal in between the prayers (Muhammad 'Ali Damolla 1905–10: I.56).

The same source reveals that the widespread Islamic belief that on the shoulders of each individual sit two scribe angels is also well known in this region. If someone has done a good deed, it is recorded within an hour. Bad deeds, however, are only recorded three days after they have been committed: this delay gives the wrongdoer an opportunity to repent. During the night of Barat, Muslims fear the horrors of hell and hope for Paradise because on this night the scribe angels look at the complete list of good and bad deeds committed over the previous year. On this basis, they increase the provisions (*risq*) of those who have done much good and decrease the provisions of the wrongdoers during the following year. This is why people hold a vigil and pray with rosaries in their hands. People are afraid and say: 'if we do not repent, our provisions will be decreased' (Muhammad 'Ali Damolla 1905–10: I.56).

In these circumstances, it was imperative to remember the dead and thereby assure their goodwill and mediation for the living. This aspect of the holiday was confirmed in the rich account given by the late nineteenth century French traveller Fernand Grenard, who explicitly attributed the

---

[14] Nikolai Nikolaevich Pantusov (1890: 145) mistakenly identified the month of Barat of the Turki lunar calendar with the seventh month of the Islamic calendar, Räjäp.

visiting of the graves and depositing of fried cakes to women. They themselves did not eat them; the cakes were supposed to be nourishment for the dead, but in fact were consumed by the *molla*s. Having presented their offerings, women lamented and kept vigil throughout the night. In each house, a banquet was held and people danced and played music for the deceased members of their family. They filled flasks with oil, which they then burnt to satisfy the souls of the dead, saying *ärwahni khoshlaymiz*, 'we welcome the spirits'. They further sang:

Barat käldi tuydunglar mu?
Bizgä poshkal qoydunglar mu?
Barat ay ulugh aydur
Uyghaqlargha jännät jaydur.

The month of Barat has come, have not you heard?
Have you offered us cakes?
The month of Barat is a noble month
Those who stay awake will find a place in Paradise (Grenard 1898: 247).

This ceremony was observed throughout Xinjiang, including the eastern oases, as is confirmed by a report from Turfan from 1891 (Katanov and Menges 1933, 1976: 1212–13). There, the Barat celebrations began on the twelfth night of the month. On this night nine different ingredients were cooked in each pot, and the women performed the Barat prayer accompanied by seventeen *räkät*s[15] before midnight. After midnight, they went to the shrines of saints where they lamented, recited the Koran, and prayed for help. Men too performed a prayer before midnight, accompanied by 27 *räkät*s. Then they too went to the cemetery, recited the Koran until dawn, and prayed for their general well-being. On this night, young children burnt homemade lanterns and went around in groups of fifteen singing:

Barat käldi, tuydunglar mu?
Manga chalpaq qoydunglar mu?

The month of Barat has come, have not you heard?
Have you offered me cakes? (Katanov and Menges 1933, 1976: 1212–13).

The vigil in the middle of the month of Barat was also observed among the Taranchi, the Turki agricultural settlers in the northern part of the region. Men and women, boys and girls stayed awake until dawn and prayed. At dawn girls went to the mosque to pray:

---

[15] A series of prescribed prayers and prostrations.

Bäkht ana, bäkht ana, bäkht dölät bär manga!
Bäkht dölät bärmäsäng säbir-taqät bär manga!
Bäkht ana, bäkht ana, bäkht dölät bär manga!
Bäkht dölät bärmäsäng yakhshi izzät bär manga!
Bäkht ana, bäkht ana, bäkht dölät bär manga!
Bäkht dölät bärmäsäng häm sa'adät bär manga!

Mother of Good Luck, Mother of Good Luck, give me blessing and good luck!
If you are not giving me blessing and good luck, then give me patience!
Mother of Good Luck, Mother of Good Luck, give me blessing and good luck!
If you are not giving me blessing and good luck, then give me honour!
Mother of Good Luck, Mother of Good Luck, give me blessing and good luck!
If you are not giving me blessing and good luck, give me happiness!
(Pantusov 1890: 63, 145–46, also quoted in Änsari, Bäshir and Xudayqul 1925: 142).

While the girls lamented and prayed, some cheeky young men mocked them with the following verse:

Bäkht ana, bäkht ana, bäkht dölät bär manga!
Bäkht dölät bärmäsäng boyun-i yoghan bär manga!

Mother of Good Luck, Mother of Good Luck, give me blessing and good luck!
If you are not giving me blessing and good luck, give me a thick neck!
(Pantusov 1890: 63, 145–46, also quoted in Änsari, Bäshir and Xudayqul 1925: 142).

So, the Taranchi in the north also kept vigil and prayed either at home or in the mosque. They put oil in gourds which were fastened to poles, lit, and carried around while people sang the following couplets:

Barat käldi, tuydunglar mu?
Bizgä chälfäk[16] qoydunglar mu?
Barat ay ulugh aydur
Uyghaqlargha jännät jaydur.
Töbä qiling xäyri sherghä,

---

[16] *chälpäk*, cf. Schwarz (1992: 345).

Mäläk yazghan kim däftärghä.
Bugün yötkär däftäringni
Mäläk söygäy khosh atingni!
Töbä qilghil bir Khudagha,
äling tafshur rahnumagha
Yanghil bu kün isyaningdin
Hajät tilä Khudaningdin!
Jümlä hajät rawa bolghay
Gaday bolsa ghäni bolghay!
Barchä ghämlär ada bolghay
Därtläringghä dawa bolghay.
Barchä baylar ihsan qilghay!
Mäshghullari asan qilghay!
Fuqaralar qiling ta'ät
Tängrim ita qilur dölät.
Bugün kechä mubaräk tün
Ötkär shäbni bidar futun.
Bolghay sanga haqq rahnumun,
Bändä seni qilmas zäbun.
Ya rabb ita qil jännätni
Bizdin raha qil mehnätni.

Barat has come, have you heard?
Have you put pancakes out for us?
The month of Barat is a great month
For those keeping vigil there is a place in Paradise.
Repent the good and the bad (deeds)
These will be entered by the angels in the book.
Today they change your book,
The angels like your good name!
Repent to the only God,
Reach out to the guide!
Today give up your rebellion!
Ask God [to meet] your needs!
May all your needs be satisfied!
May the poor become rich!
May sorrows be dealt with!
May there be a cure for all your pain!
May all rich people be made benevolent!
May all difficult things be made easy!
Poor people, submit to God!

God will give you happiness.
This night is blessed,
Pass the night alert.
May God be your guide,
He does not make his servants weak.
Oh, God, give us Paradise,
Deliver us from hardship! (Pantusov 1890: 67–68, 149–50).

Based on the ethnographic evidence, we may conclude that the funerary and commemoration rituals complement each other, and that they stand in structural opposition to the Barat. In the former, it is the dead who are interrogated and who have to account for their deeds during their lifetime. The living try to ease the burdens of the dead through taking part in the *namaz* in the mosque, through the payment of *isqat* and of real or assumed debts, and by keeping the spirit of the dead company with Koran recitations, thus easing its integration into the other world. The weak spirit is nourished through cooking, in particular through the smell of fried oil. Most of the funerary and commemoration rituals are monopolised by men because important aspects of these rituals take place in public space – the mosque and cemetery – which are normatively defined as male areas. However, the sacrificial meal is provided by women within the home and gifts are also transmitted by women.

In contrast, during the Barat, the living are at the centre of the ritual, since it is they who must account for their own sins. To ease their burdens, they appeal for the help of the dead. But to regard the Barat as a mere inversion of the death rituals would be a simplification. Although most of the praying takes place in the domestic space, we know that in the past it used to spill over into public spaces: the streets, cemetery, or saintly shrines. Male participation and male and female attendance in the graveyards at different times are also well documented. Women appear to have played a more central role in this ritual, partly because the nourishment of the dead through the smell of fried cakes at home and by the graves appears to be a central idea. Ritualised female attendance at the graves at this time can be interpreted equally as a subversion, rather than a mere inversion of normative rules. Taranchi girls could even attend the mosque at dawn, another invasion of 'male public space'. The primarily female associations of the ritual are also emphasised here through the girls' prayer addressed to *Bäkht ana* (Mother of Good Luck), which was then mocked by boys.

These implicit gender associations – that is the primarily male character of the death rituals and the primarily female associations of the Barat – are highlighted in the changes these rituals have undergone during the socialist period. Although in principle both sexes should participate in the *näzir-chiraq*, during the years of food rationing and widespread poverty in villages, expenses were often reduced by the exclusion of women who were not close relatives of the mourning family, even if they belonged to the same mosque community. Ironically, a similar trend can be observed in recent years in more prosperous villages. Like weddings, commemorations of the dead are seen by many as occasions for flaunting one's wealth. Social pressure has increased on the organisers to invite many people and provide them with elaborate meals; pressure has likewise increased on participants to bring food and fabric. Many villagers face difficulties in meeting these demands. To avoid the accentuation of the economic and social differentiation brought about by the market reforms of the early 1980s, increasing pressure is put on villagers to keep the expenses of commemoration rituals low both by the Chinese communist authorities and by the religious orthodoxy. This has led to limiting female participation to members of the dead man's family. In contrast, all men of the mosque community are expected to attend, which further emphasises the male associations of the funerary rites.

Plate 10. Men gathered for a funeral outside a mosque, Southern Xinjiang (Photo: Chris Hann).

The Barat on the other hand, has undergone further marked feminisation. Before 1949, male and female participation had been common, although the vigils were segregated. After 1949, owing to continuing religious repression, the ritual acquired a semi-clandestine character, and many of my interview partners claim that it has become increasingly feminised, with many more women taking part than men. In some villages, participation in the Barat is said to be exclusively female. To the best of my knowledge, funerary rites and the commemoration of the dead have never been labelled overtly by the secular authority as superstition, and participation in the communal prayer for the dead in the mosque has largely remained unchallenged. In the villages where I worked in 1996 even Communist Party members continued to attend both the funeral service and the *näzir-chiraq*, an indication that death-related rituals have been generally regarded to be at the heart of local Uyghur Islamic practices. In contrast, owing to religious repression, the Barat is considered by many as mere superstition and has withdrawn entirely into the domestic space. Although not necessarily condemned by all religious office holders, it does not enjoy their full support, perhaps partly due to its primarily female associations.[17]

Personal Piety – *Yagh Puritish*

Both the above-discussed rituals include the preparation and consumption of fried cakes, a task which, according to the traditional division of labour, is always associated with women. The cakes are believed to nourish the spirit of the dead with the smell of hot oil. Textual sources confirm that, despite the normative prohibition on women's presence in the cemetery, it was women who took the cakes there. The ritual orientation of this type of food preparation is known as *yagh puritish* (making the oil fragrant).

In Southern Xinjiang today, the frying of cakes and the visiting of graves by women persists beyond the well-defined ritual realm of the Barat. For some women, it is an integral part of their weekly routine, and therefore much more frequent than formalised rituals involving men. As in some other parts of the Islamic world, women are excluded from the mosque, from the communal prayer for the dead, and from attending the funeral in the cemetery. Nevertheless, women appear to play a central role in the veneration of the dead. They are active participants, either as organisers or as guests in the two rituals described above, where they are in charge of the preparation of the ritual food for nourishing the dead and of taking this food to the graves.

---

[17] Partly because of its unorthodox, folk character. There are indications that both the Barat and the *näzir-chiraq* (or at least parts of the *näzir*) were in the past challenged by some religious authorities. In 1902, one mosque in the northern suburb of Kashgar started advocating ideas of uncontaminated Sunni orthodoxy, and condemned the celebration of both rituals (Wang n.d.: 15).

Yagh puritish or preparing ritual food continues to be routinely performed by Uyghur women in villages in Southern Xinjiang as well as among Uyghur refugees from Northern Xinjiang in Almaty, Kazakhstan. It is virtually obligatory on every Thursday during the first 40 days following death. *Yagh puritish* is also performed throughout the year outside ritual obligations on a weekly basis, mainly on Tuesdays and Thursdays. Nur Luke from Khotan reported pre-1949 conditions. According to him, it was essential to make the oil fragrant on certain days of the week (he specified Thursday or Friday) as well as on the night of Barat and on religious festivals, because on these days the spirits of the dead go to visit their homes and to see their respective families and relatives. Women cooked the favourite food of their dead relative; when the cooking oil was hot they sprinkled fragrant spices into it, thus creating an incense which spread all over the house. When the spirit sniffed this scent he knew he was remembered and was pleased. He would praise God, and ask him to give his blessings (*bärkä*) to his family and relatives. But if he found that his family and relatives were not living peacefully and did not remember him, he would become angry and sad; he would cry and curse them. The food would be eaten by members of the household but could also be shared with strangers. The *sawap* (merit) generated in this way was dedicated to the spirit of the dead (Nur Luke 1950: 114–22).

Consistent with this account, I have been informed that preparing ritual food in commemoration of the dead is not the only way to pay one's respect. It is sufficient to cook any meal which requires the heating of cooking oil 'to make the oil fragrant' and to consciously remember the dead while reciting the short formula: 'may this reach the spirit of my ancestors' (*äjdatlarimning rohigha tägsün*). Although this can be done on any day, it is most commonly done on Thursdays, because it is believed that on this day the spirits fly to Mecca, to return only on Saturday. The smell of hot oil invigorates the spirits and makes them strong, so they can reach Mecca more quickly (Rakhman, Hämdulla and Khushtar 1996: 134). The regular burning of the lamp (*yid chiragh*), and making the oil fragrant ensure the frequent return of the spirit to the house and his favourable intercession with God on behalf of the living (Nur Luke 1950: 114).

Women's commemoration of the dead is achieved through the idiom of food and the act of cooking. Within the domestic space, women are the exclusive controllers of food. Their participation in all rituals is characterised by the carrying of gifts, which often include fabric as well as cooked food and bread. Nowadays, both men and women may contribute money as a ritual gift, but contributing food and textiles remains the exclusive prerogative of women. Women's close association with food is part and

parcel of their daily experience. In addition to contributing food to particular
rituals, they are also able to turn their daily activities into a private and
virtually invisible act of negotiating with the spirit world. Through their
control of food, Uyghur women's participation in the more formal, ritualised
commemoration of the dead becomes central, despite its not being
articulated as such, since their contribution is essential to the nourishment of
the dead. This appears to have taken on an additional significance
throughout the years of extreme religious repression and persecution. During
the Great Leap Forward of the late 1950s, locally known as the era of the
Big Cooking Pot (*chong qazan*), the setting up of communal eating halls in
villages near Kashgar meant that for several years villagers were not allowed
to cook at home. Many remember bitterly how even their cooking utensils
were taken away to prevent private cooking. The denial of cooking at home
meant an enormous disruption not only in family and communal life. It was
also a drastic interference with spiritual life because it rendered impossible
daily, routinised domestic rituals, such as remembering the dead (and
ensuring their goodwill). This aspect presumably remained hidden to the
Chinese authorities imposing the regulations.

Because it is so ordinary and embedded in daily life, *yagh puritish* can
also be performed on any other occasion when the spirits' help is particularly
needed. For instance, seeing one's dead parent or close relative in a dream
could be interpreted to mean that the spirit had become weak and needed
assistance. To meet this need, one should fry oil and pray (Rakhman,
Hämdulla and Khushtar 1996: 184). It can also be done before a family
member sets out on a long journey, or whenever somebody has a bad dream.
After the first two to three *poshkal*s are fried, the woman cooking says: '*Ya,
bismillah! Bowilirim, momilirimning rohigha tägsün!*' (Oh, Bismillah[18], may
it reach the souls of my grandfathers and grandmothers!), or: '*Bowilirim,
momilirimning rohi mädät qilghay!*' (May it help the souls of my
grandfathers and grandmothers!) (Häbibulla 1993: 398).

Further vestiges of the veneration of the dead also involve food
sacrifice. Sources describing daily practice in Xinjiang prior to 1949 mention
how dried apples and quince were placed in the four corners of a house. One
explanation was that it ensured that angels entered the house, but some
claimed that this was done to please the spirits of deceased relatives entering.
'Abdul-Qadir from Yarkand informs us that dried fruit could also be placed
on the graves of deceased parents and relatives, while others would leave
them at saintly shrines. Furthermore, shamanic healers (*dakhan*s, *perikhon*s)
would put down dried fruit in their houses to prevent evil spirits from

---

[18] The Arabic formula meaning 'In the name of God'.

entering ('Abdul-Qadir 1930: 46). The spirits of the dead were thought to benefit from the dried fruits through the smell, since the act of placing dried fruits in various corners of the house was known as *buy sälish* (creating a fragrance). It is possible that for some, namely the poor, this was a more easily accessible strategy than *yagh puritish* because summer fruit was much cheaper than oil.[19] For others it was yet another option to interact with the supernatural. This last reference takes us back to our starting point, since the source explicitly mentions that dried fruit could be taken to the graves of dead relatives, also to shrines, and that it was also employed with the purpose of averting evil spirits by the *dakhan* and *perikhan*, those figures with magical powers whom some scholars like to describe as shamans. This short indigenous reference is an apt encapsulation of the convergence of diverse traditions. My materials are not sufficient to allow me to elaborate on the equivalencies to be found between ancestor cults and shamanic traditions, but appealing to the spirit of the dead for help through mediation and techniques of transferral, transmission, and sacrifice are common to both.

Similar expressions of personal piety may be found in other domestic acts: Patimäm's hand is frequently invoked when dough is prepared.[20] In village households, bread is normally baked every week or once every ten days, but dough making is more frequent since most dishes require the preparation of noodles. When starting this job many village women whisper quietly, 'this is not my hand, it is the hand of Mother Patimäm which is doing this job' to ensure the saint's blessing and good luck for her family which as they consume the blessed food. As one elderly woman explained: 'few women know exactly who Patimäm is, but her hand is firmly imprinted on our minds'.

The practice of *yagh puritish* as a weekly ritual accompanied by private prayer to appease the spirit of the dead has survived the Soviet period among Uyghur migrant families in Kazakhstan. It is often routinely observed even by women whose religiosity may be best described in terms of scepticism. Today, it plays an important part in pilgrimages and in modern

---

[19] My interview partners making reference to the serious food shortages during the late 1950s and early 1960s recalled that poverty was so great that some people started selling the fruit of trees normally regarded as common property to which all, including the poor, had free access. Molla 'Abdul-Qadir from Yarkand (c. 1930) informs us that local custom demanded that mulberry trees should be planted on the common land outside private gardens. In this way nobody could be angry if people ate the mulberries, and both rich and poor had equal access to it ('Abdul-Qadir 1930: 1).

[20] Patimäm is undoubtedly identical with Fatima, daughter of the Prophet Muhammad, a female saint venerated throughout the Islamic world. Her hand is a well-known symbol in Muslim popular religion which serves to avert the evil eye (Schimmel 1990: 264).

healing rituals. It has persisted in Xinjiang throughout the repression of the Maoist years. We know of the pre-1949 existence of the practice as a ritual action, but it is harder to establish to what extent it continued to remain part of women's daily routine during the Maoist era, at times of serious food shortages and rationing. It is possible that its significance as a private, female manifestation of personal piety within the domestic space has increased as ritual forms of religious expression have shrunk owing to political pressure. Even if this cannot be proved, the mere fact of its routinised persistence among Xinjiang villagers and Kazakhstani migrants in changing economic and political climates can be at least partly interpreted as a consequence of decades of religious persecution, which confined the extension of religious ritual to the domesticity of the female world.

Conclusion

Emphasising the composite, syncretic nature of prevailing practices, I have shown that instead of attempting to discern the separate, largely imaginary 'building blocks' of popular practices, assumed to be pure and authentic, it is through examining the complicated interplay of various practices with each other and with normative rules that we can make better sense of strategies to deal with the supernatural and to the gendered core of persisting Uyghur cultural identity. Ultimately, all practices pertaining to the dead serve a double purpose: through performing sacrifices for the dead, social actors hope to ensure at the same time the well-being of both the spirits of the dead and the living. In this respect, saint worship through pilgrimages to shrines may appear to actors as virtually synonymous with more general veneration of the dead. I have argued that funeral and commemoration rites are ostensibly male rituals supported by female participation which has varied over time. They involve participation in public spaces, notably the mosque and the cemetery, which at the normative level are identified as male spheres. The obligation to pray at the dead parents' graves is also regarded as an exclusively male obligation. The connection of death rituals to official Islamic practice is ensured through the obligatory participation of male members of the mosque community at the communal prayer for the dead in the mosque and in the presence of members of the Muslim spiritual authorities. The Barat, like the commemoration of the dead, aims at attaining forgiveness and redemption for the dead. But through ensuring good relations with the spirit world, this ritual also focuses on the welfare of the living. Although before 1949 it had a partly public and emphatically communal character and was closely associated with women, as a result of religious repression and its definite classification as a feudal superstition, it has undergone further feminisation and domestication. This transformation was made possible partly by the fact that it has never been connected to the mosque and that it allows full female participation. I suggest that the primarily male association of the veneration of the dead through the funeral, the commemoration of the dead, and praying by the graveside are merely normative. Through the subversive, more female ritual of Barat and through the most important female symbol of food, expressed in *yagh puritish* or the nurturing of the dead, women's central role in dealings with the supernatural is given expression, even though it remains muted.

References

'Abdul-Qadir. ca. 1930. *A Collection of Eastern Turki Folkloristic Texts.* Unpublished manuscript. Yarkand, Jarring Collection, Lund University Library. Prov. 464. (Turki).

Ardener, E. 1975. Belief and the Problem of Women. In S. Ardener (ed.), *Perceiving Women*, pp. 1–17. London: Dent.

Änsari, L., Z. Bäshir, and I. Xudayqul (eds.). 1925. *Uyghur äl ädäbiyatidin beyit, näkhsha, qoshaqlar, maqal, täpishmaq, chöchäklär.* Moscow: SSSR Xälqläring Ozäk Näshriyati.

Basilov, V. N. 1987. Popular Islam in Central Asia and Kazakhstan. *Journal of the Institute of Muslim Minority Affairs* 8 (1): 7–17.

Basilow [Basilov], W. N. 1995. *Das Schamanentum bei den Völkern Mittelasiens und Kazachstans.* Berlin: Reinhold Schletzer Verlag.

DeWeese, D. 1994. *Islamization and Native Religion in the Golden Horde: Baba Tükles and Conversion to Islam in Historical and Epic Tradition.* University Park: Pennsylvania State University Press.

van Gennep, A. 1960 [1909]. *The Rites of Passage.* London: Routledge & Kegan Paul.

Gibb, H. A. R., and J. H. Kramers (eds.). 1974. *Shorter Encyclopaedia of Islam.* Leiden: Brill.

Gladney, D. 1994. Representing Nationality in China: Refiguring Majority/ Minority Identities. *Journal of Asian Studies* 53 (1): 92–123.

Grenard, F. 1898. *Le Turkestan et le Tiber. Étude éthnographique et sociologique.* (J.-L. Dutreuil de Rhins: *Mission Scientifique dans la Haute Asie 1890–1895*). Paris: Ernest Leroux.

Häbibulla, A. 1993. *Uyghur Etnografiyisi.* Ürümchi: Shinjang Xälq Näshriyati.

Jarring, G. (ed.). 1980. *Literary Texts from Kashgar.* Lund: CWK Gleerup.

——. 1986a. Ramazan Poetry from Charchan. *Orientalia Suecana* 33/35 (1984/86): 189–194.

——. 1986b. *Return to Kashgar: Central Asian Memoirs in the Present.* (trans. Eva Claeson). Durham: Duke University Press.

——. 1987. *Dervish and Qalandar: Texts from Kashgar.* Stockholm: Almqvist & Wiksell International.

Katanov, N. T., and K. H. Menges. 1933, 1976. *Volkskundliche Texte aus Ost-Türkistan.* Proceedings of the Prussian Academy of Sciences, Section of Philology and History, 1933. Leipzig: Zentralantiquariat of the German Democratic Republic.

Mackerras, C. 1995. *China's Minority Cultures: Identities and Integration since 1912.* New York: St Martin's Press.

Muhammad 'Ali Damolla. ca. 1905–10. *A Collection of Essays on Life in Eastern Turkistan.* Unpublished manuscript. Kahsgar, Jarring Collection, Lund University Library. Prov. 207. I.–II. (Turki).

Nur Luke. ca. 1950s. *A Collection of Essays on the Habits and Customs of Eastern Turkestan.* Unpublished manuscript. Jarring Collection, Lund University Library. Prov. 212. (Turki).

Ölüklärning qomaqining bäyani. n.d. Unpublished manuscript. Jarring Collection, Lund University Library. Prov. 29. (Turki).

Pantusov, N. N. 1890. *Taranchinskiie pesni.* Saint Petersburg: Imperatorskoi Akad. Nauk.

Rakhman, A. R., R. Hämdulla, and Sh. Khushtar. 1996. *Uyghur Örp-Adätliri.* Ürümchi: Shinjang Yashlar Ösmürlär Näshriyati.

Reetz, D. 1999. Islamic Activism in Central Asia and the Pakistan Factor. *Journal of South Asian and Middle Eastern Studies* 23 (1): 7–10.

Rudelson, J. J. 1997. *Oasis Identities: Uyghur Nationalism along China's Silk Road.* New York: Columbia University Press.

Schimmel, A. 1990. Traditionelle Frömmigkeit. In D. Ahmad Munir et al. (eds.), *Der Islam. III. Islamische Kultur Zeitgenössische Strömungen–Volksfrömmigkeit,* pp. 242–266. Stuttgart: Kohl-hammer.

Schwarz, H. G. 1992. *An Uyghur-English Dictionary.* Bellingham: Western Washington University.

Skrine, C. P. 1971 [1926]. *Chinese Central Asia.* New York: Barnes & Noble.

Stewart, C., and R. Shaw. 1994. Introduction. In C. Stewart, and R. Shaw (eds.), *Syncretism/ Anti-syncretism: The Politics of Religious Synthesis,* pp. 1–26. London: Routledge.

Sukhareva, O. A. 1960. *Islam v Uzbekistane.* Tashkent: Izdatel'stvo Akademii Nauk Uzbekskoi SSR.

Turner, V. 1974. *Dramas, Fields, and Metaphors.* Ithaca: Cornell University Press.

Wang J. n.d. *Islam in Kashgar in the 1950s*. Unpublished paper.

Warikoo, K. B. 1985. Chinese Turkestan during the Nineteenth Century: A Socio-Economic Study. *Central Asian Survey* 4 (3): 75–114.

Welch, A. T. 1977. Death and Dying in the Qur'an. In F. E. Reynolds, and E. H. Waugh (eds.), *Religious Encounters with Death: Insights from the History and Anthropology of Religions*, pp. 183–213. University Park: Pennsylvania State University Press.

Wensinck, A. J., and A. S. Tritto. 1960. Adhab al Kabr. In H. A. R. Gibb et. al., *The Encyclopaedia of Islam*, pp. 186–187. Leiden: Brill.

——. 1997. Sha'bān. In C. E. Bosworth et. al., *The Encyclopaedia of Islam*, New Edition, p. 154. Leiden: Brill.

Chapter 9
Rivalry and Solidarity among Uyghur Healers in Kazakhstan[1]

A powerful current in recent scholarship has emphasised the constructed nature of all social phenomena, from economic institutions to ritual and belief systems. Many scholars have insisted that tradition itself is invented (Hobsbawm and Ranger 1983). While recognising the validity of this perspective, this chapter draws more from the counter-trends which put greater weight on continuity and the persistence of tradition: primordiality is a myth, but resonance with a given cultural stream always constrains the scope for construction and invention (Sahlins 1999). According to this view cultural patterns are passed on, often in highly structured ways, and it is time that sceptical debunking gave way to more generous recognition of local authenticities.

The recent efflorescence of healers in Inner and Central Asia is not an entirely new phenomenon. Many magical and healing practices have a demonstrable tradition in both Eastern and Western Turkestan and elsewhere in Asia, and they have been documented, described, and analysed in an extensive literature.[2] As Vladimir Basilov showed, shamanistic practices in large areas of Central Asia share many commonalities, regardless of the ethnic affiliation of the practitioners. Some healing rituals continued under socialism, albeit in a cautious and limited manner (Basilov 1987; Basilow 1995). Despite the disruptions and changed circumstances, the claim of contemporary Central Asian healers to local antecedents (and thereby to tradition) is not unfounded. Continuities with the past form the backbone of the healers' activity and are explicitly emphasised by the actors. The healing ritual itself is said to be based on 'centuries old' practice. Before practising, the healer must receive the blessing of another, senior healer. Once an established professional, she or he is able to bless new, junior practitioners.

---

[1] Published in *Inner Asia* 2001, 3: 73–98.
[2] For bibliographies, see Voigt (1977); Hoppál (1985); Alekseev (1987); for a general volume see Schenk and Rätsch (1999).

In this way healers legitimise themselves through latching on to the past, joining a chain of predecessors from whom the blessing comes.

At the same time, the rituals which I observed in Almaty in 1997 have undergone important changes and differ in significant ways from the descriptions of such 'classical' performances. As Caroline Humphrey found among the modern Buryat, so too in Almaty: 'elaborate costumes, drumming, and above all the presence and participation of an audience – the "society" which according to some theories of shamanism is supposed to be so essential to validating the shaman's efforts – have all gone' (Humphrey 1999: 8). Humphrey explained this retreat of the shamanic ritual into simplified domesticity among the Buryat as a reaction to the 'enforced communality' of Soviet times, an argument which could equally be applied to Kazakhstan and to the Xinjiang Uyghur Autonomous Region in the People's Republic of China.[3] Humphrey's further observation, that the Buryat shaman does not fly to the other world as in most anthropological accounts of shamanism, but rather summons the spirits to him or her, also applies to Uyghur healers whom I encountered in Kazakhstan (Humphrey 1999: 4).

Descriptions of Central Asian healing rituals in European sources over the last hundred years were generally fixated on the figure of the shaman. They presented shamanism as 'an exotic essence, a romanticised inversion of Western rationalism rather than a scholarly category' (Thomas and Humphrey 1994: 2). In the Turki/Uyghur case, the scholarly preoccupation with the shaman (*perikhan, dakhan, bakhshi*) has led to a neglect of other specialists whose methods were less spectacular. These other performances did not acquire the character of a communal ritual and by and large remained within the boundaries of domesticity and therefore within daily practice.[4] My observations among the Uyghur in Almaty confirm this pattern. Following Humphrey, I find it useful to explore the activities of practitioners who are not strictly speaking considered shamans, since 'in no society in Inner Asia, including even the smallest tribe, was trance shamanism all that was going on in religious life' (Humphrey 1994: 192–98). Similarly, writing from a text-based, historical perspective, Devin DeWeese pointed out that an exaggerated emphasis on the figure and performance of the shaman diverts attention away from more central aspects of religious belief, such as the domestic cult (DeWeese 1994: 32–39, chapter 8). It is time to move away

---

[3] Humphrey (1999: 7–8). For a study of the ethnic composition of Xinjiang see Hoppe (1998).

[4] Descriptions point to the existence of a number of such specialists, although their exact function is usually not spelt out. For a summary of sources on shamanism among the Turki/Uyghur of Eastern Turkestan/Xinjiang, see Basilow (1995). For a list of other specialists, see Katanov and Menges (1933, 1976: 1250–63); Du Shaoyuan (1995).

from the fixation on shamanic ritual and to enquire more generally into the meaning of inspirational practices, both for the practitioner and for the clients.

This chapter therefore approaches the healer's sessions as social action and one of many forms of curing practices currently available to patients. I shall show that within the informal surroundings of the neighbourhood, the healer and her circle of patients may constitute informal religious associations which offer companionship and solidarity to their members, but are simultaneously an arena of contested authority. The chapter explores the ways in which a healer establishes and maintains the credibility from which her authority derives.[5] It further suggests that modern healers' activities may have important but largely hidden underpinnings, which derive from intra-group differentiation. It combines attention to long-term cultural continuities with a consideration of more proximate social differentiating factors in order to tease out the social meanings of this form of healing today.

The Setting

My two months' stay in Kazakhstan in 1997 was an extension of earlier research in Xinjiang, described in the preceding chapters. I was able to stay with a Uyghur family, an opportunity I did not have in Xinjiang. My host family helped me to integrate into the neighbourhood. I took part in daily life and became involved in the various social activities of my landlady. I soon realised that occasional visits to a healer formed part and parcel of neighbourhood life.

The composition of the neighbourhood reflected the ethnic, linguistic, cultural, and religious diversity of the city: it included Russians, Kazakhs, Uyghurs, some ethnic Germans, Tatars, Uzbeks, and others. All these people were trying to come to terms with the social consequences of post-Soviet economic hardship and they did so in culturally diverse ways. Those able to keep their former jobs continued to work there, though some sought additional sources of income. Those who lost their old jobs tried to find employment in the private sector or in self-employment, such as working as a driver or as a seamstress. Letting out one's city centre flat to a foreign firm was one strategy for making ends meet, and the new petty markets opened up others. Work as a healer was also an option taken up by many, both men and women.

---

[5] In this respect my approach overlaps with that of Manduhai Buyandelgeriyn (1999), who focused on power struggles among Buryat shamans.

Almaty offered a wide variety of healing methods and healers, but my investigations focused around the activities of one Uyghur neighbourhood healer whose clientele was mostly recruited from within the neighbourhood. I first visited this lady with my landlady when she needed the healer's services. After this initial introduction, I became a regular visitor. I sat through many of the healer's seances and accompanied her on home visits and on a pilgrimage (chapter 10). Later I met some other healers, but I continued to focus on this lady. I learned about her background, her methods, her ideas, and also the opinions held by others about her.

The neighbourhood in question, Mir (Peace)[6], had been officially attached to the city of Almaty only three years previously. Throughout the years of Soviet socialism it was inhabited principally by refugees and migrants, who were settled here to work in the local collective farm (*kolkhoz*). Perched on the very edge of a large city, the neighbourhood displayed both urban and rural characteristics.[7] The city centre was 40 minutes away by bus and the modern housing estates in the vicinity were constant reminders of the city's proximity. But gentrification also started as new villas were being built by the nouveaux riches. Nonetheless, at the time of my stay this neighbourhood still retained much of its 'traditional' character.

Although primarily regarded as a Uyghur neighbourhood, according to some people it had been founded originally as a settlement for Meskhetian Turks. Many houses had been occupied by ethnic Germans who 'repatriated' to Germany in the early 1990s. Most of these houses were either still up for sale or had been sold to incoming Kazakhs and others. Some Russian and Tatar families were also living in the neighbourhood, and ethnically mixed marriages were not uncommon. Not all Almaty Uyghurs lived in this neighbourhood. Many lived in ethnically mixed apartment blocks on housing estates in other parts of the city, but Mir had a larger concentration, and even boasted a Uyghur primary school and the neighbourhood leadership was predominantly Uyghur.

This Uyghur diaspora community is far from homogeneous. The main internal divisions were not simply based on oasis identities, as one might expect on the basis of the anthropologist Justin Rudelson's study of ethnic identity in the Uyghur homeland (Rudelson 1997). Rather, the divisions were based on migration history and followed a temporal axis. Responding to the changing political and economic climate, over the last hundred years many Uyghurs have left China as migrants and refugees to neighbouring

---

[6] The name of the neighbourhood and the names of all individuals have been changed.

[7] At the time of my stay, Almaty was still the capital of Kazakhstan. Soon after my departure the capital was transferred to Astana.

Central Asia. Some families have a history of several such resettlements. As a result of these movements, the Uyghur living in Kazakhstan today emphasise intra-group differences based on the migration history of their families, which significantly affect and reflect their level of integration into their surroundings. People whose families had come to what is Kazakhstan today are considered well-integrated and referred to as local (*yärlik*) Uyghurs. Those with a more recent migration history (arrival in 1962) are described as Chinese (*Khitay*) Uyghur.[8] Sunni Islam is the dominant religion among them, but collective and individual memory recalls long periods of religious oppression in the Soviet Union and, in the case of the recent migrants, also in the People's Republic of China. Both groups have retained the Uyghur language as a primary ethnic marker and as the main means of communication within the group, and they both share some idea of a homeland back in Eastern Turkestan/Xinjiang. However, only the recent migrants have retained active family ties with relatives left in the homeland. For many local Uyghur, Eastern Turkestan/Xinjiang has taken on the dimension of a mythical homeland, though some might visit the place for commercial or religious purposes. These and other perceived differences were articulated through the construction of mutual stereotypes. Chinese Uyghur claimed that the local Uyghur had forgotten their national traditions and had been alienated from Islam, as manifested in their consumption of pork. They were also said to have become ignorant of traditional customs, including the preparation of authentic Uyghur food. Furthermore, having adapted to Russian ways, their temperament had become Russian (*mijäzi orus*, chapter 7), an outcome accentuated by frequent intermarriage with Russians. In contrast, the Chinese Uyghur were projected by both groups as embodiments and maintainers of tradition who could help local Uyghur to relearn what they had forgotten. For their part, local Uyghur described the recent migrants as being more conservative and less educated than themselves, but – when in a more charitable mood – some might add that the Chinese Uyghur were indeed more knowledgeable in matters of religion and better upholders of Uyghur tradition as manifest in customs, language use, and cooking.[9] Both groups emphasised that intermarriage between them was

---

[8] This simple model does not do justice to the complex realities experienced by many families who went through several phases of migration. Some of those who left China in the end of the nineteenth century returned a few decades later, fleeing religious persecution in the Soviet Union, only to make their way back again in the 1950s or 1960s. A number of those who returned to China from the Soviet Union in the 1930s never gave up their Soviet passports and used these during the time of the most recent wave of re-migration.

[9] At the time of my stay, a dissident imam from Kashgar was serving in the neighbourhood mosque. His studies in the Middle East coupled with his origins in Kashgar (which is widely

infrequent, a claim I found difficult to substantiate. There was certainly a great deal of interaction between the two sub-groups. Like other first generation migrants, the Chinese Uyghur were disadvantaged initially in their new place of residence because they did not speak Russian and were unable to use their qualifications acquired in China. Initially, inter-group relationships often followed a pattern of asymmetrical patron-client relations, in which the Chinese Uyghur sought favours from influential local Uyghur. Such favours could include help with the admission of a son or a daughter to university or securing a job for adult children. Local Uyghur clearly enjoyed a more favourable position in Soviet Kazakhstan, especially in the labour market. By the late 1990s the 'newcomers' had mastered Russian well enough to get by in daily life and their children were all fluent Russian speakers. However, they still appeared to be more vulnerable to postsocialist unemployment than the same generation of local Uyghur.

In Mir, relations between the sub-groups were generally good. Hostility was more often expressed on the interethnic level. Many first generation Chinese Uyghur continued to regard the Han and the Chinese state with a great deal of hostility. Their children, however, directed their discontent toward the Kazakh leadership, whom they blamed for the economic mismanagement of the country and discriminatory policies against small groups like themselves. All Uyghurs liked to claim a higher level of family cohesion than other ethnic groups (e.g. Kazakhs or Russians). Within their group, this characteristic was more likely to be attributed to the Chinese Uyghur, who were said to be more endogamous than the locals and to maintain close contacts with people who originated in the same Xinjiang oasis.[10]

Social life was not confined to the neighbourhood, and ritual action (mourning, circumcision, and wedding celebrations), informal socialisation, and kinship and support networks reached far beyond its physical boundaries. Not all members of Mir knew each other well: it was by no means a self-sufficient, closed *Gemeinschaft*, but a space attached to a highly

---

regarded as the Islamic heartland of Xinjiang) automatically credited him with a great deal of respect and authority in spite of his young age.

[10] The oasis affiliations of the Chinese Uyghur were not always clear-cut. On the composite origins of the Uyghur coming from the Ili valley, north of Xinjiang, see Roberts (1998: 697). If a person had one parent from Ili, and another from Ürümchi, she or he could foreground the descent line as the situation required. Similarly, a person born in Kashgar but brought up in the northern city of Chöchäk could lay claim to either as a place of origin. In such cases people usually insisted on the northern line of descent because this ensured more immediate acceptance by their predominantly northern neighbours, who regarded southerners as ignorant and boorish. In contrast, local Uyghur often claimed ignorance of the precise origins of their families.

complex urban milieu in which neither residence, nor ethnic affiliation, nor language, nor religion provided people with absolute identities. Ethnicity seemed generally to be the most important form of identity, but this too was far from being absolute, either under or after socialism. The collapse of the Soviet Union and the abandoning of a planned economy in favour of the free market exposed the population to a multitude of new ideas and religious movements, ranging from various forms of evangelical Christianity to New Age cults and the Hare Krishna movement.[11] These new ideologies were paralleled by the revival of numerous traditional ritual practices, often with eclectic new techniques. Thus spirit possession was accompanied by the use of electrical currents, massages, herbal cures, yoga, and transcendental meditation.

The dominant element in the revival of ritual practices was that of healing, a consequence of the economic uncertainties of the transition, accentuated by a crisis in the old health care system. The market for alternative solutions to social and medical problems was conditioned by poverty on both demand and supply sides. Some forms of folk medicine persisted throughout the Soviet era on a limited scale but the ideological permissiveness of the post-Soviet era has allowed a veritable efflorescence. As in Siberian cities, in Central Asia too, 'it has become normal for anyone with a misfortune or quandary to visit a shaman' (Humphrey 1999: 3).[12] The Kazakh government tried to regulate the proliferation of alternative healers by act of parliament in 1997. This restricted the practice of folk medicine to the holders of certificates and licenses. The certificates were to be issued jointly by the Centre of Eastern and Contemporary Medicine and the Ministry of Health and the licenses were newly obtainable from the local authorities. However, controls were ineffective and, during my stay a number of unregistered private practitioners were active in Mir.

In what follows, I shall concentrate on the activities of one Uyghur female healer who habitually described herself as a *qumilaqchi* (diviner, fortuneteller). Although she did not call herself a *bakhshi* (shaman)[13], I shall argue that her methods and activities overlap substantially with those of Muqäddäs, the *bakhshi* (to be introduced below) from whom she learned her trade. The sessions were usually referred to as *dawalash* (healing, curing), although the practitioners themselves sometimes used the Russian term

---

[11] For an excellent survey of the range of complementary medicine available in post-Soviet Almaty, see Penkala-Gawęcka (2006).

[12] A dramatic increase of shamans has also been reported among the Buryats in Mongolia (Buyandelgeriyn 1999: 221).

[13] Schwarz gives the following meanings: shaman, witch doctor, sorcerer, magician (1992: 53). The healers themselves sometimes translated the word into Russian as *shamanka*.

seans. I begin by describing the healing methods of Muqaddäs the *bakhshi*, since this is the yardstick against which the activities of the lower level specialist, the *qumilaqchi* can be measured. This is followed by a description of the working methods of the *qumilaqchi*. Finally, this healer's ideological stance to her teacher and patients will be evaluated in terms of solidarity, rivalry, and conflicting interests. I argue that she had to perform a careful balancing act to maintain her own credibility without allowing her clients to become either too sceptical or to become business rivals.

The Teacher: Muqäddäs, the *Bakhshi*

Muqäddäs was an attractive, charismatic woman in her late forties. She was a local Uyghur, the mother of three children. After two divorces, in 1997 she was living again with her first husband. Having attended a three months' course at the Centre of Eastern and Complementary Medicine, Muqäddäs has acquired a certificate as a recognised folk healer and claimed to be a 'psychologist-healer', rather than an exorcist. As a licensed healer she had, together with a number of other alternative practitioners, integrated into the new and chaotic medical system of independent Kazakhstan. In 1997 she was practising in her small surgery in the basement of a big polyclinic in the centre of Almaty. As a registered healer, she received a set fee from her patients (400 *sum* per visit), and she had to pay taxes to the state.[14] Each consultation was by appointment and lasted approximately 30 minutes.

Muqäddäs claimed that she was capable of dealing with a wide range of health and social problems. She also asserted that all such problems could be caused by evil spirits, and that belief formed the ideological basis of her holistic approach. Through summoning her helping spirits she could expel the trouble-making ones from the patients' body. Her patients included men and women of various ethnic groups – Uyghur, Kazakh, and Russian. They represented diverse social groups, although the high fees which she charged at the polyclinic could generally be afforded only by members of the more affluent middle class. She usually summoned the spirits in a mixture of the Uyghur and Kazakh languages, but to her patients she normally spoke in Russian. During her sessions, she stood facing the patient who also remained standing. She asked the patient to close his or her eyes and started chanting. Soon she gave the impression of herself being in a trance. Having summoned the spirits by lifting her hands up in praying position, she then drew on a repertoire of bodily techniques, which included serial belching, loud laughter, screaming, whistling, bending her whole body to and fro, rhyth-

---

[14] The official currency is tenge, but locals prefer the word *sum*. In 1997, 1 US dollar was equal to 185.80 Kazakh tenges.

mical stamping of her feet, and the repeated touching of the patient's body. Ailments such as backache were treated with massage (for which the patient should bring a clean sheet and a pot of honey). On a typical day in 1997 I recorded the following visitors to Muqäddäs' surgery:

- A Kazakh woman aged 40 and her son aged 17. The son had been showing signs of mental disturbance, which Muqäddäs explained as having been caused by the evil eye (*yaman köz*). The mother suffered from backache. As requested by the mother, Muqäddäs at first treated mother and son simultaneously, applying the technique of hypnosis. After this, the son was sent outside, and the mother was given a very thorough and even painful massage. The healer explained the backache exclusively as a physical problem: too much salt had been trapped under the patient's skin. To eliminate the accumulated salt, she applied honey on the lady's back and massaged it. This was the woman's seventh visit to Muqäddäs.

- A Kazakh woman and her teenage daughter. The woman was director of a scientific institute at the Kazakh Academy of Sciences, and was embarrassed about consulting an alternative practitioner. She was visiting for the first time, and confessed that she never used to believe in 'such things'. Following an operation, the daughter had become very weak, lethargic, and pale, and had bad dreams. Doctors had not been able to find anything wrong with her. Muqäddäs assured the mother that the girl had been possessed by spirits (*arwahlar*), probably including that of her grandfather. The spirits could not be fully released from her because she could 'not be opened' (*echilmäydu*). Muqäddäs could nonetheless help by purifying her (*tazilish*). In the 40-minute healing session which followed, Muqäddäs employed all her exorcising techniques. She went very close to the girl, who appeared to be in trance, held her arms and made her bend in various directions, her own body following the patient's movements. She chanted, belched, and shouted, repeatedly calling on her helping spirits to remove (*kötärsün, kötärsün!*) the polluting elements (i.e. the bad spirits) from the girl. At the end of the session she said that the girl could possibly become a healer herself when she grew up. The girl's mother produced a big jar which had been filled with water. Muqäddäs recited (*oquydu*) a short prayer over this water. Then she prayed and blew over a packet of tea, also brought by the girl's mother, which the girl was to prepare with this water and consume.

- A Russian woman (aged about 50) complained of pain all over her body. She was treated with the exorcism seance as described above.

She was not a first time visitor, and the seance was more routinely performed. It lasted for 15 minutes only.

- A Uyghur boy aged 12 with earache complaints. Muqäddäs performed the seance briefly. Then she sat the boy down and held his head in her hands, without talking much. She chanted, but without the elaborate formalities of the previous sessions.

- A young Uyghur girl who complained of stomachache. She was told by Muqäddäs that her illness was caused by evil spirits. Muqäddäs proceeded to exorcise the spirits, using the methods of chanting, praying, shouting, belching, whistling, and touching the girl's body from top to toe, but especially the stomach area. This lasted for about 30 minutes.

- A Uyghur lady called Büwükhan, aged 47, who was a former pupil, confidante, and friend of Muqäddäs and now herself a practising healer. Büwükhan came partly to have her persistent cough treated, and partly to ask Muqäddäs why her own previously flourishing healing business was declining. Muqäddäs told Büwükhan that she had been bewitched. Evil people jealous of her business success had cast a spell on her. She then performed a proper, long seance, with all her usual techniques. Büwükhan did not pay a fee, unlike all the earlier clients that day.

The Lesser Religious Specialist: Büwükhan, the Diviner

Büwükhan was also a local Uyghur. She called herself a *qumilaqchi* (diviner, fortune-teller, or seer) (see Schwarz 1992: 657). Her patients usually called her a female healer (*dawalaghan ayal*). Although she had been instructed by the acknowledged *bakhshi* Muqäddäs, Büwükhan insisted that she herself was not a shaman. First, she told me that when she was 15 (during Soviet times) she had been abducted by a married man who had kept her in his house for a month while his wife was away visiting her mother. Later Büwükhan clarified the story: she had gone to this man's house after he had paid money to her parents, who were very poor. When the wife returned home and realised what had been going on, she filed a complaint against her husband. He was condemned to four years' imprisonment, since Büwükhan at the time was still a minor. Büwükhan returned to the parental home pregnant, and married another man soon after the birth of her first child. He was a cook and barber, a Chinese Uyghur from the north of Xinjiang whose family had settled in Almaty; he was 13 years her senior. From this marriage she had four further children. Of the 16 years of their marriage, the couple had spent 6 years in Bukhara at her mother-in-law's house. Büwükhan had very negative memories of this period. Her mother-in-law had treated her badly and made her work extremely hard. Eventually the couple returned to Almaty, where they had built the house where she was still living in 1997. A few months after they had moved into the house her husband died. She had married again, but this marriage had ended after only five months. She had thrown out her husband because he turned out to be a man of bad disposition. Since her divorce she had lived with her two youngest children. She explained that, although marriage was an option for her, for a female healer it was better to remain single because she could remain clean (*pakiz yürüdü*) more easily.[15]

During socialism, Büwükhan had performed odd jobs on the collective farm. After the collapse of the Soviet Union, like many others, she experienced economic hardship. She had met Muqäddäs in 1993 when the latter was already a practising healer. Although Muqäddäs had a husband and children, she had come to live in Büwükhan's spacious house for a year because her family was poor and their own house very small. She needed to make money, and she needed space to practise.[16]

Büwükhan provided Muqäddäs with rooms and the neighbourhood proved to be a convenient location for establishing a healing business. Büwükhan gave Muqäddäs spiritual support and became her assistant. During this period she also paid the *bakhshi* substantial sums of money (2,500 *sum* altogether). She had attempted fortune-telling before, but Muqäddäs told her that she had many spirits and therefore had the potential to heal. After this revelation Büwükhan became very ill, so ill that she had to stay in bed for weeks. No doctor could help her. She learnt from Muqäddäs that she must have been possessed by spirits as a four-year-old. Muqäddäs also helped her understand that she had to take up the challenge, and in order to recover she had to become a healer herself. Büwükhan referred to this revelation as the time when she 'opened up' (*echildi*). Since that time she has been making a living from healing. During much of my stay in the neighbourhood, following a short period of stagnation, her business was booming and some neighbours estimated that she could make as much as 2,000 *sum* per day.

---

[15] This emphasis on the importance of cleanliness, which has both physical and ritual dimensions, has clear Islamic connotations. When I pointed out that Muqäddäs herself was living with her former husband, Büwükhan replied that, as a *bakhshi*, Muqäddäs knew very well how to keep herself clean, thus implicitly attributing superiority to Muqäddäs.

[16] I was never told how the two women met, nor did I learn how Muqäddäs organised her family while she was staying with Büwükhan. It is likely that she could rely on family support and in any case she often visited her family. It was presumably during this period that Muqäddäs established herself as a well-known, charismatic, and strong shamaness within the neighbourhood, and through informal networks also in wider circles in Almaty. Soon she had enough money to be able to afford a large house herself in another district of the city.

Unlike Muqāddäs, Büwükhan worked from home. Her 'surgery' was a rectangular side room opening from her kitchen; it was furnished with carpets and mats both on the walls and on the floor. Cushions were arranged along the two longer sides. Facing the entrance, at the far end of the room stood a small table with the tools of her trade: a copy of the Koran, a handful of white beans (used for divination) wrapped in a piece of white cloth, a whip (*qamcha*), a knife (*bichaq*), a rosary (*täspih*), a spare headscarf for female patients who happened to come for a healing session without a scarf[17], and some money. The rosary and the Koran were important markers of Büwükhan's Muslim identity. In fact she never used the Koran, even though the magical use of the Holy Book for divination among the Uyghur (and Central Asian Muslims in general) is well documented (Katanov and Menges 1933, 1976: 1250–53).[18] In between seeing patients who waited in her kitchen, she did a bit of cooking, ate, drank water, and even watched television, sometimes accompanied by her patients. Outside surgery hours and between consultations she was casual, relaxed, and friendly.

Büwükhan relied mostly on a limited repertoire of prayers, though with new patients she usually started with a divination session. Healer and patient sat on mats facing each other. Praying quietly, Büwükhan opened the white tissue and organised the white beans in groups of two, three, or four; then she re-organised them, pushing the small groups here and there. She then showed signs of getting into trance, made strange noises, trembled, and shook her body. Eyes closed, she would speak in a distorted voice, so that she could barely be understood. Occasionally she started the session by fingering the rosary for inspiration.

Like Muqāddäs, Büwükhan also treated both physical symptoms and social problems. She claimed to be a *qumilaqchi* from birth but after her apprenticeship with Muqāddäs she had progressed to become a healer (*dawalaghan ayal*). Her trademark method of diagnosis remained divination. The diagnosis was commonly that the patient was afflicted by evil spirits, or by the evil eye, or that someone had cast a spell. During the divination and the ensuing healing, the healer appeared to be in an altered state of consciousness. In contrast to descriptions of 'classical' shamans, Büwükhan, like Muqāddäs, never claimed that her soul left her body. On the contrary, in

---

[17] Female patients and the healer herself are expected to show outward signs of modesty. The headscarf expresses moral propriety, piety, belief in God and therefore in the healer.

[18] The Koran was a Uyghur edition from Xinjiang in the Arabic script, which she could not read. As a local Uyghur, Büwükhan had been educated in Russian schools and was familiar only with the Cyrillic alphabet. The whip and the knife belonged to the traditional shaman's equipment. In modern Xinjiang, the knife and more specifically its metal part is still widely believed to scare off the evil spirits.

her incantations she was – she said – explicitly summoning the spirits, who then used her body as a medium through which they could speak. She addressed her helping spirits as *igä* (master, owner), usually in the plural.

Plate 11. Healing ritual at home, Almaty, Kazakhstan (Photo: Ildikó Bellér-Hann).

Here are some examples of Büwükhan's healing sessions, taken from those I observed in the autumn of 1997.

- A Uyghur woman (aged 35–40) brought along her husband's picture. He had left her for another woman and she wanted him back. The photograph showed the married couple together, but the woman had covered her own image with a piece of paper, so that she would not be subjected to magical forces. Büwükhan started her incantations, summoned the spirits, and asked them for their help. She appeared to be in a trance, addressing God and the spirits repeatedly. She carried on this incantation for about 15 minutes, then approached the patient, and touched the photograph of the husband. After the session was over, the woman offered to bring along some of her husband's clothes for further, more effective magic, but Büwükhan opposed this vehemently. That would amount to black magic (*qara magiya*) and she specialised only in white magic (*aq magiya*).

- A middle-aged man (about 40) came accompanied by his elder sister. Apparently she had persuaded him to come because he was suffering from depression and insomnia. Since it was his first visit, Büwükhan began with divination. Communication with the spirit world with the help of the white beans revealed that he was tortured by many worries. Büwükhan's helping spirits told her that the man had several enemies and what was worse, aliens (*asman adamliri*) were troubling him. Aliens, as known from American science fiction films, had taken up residence inside his house, and made him tell lies to her. Büwükhan explained that for this reason she was unable to help him. After the session, persuaded by his sister and Büwükhan, the man agreed to make an appointment for the healer to visit his home to exorcise the trouble-maker aliens.

- The brother of a male patient, who otherwise would not have visited the healer, took the opportunity (as did many such accompanying relatives) to have his own future predicted. Büwükhan knew practically nothing about him apart from the fact that he was planning to travel to Tashkent in the near future. During trance she told him that in the near future he would make a lot of money, which she predicted would be connected to a journey that he was about to undertake. On the negative side she said that he had been living under a curse (*qaghish*) which needed to be lifted. He would require several healing sessions with her to be cured.

- An elderly woman came with her grown daughter to complain about the disappearance of her other daughter, aged 22. Using the beans for divination, Büwükhan reassured the mother that her daughter would return soon. After the session, however, she told me that the spirits had told her otherwise; the girl, like many other students in post-Soviet Almaty, had fallen into bad ways and was unlikely to return. Nevertheless, she had no choice but to tell a white lie. She could not bring herself to tell the truth to the mother.

- An elderly lady, whose two married sons had both been left by their wives, came to ask the healer to get back her fugitive daughters-in-law. She prayed over the women's photographs and predicted that the women would return.

- A woman brought along the photograph of her unfaithful husband. The divination session revealed that he had the devil himself inside him (*ichidä shäytan bar*). Only further seances performed over his photograph would help.

- The brother of a female patient was a construction worker (aged about 35) who lived in the neighbourhood and complained of incessant migraine. It had originally been triggered by a heavy drinking bout. It was widely known that the man had been in prison twice because, under the influence of alcohol, he had been involved in fighting and injured others with a knife. For a year he had not touched a knife, and now he was suffering from migraine attacks. Büwükhan performed the usual healing seance during which she gently massaged the patient's head. Unlike her female patients, this man was unable to keep his eyes closed during the session. As Büwükhan told the spirits to purify the patient's body (*tazawalinglar*), the patient himself repeatedly shook the invisible dirt caused by the harmful black spirits (*qara arwahlar*) off his clothes. He thoroughly shook his shirt as well as the legs of his trousers to aid the cleansing process. After the seance, Büwükhan talked to her client for another half an hour. She admonished him for his previous behaviour and gave him some no-nonsense advice concerning his lifestyle. She warned him to give up drinking once and for all. She added that the spirits simply would not tolerate this kind of behaviour. She advised him to have a rest, to remain for three days in seclusion in his home, and to abstain from sexual relations with his wife during this period. When he returned to her to complete his course of treatment some weeks later, he claimed that he had followed her advice and reported a marked improvement in his symptoms.
- An unemployed man (30) from the nearby housing estate, whose circumstances Büwükhan did not know, came for help. Büwükhan diagnosed that his good luck was blocked by evil spirits (*jinn*) and performed one healing session. Later she explained that it would have been pointless in this case to recommend the usual curing course of several sessions because he was unemployed and short of money. One simply had to hope that one session would help.
- A Kazakh woman (29) who had studied biology and mathematics at the university but failed to graduate, came along to complain about her unemployment. She was treated with the usual methods – chanting and incantations, but in Kazakh – to bring her good luck.
- A Russian woman (39) wanted to have her 18-year-old son's fortune told, using his photograph. During divination the spirits revealed through Büwükhan that he was going to have a stable life, neither too good nor too bad. This time the spirits spoke in Russian.

- A Uyghur lady, in her early forties, had progressed from being Büwükhan's regular patient to becoming her friend. She herself had been an alternative practitioner who treated others using the electrical currents (bio-energy) emanating from her own body. Influenced by her sister, also a regular patient of Büwükhan and a pious Muslim, this lady too began actively observing the basic tenets of Islam. She reported that she had been bothered by the spirits for four years. After she had given up her regular job as a hairdresser she also started performing divination (*qumilaq echish*) and healing (*dawalash*). But her powers had declined and to regain her healing abilities she needed Büwükhan's help. The ensuing healing session followed the normal pattern described above.

- A deeply pious and elderly Uyghur lady from China (64) who had already made the pilgrimage to Mecca, came several times for a variety of reasons. She had a relative in Mir, and came to spend long months with her each year. She was worried about her children, especially her son, who was single and made his living from the cross-border trades of drug-dealing and smuggling. Through divination Büwükhan learnt from the spirits that the son had been bewitched. She advised that he should visit her for a few healing sessions, to lift the curse which had been cast on him and enable him to marry. This was the only time I saw Büwükhan do divination without beans: she simply summoned the spirits and they immediately started speaking to her. She reassured her visitor that the son would marry eventually. She also warned the lady that she herself was under an evil spell, and was in need of treatment. The lady quickly agreed, after which Büwükhan explained to her that she too had spirits in her, which was a potentially good thing. The lady at this point told Büwükhan that once she had fallen very ill, and had to stay in bed for a long time. It was then that she had realised that her body was full of spirits. Büwükhan convinced her that during her pilgrimage to Mecca the spirits of two saints had permanently settled in her.

This lady became a regular patient. After one session she reported that, during the seance, she had seen the spirits of both her dead parents and of her dead husband. She also explained how in her rented house in the neighbourhood she often heard noises of merry-making in the middle of the night. On one occasion she had even heard someone call out her name. However, when she looked she saw no one. During the night before one of her visits to the healer she felt that somebody had embraced her and showed the blue marks on her body. The diviner explained to her client that all this was due to the activities of the spirits. The fact that they had embraced her in a dream was a sign of their pleasure over her agreement to do a healing course with Büwükhan.

Like Muqäddäs, Büwükhan also often encouraged her patients to give way to their emotions during the healing session: to cry, to shout, and to make whatever noises they liked. After the seance, especially with new patients, both practitioners asked their patients how they felt. Both warned that the patients should remember their dreams on the night following a session, because they would have special significance for the outcome of the treatment.

Most of Büwükhan's divination projected an optimistic outcome. A negative diagnosis was never final. It could always be rendered positive provided that the patient followed her advice and underwent a whole course with her. The very word for curing (*dawalash*) had implications of improvement.

The opinions of healers and patients did not constitute a unified system of beliefs. Although the healer's role as medium between the human world and the realm of the spirits was commonly accepted by patients, opinions differed concerning the nature and the precise dwelling of the spirits. Some claimed that all humans had spirits in them, while others, including Muqaddäs and Büwükhan, maintained that only a chosen few were possessed by helping spirits or 'masters'. The spirits could be good/white (*aq*) or evil/black (*qara*). Those who performed good (i.e. white) magic had good spirits serving them, while others engaged in black magic were harmful. It was also possible for the 'white hegemony' in a healer's body to be toppled by evil spirits. The healer's body was perceived as a permanent vessel of spirits. This was demonstrated regularly through unexpected and exaggerated bodily manifestations, such as excessive trembling, shaking, belching, or crying, both during and outside the healing ritual. For example, when Büwükhan was walking or travelling in a car past a cemetery or a saintly tomb, she demonstrated that she could feel the presence of the dead spirits even from a distance, and her own spirit masters reacted to this through her body. She showed similar reactions to indicate the physical proximity of people possessed by evil spirits but she also claimed that she herself had little control over her own master spirits. When summoning helping spirits during a seance, she could never be sure who would come, and since a different set of spirits could be expected each time, each seance was bound to be slightly different. Her helping spirits consisted of her own dead ancestors as well as the spirits of well-known Islamic saints. Among these she attributed a prominent role to those whose tombs she had visited in the course of pilgrimages (chapter 10).

Büwükhan's activities were not restricted to her home. She sometimes took barren women to a large tree in the neighbourhood, where she prayed, and where the patient could leave a votive rag to ensure pregnancy. She also paid home visits to certain patients. These were deemed necessary when a patient was too old or too sick (or both) to leave his or her bed. Occasionally, home visits were paid when the healer herself had been told by the spirits that the patient's home needed purification after a series of misfortunes. The purification process could include the performance of the usual incantations by the healer in every room of the flat, the baking of ritual cakes by the healer to nourish the good spirits with its smell (chapter 8), the fumigation of the rooms by burning a dried plant (*adrasman*), and the chasing out of bad spirits with her whip. The harmful spirits were supposed to escape through the open windows.

Once Büwükhan was called upon to inaugurate a new business by purifying the premises. This was considered particularly important since the new firm was taking over the offices of another business which had gone bankrupt. Fumigation with *adrasman* and incantations had to be accompanied by the ritual sacrifice of a sheep in the office building. Other assignments included participation in special, home-based rituals organised by and for women, taking the form of communal thanksgiving prayers. Büwükhan also took patients occasionally to a big shrine in Almaty, and regularly organised major pilgrimages for female patients to Turkistan and surroundings in south-western Kazakhstan. The main destination here was the shrine of the famous Central Asian Muslim saint, Aḥmad Yasawī (chapter 10).

Further patients were usually recruited from the circle of close relatives and friends of her regular visitors. With some female patients, Büwükhan could establish quasi-friendly relations through having long conversations following a healing session. She got to know their family circumstances, their financial and social background, and their personal histories. As an outgoing, highly sociable person, Büwükhan clearly enjoyed some of these conversations and genuinely valued the friendship of these patients. Her problem was how to ensure a sufficient number of regular clients to provide her with a basic income. Evidently a great deal depended on the religiosity of the patient. With new patients, especially with those who appeared to belong to the sceptical kind, the healer took great pains to give her best performance. With people whose piety she did not doubt, she was more off-hand. With those women, whom she saw as potential long-term clients on account of the strength of their beliefs, she applied the same method that Muqäddäs had applied with her before: she declared that the woman in question was possessed by spirits herself. This knowledge imposed tremendous responsibility on the client, because once a person knew that she had spirits, she had an obligation to become a healer herself. By refusing, she risked illness and worse. Nevertheless, willingness was not enough. The person who was possessed by spirits could only become a healer if 'her way opened up' (*yoli echilidu*). The notion of 'opening' was used positively and loosely, and could refer to the healing process, an improvement in the patient's condition, and the ability of a person who had spirits (in her body) to cure others. With ordinary patients Büwükhan usually diagnosed the presence of bad spirits or the influence of the evil eye or a spell, with clients who showed a particular interest in the spirit world and who appeared to be potential regulars, she added that the person also had potential helping spirits herself. In such cases, a bad spell or evil spirits might be presented as obstructing the person's way to a cure. By telling some clients that they were possessed by spirits, Büwükhan ensured that she had a circle of women on whom she could count for regular visits, but at the cost of having to keep them under control and prevent them from declaring themselves independent healers who, if based in the same neighbourhood or close by, might endanger Büwükhan's livelihood.

With young women the problems were easily solved. She simply warned them that they were too young to become healers and that they would have to wait until they were at least 40. Older women, on the other hand, were habitually told that their way had been blocked and this prevented them from becoming healers. During my stay several of her regular clients, with whom she had established special, close relationships through revealing to them that they had been possessed, showed an interest in setting themselves up as healers. One young 22-year-old client, a local Uyghur and unemployed single mother living with her parents after her divorce, showed particular talent for communicating with the spirits. She appeared to be a good medium and discrediting her on the grounds of her age would have been difficult. Instead Büwükhan started taking the girl around with her on visits to patients, and she also sat through many of Büwükhan's healing sessions in her home. She was often asked how she felt after a session. She claimed to have had visions during Büwükhan's incantations, and in general she appeared to have lent a great deal of credibility to Büwükhan's activities. The age difference and her apparent willingness to submit to Büwükhan's authority laid the foundations of a potential master-apprentice relationship, analogous to that between Muqäddäs and Büwükhan.[19]

---

[19] I have no knowledge if this ever became formalised or if the relationship continued at all.

Analysis: The Force of Tradition

Büwükhan obviously followed practices introduced to her by Muqäddäs. She was also open to other ideas from neighbourhood women, other healers, and even television, creatively adopting all these stimuli in her own way. It was in Muqäddäs' company that Büwükhan undertook her first pilgrimage to Turkistan, and another to the Uyghur homeland in Xinjiang. For other women visits to shrines served the purpose of enlisting the help of dead saints to regain their health and to ensure good luck for themselves and their family. For the healer such visits had further significance. The healing sessions cost a lot of energy, and frequent exposure to evil spirits was detrimental to one's own health. Occasional pilgrimages to shrines helped the healer to regain strength through the blessings of the saints, enabling her to continue healing. They also generated a great deal of 'symbolic capital' for the healer (i.e. religious prestige that enhanced her credibility) especially when, upon their return, the party of pilgrims could relate miraculous events occurring during the journey.[20] Compared to the recognised, prestigious *bakhshi*, Büwükhan operated on a more modest scale in terms of both income and healing methods, but she too covered a wide range of events and activities. Divination was her main profile, but it rarely formed the sole focus of her sessions. Rather it was used to formulate a diagnosis and recommend a cure. Like Muqäddäs, Büwükhan claimed that spirit possession had been signalled to her through a long and painful illness, but as a lower ranking specialist, she relied much more heavily on verbal communication, including divination, rather than on other bodily expressions.

Muqäddäs became a tax-paying healer with an official certificate and license to practise with a multi-ethnic clientele in a busy hospital. She was well known in various circles in Almaty, her prestige firmly founded on a combination of factors, including her exceptional performing abilities, and her impeccable claims to what is widely perceived as a shared Central Asian Muslim Turkic tradition. She claimed that she had studied with three instructors; a Uyghur man aged 106 at the time, an Uzbek man, and a

---

[20] This was the case during the pilgrimage in which I too joined the neighbourhood women (chapter 10).

Kazakh healer.[21] She had acquired the blessing of all three, (*du'a aldi*), a necessary precondition to become a *bakhshi*.[22]

Büwükhan's credentials were much more modest. Although a woman with considerable charisma and many talents, she lacked Muqäddäs' performing abilities. She did not have a healer's certificate and remained an unregistered healer, with a primarily, though not exclusively Uyghur, neighbourhood-based clientele, and an altogether more precarious existence. She insisted that, although she had hosted Muqäddäs in her house for a whole year, she had not received the blessing from her necessary to start work as a healer. In fact she had not received the blessing from any living healer, but from the spirit of dead Muslim saints. With this statement Büwükhan emphasised her spiritual independence from Muqäddäs, to whom she denied any formal apprenticeship, even though it was common knowledge that the two cohabited in her house for a year. Muqäddäs' account of this part of their relationship made explicit references to the donations of money and clothes that Büwükhan made to her during this period, which are among the well-known requirements of ritualised and formalised apprenticeship among the Uyghur.

Büwükhan emphasised that she was not a *bakhshi*, and insisted that she could never become one. Her destiny was to remain a diviner, since she had particularly strong diviner spirits (*qumilaqchi arwahlar*). She repeatedly and publicly acknowledged Muqäddäs' superiority. She not only disclaimed being a *bakhshi* herself, she also stressed that, whenever she was sick or had other trouble, she herself needed the strong and more powerful Muqäddäs to heal her. Muqäddäs's authority was regularly evoked, for example when as a last step in her preparations for a major pilgrimage to the shrines of Central Asian saints, she asked Muqäddäs to purify her body with fumigation before departure. In private conversation with clients, Büwükhan often evoked her close relationship with Muqäddäs or quoted Muqäddäs' words to reinforce a particular point.

Büwükhan's attitude towards the *bakhshi* was a subtle mixture of dependence and independence. The relationship between the two healers was a mutually advantageous bargain. Büwükhan accepted Muqäddäs' superiority and admitted her own more limited abilities as a healer. In

---

[21] This Kazakh man, whom I met during a pilgrimage to famous Muslim shrines in Turkistan, was said to have become later possessed by evil spirits, who started causing harm to both Muqäddäs and Büwükhan. He too was a holder of a healer's certificate issued by the Centre of Eastern and Contemporary Medicine and the Ministry of Health.

[22] In subsequent years Muqäddäs further widened her horizon. She spent several months in India accompanied by a male guru. On her return she claimed to have mastered techniques of meditation and to have acquired further knowledge. She also expressed her wish to give up her hospital praxis and continue to work freelance from her own home.

exchange, she could rely on Muqäddäs authority to help her attract patients: she was the cheap alternative. As long as Büwükhan kept to these rules, Muqäddäs also benefited because the success of her former helper was also a feather in her own cap and underlined her own achievements as a *bakhshi*. The two women were not rivals, partly because Büwükhan submitted to Muqäddäs' authority, partly because their 'catchment area', in geographical, social, and ethnic terms did not coincide. Working for a relatively high fee on the premises of a central polyclinic, Muqäddäs attracted an affluent clientele with diverse ethnic affiliations, while Büwükhan remained a neighbourhood healer.[23]

The credibility of both healers was to a large extent rooted in Central Asian traditions which could be termed the domestic cult. These traditions assume that after death the spirits of dead relatives continue to take an interest in the life of the living, and that remembering these spirits, praying for them, and making offerings to them ensures their benevolence. Such beliefs continue to have some currency among the Uyghur diaspora in Kazakhstan and in the Xinjiang homeland (chapter 8).[24]

Chinese Uyghur, usually credited with closer adherence to traditional culture and religion, also regularly reinforced assumptions concerning the efficacy of the dead. Many women (including the sceptical ones) used a trip back to Xinjiang to visit a healer there because they were supposed to be better than the ones in Kazakhstan. They also told stories from their childhood about the proper (i.e. more authentic) *bakhshi* ceremony, about old and new miracles which they themselves had experienced or about which they had heard. On the surface, these stories emphasised the greater spirituality of the homeland and in some ways denigrated the magical potential of healers in Kazakhstan, but at the same time they also reinforced the idea of the efficacy of spirits. Decades of religious repression in China could not suppress such beliefs. Contemporary healing practices certainly built on such sentiments by calling upon the help of dead saints as well as one's own spirit helpers. The same basic idea gets expression in saint cults articulated through pilgrimages to shrines: pilgrims pray to saints, addressing

---

[23] Both healers maintained that ideally, money should not play a role in healing, and it should be left to a client's discretion how much to give. If a patient gave nothing, in principle that too was acceptable. In 1997 most patients habitually gave a fee of 100 *sum* for a visit to Büwükhan, which was one-fourth the fee due to the clinic-based certified practitioner. For a series of sessions Büwükhan sometimes received much more than 100 *sum*, especially from regular clients who were devoted to her. In place of money, but sometimes in addition to it, she would also be given presents, such as food or cloth. When her business was going well, her daily income could be as high as 2,000 *sum*.

[24] Although scepticism and disbelief are just as important, we have no reason to assume that in traditional Uyghur society such elements were entirely lacking.

them by kinship terms, as *ata* or *ana* (father or mother). More significantly, Chinese Uyghur women often performed sacrifices to their dead in the privacy of their own homes (chapter 8). Significantly, on home visits Büwükhan sometimes made ceremonial pancakes with the purpose to please the spirits and support the healing process.

Nawat, the Rebel

In contrast to the example given at the end of the preceding section, another woman belonging to Büwükhan's circle, who had been showing manifest signs of spirit possession, rebelled against the diviner's authority. Nawat was a married woman aged about 50, with grown children. She decided to establish herself as a healer on her own right in the neighbourhood. Lacking both the charisma and the various performing talents of both Muqäddäs and Büwükhan, she tried to establish her own credentials at the expense of the latter. At mourning rituals and religious gatherings she started displaying symptoms of spirit possession, shaking and trembling, closing her eyes, and producing tears at the most unexpected moments. Nawat was due to join Büwükhan and some other women from the neighbourhood on the pilgrimage to Turkistan (chapter 10) but this was not to happen. As she began talking about the possibility of setting herself up as a healer, Büwükhan felt threatened. She repeatedly told Nawat that she was being possessed by evil spirits instead of helpful protective ones, and cleansed her several times with fumigation. Nawat, however, continued her rebellion. Claiming to have been advised by her good protector spirits, she prophesied that the planned pilgrimage was going to be a failure and that she would not take part in it anyway, because she had more important things to do. Soon after we heard about this, her half-sister (my landlady) and I paid Nawat a visit. She was praying as we arrived. Wearing a large scarf covering most of her upper body, a sign of great piety, she sat us by the table, on which stood a pile of ritual cakes, prepared to nourish the spirits. She had switched off the electric light and her dark room was lit only by a single candle standing on the table. She explained to us that, while praying in a *haji* lady's house, the spirits had revealed themselves to her.[25] They had ordered her to stay at home for 40 days in seclusion, and thereby miss the pilgrimage, which in any case was doomed to failure. After the 40 days she was to sacrifice a sheep and hold a ritual meal (*näzir*), normally associated with mourning for the spirit of the dead. Having completed these tasks she would be declared a *haji*, or even a saint (*äwliya*). After announcing all this, she closed her eyes, and in a trancelike state started moving her upper body rhythmically. She breathed in

---

[25] A *haji* is a person who has completed the great pilgrimage to Mecca.

and out deeply and eventually started speaking, eyes still closed, in a manner implying that now the spirits were addressing us. The spirits were speaking to both Nawat and her half-sister, who was sitting there bewildered. Nawat, sometimes unsure how to continue, stopped and listened to her spirit protectors. Only her closed eyes and rhythmically moving body indicated that she was supposed to be in an altered state of consciousness. In the following two hours the spirits, speaking through Nawat, made a number of unpleasant allegations against her half-sister. She and her family were accused of not performing the ritual ablution regularly, of not praying, and of having turned the commemoration feast (*näzir-chiraq*) for her dead father-in-law into a secular party (*mäshräp*) (chapter 3). Of all the accusations, the half-sister took the last one as the most serious insult.[26]

Deeply offended, she was unsure whether Nawat was genuinely turning into a healer and was being possessed by spirits, or whether she was just pretending and using spirit possession as an excuse to slander her family members and to establish herself as a healer in order to make money. A few days later she gave an account of this meeting in women's circles, publicly discrediting Nawat. To offend her half-sister was clearly a grave mistake on Nawat's part. She also tried to discredit repeatedly both Büwükhan and Muqäddäs. Büwükhan's reaction to this was cautious. She never poured scorn on Nawat, even though she was greatly annoyed by her actions. She was aware that to discredit anyone else claiming spirit possession risked diminishing her own credibility. Instead, she admitted that Nawat was truly possessed by spirits, but continued to hold that these were bad spirits of whom Nawat should be urgently cleansed. However, when Nawat went further with her accusations, and announced her seclusion and imminent elevation to healer and even saintly status, Büwükhan turned openly against her. Nawat could be easily discredited. Her half-sister's indignation was paving the way, and after the pilgrimage undertaken by a group of Uyghur women from the neighbourhood to Turkistan proved to be a success, and the participants returned with miraculous stories, it was easy to dismiss Nawat's prophesy as a fabrication.

Nawat had violated the unwritten rules of hierarchy which had been so carefully observed by Büwükhan. Not only did she turn against her own teacher, but she also challenged the credibility of her teacher's teacher,

---

[26] Although the half-sister had always doubted the magical powers of some healers and was inclined to believe that many of them were fraudulent, she did have a fundamental belief in the spirit world. This was based on her childhood experiences in Xinjiang where she took part in communal healing sessions and other rituals led by religious specialists. Later encounters with Uyghur healers during her visits to Xinjiang in the late 1980s and early 1990s further contributed to maintaining her fundamental acceptance of the spirit world and the possibility of communicating with it.

whose prestige had won even wider recognition. One further factor contributing to Nawat's failure to enter the ranks of healers may have been her intra-group affiliation. While both Muqäddäs and Büwükhan were local Uyghur, Nawat belonged to the first generation of migrants from China, even though she arrived as a young person. As noted above, local Uyghur were better integrated into Soviet society, tended to have higher levels of education, better Russian, and better knowledge of how things worked in Kazakhstani society. In employment prospects and achievements, the Chinese Uyghur still lagged behind. All of the successful healers in this neighbourhood were local Uyghur.[27] Being a Chinese Uyghur may have worked against Nawat because it seems that individuals from this group still lack the necessary social capital to build up credibility in the art of healing when claims to authenticity are continuously put to the test. First generation Chinese Uyghur are prominent in creating and maintaining the healer's prestige, since they are believed to be more knowledgeable than the local Uyghur in both Uyghur traditions and in religious issues. However, this does not suffice for them to establish themselves as credible healers in their own right. Chinese Uyghurs' contribution to the perpetuation of such traditions consisted in their acceptance of and participation in spirit possession and religious healing. Healers like Büwükhan were able to establish themselves not so much because they represented the unbroken continuation of a local tradition (i.e. the so-called shamanic practice), but because of their clients' close familiarity with domestic rituals that also involved the idea of spirit cult.

Conclusion

Büwükhan claimed repeatedly that she was not a *bakhshi*, but she operated on very much the same principles as Muqäddäs: spirit possession was central to both. Their claims to authenticity relied on assumed tradition. Büwükhan derived her credentials from the well-known *bakhshi* who had lived in her house, but she also insisted that she received the necessary blessing directly from Islamic saints. Praying to these saints and undertaking pilgrimages to the shrines of Muslim holy persons served to enhance her credibility. But these acts, her personal charisma, and performing talents can give only a partial explanation to her success as a healer. This depended also on the widespread belief in the efficacy of the spirits of the dead, a belief closely

---

[27] One was a miraculously talented 12-year-old girl, who appeared to have been possessed by spirits for some time. Another was a man said to perform the classical shaman seance as described by several observers from the late nineteenth and early twentieth centuries. A third man used techniques similar to Büwükhan, but treated groups of people rather than individuals.

intertwined with the domestic cult of one's deceased relatives, which plays a central role both in popular ritual and in daily life.

My observations and research have been limited to the Uyghur of Xinjiang and Kazakhstan, but it is possible that they have a much wider currency for Inner Asia. Following Devin DeWeese, who works with historical narratives, these materials also suggest that studies of Inner Asian religious life have paid excessive attention to the figure and experiences of the shaman, and lost sight of the centrality of domestic cults in everyday religious life (DeWeese 1994: 32–50). In the inspirational practices of the contemporary Uyghur the cult of ancestors has continued to provide the underpinnings of religious life. Even women who describe themselves as modern or non-practising Muslims are inclined in certain contexts to accept that the dead could interfere with the life of the living. This domestic cult is compatible with the cult of Islamic saints, which is also rooted in the belief of the efficacy of the dead. This may also explain why the postsocialist healer needs respectable Islamic credentials and the authenticity of local tradition.

The persistence of beliefs and practices aimed at ensuring the efficacy of the spirits (of the dead or of Muslim saints) is reinforced in Almaty by the stories of Chinese Uyghur women evoking spiritual experiences in the homeland. This allure of Xinjiang as the land of a higher level of spirituality is also expressed in some women's preference for visiting religious specialists there because they are perceived as particularly knowledgeable. The greater degree of religiosity attributed to first generation Chinese Uyghur plays an important role in the legitimisation of traditional healers who tend to be local Uyghur. But the symbolic capital of the former is insufficient for them to compete successfully as healers with the social capital deployed by the latter.

The Uyghur are a stateless minority in China and the diaspora in Kazakhstan is still more marginalised in the wider society. The emergence of numerous healers and the disproportionate levels of participation of unemployed, middle-aged women support the theory that spirit possession is a distinctive style of 'bargaining from weakness' (Gomm 1975; cited in March and Taqqu 1982: 76). However, the equation of spirit possession with the domain of the most marginalised needs refinement, since the better integrated members of the minority, the local Uyghur, seem able to exclude recent arrivals from this lucrative market.

References

Alekseev, N. A. 1987. *Schamanismus der Türken Sibiriens: Versuch einer vergleichenden arealen Untersuchung.* (trans. Reinhold Schletzer). Hamburg: Reinhold Schletzer.

Basilov, V. N. 1987. Popular Islam in Central Asia and Kazakhstan. *Journal of the Institute of Muslim Minority Affairs* 8 (1): 7–17.

Basilow, W. N. [Basilov, V. N.]. 1995. *Das Schamanentum bei den Völkern Mittelasiens und Kaschstans.* Berlin: Reinhold Schletzer Verlag.

Buyandelgeriyn, M. 1999. Who 'Makes' the Shaman? The Politics of Shamanic Practices among the Buriats in Mongolia. *Inner Asia* 1 (2): 221–244.

DeWeese, D. 1994. *Islamization and Native Religion in the Golden Horde: Baba Tükles and Conversion to Islam in Historical and Epic Tradition.* University Park: Pennsylvania State University Press.

Du S. 1995. Pratiques chamaniques des Ouïgours du Xinjiang. *Études mongoles et sibérienne* 26: 41–62.

Gomm, R. 1975. Bargaining from Weakness: Spirit Possession on the South Kenya Coast. *Man* 10 (4): 530–543.

Hobsbawm, E., and T. Ranger (eds.). 1983. *The Invention of Tradition.* Cambridge: University Press.

Hoppál, M. 1985. Shamanism: An Archaic and/ or Recent System of Beliefs. *Ural-Altaische Jahrbücher* 57: 121–140.

Hoppe, Th. 1998. *Die ethnischen Gruppen Xinjiangs: Kulturunterschiede und interethnische Beziehungen.* Hamburg: Institut für Asienkunde.

Humphrey, C. 1994. Shamanic Practices and the State in Northern Asia: Views from the Center and the Periphery. In N. Thomas, and C. Humphrey (eds.), *Shamanism, History and the State*, pp. 191–228. Ann Arbor: University of Michigan Press.

——. 1999. Shamans in the City. *Anthropology Today* 15 (3): 3–10.

Katanov, N. T., and K. H. Menges. 1933, 1976. *Volkskundliche Texte aus Ost-Türkistan.* Proceedings of the Prussian Academy of Sciences, Section of Philology and History, 1933. Leipzig: Zentralantiquariat of the German Democratic Republic.

March, K., and R. L. Taqqu. 1982. *Women's Informal Associations in Developing Countries: Catalysts for Change? Women in Cross-Cultural Perpsective.* Boulder: Westview Press.

Penkala-Gawęcka, D. 2006. *Medycyna komplementarna w Kazachstanie: siła tradycji i presja globalizacji.* Poznan: Wydawnictwo Naukowe UAM.

Roberts, S. 1998. Negotiating Locality, Islam and National Culture in a Changing Borderland: The Revival of *Mäshräp* Rituals among

Young Uighur Men in the Ili Valley. *Central Asian Survey* 17 (4): 673–699.

Rudelson, J. J. 1997. *Oasis Identities: Uyghur Nationalism along China's Silk Road*. New York: Columbia University Press.

Sahlins, M. 1999. Two or Three Things that I Know about Culture. *The Journal of the Royal Anthropological Institute* 5 (3): 399–421.

Schenk, A., and C. Rätsch (eds.). 1999. *Was ist ein Schamane? Schamanen, Heiler, Medizinleute im Spiegel westlichen Denkens*. Berlin: Verlag für Wissenschaft und Bildung.

Schwarz, H. G. 1992. *An Uyghur-English Dictionary*. Bellingham: Western Washington University.

Thomas, N., and C. Humphrey. 1994. Introduction. In N. Thomas, and C. Humphrey (eds.), *Shamanism, History and the State*, pp. 1–12. Ann Arbor: University of Michigan Press.

Voigt, V. 1977. Shamanism in Siberia (A Sketch and a Bibliography). *Acta Ethnographica Academiae Scientiarum Hungaricae* 26: 385–395.

Chapter 10
The Micropolitics of a Pilgrimage[1]

Pilgrimages and other types of travel in Islamic societies constitute forms of social action which can be studied from different perspectives (Eickelman and Piscatori 1990: 3).

While Victor and Edith Turner defined pilgrimage as ritual action, a kind of rite of passage, and subjected it to structural analysis (Turner and Turner 1978), in a recent study of local pilgrimages performed by women in post-Soviet Azerbaijan, Ingrid Pfluger-Schindlbeck suggested shifting the focus from the structure to the social context of the pilgrimage (Pfluger-Schindlbeck 1997). On the basis of ethnographic materials concerning a regional pilgrimage organised by women in postsocialist Kazakhstan in the late 1990s, in this chapter I shall attempt to give equal weight to both approaches, taking both social context and structure into account. The chapter considers aspects of religious experience in post-Soviet Central Asia and the multiple motivations for and meanings of pilgrimage to participants and their environment. It also examines how the modern pilgrimage relates to classical analyses of ritual behaviour.

The Protagonists and the Social Setting

The women pilgrims in this case study are ethnic Uyghurs, Turkic-speaking Sunni Muslims from north-west China.[2] Responding to fluctuations in politics and economics, over the last hundred years many left China as migrants and refugees.[3] The idea of the pilgrimage was introduced to the

---

[1] Published in G. Rasuly-Paleczek and J. Katschnig (eds.), *Central Asia on Display. Proceedings of the VII. Conference of the European Society for Central Asian Studies*, pp. 325–38. Münster: LIT Verlag, 2005.

[2] Although the data concern female participants only, gender is by no means the only relevant factor in women's ritual behaviour.

[3] For a general overview of the Uyghur in Kazakhstan see Roberts (1998). For details of my fieldwork and the intra-group differences among Uyghur in Almaty, see chapter 9, this volume.

neighbourhood women gradually by a local Uyghur woman who practised as a self-employed healer. She claimed not to be a traditional shaman (*bakhshi*), as her own teacher had been, but merely a seer (*qumilaqchi*).[4] Among the healer's clientele a group of particularly pious women crystallised, most of who expressed an interest in taking part in the healer's planned visit of the saintly tomb of Aḥmad Yasawī in Turkistan, in western Kazakhstan.[5] The healer claimed to have completed this pilgrimage several times before in the company of her teacher. The latter had indeed made the trip three times which, given the long distance of the shrine from Almaty, is said to equal the Hajj. The former clearly saw the enterprise as a long-term investment in her business. Although successful at the time in the neighbourhood, her position was continuously threatened by neighbourhood gossip which branded her a swindler by rival healers and by ambitious clients who themselves were hoping to become established healers. Her credentials gained strength from her close associations with the respected shamaness, but she also tried to establish her separate identity as an independent healer. She claimed that unlike other practitioners, who received the necessary blessing from senior healers, she had received hers directly from the saints buried in Turkistan. Following her teacher's example, taking pilgrims there on her own appeared an ideal way to reaffirm her own uncertain position. In this respect she had some followers: several women in the neighbourhood with an aspiration to start their own business as healers said that they could do so only after they had made the pilgrimage to Turkistan and had received the blessing of its saints (*dua älish üchün*).

Participation was discussed by a relatively large number of women, but recruiting pilgrims proved to be difficult. After 1991 many people previously in state employment lost their jobs, women in particular.[6] The pilgrimage was expensive in local terms, notably the cost of a hired car and two drivers. Further expenses included sharing the cost of sacrificial meals and making donations to the shrines. Many women simply did not have the money. Others did not gain their husbands' permission to go for a variety of reasons, which included suspicion of the healer's alleged supernatural powers or doubts as to the compatibility of her activities with Islam. Others could not take time off because of employment or domestic responsibilities. One elderly lady turned down the invitation because, as a visitor from the

---

[4] Nevertheless, at the time of my stay in the neighbourhood she was exorcising spirits from patients with psychological and physical complaints using techniques quite similar to those employed by shamans (chapter 9).

[5] On Yasawī, see Iz (1960).

[6] On the general situation in Kazakhstan following the collapse of the Soviet Union, see Olcott (1993) and Holm-Hansen (1997). On the position of women, see Michaels (1998).

XUAR with a Chinese passport, she was afraid that the Chinese authorities would somehow learn about her trip, and that she would be penalised upon her return. Yet others withdrew because they were afraid that they could not cope with a journey of 900 kilometres (one way), given their bad health or old age. One young woman who worked in a research institute was putting off the time when she would go. Another woman's withdrawal was a deliberate challenge to the healer. She predicted that the pilgrimage was going to be a failure and claimed that she had been advised by the spirits of the saints of Turkistan to retreat and stay in isolation for 40 days, in order to gain religious merit. Her extravagant behaviour invited much gossip and criticism in the neighbourhood (chapter 9).

Strategies of Recruitment

To give women a foretaste of the Turkistan pilgrimage, an idea of the spiritual experience that awaited them there, the healer organised brief visits to a local shrine in Almaty. This was the shrine of Räyim Batir (1705–85), a 'great saint' (chong äwliya), whose new shrine had been built with government support in 1994 as part of the Kazakh government's effort to construct a national history of which Islam became an integral part. Such visits served as both a recruitment strategy as well as a rehearsal for the pilgrimage to Turkistan. They included many elements which are locally conceived as part of Islamic traditions, such as listening to the recital of Koranic verses by the guardian of the shrine, presenting him ceremonial cakes fried in oil (zhit)[7], showing respect by bowing in front of the shrine, circling the saintly tomb, praying to the saint, and drinking from the miraculous water in the nearby well. At a stall outside the shrine, women also bought small charms (tumar) imported from Turkey to protect themselves from the evil eye.

Another strategy used by the healer to recruit women for the pilgrimage was to persuade one of her clients to hold a religious ceremony called mothers' tea (anilar cheyi) in her home to commemorate the spirits of seven female saints (yättä äwliya rohigä näzir), some of whose shrines were located in the vicinity of Turkistan. During the ritual the female saints of Turkistan and the forthcoming pilgrimage were mentioned repeatedly.[8]

---

[7] These may be seen as a substitute for animal sacrifice. These cakes are usually prepared in honour of the spirits of the dead. On nourishing the spirits of the dead with the smell of fried oil see chapter 8.

[8] The women taking part all appeared to have experienced spirit possession as manifest in bodily signs such as shaking, trembling, belching, and the like. Some women prayed almost incessantly. The healer's incantations were followed by another woman's account of how God created woman from Adam's rib, and how they were sent to heaven. She was listing the

Pilgrimage

In spite of these efforts to generate interest in the pilgrimage, it proved difficult for the healer to find the necessary six women to accompany her on the journey.[9] Eventually a group of seven women (six Uyghur and me) and two Kazakh drivers set out on a Saturday morning, when the car became available. The women were mostly residents of the neighbourhood, though two of them lived on a more distant estate. All were paying clients of the healer. Two middle-aged sisters were Chinese Uyghur. For the three married women the pilgrimage may have provided a way of temporarily escaping male authority, but this was not a significant motivation. The other three women were divorced. Two of the local Uyghur were mother and daughter, but given the complicated settlement history of the neighbourhood, which had grown out of a *kolkhoz*, it is not surprising that kinship was of limited significance in women's ritual action.[10] The recruitment of pilgrims had much more to do with the difficult economic situation of the post-Soviet era, in which middle-aged Muslim women with few qualifications, in an atmosphere of uncertainty, were trying to improve their lives.

All six stated some form of ailment as their most important reason for going on the pilgrimage, but additional reasons were also articulated. One woman hoped to have her marital problems solved; a divorcee wished for a new husband. All wished to ask the saints' assistance for financial success, or at least security, and all hoped to gain religious merit (*sawap*). The healer needed the trip to increase her religious prestige and symbolic capital in order to strengthen her position as a leading healer in the neighbourhood. She stressed that a person who constantly worked with spirits was especially vulnerable to being harmed or weakened by them, and therefore needed to gain strength from the saints in order to continue healing. She also had a bad cough at the time, which she attributed to the work of some harmful spirits. By gaining strength from the spirits of the saints she hoped that her cough would be cured. Although God was ultimately responsible for cures and for blessings (*bärkä*), she explained that the saints' intervention was also

---

functions of the four archangels when she was interrupted by another woman, who fell into trance and gave ecstatic signs of spirit possession. After she was calmed down the others present asked the healer for further instructions. She warned them that they were all novices and therefore not yet capable of working as healers themselves: nevertheless, taking part in the pilgrimage would certainly help them gain religious merit.

[9] The healer needed to take a full car and, although my initial interest was met with some suspicion, I was able to participate because I could share the cost of the rented car and the sacrificial animals.

[10] This contrasts to the situation in a postsocialist Azerbaijani village where familial relationships in pilgrimage play an important role (Pfluger-Schindlbeck 1997).

necessary. One woman from outside the neighbourhood took part in the pilgrimage in order to be freed from the evil forces which had prevented her from becoming a healer. She looked to the spirits of the saints to give her strength and to allow her to cure others.

Plate 12. Pilgrims at the shrine of Aristan Baba, Türkistan, Kazakhstan (Photo: Ildikó Bellér-Hann).

The Holy Places Visited

The pilgrimage took altogether five days. This included the long car journey there and back, and visiting seven shrines in and around Turkistan. Two of these, the shrines of Aristan Baba Atam and Qurban Baba, were located very near each other. Both were said to be Kazakh saints, the former of whom had lived in the twelfth century. Their shrines, two domed stone buildings, had been restored recently by the Kazakh government. Further saintly shrines visited by the group included the Üshik Baba shrine; the famous mausoleum of Aḥmad Yasawī, founder of the Yasawiyya Brotherhood; and the tombs of two female saints. One of these was Jawhar Anam, daughter of Aḥmad Yasawī, whose shrine was a small, modest building in natural surroundings, recently built with financial support from Turkey. The other belonged to Domalaq Anam, whose shrine was situated in a natural beauty spot, not far from the main road. The small domed building had been renovated recently. At the time of our visit, the large imposing building of the Yasawī shrine, situated in the town of Turkistan, was under restoration. We were informed that financial support for the works was provided by a Turkey-based pious foundation and even the construction workers had been brought from Turkey. The final, seventh stop differed from all the previous places visited in possessing no saintly grave. Nevertheless, the place was known as *Yighlaghan Ana* (Crying Mother) after a mother who, so the legend goes, had been left alone with her two small children. The spot was also known as *Altun Bulaq* (Gold Spring), and it was indeed a beautiful natural phenomenon: seven springs met here and formed a multitude of small waterfalls, all surrounded by forest. The trees and bushes in the vicinity of the waterfalls were covered in votive rags, testifying to the number of pilgrims who had been here and made their wishes.

The Pilgrims' Experiences

During the five days of the journey a flexibly observed routine was established. Nights were spent at the pilgrims' guest-room of a shrine, which we shared with other visitors. The day began at dawn with performing the ritual ablution (*tärät*), which was followed by a visit to a shrine. There communal prayer led by the guardian of the shrine was followed by listening to the recital of Koranic verses. Each pilgrim would also pray to the saint silently, making her private wishes. This was, in most cases, confirmed by tying votive rags on the nearby bushes (*niyät baghlanish*). Most saintly tombs had a well with water ostensibly endowed with curative powers. The visit to the shrine was routinely followed by drinking some of this water, and filling flasks with it to be taken home.

Meals were cooked in the communal pilgrims' kitchen. All cooked meals had a sacred character. The pilgrims were offered meals cooked by other pilgrim groups from the flesh of a sacrificial animal, and when it was their turn to cook the ceremonial dish, they also shared it with newcomers and the guardians of the shrine. Cooking was only possible at shrines which had a pilgrims' room. Due to the unavailability of such facilities at some shrines and to financial restraints, our group twice sacrificed a sheep and cooked the ceremonial meal. The ceremonial meal consisted always of pilaf (*polo*) – rice cooked with carrots, mutton, and raisins.

Spirituality

One major departure from women's daily routine at home was that they all tried to observe what they regarded as basic religious prescriptions, namely the ritual ablution and the ritual prayer five times a day. Our busy schedule, however, did not make this always possible and most days the ritual prayer was performed only four times, and not at all during the car journey. A special atmosphere was ensured by all the women donning the pilgrims' white headscarf, and by trying to stay awake praying at least one night. In one pilgrims' centre the group listened to Uzbek women conducting a loud, public commemoration ceremony (*zikr*), and upon arrival to another pilgrims' centre late at night we heard how a male healer was exorcising spirits from the body of a sick woman. One member of our group, a young woman, had a vision during broad daylight which was explained by the healer as a sign of her body purifying itself under the influence of the dead saints' proximity. Bodily processes such as having a cold or developing a pimple or a rash were all explained in similar terms, as evidence of saintly presence.

The women told and listened to legends connected to some of the shrines. One such story was told about the present guardian of the shrine of Jawhar Anam. He was an elderly Kazakh man who had led an ordinary life until he became ill with cancer. He nearly died, but was then miraculously saved by doctors. During his illness he started having visions. He was visited by spirits (*ärwahlar*), who recommended that he come to Turkistan and take care of the saintly tomb of Jawhar Anam to express his gratitude and ensure future health. At about the same time, a rich businessman in Turkey had a dream in which he was ordered by the spirits to build a new shrine in Turkistan for this particular saint. The two narratives thus combined to explain the presence of the new shrine as well as its guardian. The guardian himself confirmed the stories, and told us another one of a young woman who had been unable to conceive but had many children after she made a pilgrimage to the shrine. When visiting female saints' tombs, women pilgrims behaved more emotionally than they had done when paying their respects to male saintly shrines, and expressed their devotion in larger donations of money for the upkeep of these tombs. The pilgrims themselves told miraculous stories, some of which were said to have taken place in the homeland of Xinjiang.

The Miracle: Punishment and Forgiveness

The pilgrim group itself experienced a series of miracles, which occurred on the last day of the pilgrimage, quite appropriately at the tomb of the most important saint, Aḥmad Yasawī.

Plate 13. Aḥmad Yasawī's shrine in Türkistan, Kazakhstan (Photo: Ildikó Bellér-Hann).

On our first visit to Yasawī's tomb in the central part of the town of Turkistan, we spent little time there. There was no pilgrim's centre, and the impressive building was scaffolded and under restoration. On the following day we returned to town, and the members of our group had a heated discussion about whether or not we should visit the market. Some of the elderly women thought that this would not be acceptable during a pilgrimage, while the younger ones were keen to see the bazaar. The argument ground to a halt when our car suddenly broke down. The healer insisted that this was an admonition from the saint, because we had spent too little time at his shrine and because we were about to go shopping during the pilgrimage. While our Kazakh drivers took the car to a workshop, our group decided to walk back to Yasawī's shrine and pray for the saint's forgiveness. This time we spent more time inside, but our visit still lacked the level of spirituality experienced at the smaller shrines before, if only because of the large-scale restoration works and the commercial atmosphere of the surroundings. We also looked around the small museum and the ongoing archaeological excavations around the tomb. As the leader of our group explained, by causing the car to break down, the saint made sure that we returned to his shrine and paid due respect to him. It all happened with God's will.

Repairing the car took a long time, so after paying our due respect to the saint we sat in an open-air tea-house situated just opposite the shrine. We observed how an elderly Kazakh beggar, dressed in dirty white clothes, approached a group of Uzbek female pilgrims sitting at the nearby table. The women refused to give alms and chased him away. Our group invited him to join us for a cup of tea. Before accepting the invitation he recited some prayers and asked us for donations. Having received our contributions, he drank some tea and blessed us all before moving on to another group. As he was just about to leave us, our drivers appeared with the repaired car. The pilgrims rejoiced and unanimously declared this to be another miracle: we had been kind and generous to the beggar and showed repentance, therefore God and the saint had shown their benevolence to us. By the evening, the talk among the pilgrims still revolved around the signs of grace manifested that day. The healer and the other pilgrims were by now certain that the beggar was no ordinary person but the Prophet Khizir, who has the habit of appearing in the disguise of an old, white-bearded beggar to test people's generosity. His blessing was the surest sign that our previous mistakes had been forgiven and that our pilgrimage was destined to be auspicious.

Tradition and Creativity

Neither the healer nor the other participants had been through rigorous religious training, although some had been taught the basic rules informally at home.[11] While certain ground rules identified as religious tradition were observed, in matters of detail the women were often uncertain. The pilgrimage was more than the simple following of an established pattern: it also served as a vehicle for re-inventing tradition and thus creating new precedence for behaviour on the level of popular religion. The major components – travelling to holy shrines, supplication to the spirits of dead saints, praying, circling the shrines, preparation of the sacrificial meal from the meat of ritually slaughtered sheep, drinking from sacred wells near the shrines, tying votive rags on trees, performing the ritual ablution, and regularly performing ritual prayers – connect the modern pilgrims to traditional religious practice in the Turco-Persian Muslim world.[12] But concerning other elements, the women were uncertain and discussed how they should proceed: the manner of saluting the saint, touching the wall of

---

[11] This was particularly true of the two sisters, who had spent their childhood in Xinjiang before they migrated to the Soviet Union in the early 1960s.

[12] For example, see Pfluger-Schindlbeck (1998: 103) who described local pilgrimages by village women in Azerbaijan. The elements of the pilgrimage also correspond closely to pilgrimages elsewhere in the Muslim world (e.g. Westermarck 1926; Kriss and Kriss-Heinrich 1960).

the shrine, walking away from it backwards, the length of a visit, the mode of reciting a prayer, making a supplication, and other aspects of general behaviour. They constantly looked to the healer, who claimed to have acquired some knowledge in the course of earlier visits to the shrines under the guidance of her mentor.

Nevertheless, she too was often visibly unsure and new situations constantly put her knowledge and authority to test. All pilgrims were eager to demonstrate their devotion, and one way of this was to display knowledge in matters of religion. So each added her own, often very fragmented knowledge or opinion of how things should be done properly. They set themselves and the others high expectations which they could not always meet. For example, they agreed that though one could not pray five times a day in normal life, during the pilgrimage one should make an effort to do so. In practice, they rarely succeeded. Some did not to know when to pray, what to say during the prayers, or were uncertain as to the various movements that should accompany praying. They constantly watched each other and other pilgrims present for examples which they could imitate.

There was disagreement concerning how the ritual ablution should be performed. Early in the morning, it was very cold and one woman suggested that it would suffice to wash our feet symbolically (i.e. without removing our stockings). Given the presence of male pilgrims and guardians, the necessity of observing the rules of modesty (chapter 4), and the fact that there were no washing facilities to speak of, performing the ablution was somewhat difficult. When the healer herself hesitated to pronounce a definite opinion, the women had a short discussion and decided that the ritual ablution had to be performed properly, with stockings removed. Sometimes rules of be- haviour were determined more pragmatically. We bought and sacrificed two lambs, one at the female saint Jawhar Anam's shrine, the other at the pilgrims' rest place near the shrines of Aristan Baba and Qurban Baba. At the other places we visited, slaughtering and cooking were impossible due to the absence of cooking facilities, although in theory a new sacrifice should have been made at each shrine.

Criticism coming from male pilgrims or shrine guardians for inappropriate behaviour also prompted the women to adjust their behaviour and formulate new rules. Although a seasoned pilgrim, the healer was scolded at one of the shrines by the male guardian because in his opinion our group did not pray long enough. She was offended, since she felt that her authority and religious knowledge were being called into question. In another place, a male pilgrim admonished a member of our group because the edge of her long underpants was showing from underneath her long skirt.

On another occasion, one woman was warned that her hair could be seen underneath her headscarf.

During the pilgrimage, mutual admonition within the group became a habit. Criticisms at holy places implied that there were set rules, which pilgrims should learn if they did not know them already. Especially the healer, in an effort to re-assert her authority over the group, developed the habit of regularly admonishing others. One morning at the well of the Aristan Baba shrine, she told a member of the group not to spit in a sacred place. The woman apologetically explained that this was a misunderstanding; she had not spat but merely bowed in front of the saint, thanking him for the miraculous water. Later that day, the healer warned an elderly member of our group not to sit with her feet stretched out in the direction of Aristan Baba's shrine because it was disrespectful and could bring bad luck. She challenged male authority whenever she could (though not in religious contexts), thus asserting her position as someone endowed with special powers. In one episode, as we were about to have breakfast after a lengthy early morning prayer session, we returned to the pilgrims' courtyard to find that a man had inadvertently used up our tea water. Water could only be boiled in a large kettle over an open fire and it was therefore a long, time-consuming procedure. In her anger, the healer made us collect our table cloth and ordered us to make preparations to leave without having breakfast. However, she quickly sensed from the grumbles of the tired women that this suggestion was not welcome. So, to save face she decided to turn to the spirits for advice. They duly told us to stay and have our morning meal in peace.

Of the seven shrines visited, the most famous one was the shrine of Aḥmad Yasawī. However, the women themselves saw this in a different light. They clearly were impressed more by the relatively modest shrines of female saints, and this was reflected in the time they spent there, the larger amounts of money they donated, and the stories they told afterwards about the pilgrimage. Yasawī's shrine commanded less interest and the punishment meted out by the saint and the subsequent miracle of meeting the Prophet Khizir were both consequences of our spending too little time there. Imposing their own hierarchy on the shrines was another creative action on the part of the women, perhaps motivated by their closer identification with female saints, and encouraged by the more personal, friendly reception they received from the guardians at these shrines. Although on an emotional level the women continued to privilege the lesser female saints in their recollections, paradoxically their account of the punishment meted out by Yasawī for their neglect of his shrine and of the ensuing grace confirmed the official hierarchy.

By all accounts it was unanimously agreed that the pilgrimage was a success.[13] We returned without major mishaps and with tales of miracles. All participants got what they hoped for: either the promise of a cure, or the fulfilment of other wishes. Nonetheless, after our return the healer's business showed signs of decline. She and the would-be healer in our group both complained that their business and their health had been adversely affected by the evil forces emanating from a Kazakh male healer who had joined us on the journey back to Almaty.

The Pilgrimage as Rite of Passage

To what extent did the pilgrimage display the structural features of rites of passage, as defined by Arnold van Gennep (1960) and elaborated further by Victor Turner (1969)? In this model, rites of passage are constructed according to a tripartite model: 1. separation from (departure from) daily life/structure, 2. liminality (anti-structure/*communitas*) 3. re-integration to structure. In many ways, the journey was indeed a departure from ordinary life, with elements of anti-structure or *communitas*. This was expressed in physical difficulties (tiredness, dirtiness, and discomfort); in the heightened sense of communality; long and frequent praying sessions; vigil; sexual abstinence; the preparation and consumption of sacrificial meals; the frequent consumption of and washing in sacred water; the increased exposure to sacred and evil forces; and the experience of miracles.

In many ways the pilgrimage appeared to promote communal spirit within the travelling group. Throughout the trip the pilgrims ate, slept, and prayed together. They also performed the ritual ablution and prepared the sacrificial meal communally. There was practically no room for individual action: even leaving the pilgrims' guest-room for a short time at night was not allowed, since *jinn* and harmful spirits pose a continuous danger to the pilgrims in sacred places.[14] This communal spirit should have extended – according to the theoretical assumptions – beyond the actual pilgrim group and transcended ethnic boundaries. At the same time most groups we encountered in western Kazakhstan (including our own) were organised along ethnic lines. Our group interacted with members of other ethnic groups, especially Kazakh and Uzbek pilgrims. A common identity and the basic equality of all Muslims were fostered by various groups praying together at the shrines, by the sharing of the guest-room, and by sacrificial

---

[13] In spite of the fact that some had initially feared that my presence (as a non-Muslim) could provoke the saints' wrath.

[14] In the Muslim world, *baraka* (holiness, blessed virtue) is not only beneficial energy but also has an element of danger (cf. Westermarck 1926: 227–28).

commensality. The acceptance of a Kazakh male healer as our travel companion on the way back to Almaty, the good relations with the Kazakh guardian of the Üshik Baba shrine, and the benevolent almsgiving to the Kazakh beggar – all these indicated the participants' willingness to disregard ethnic boundaries in favour of *communitas*. However, the evil forces thought to lurk around sacred places were frequently associated with another ethnic group or individuals of different ethnicity. Kazakh and Uzbek female pilgrims were often suspected of approaching our group with evil intentions. This prompted the healer repeatedly to ritually purify the communal guest-room after their departure. One Uzbek pilgrim group was condemned for refusing to share their sacrificial meal with others, and it was Uzbek female pilgrims who chased away the Prophet Khizir at Yasawī's shrine. Some time after our return to Almaty, two members of our group complained that the Kazakh healer had cast a spell on them, causing one of them to have migraines; he was also said to have brought about a decline in the healer's previously booming business.

The issue of ethnicity repeatedly came up in discussions concerning saints and spirits. The healer's personal vision of religion transcended ethnic boundaries. She took it for granted that in multi-ethnic Kazakhstan what mattered most was the common, shared Islamic tradition. During her healing sessions she summoned her helping spirits in both Uyghur and Kazakh, and she was eager to socialise with healers of various ethnic groups. No doubt pragmatic considerations played a part in this; all healers were keen to have as many clients as possible, regardless of ethnic background or mother tongue. All had to increase their religious knowledge to reconfirm their reputation as healers, and the source of this knowledge had to be Islamic. Some of the other pilgrims however, were suspicious of this disregard of ethnic boundaries in the supernatural realm. They repeatedly enquired about the ethnic affiliation of the healer's helping spirits, and of the saints whose shrines they visited. They doubted the efficacy of Kazakh healers, spirits, and saints. This prompted the healer to pronounce an opinion on the issue several times, although she failed to come up with a consistent view. During the pilgrimage she repeatedly stressed that it was religious devotion that mattered, and – after all – in Kazakhstan one would expect to find mostly Kazakh saints. On the other hand, during our visit to the museum attached to the Yasawī shrine, she discovered that Yasawī was a Uyghur rather than a Kazakh saint. In revealing this to the group, she probably hoped to please her fellow pilgrims rather than voice her own personal opinion. All these examples indicate that *communitas* was only partially realised during the pilgrimage: the full realisation of *communitas* spirit was impeded by the ethnicisation of popular religion, and rather than blurring ethnic boundaries, the interaction of pilgrim groups reinforced ethnic separation.

The structure of the pilgrimage as a rite of passage also failed to live up to the ideal as formulated by Arnold van Gennep (1960) and Victor Turner (1969). The phases of separation and re-integration were not marked sharply: neither the departure nor the return of the pilgrims was celebrated in any special way. Apart from the white headscarf donned by all the women, there was no special clothing or other outward sign to indicate their pilgrim status. In fact the women only began wearing the scarf after arriving at the first shrine. On the way to the shrines, popular music was played in the car, jokes were told, and some of the women flirted with the drivers. Only as we proceeded from shrine to shrine did the atmosphere gradually become more solemn, and it stayed that way on the long return journey. This time only religious music was played, all the women wore their pilgrims' scarves, and took care that their hair was not showing. They prayed frequently and conversation revolved around the miraculous events of the pilgrimage, the shrines, and the saints. The efforts of the Kazakh male healer who joined us for the return journey to flirt with the women were met with indignation. The healer did impose avoidance rules in the period after their return from the pilgrimage (re-integration) by insisting that participants should abstain from all kinds of entertainment for seven days (only attending the commemoration of the dead during this period was deemed acceptable). Nevertheless, no celebration or ritual marked the return of the pilgrims, and they re-integrated quickly into their usual daily routine. After their return, there was no change in the social status of the women in the wider community. While devout Muslims showed interest in and appreciation of their experiences, others laughed and called them ignorant.

On the whole, this major regional pilgrimage showed no clear tripartite structure defined by theoreticians of rites of passage. Instead, it revealed a greater measure of continuity. The historian Caroline Bynum (1988) made a similar argument in a very different context. Applying Victor Turner's model of social dramas (an extension of van Gennep's schema of ritual action) to the life histories of male and female Christian saints, she found that while the life stories of male saints displayed abrupt changes and therefore conformed to the model, female saints' lives showed much more continuity and thus defied the clear tripartite division. It remains a question for future research to determine to what extent my observations have wider currency in Central Asia, and whether the continuities observed on the micro-level of a pilgrimage are simply due to gender differences, or perhaps more complex factors arising from the realities of post-Soviet Central Asia also play a part.

Conclusion

Despite the small number of participants, this pilgrimage was for some time the talk of the neighbourhood and had an impact beyond the actual circle of participants. Complex factors influenced women's decisions to participate in it or withdraw from it, and community members' decisions to condemn it or approve it. The pilgrimage was emphatically a female undertaking and expressed women's religious commitment. Interethnic contacts during the liminal period of the ritual did not lead to a transcending or blurring of these boundaries in the more global context of Islam. Rather, popular ideas concerning heightened danger in and around sacred spaces caused such boundaries to be reinforced. The attribution of ethnic identity to dead spirits also shows the assertion of boundaries. In this way the macro-structural features of postsocialist society were reflected in the micro-interaction of this small group of pilgrims.

Against a background of general economic hardship, some citizens of postsocialist Kazakhstan have tried to acquire the symbolic capital needed to practise as healers. The chaotic health care system and the religious liberalism of the new Kazakh state have both contributed to the popularity of alternative healing practices. Informal religious gatherings and communal experiences provide single women, divorcees, and widows with a sense of comfort and companionship, and such opportunities are also attractive to married women, given the domination of patriarchal conditions. In some respects, religious undertakings such as a pilgrimage do have an integrating effect since in principle they can reinforce gender and ethnic solidarity. However, a close observation of a pilgrimage reveals that it does not necessarily conform fully to the tripartite schema of ritual action or social dramas as formulated by some anthropologists. Women's communal ritual action seems to be more of a continuation and extension of daily routine, where they integrate perceived tradition with pragmatic considerations. They respond to the new challenges posed by the unusual circumstances with the same creative spirit as they do to the economic challenges of postsocialist society. The phase of anti-structure does not lead to full *communitas*, but paradoxically reinforces group differences on the interethnic level. But only further extensive research into the rituals and daily practices of marginal groups in the region can shed more light on the interaction between ritual practice, religion, ethnicity, and gender.

References

Bynum, C. W. 1988. *Holy Feast and Holy Fast: The Religious Significance of Food to Medieval Women*. Berkeley: University of California Press.

Eickelman, D. F., and J. Piscatori. 1990. Social Theory in the Study of Muslim Societies. In D. F. Eickelman, and J. Piscatori (eds.), *Muslim Travellers: Pilgrimage, Migration, and the Religious Imagination*, pp. 3–25. Berkeley: University of California Press.

van Gennep, A. 1960. *The Rites of Passage*. London: Routledge and Kegan Paul.

Holm-Hansen, J. 1997. *Territorial and Ethno-Cultural Self-Government in Nation-Building Kazakhstan. NIB Report*, Vol. 7. Oslo: Norwegian Institute for Urban and Regional Research.

Iz, F. 1960. Aḥmad Yasawī. In H. A. R. Gibb et. al., *The Encyclopaedia of Islam*, New Edition, pp. 208–209. Leiden: Brill.

Kriss, R., and H. Kriss-Heinrich. 1960. *Volksglaube im Bereich des Islam. I. Wallfahrtwesen und Heiligenverehrung*. Wiesbaden: Otto Harrassowitz.

Michaels, P. A. 1998. Kazak Women: Living the Heritage of a Unique Past. In H. L. Bodman, and N. Tohidi (eds.), *Women in Muslim Societies: Diversity within Unity*, pp. 187–202. London: Rienner.

Olcott, M. B. 1993. Kazakshtan: A Republic of Minorities. In I. Bremmer, and R. Taras (eds.), *Nation and Politics in the Soviet Successor States*, pp. 313–330. Cambridge: Cambridge University Press.

Pfluger-Schindlbeck, I. 1997. Politische Implikationen der lokalen Wallfahrt von Frauen in Aserbaidschan. *Zeitschrift für Ethnologie* 122: 169–182.

———. 1998. Beispiele islamischer Rückbesinnung aus dem postsowjetischen Aserbaidschan. *Mitteilungen der Berliner Gesellschaft für Anthropologie, Ethnologie und Urgeschichte* 19: 97–106.

Roberts, S. 1998. Negotiating Locality, Islam, and National Culture in a Changing Borderland: The Revival of the *Mäshräp* Ritual among Young Uighur Men in the Ili Valley. *Central Asian Survey* 17 (4): 673–699.

Turner, V. 1969. *The Ritual Process*. Harmondsworth: Penguin.

———., and E. Turner 1978. *Image and Pilgrimage in Christian Culture*. Oxford: Blackwell.

Westermarck, E. 1926. *Ritual and Belief in Morocco*. London: Macmillan.

Index

adoption 40, 79, 139, 140, 185, 189, 199

agriculture 13, 26, 27, 27n, 29, 33, 46, 64, 66, 73, 74n, 75n, 106, 114, 115n, 122, 140, 150, 155, 157, 158

All-China Women's Federation 25n, 41, 67, 86, 176

Almaty 11-2, 85n, 213, 222, 224, 224n, 227n, 228, 230, 231, 231n, 233-4, 238, 240, 246, 249n, 250-1, 260-1

alms 202-3, 257, 261

Altä Shähär 153

altruism 36, 79, 87

animal husbandry 64-6, 72, 74, 81, 98, 114, 160

Aqsu 30, 114n, 123, 135, 153, 153n

archives 6, 119

authority 8, 9, 10, 23, 24n, 28, 31, 33, 36, 40, 42, 43-7, 63, 67, 82n, 106n, 114, 123, 125-9, 223, 225n, 239, 241, 242; local 8, 9, 12, 43, 77, 125, 135, 149, 227; male 30, 252, 259; religious 24, 44, 47, 123, 125, 127, 129, 212n, 239, 241-3, 258-9; secular 24, 44, 46, 47, 87, 89, 127, 212

bakhshi 200, 222, 227-8, 230-1, 231n, 240-2, 245, 250

Barat 45n, 161, 200, 205, 205n, 206, 206n, 207-13, 216-7

bek 127, 127n, 128, 130

birth 29, 30, 34, 39, 39n, 40, 47, 58-9, 61, 99-101, 106n, 107-8, 110-3, 119n, 138-9, 161, 171, 176n, 185-6, 189n, 191, 230, 232

budget 60, 61, 65; domestic 55, 56, 132, *see* household, budget

cadre 7, 9, 10, 13, 24n, 25n, 26, 33, 34, 35, 38, 39, 41, 42, 42n, 43-4, 46, 47, 58-9, 60n, 78, 82, 84-7, 87n, 106n, 171, 175-7, 182-4

Central Asia 2, 6, 12, 47, 71, 84, 122-3, 152, 153n, 172, 198-9, 200n, 221-2, 225, 227, 232, 238, 240-2, 249, 262

China 1-3, 5, 6, 21, 21n, 22, 23n, 25n, 28, 39, 58n, 68, 71-2, 72n, 73n, 74n, 84, 86, 106n, 141-2, 146, 149, 150, 150n, 167, 171; elsewhere in 9, 10n, 14, 23, 27, 32n, 41, 43, 51n, 56-7n, 58, 60, 150n, 154, 177; Imperial 148, 178n; interior of 79, 147, 181, 183, 184; minorities of 5, 21n, 167n, 197n, 246; north-west 71, 106, 249; outside 5, 84, 183, 184; People's Republic of 2, 21, 51, 71, 112, 136, 150, 167, 197, 222, 225; post-Mao 14; rural 21, 51, 52, 58n, 63n; socialist 23n, 169; western 8

Chinese Muslims 121, 169, 170n, 174, 174n, 176, 176n, 177n, 182

collectivisation 21n, 23, 25, 28, 33, 36, 51-2, 57-60, 61, 63-4, 72, 78, 80, 89, 90, 106-7, 138, 146, 151, 157, 159, 169; decollectivisation 1, 10, 25

commemoration of the dead 212-4, 216, 217, 262, *see* death rituals

commensality 128, 162, 187n

commerce 27, 71, *see* trade

commune 13, 23, 31, 34n, 41, 57, 59, 60, 68, 72, 149, 151; period 23, 34, 38-9, 52, 83, 149, 151, 156, 160

corvée 23, 23n, 37, 46, 63

crafts 27, 62, 64-6, 67, 71-3, 75, 75n, 77, 78-9, 81, 88, 90, 156, 160, 174, *see also* production, sideline

craftsmen 58, 60, 64, 71, 90, 123, 184

cultivation 26, 28, 30-3, 40, 46, 54, 63, 80, 96, 102, 115n, 122, 155, 158, 160, *see* production
Cultural Revolution 23, 67, 136, 146, 150, 182, 182n

dakhan 200, 214-5, 222
death 8n, 30, 33, 34, 44-5, 81, 86n 130, 150, 184, 200, 202-4, 213, 242; payments 201-3, 210; rituals 56, 184, 188n, 200-13, 216
demography 147, 180
dispute settlement 128, 129, 137
divination 232, 234-7, 240
diviner 227, 230, 236, 241, 243
divorce 29n, 53, 55-6, 62, 89n, 100, 103n, 110n, 113, 126, 129-30, 131n, 131-2, 134, 135, 136-7, 139, 178, 190, 191, 228, 231, 239; in case of 100, 103, 110n, 126, 136, 139; marriage and 55, 56, 108, 137; rate 56n, 57n, 102; settlement 62, 81
divorced women/ divorcée 87, 100, 103, 110, 252, 263
doppa 53, 62, 66, 67, 73, 75, 75n, 76-9, 86-90, 114, 182

Eastern Turkestan 121n, 122, 123n, 124, 134, 136, 136n, 152, 200, 222n, 225
economy 89, 97n, 102, 106, 150, 226; household 59; market 30, 162; planned 72, 227; socialist 28; socialist commodity/ market 46, 68, 71, 90, 138, 146, 150
education 5, 28, 29-31, 45-6, 53, 84, 99n, 101, 149, 168n, 174, 176-9, 186, 192, 245, *see also* religious education
ethnic; boundaries 139, 170, 173, 189, 191, 260-2; conflict 6, 8, 167, 169, 179-80, 191, 263; group 2, 2n, 7, 21, 105, 115, 151, 167, 169, 171,

192, 197, 226, 228; minority 1, 6, 22, 177, 192; nationalism 150; relations 5, 6, 11, 13, 21, 168n, 181
ethnicity 7-9, 139-40, 145n, 151, 169-70, 174n, 178, 192, 197n, 227, 261, 263

family; planning 28, 39, 39n, 40, 42, 45, 106n, 110n, 139, 146, 161-2, 180, *see also* law, family
farming 36, 51, 114, 140, 155, *see* agriculture
food 28-9, 29n, 33, 39, 52-3, 56-7, 59-61, 83, 85, 88, 109, 109n, 110n, 134, 138, 157, 160, 174n, 184n, 186-7, 187n, 188-9, 191, 198, 204-6, 211, 212-7, 225, 242n
funeral 34, 202-4, 211-2, 216-7, *see* death rituals

gender; asymmetry 96, 101, 108-9, 109n; inequality 52; relations 6, 51, 55-6, 131-2, 179, *see also* labour, division of
generosity 133, 257
geography 4, 5, 13, 98, 101, 145, 167, 199, 242
Ghulja 168n
Great Leap Forward 57, 136, 149, 214

hair-tying ritual 112, 185, 185n
Han Chinese 22, 22n, 39, 41, 46, 51, 68, 167-8, 181, 185, 188, 190, 200
healing 11, 157, 161, 200, 200n, 216, 221-4, 226-40 *passim*, 242-5, 252, 261, 263, *see* religious healing
honour and shame 137, *see* modesty
hospitality 59, 170n, 187-8, 188n
household; allowance 132; budget 55, 60; head 34, 35, 55, 60, 61, 87, 88,

89, 131, 203, *see also* economy, household

Hui 147, 182, *see* Chinese Muslims

illness 33, 81, 110, 230, 239, 240, 255

inheritance 57, 81, 108, 109n, 126, 129-30, 137-8, 159

irrigation 25n, 36, 38, 58, 61, 63, 73n, 75, 115n, 122-5

Islam 5, 6, 22, 24, 43n, 44, 56, 68, 97, 106, 113, 140, 147-52, 156, 161, 173, 197-9, 205, 225, 235, 246, 250-1, 263

Islamic; courts 119, 121, 126-7, 130, 136; festivals 33, 59, 66, 184n, 213; mysticism 168, *see* Sufi/ Sufism

isqat 201-3, 203n, 210

Kashgaria 152

Khizir 257, 259, 261

Khotan 66, 80, 128-9, 153, 153n, 201, 204, 213

kinship 6, 78n, 90, 91, 96, 111, 138, 226, 243, 252

Koran 60, 104, 108, 129, 135n, 200-7, 210, 232, 232n, 251, 254

Kucha 11-2, 71, 85, 114n, 120, 123, 153, 167-9, 171-2, 174-80, 184-5, 189, 189n, 190, 191, 193, 204

labour; division of 3, 10, 51n, 52, 57, 67, 68, 73n, 76, 90, 105n, 121, 156, 159-60, 174, 186n, 212; migration 22, 101-3, 180

labourer 54-5, 64, 74, 102, 105, 123, 173, 175, 177

land; arable 26, 73, 80; attachment to 155, 162; ownership 25, 43, 160; reform 23, 25-6, 80, 80n

language 1, 4-5, 8, 22, 71, 96-7, 99, 107, 109, 111, 152, 153n, 167,

170, 173, 174n, 176, 177n, 179-80, 192, 225-8

law; customary 108, 119-25, 128-32, 136-41; family 126, 137; Islamic 119, 121-2, 126-30, 133-4, 137, 139, 149, 159, 187n; state 119-21

mahr/ mähr 134-6, *see* marriage, payments

Manchu 3, 5, 147-8, 152, *see* Qing dynasty

Mao [Zedong] 14, 150, 151

market; economy 30, 46, 90, 138, 146, 150, 162; forces 23; liberalisation of the 72, 90, 146, 150n, 158

marriage; ceremony 103, 128, 130, 181, 202, 204, 207, 242, 251, 255; close-kin 111, 137; intermarriage 189-90, 225; negotiations 9, 133, 198; payments 110n, 132-5

mäshräp 82-5, 85n, 90, 244

migration 12, 22, 28, 29, 80n, 96, 101-3, 106, 147, 149, 180, 191, 224-5, 225n

mijäz 110, 171, 178, 186-7, 187n, 225

mirab 124-5

modesty 56-7, 62, 74, 77, 103-4, 114, 183, 232n, 258, *see also* namahram

molla 4, 53n, 106, 125, 127, 130, 131n, 135, 201, 204, 207, 215n

mosque 35, 36, 39n, 43-4, 52, 119, 128, 130-1, 133, 148-9, 161, 172-3, 182, 202-3, 207-8, 210-2, 212n, 216, 217, 225n

namahram/ namähräm 56, 74, 103-4, 104n, 114, 132, 137, *see also* modesty

näzir-chiraq 211, 212, 212n, 244

neighbour 5, 11, 38, 66, 75, 77, 90, 102, 105, 167, 179, 181, 183, 188n, 224, 226n, 231

neighbourhood 9, 11-2, 13n, 35, 41-2, 60, 61, 62, 75-80, 82, 84, 86, 127-8, 173, 181, 186, 188, 201, 206, 223-6, 231, 231n, 235, 236, 239-45, 250-3, 263

officials 8, 24, 31-4, 34n, 39-42 60, 86, 114, 123-5, 127, 127n, 170, 178-9, 186, 193, *see also bek*; cadre

örp-adät 136-7, 139, 141, 197

patriarchy 51, 55, 68, 97, 101, 114, 116

pilgrimage 11, 77, 148-9, 161, 198, 215-6, 224, 236-45,

pollution 54, 110, 111n, 187

post-reform 5, 14, 63, 66, 79, 152, 158

postsocialism/ postsocialist 14, 226, 246, 249, 252n, 263

poverty 23, 32, 56n, 67, 72, 86, 102, 157, 180, 181, 211, 215n, 227

procreation 11, 95-6, 99n, 101, 103, 106-7, 109, 111, 113, 115

production 26, 27, 30-1, 57n, 58, 61, 65, 67, 74, 75, 78, 78n, 90, 96, 99-102, 113-6, 146, 149-50, 157, 159, 161, 205; agricultural 23, 52, 54, 80, 95, 122, 156; brigade 13, 13n, 34n, 59, 78, 151; knowledge 4, 4n; methods 42; private 57, 90; ritual 158; sideline 27, 31, 36, 58, 60, 63-6, 71-5, 77-9, 81, 83, 85, 87-90, 114, 123, 156, 160, 166, 184, 186, *see also* crafts, craftsmen; status 55n; team 13, 13n, 25, 25n, 26n, 31, 34, 34n, 37, 41, 59, 76, 78, 151; team leader 35, 41, 59, 78, 78n

property 43, 101, 108, 110n, 122-6, 129-30, 155, 155n, 158-9; common 26n; private 2n, 57, 80, 81, 123, 151, 159, 160, 215n; relations 57, 129, 130, 149, 155n, 158-9; rights 25n, 126, 129

Qing dynasty 126, 148

Qurban 33, 205, 253, 258, *see also* Islamic festivals

Ramadan 85, *see also* Islamic festivals

reform(s) 1, 2n, 23, 28, 44, 51, 72, 72n, 78, 82-3, 150, 152, 159-60; agrarian 57; economic 21, 46, 72, 72n, 80-1, 84, 106, 109n, 114, 152, 160, 180n; era 23, 28, 43-6, 109n; market 5, 211; period 14, 23, 32, 40, 41, 51, 56n, 61-3, 78, 90, 146, 155; post-reform 5, 14, 63, 66, 79, 152, 158; rural 21, 61n, *see also* land, reform

religion 3n, 7, 11-3, 43, 95, 97, 106, 115, 137, 151, 154, 160, 161, 170, 177n, 182, 192, 197-9, 199n, 215n, 225, 227, 242, 257-8, 261-3

religiosity 215, 238, 246

religious 4, 7, 12, 78, 83-90, 120-3, 126-31, 151, 154, 158, 160, 182, 182n, 198n, 205, 211-6, 222-6, 230, 240, 243-6, 249, 251-4, 257-63; authority 24, 43-7, 89, 123, 127, 212n; dignitaries/ elite 5, 43, 44, 45, 126, 127n, 128, 149, 179, 179n; duties/ obligations 87; education 148; freedom 1, 24n, 146; healing (rituals) 161, 215, 221-2; holidays/ festivals 59, 66, 89n, 138, 161, 184n, 205, 213; law 121, 122, 127n, 128; policies 140, 149, 171, 173n, 193; practices 2, 11, 12, 43n, 136, 197-8, 257; repression 44, 147, 162,

191, 212, 214, 216, 225, 225n, 242, *see also* rituals

Republican era 135

responsibility system 28, 30, 46, 72, 150

rituals 2, 4, 43, 160-1, 184n, 184, 188n, 197-8, 200-1, 205, 210-4, 216, 221-2, 238, 243-5, 263; life-cycle 33, 56, 59, 138, 183n, 203; religious 83, 159

rotating savings and credit associations 82, 85, 85n

shaman/ shamanism 198-200, 215, 222, 222n, 223n, 227, 227n, 230, 232, 232n, 245n, 246, 250, 250n

Sharī'a 121, 130, *see* law

Shi'ism/ Shi'ite 104n

shrine 44, 109, 130-1, 149, 153, 154n, 173, 200, 206-7, 210, 214-6, 238, 240-2, 245, 250-62

socialism 2, 4, 7, 23n, 56n, 57, 136, 141, 149, 151, 161, 172, 197, 221, 224, 227, 231

Soviet Union 148, 169, 225, 225n, 227, 231, 250n, 257n

state 10, 14, 22n, 23-28n, 30-32n, 35-7, 40, 41-7, 68, 80, 82, 90, 102, 110n, 114, 136-7, 140-1, 146, 151-4, 158, 162, 169, 173n, 176-7, 181, 192, 226, 228, 263; authority 43-7, 122, 141; control 28, 47, 138, 158; employee 24n, 41, 250; interference 32, 138, 147, 158, 160, 169; law 119-20, 136, 141; ownership 31, 32, 66; policies 146, 162; representatives 8, 41, 43, 87

subsistence 12, 27, 31-2, 73, 80, 82, 97, 114, 155

Sufi/ Sufism 43-4, 84, 149, 160, 161, 198

Taranchi 207, 208, 210

Tarim basin 122, 127

tax/ taxation 31, 123-4, 147-9, 228, 240

Tian Shan 122, 153

toyluq 110n, 133-6

trade 37, 58, 63, 64, 71-2, 100, 160, 227, 232, 236

Turfan 203, 203n, 207

Turkey 11, 88n, 95, 97-8, 100n, 102, 104n, 206, 251, 253-5

Turkistan 238, 240, 241n, 243-4, 250-1, 253-5

UNICEF 13, 78, 86-7, 91

water (as resource) 31, 38, 53-4, 61, 122-5, 128, 155n, 186, 229, 232, 251, 254, 259, 260

wealth 26-8, 54, 57, 80-1, 91, 130, 133, 138, 155-6, 211

Western/ Russian Turkestan 122, 124, 221

women; Women's Federation 25n, 41, 60-2, 67, 68, 86, 176, *see* All-China Women's Federation; women's work 52-3, 57n, 68, 74n, 86, 95-6, 104, 105, 113, *see also* labour, division of

work; communal 36-9; fieldwork 1, 6-8, 10-3n, 52, 54n, 72, 74, 95, 97, 99, 99n, 105, 138, 150n, 168n, 186n; framework 5, 6, 11, 27, 57n, 83-5n, 89, 120-1

Xinjiang Uyghur Autonomous Region 2, 21, 145, 147, 151, 167, 222

Ya'qūb Bek 121, 121n, 131, 149, 153

Halle Studies in the Anthropology of Eurasia

1 Hann, Chris, and the "Property Relations" Group, 2003: *The Postsocialist Agrarian Question. Property Relations and the Rural Condition.*

2 Grandits, Hannes, and Patrick Heady (eds.), 2004: *Distinct Inheritances. Property, Family and Community in a Changing Europe.*

3 Torsello, David, 2004: *Trust, Property and Social Change in a Southern Slovakian Village.*

4 Pine, Frances, Deema Kaneff, and Haldis Haukanes (eds.), 2004: *Memory, Politics and Religion. The Past Meets the Present in Europe.*

5 Habeck, Joachim Otto, 2005: *What it Means to be a Herdsman. The Practice and Image of Reindeer Husbandry among the Komi of Northern Russia.*

6 Stammler, Florian, 2009: *Reindeer Nomads Meet the Market. Culture, Property and Globalisation at the 'End of the Land'* (2 editions).

7 Ventsel, Aimar, 2006: *Reindeer,* Rodina *and Reciprocity. Kinship and Property Relations in a Siberian Village.*

8 Hann, Chris, Mihály Sárkány, and Peter Skalník (eds.), 2005: *Studying Peoples in the People's Democracies. Socialist Era Anthropology in East-Central Europe.*

9 Leutloff-Grandits, Caroline, 2006: *Claiming Ownership in Postwar Croatia. The Dynamics of Property Relations and Ethnic Conflict in the Knin Region.*

10 Hann, Chris, 2006: *"Not the Horse We Wanted!" Postsocialism, Neoliberalism, and Eurasia.*

11 Hann, Chris, and the "Civil Religion" Group, 2006: *The Postsocialist Religious Question. Faith and Power in Central Asia and East-Central Europe.*

12 Heintz, Monica, 2006: *"Be European, Recycle Yourself!" The Changing Work Ethic in Romania.*

13 Grant, Bruce, and Lale Yalçın-Heckmann (eds.), 2007: *Caucasus Paradigms. Anthropologies, Histories and the Making of a World Area.*

14 Buzalka, Juraj, 2007: *Nation and Religion. The Politics of Commemoration in South-East Poland.*

15 Naumescu , Vlad, 2007: *Modes of Religiosity in Eastern Christianity. Religious Processes and Social Change in Ukraine.*

16 Mahieu, Stéphanie, and Vlad Naumescu (eds.), 2008: *Churches Inbetween.Greek Catholic Churches in Postsocialist Europe.*

17 Mihăilescu, Vintilă, Ilia Iliev, and Slobodan Naumović (eds.), 2008: *Studying Peoples in the People's Democracies II. Socialist Era Anthropology in South-East Europe.*

18 Kehl-Bodrogi, Krisztina, 2008: *"Religion is not so strong here". Muslim Religious Life in Khorezm after Socialism.*

19 Light, Nathan, 2008: *Intimate Heritage. Creating Uyghur Muqam Song in Xinjiang.*

20 Schröder, Ingo W., and Asta Vonderau (eds.), 2008: *Changing Economies and Changing Identities in Postsocialist Eastern Europe.*

21 László, Fosztó, 2009: *Ritual Revitalisation after Socialism: Community, Personhood, and Conversion among Roma in a Transylvanian Village.*

22 Hilgers, Irene, 2009: *Why Do Uzbeks have to be Muslims? Exploring religiosity in the Ferghana Valley.*

23 Trevisani, Tommaso, 2010: *Land and Power in Khorezm. Farmers, Communities, and the State in Uzbekistan's Decollectivisation.*

24 Yalçın-Heckmann, Lale, 2010: *The Return of Private Property. Rural Life after the Agrarian Reform in the Republic of Azerbaijan.*

25 Mühlfried, Florian, and Sergey Sokolovskiy (eds.), 2011. *Exploring the Edge of Empire: Soviet Era Anthropology in the Caucasus and Central Asia.*

26 Cash, Jennifer R., 2011: *Villages on Stage. Folklore and Nationalism in the Republic of Moldova.*

27 Köllner, Tobias, 2012: *Practising Without Belonging? Entrepreneurship, Morality, and Religion in Contemporary Russia.*

28 Bethmann, Carla, 2013: *"Clean, Friendly, Profitable?" Tourism and the Tourism Industry in Varna, Bulgaria.*

29 Bošković, Aleksandar, and Chris Hann (eds.), 2013: *The Anthropological Field on the Margins of Europe, 1945-1991.*

30 Holzlehner, Tobias, 2014: *Shadow Networks. Border Economies, Informal Markets and Organised Crime in the Russian Far East.*